INTERNATIONAL DIMENSIONS OF

Organizational Behavior

THIRD EDITION

NANCY J. ADLER
McGill University

SOUTH-WESTERN College Publishing

An International Thomson Publishing Company

Acquisitions Editor: Randy G. Haubner
Project Leader: Christine O. Sofranko
Production House: Justified Left
Internal and Cover Designer: Joseph M. Devine

2 3 4 5 6 7 MT 2 1 0 9 8 7 6
Printed in the United States of America

Library of Congress Cataloging-in-Publication Data
Adler, Nancy J.
        International dimensions of organizational behavior / Nancy J.
        Adler. — 3rd ed.
                p.   cm.
        Includes bibliographical references and index.
        ISBN 0-538-86136-3
        1. Organizational behavior—Cross-cultural studies.   I. Title.
        HD58.7.A33   1997   96-19520
        658—dc20   CIP

I(T)P   International Thomson Publishing.
         South-Western College Publishing is an ITP company. The ITP
         trademark is used under license.

To my mother, Liselotte Adler, who brought together two worlds and two very different cultures in creating the home in which I grew up.

Preface

The world of organizations is no longer defined by national boundaries. *International Dimensions of Organizational Behavior* breaks down the conceptual, theoretical, and practical boundaries limiting our ability to understand and work with people in countries around the world. Until recently, much of the published understanding of management came from the American experience: American managers and American-trained researchers observed the behavior of people in U.S.-based organizations. From their observations and research, they developed models and theories to explain organizational and managerial behavior. The problem was in their assumption: they implicitly assumed that what was true for Americans working in the United States was also true for people from other countries. Both managers and researchers assumed that American work behavior was universal. They were wrong. *International Dimensions of Organizational Behavior* challenges us to go beyond our parochialism and to see the world from a global perspective.

Today, managers no longer have the luxury of reducing global complexity to the simplicity of assumed universality; they no longer have the luxury of assuming that there is only one best way to manage. Luckily, we have learned that global complexity is neither unpredictable nor random. Variations across cultures and their impacts on organizations follow systematic, predictable patterns. Starting with a core of traditional, primarily United States-based understandings of the behavior of people in organizations, *International Dimensions* becomes a guide to modify our attitudes, thinking patterns, and behavior. Far from ignoring the historical body of managerial knowledge, *International Dimensions* expands our understanding of people's behavior at work to include the diversity and complexity of today's global business environment.

International Dimensions of Organizational Behavior is divided into three sections. The first section, "The Impact of Culture on Organizations," describes the ways in which cultures vary, how that variance systematically affects organizations, and how people can recognize cultural variance within their own work environments. The second section, "Managing Cultural Diversity," presents an integrated approach to managing in multicultural work environments. Chapter 4 investigates cross-cultural problem solving and organizational development; Chapter 5 presents the dynamics of multicultural teams; Chapter 6 reviews leadership, motivation, and decision making from a global perspective; and Chapter 7 summarizes global approaches to managing conflict and to negotiating.

The third section, "Managing Global Managers," presents a series of issues that are unique to global management. It addresses the human resource management questions involved in managing one's life and career while moving across international borders. Chapter 8 describes the cross-cultural entry and reentry transitions from the employee's perspective and addresses such questions as: What is cultural shock? How does one adjust to a new culture? How should international employees manage reentry back into their home country and organization? Chapter 9 also presents global transition issues, but from the spouse's perspective. Chapter 10 introduces the challenges of managing global careers. How do the routes to the top of major companies vary from country to country? What do managers see as the most important benefits and drawbacks in pursuing global careers? Given its focus on global managers, this section goes far beyond the scope of domestically oriented books on either management or organizational behavior.

International Dimensions of Organizational Behavior has been used by executives, managers, and college students in a number of ways. First, it is used as the basis of independent cross-cultural management seminars in which each chapter of the book forms the core of a course module. When used in this way, the book is often supplemented with current readings providing a more in-depth look at specific areas of the world as well as with news articles on contemporary world business events. For example, while introducing each module with a chapter from *International Dimensions*, seminar participants might expand the material in the book, based on their current interests and experience, by looking at how it applies to, for instance, Eastern European or Pacific Rim countries.

Alternatively, the book is used as a supplement to a standard organizational behavior course. In this case, professors first use their standard introduction to the study of people's behavior in organizations. Using Chapters 1 and 2, they then introduce a module on international dimensions of organizational behavior. Following this introduction, they then pair a chapter from *International Dimensions of Organizational Behavior* with each of the modules of their standard course. For example, they pair

Chapter 3 with the perception and/or communications module; Chapter 4 with the problem solving and/or organizational development and change module; Chapter 5 with the module on group dynamics and team building; Chapter 6 with the discussion of leadership, motivation, and decision making; and Chapter 7 with material on conflict management and negotiation. In addition, either in combination with a module on career management or as an independent module, professors then present Part 3 of the book on managing global managers. Participants complete the course with an in-depth understanding of organizational behavior issues from both a global and a domestic perspective.

As a third alternative, *International Dimensions of Organizational Behavior* is used as a self-contained section of a traditional organizational behavior, management, human resource management, or international business course. In this case, professors present their traditional, often more domestically oriented, material and then add on a section on international dimensions. Whereas participants have the opportunity to read the entire book, the professor selects those international aspects of the material that appear most important and relevant to the entire course to present during class sessions.

Because the vast majority of traditional management literature and practice is still based on the behavior of Americans, *International Dimensions* often uses the United States as a reference point and as a point of comparison. American readers will recognize the familiar ways in which organizational behavior is usually described and be able to add a more global perspective to that knowledge. Readers from all countries will gain a better understanding of their own culture's practices and ways of conducting business, both relative to traditional U.S.-based descriptions and, more importantly, relative to a wide variety of countries worldwide. No country's system or perspective is any better or worse—any more or less effective—than any other country's; rather, each is distinct and therefore must not be understood as a replica of any other nation.

Cross-cultural management (i.e., studying the international dimensions of people's behavior in organizations) is a new field relative to the traditional study of management. *International Dimensions of Organizational Behavior* integrates what is known in the field as the final decade of the twentieth century. There is no doubt that by the twenty-first century, our knowledge will have grown far beyond today's understandings. Whereas the limits of our understanding at times restrict us, they also define the boundaries and excitement of an important, rapidly expanding field of knowledge. Far from leaving with a sense of knowing all there is to know,

it is hoped that readers will finish the book with a sophisticated awareness of the world beyond their own national boundaries, an understanding of the limits of their own knowledge, and a set of questions to guide
their management decisions and future inquiry.

ACKNOWLEDGMENTS

The process of understanding the human dynamics in global management
has brought together some of the best thinking and insights from consultants, executives, managers, scholars, and researchers worldwide. The
process is evolving. What we know today is so much more than what we
understood yesterday, and yet so much less than what we will need for
tomorrow. The excitement and passion in the search is predicated on our
need to understand ourselves in a world in which no part of humanity is
very far away, a world in which our success as well as our very survival
depends on our understanding and respect for each other.

I would like to thank the many, many people who have contributed to
this book, each from his or her unique perspective and expertise. The
quality of this book is shared by all, the errors and limitations are mine
alone. My thanks to: Liselotte Adler (USA), Arshad Ahmad (Pakistan),
Nakiye Boyacigiller (Turkey), Jill de Villafranca (Canada), Joseph J.
diStefano (Canada), Angela Dowson (Canada), Paul Evans (England),
John Graham (USA), Jon Hartwick (Canada), Mary Hess (USA) Maryann
Jelinek (USA), André Laurent (France), Phyllis Lefohn (USA), Robert T.
Moran (USA), Eileen Newmark (USA), Pri Notowidigdo (Indonesia),
France Pepper (Canada), Roger Putzel (USA), Vijit Ramchandani (India),
Indrei Ratiu (Britain/Romania), George Renwick (USA), Stephen
Rhinesmith (USA), David Ricks (USA), Karlene Roberts (USA), Anita
Salustro (USA), Suzanne Sellitto (Canada), Richard Vilas (USA), and
Frances Westley (Canada).

A very special thank you goes to Robine Andrau for her excellent edit-
ing of the second and third editions, to Rosalind Finlay for her patient and
conscientious typing and organizing of each new revision until the chapters finally became the third edition, to Christine Sofranko of South-
Western College Publishing for her professionalism and enthusiasm in
managing the entire project, to Sue Ellen Brown of Justified Left for
expertly supervising every aspect of the production process, and to Louise
Dubreil, without whose help, encouragement, and insight this book would
have never become a reality.

About the Author

Nancy J. Adler is a Professor of Organizational Behavior and Cross-Cultural Management in the Faculty of Management of McGill University in Montreal, Canada. She received her B.A. in economics, M.B.A. and Ph.D. in management from the University of California at Los Angeles (UCLA).

Dr. Adler conducts research and consults on strategic international human resource management, expatriation, women in international management, international negotiating, developing culturally synergistic approaches to problem solving, and international organization development. She has authored numerous articles, produced the film *A Portable Life*, and published the books, *International Dimensions of Organizational Behavior* (third edition 1997), *Women in Management Worldwide* (1988), and *Competitive Frontiers: Women Managers in a Global Economy* (1994).

Dr. Adler has consulted to private corporations and government organizations on projects in Europe, North and South America, the Middle East, and Asia. She has taught Chinese executives in the People's Republic of China, held the Citicorp Visiting Doctoral Professorship at the University of Hong Kong, and taught executive seminars at INSEAD in France and Bocconi University in Italy. She received McGill University's first Distinguished Teaching Award in Management (1986) and was its recipient again in 1990.

Dr. Adler has served on the Board of Governors of the American Society for Training and Development (ASTD), the Canadian Social Science Advisory Committee to UNESCO, the Strategic Grants Committee of the Social Sciences and Humanities Research Council, and the Executive Committees of the Pacific Asian Consortium for International Business, Education and Research, the International Personnel Association, and the Society for Human Resource Management's International Institute, as well as having held leadership positions in the Academy of International Business (AIB), the Society for Intercultural Education, Training, and Research (SIETAR), and the Academy of Management. Dr. Adler received ASTD's International

Leadership Award and SIETAR's Outstanding Senior Interculturalist Award. She was selected as a 3M Teaching Fellow honoring her as one of Canada's top university professors, and elected to both the Fellows of the Academy of International Business and the Academy of Management Fellows.

Film Notes

This third edition highlights places where videos may be used appropriately for further learning. Nancy Adler has participated in several highly regarded video programs that enhance the study of work beyond national boundaries.

"A PORTABLE LIFE"
MCGILL UNIVERSITY
Instructional Communications Centre
A Videocassette Program with Nancy J. Adler

"A Portable Life" is a 30-minute videocassette program on the role of the spouse in cross-cultural transfers. It describes the personal experiences of the spouse as seen through the eyes of four executive wives: one English Canadian, one French Canadian, one Australian, and one British. The four have lived in Africa, Asia, Europe and North and South America. In all cases, the cultural immersion of the wife was greater than that of the executive and therefore the challenges for successful cross-cultural adjustment were different and greater.

In "A Portable Life," the spouse of the international executive is portrayed as the wife. The reason is not that all spouses are wives; they are not. The reason is that to date, very few married women have been sent abroad in expatriate status and even fewer have been accompanied by a male spouse.

Purchase in the U.S.A., Canada and other countries:

Instructional Communications Centre
McGill University
550, rue Sherbrooke ouest
Montreal, Quebec, Canada H3A 1B9
Tel: (514) 398-7200
Fax: (514) 398-7339

BRITISH BROADCASTING CORPORATION:

"It's a Jungle Out There!" (Part 1) and "The Survival Guide" (Part 2)

This two-part series follows the development of a multinational team on a project in Africa. Part 1, "It's a Jungle Out There," presents the experiences of the team from their formation in England through their various experiences in Africa. Part 2, "The Survival Guide," presents commentary by Professor Nancy J. Adler of McGill University in Montreal, Canada, assessing the areas in which the team functioned well and those in which it functioned poorly. Professor Adler gives recommendations for improving the multinational team's effectiveness, including emphasizing those areas in which they could use the team's international cross-cultural background to increase its effectiveness. Adler discusses the problems involved in communiation and decision-making across cultures, as well as the basis for creating cultural synergistic solutions to the problems faced by multinational teams.

"World Without Borders"

This video program documents the evolution of a multinational firm, Cable and Wireless, from its domestic origins, through the multidomestic stage, and into its current multinational and planned transnational strategies. A set of European and American professors comment on the strategic evolution of Cable and Wireless, while presenting frameworks for understanding and managing the evolution of global firms.

To order the video programs, please contatct:

CANADA:	UNITED STATES:	INTERNATIONAL
BBC Worldwide Americas	BBC Worldwide Americas	British Broadcasting Corporation
65 Heward Avenue	747 Third Avenue	Open University Production Centre
Toronto, Ontario	6th and 7th Floors	Walton Hall, Milton Keynes
Canada M4M 2T5	New York, NY, USA 10017	England MK7 68H
Tel: 416-469-1505	Tel: 212-705-9300	Tel: 44-1908-665-343
Fax: 416-469-0642	Fax: 212-888-0576	Fax: 44-1908-665-300

Table of Contents

The Impact

of Culture on

Organizations

CHAPTER 1
Culture and Management

Verité en-deçà des Pyrénées, erreur au-delà.
("There are truths on this side of the Pyrenees which
are falsehoods on the other.")[1]

— Blaise Pascal

Capital raised in London in the Eurodollar market by a Belgium-based corporation may finance the acquisition of machinery by a subsidiary located in Australia. A management team from French Renault may take over an American-built automotive complex in the Argentine. Clothing for dolls, sewn in Korea on Japanese-supplied sewing machines according to U.S. specifications, may be shipped to Northern Mexico for assembly with other components into dolls being manufactured by a U.S. firm for sale in New York and London during the Christmas season. A California manufactured airbus . . . is powered by British . . . engines, while a competing airbus . . . flies on Canadian wing assemblies. A Frenchman is appointed president of [a] U.S. domiciled . . . corporation, while an American establishes . . . a Swiss-based international mutual fund (18:1–2).

Managing the global enterprise and modern business management have become synonymous. The terms *international, multinational, transnational,* and *global* can no longer be relegated to a subset of organizations or to a division within the organization. Definitions of success now transcend national boundaries. In fact the very concept of domestic business may have become anachronistic.

Today "the modern business enterprise has no place to hide. It has no place to go but everywhere" (40:xiii).

Executives no longer question the increasing importance of global business. As reported in the *21st Century Report* (27), more than two-thirds of the world's CEOs view foreign competition as a key factor in their firm's future business success. Similarly, two-thirds of the world's CEOs expect to generate employment and revenues increasingly from outside of their firm's home country (27:30,31). These same executives believe that effectively managing human resources is critical to global success (27:2).

The post–World War II years saw a major expansion of world trade. From 1948 through 1972 world exports grew from $51 billion to $415 billion, representing a sevenfold increase in monetary terms and a fourfold increase in volume (16:23).[2] In the five years from 1975 to 1979, world trade increased by about 32 percent in real terms (32). By 1980 international trade volume exceeded $1 trillion as compared with $800 billion in 1975 (32). By 1982 world exports amounted to $1.4 trillion (33). By the 1990s Coca-Cola, for example, earned more money selling soda to the Japanese than to Americans (60:5). Today's world trade dwarfs all prior statistics.

By the mid-1980s the U.S. Commerce Department estimated that some 70 percent of American firms faced "significant foreign competition" in U.S. domestic markets, up from only 25 percent a decade earlier (49:11). By the end of the 1980s, the chairman of the Foreign Trade Council estimated the figure to be 80 percent. Today global competition is serious, pervasive, and here to stay (34).

What does the future portend? According to *The Economist*, "Over the next 25 years, the world will see the biggest shift in economic strength for more than a century" (23:3). Emerging economic giants will dwarf developed industrial economies so that "within a generation, China will overtake . . . [the United States] as the world's biggest economy; . . . [moreover,] as many as nine of the top 15 economies will be from today's Third World—[with] Britain overtaken by such countries as Taiwan and Thailand . . . The Third World's share of world exports of manufacturered goods [already] jumped [over 400%], from 5 percent in 1970 to 22 percent in 1993" (23:4).

Will today's economically developed countries continue to prosper or will they lose out to the gains forecast for developing economies?[3] Pessimists argue that with increasing access to First World technology, cheap educated labor in Third World countries will force workers from rich countries to lose their jobs. They claim that free trade with developing countries is a recipe for mass unemployment, huge wage inequalities, and a massive migration of firms to low-wage countries. In a dramatic role reversal, Third World countries that historically were considered victims of multinational exploitation would now be viewed as villains, stealing capital and jobs and, ironically, creating inequities by destroying the wealth of developed economies.

On the surface this pessimistic scenario appears persuasively true, especially when comparing the hourly wages of production workers. "It costs $25 an hour to employ a production worker in Germany, $16 an hour in [the United States]; but only $5 in South Korea, $2.40 in Mexico, $1.40 in Poland, and 50 cents or less in China, India and Indonesia" (23:14). According to the president of the World Economic Forum, it will soon be possible to have high productivity, high technology, and low wages (59). For example, a French consumer electronics group already employs three times as many highly skilled workers in Asia as in France. Similarly, the Italian sportswear maker Fila produces only 10 percent of its sportswear in Italy; it subcontracts the rest in lower wage Asian economies.

Optimists, however, predict a very different scenario. According to the optimists, developed countries, far from losing out to the growing prosperity of developing countries, will benefit from it, primarily due to the increased demand from bigger export markets in developing countries, containing billions of consumers. Already today, "over 42 percent of America's exports, 20 percent of Western Europe's, and 48 percent of Japan's now go to the Third World or countries of the former Soviet block" (23:14). In addition, the optimists contend that both developed and developing economies benefit from increased competition. Greater economies of scale and better allocation of resources resulting from increased competition and financial diversification should improve expected rates of return for all players. Nevertheless, the inflows of foreign direct investment into developing countries are impressive, having increased from $3 billion in 1990 to $80 billion in 1993, of which approximately 60 percent has gone to Asia (39). However, investment in developed economies has been greater—over $110 billion in 1993 (39). Since 1990, far from dramatically losing out, the rich world's capital stock has decreased by a mere 0.5 percent from what it would have been without the increased investment in the developing world (39).

Although international businesses have existed for centuries, the world has clearly entered an era of unprecedented global economic activity, including worldwide production, distribution, and, in increasingly large numbers, international joint ventures and global strategic alliances. Examples of new global operations and alliances abound, with most major firms earning more from their international than from their domestic operations. Global companies such as Asea Brown Bovari, Honda, British Petroleum, Siemens, Motorola, and Eastman Kodak each do business in more than 50 countries (35:3). The 1992 economic integration of the European Economic Community focused the world's attention on transborder business activity and the importance of trading blocks. Although the United States and Canadian economies have been inextricably linked to the world economy for years, the signing of the North American Free Trade Agreement refocused American, Canadian, and Mexican attention on international business.

As Professor Ian Mitroff observes, "For all practical purposes, all business today is global. Those individual businesses, firms, industries, and whole societies that clearly understand the new rules of doing business in a world economy will prosper; those that do not will perish" (46:ix). Mitroff challenges us to realize that "It is no longer business as usual. Global competition has forced . . . [executives] to recognize that if they and their organizations are to survive, let alone prosper, they will have to learn to manage and to think very differently" (46:x).

GLOBAL STRATEGY AND CULTURE[4]

To succeed, corporations must develop global strategies. The 1980s made the importance of such recognition commonplace, at least among leading firms and management scholars; the 1990s made it imperative. Incorporating today's global realities, new time- and quality-sensitive approaches to managing research and development, production, marketing, and finance evolved rapidly. Yet, only in the last decade has an equivalent evolution in understanding international organizational behavior and managing global human resource systems begun to emerge. Although the other functional areas increasingly used global strategies that were largely unheard of—or would have been deemed inappropriate—only one or two decades ago, many firms continued to conduct the worldwide management of people as if neither the external economic and technological environment nor the internal structure and organization of the firm had changed.

Focusing on global strategies and management approaches from the perspective of people and culture allows us to understand the influence of national cultures on organizational functioning. Rather than becoming trapped within the most commonly asked, although unfortunately misleading, question of *whether* organizational dynamics are universal or culturally specific, this book focuses on the crucially important questions of *when* and *how* to be sensitive to national culture.

PHASES OF DEVELOPMENT

As we investigate the influence of cultural diversity on multinational and global firms, it becomes clear that national cultural differences are important but that their relative impact depends on the stage of development of the firm, the industry, and the world economy. Using the model shown in Table 1-1, which traces the post–World War II development of

TABLE 1-1 *Multinational Corporate Evolution*

	Domestic	**Multi-domestic**	**Multi-national**	**Global**
Primary orientation	Product/Service	Market	Price/Cost	Strategy
Competitive strategy	Domestic	Multidomestic	Multinational	Global
Importance of world business	Marginal	Important	Extremely important	Dominant
Product/service	New, unique	More standardized	Completely standardized (commodity)	Mass-customized
Development	Product engineering emphasized	Process engineering emphasized	Engineering not emphasized	Product and process engineering emphasized
Technology	Proprietary	Shared	Widely shared	Instantly and extensively shared
R&D/sales	High	Decreasing	Very low	Very high
Profit margin	High	Decreasing	Very low	High, yet immediately decreasing
Competitors	None	Few	Many	Significant (few or many)
Market	Small, domestic	Large, multidomestic	Larger, multinational	Largest, global
Production location	Domestic	Domestic and primary foreign markets	Multinational, based on least cost	Global, least cost
Exports	None	Growing, high potential	Large, saturated	Imports, exports, and "transports"
Structure	Functional divisions	Functional with international division	Multinational lines of business	Global alliances, heterarchy
	Centralized	Decentralized	Centralized	Coordinated, decentralized

Source: © 1989 by Nancy J. Adler. See Adler and Ghadar (4). Phases I–III are based on Vernon (68).

global enterprises (3;4;68), we can trace distinct variations in the relative importance of cultural diversity and, consequently, equally distinct variations in the most appropriate approaches to managing people worldwide. Whereas historically the order of the phases has varied, primarily depending on the organization's age and origin as an Asian, European, or North American firm, the order presented here reflects the most common evolution for North American firms. Today, as transnational dynamics increasingly define global business competitiveness, firms frequently skip specific phases in order to position themselves to more rapidly maximize their global competitive advantage within a particular industry.

Domestic Phase

As shown in Tables 1-1 and 1-2, immediately following World War II most firms operated primarily from a domestic, ethnocentric perspective. Firms produced unique products and services that they offered almost exclusively to the domestic market. The uniqueness of the product or service and the lack of international competition negated the firm's need to demonstrate sensitivity to national cultural differences. When firms exported products, they often did so without altering them for foreign consumption. Foreign buyers, rather than the home country product design, manufacturing, or marketing teams, absorbed the inconvenience of any cultural differences. In some ways the implicit message sent to foreigners was "We will *allow* you to buy our product"; and, of course, the assumption was that foreigners would want to buy. During this initial

TABLE 1-2 *Corporate Cross-Cultural Evolution*

	Domestic Phase	Multidomestic Phase	Multinational Phase	Global Phase
Primary orientation	Product/Service	Market	Price/Cost	Strategy
Strategy	Domestic	Multidomestic	Multinational	Global
Perspective	Ethnocentric	Polycentric/ regiocentric	Multinational	Global/ multicentric
Cultural sensitivity	Marginally important	Very important	Somewhat important	Critically important
With whom	No one	Clients	Employees	Employees and clients
Level	No one	Workers and clients	Managers	Executives
Strategic assumption	"One way" or "One best way"	"Many good ways" Equifinality	"One least-cost way" Simultaneously	"Many good ways"

Source: © 1989 by Nancy J. Adler. See Adler and Ghadar (4).

phase, nationals and philosophies from the headquarters' country dominated management: firms in the domestic phase regarded culture and
global human resource systems as largely irrelevant.

Multidomestic Phase

Domestic competition ushered in the second phase and with it the initial
need to market and produce abroad. Totally unlike its irrelevance during the initial domestic phase, sensitivity to cultural differences became
critical to implementing effective corporate strategy in the multidomestic
phase. The domestic phase's product orientation shifted to a market orientation, with companies now needing to address each foreign domestic
market separately and differently.

Whereas the unique technology of the domestic phase's products and
services fit well with an ethnocentric "one-best-way" approach, during
the multidomestic phase firms began to assume that there were "many
good ways" to manage, with each dependent on the particular country
involved. Successful companies no longer expected foreigners to absorb
cultural mismatches between buyers and sellers. Rather, home country
representatives modified their style to fit with that of their clients and colleagues in foreign markets. Moreover, while cultural differences became
important in the design and marketing of culturally appropriate products,
these differences became *critical* in their production in factories worldwide. Managers had to learn culturally appropriate approaches to managing people in each of the countries in which they operated.

Multinational Phase

By the 1980s many industries had entered the multinational phase. The
competitive environment for these industries had changed again and with
it the demands for culturally sensitive management practices. In multinational industries, a number of companies produce almost indifferen-
tiable products (practically commodities), with the only significant competition being on price. From this global price-sensitive—and therefore
cost-sensitive—perspective, cultural awareness declines in importance.
Price competition among almost identical products and services produced by numerous multinational competitors negates the importance
of most cultural differences and almost all advantages gained by
cultural sensitivity.

As shown in Table 1-2, the primary product design and marketing
assumption is no longer the domestic phase's "one best way" or even the

multidomestic phase's "many good ways" but rather "one least-cost way." The primary market becomes global, with no significant market segmentation. Firms can gain competitive advantage only through process engineering, sourcing critical factors on a worldwide basis, and benefiting from economies of scale. Price competition significantly reduces the influence of cultural differences.

Global, or Transnational, Phase

Some managers believed that the multinational phase would be the ultimate phase for all industries. This assumption did not prove to be true. Although a number of industries today continue to operate under the norms of the multinational phase, a fourth phase has emerged for firms in the most globally competitive industries. In it, top quality, least-possible-cost products become the baseline, the minimally acceptable standard. Competitive advantage comes from strategic thinking, from mass customization, and from outlearning one's competitors. Product and service ideas are drawn from worldwide sources, as are the factors and locations of production. However, companies tailor final products and services and their marketing to very discrete market niches. One of the critical components of this market segmentation is nationality and ethnicity. Culture, once again, becomes a critical competitive factor.

Successful global firms competing under transnational dynamics need to understand their potential clients' needs, no matter where in the world the clients live. They then need to quickly translate these worldwide client needs into products and services, produce those products and services on a timely and least-cost basis, and then deliver them to clients in a culturally acceptable fashion for each of the national and ethnic communities involved.

By this global phase, the exclusive product, sales, or price orientation of past phases almost completely disappears. Companies replace these individual orientations with a culturally responsive design orientation, accompanied by a rapid, worldwide, least-cost production function. Needless to say, culture is critically important to this most advanced stage. Similarly, the ability to manage cross-cultural interaction, multinational teams, and global alliances becomes fundamental to overall business success. Whereas effective global human resource management strategies varied in past phases from being irrelevant to being helpful, by the global phase they become essential, a minimum requirement for organizational survival and success.

CROSS-CULTURAL MANAGEMENT

The growing importance of world business has created a demand for managers sophisticated in global management and skilled at working with people from other countries. Cross-cultural management explains the behavior of people in organizations around the world and shows people how to work in organizations with employee and client populations from many different cultures. Cross-cultural management *describes* organizational behavior within countries and cultures; *compares* organizational behavior across countries and cultures; and, perhaps most importantly, seeks to understand and improve the *interaction* of co-workers, managers, executives, clients, suppliers, and alliance partners from countries and cultures around the world. Cross-cultural management thus expands the scope of domestic management to encompass international and multicultural dynamics. Rather than global management being a subset of traditional domestic management approaches, it is clear that single-culture, domestic management has become a limited subset of global, cross-cultural management.

Parochialism

Parochialism means viewing the world solely through one's own eyes and perspective. A person with a parochial perspective neither recognizes other people's different ways of living and working nor appreciates that such differences have serious consequences. People in all cultures are, to a certain extent, parochial. Journalists, politicians, and managers alike have frequently decried Americans' parochialism.[5] Americans speak fewer foreign languages, demonstrate less interest in foreign cultures, and are more naive in global business situations than the majority of their trading partners. In *The Tongue-Tied American* (61), United States Congressman Paul Simon deplored the shocking state of foreign language illiteracy in the United States and emphasized the heavy price Americans pay for it diplomatically, commercially, economically, and culturally. His message was a "shocking indictment of the complacent, potentially catastrophic monolingual arrogance of . . . [Americans], from top government leaders to the . . . [person] in the street" (65). Echoing Simon's sentiments in reference to South America, former United States Congressman James Symington explained the problem as Americans'

> fundamental, dogged, appalling ignorance of the Latin mind and culture. Foreign students and statesmen refresh their perceptions of the United States

by reading our poets, essayists, novelists and humorists. But our approach is like that of the man who, when asked which hurts most, ignorance or apathy, replied, "I don't know and I don't care." Such indifference cannot be justified by our otherwise commendable concern for what people do rather than what they think. . . . Preoccupied with acting, we seldom miss opportunities to ignore thought. [Perhaps, in the future] . . . diplomats—possibly even presidents—might know something of the cultural lessons that stir our neighbors' hearts (62).

Fortune magazine reports that "A 'Copernican revolution' must take place in the attitudes of American CEOs as the international economy no longer revolves around the U.S., and the world market is shared by many strong players" (37:157). Lester Thurow, former dean of MIT's Sloan School of Management, asserts that CEOs "must have an understanding of how to manage in an international environment. . . . To be trained as an *American* manager is to be trained for a world that is no longer there" (24:50). Many business leaders predict that the next generation of top executives will have to have multiple global assignments to reach the top (9:B18;13). Royal Dutch Shell, for example, already requires four global expatriate assignments before it will consider a manager for promotion into senior management. Yet, in the United States such global exposure and experience has neither been the norm in the past, nor, unfortunately, is it very common today.

Two decades ago a *Dun & Bradstreet* survey found that only a handful of the 87 chairmen and presidents of the 50 largest American multinational corporations could be considered career internationalists. Of the 87 top executives, 69 had had no international experience at all, except for inspection tours (19). Today, executive recognition of the importance of global experience has increased, but not as rapidly as one might have predicted. For example, whereas almost two-thirds (62%) of today's American executives see "emphasizing an international outlook" as very important for the CEO of tomorrow, only a third (35%) consider experience outside of the United States as very important, and fewer than one in five (19%) consider foreign language training as very important (37:158). By comparison, 82 percent of non–American executives consider an international outlook as very important for future CEOs; twice as many (70% versus 35%) consider experience outside of their home country as very important; and more than three times as many (64% versus 19%) consider foreign language training as very important (27;37:158).

Why have many Americans ignored the need to think and act global-ly? Americans' historic parochialism is understandable and at the same time unfortunate. Because the United States has such a large domestic market (over 250 million people) and English became the international business language, many Americans assume that they need to neither speak other languages nor go to other countries to succeed in corporate work. This parochial assumption is certainly not true for young Brazilians, Swedes, Israelis, or Thais.

The United States's former political and technological dominance also led many Americans to believe that they could conduct business strictly from an American perspective. In many fields in which American tech-nology was the only advanced technology available, potential clients and trading partners from around the world have had no option but to "buy American." Global business expertise was unnecessary because the product sold itself (Domestic Phase). In the public sector, projects trans-fering technology from the United States to Third World countries further encouraged Americans to view the world from an American perspective (Multidomestic Phase). An Indonesian's comments about Americans' views of Third World people capture this technologically based parochialism:

> The questions Americans ask me are sometimes very embarrassing, like whether I have ever seen a camera. Most of them consider themselves the most highly civilized people. Why? Because they are accustomed to technical inventions? Consequently, they think that people living in bamboo houses or having customs different from their own are primitive and backward (58).

The academic community often further reinforced American man-agers' tendency toward parochialism. Most management schools are in the United States; the vast majority of management professors and researchers are American trained; and the majority of management research still focuses on U.S. companies. Out of over 11,000 articles published in 24 management journals between 1971 and 1980, approxi-mately 80 percent were studies of the United States conducted by Americans (1). Fewer than 5 percent of the articles describing the behav-ior of people in organizations include the concept of culture (1). Fewer than 1 percent focus on people from two or more cultures working together, a crucial area for global business (1). The publishing of cross-cultural management articles increased only slightly during the 1980s (25;41;43;48).

By 1990 only 6.5 percent of organizational behavior and human resource management (HRM) articles published in leading U.S. management journals were international; however, almost three times as many (17.5%) organizational behavior and HRM articles in leading management journals published outside of North America were international (3). Of these international articles, almost every article (96%) found that culture had a significant impact on managerial styles and organizational success (3). The manager about to negotiate a major contract with a national of another country, the executive about to become a director of Asian, Latin American, or European operations, and the newly promoted vice president for global marketing, all receive less guidance than they need from the available management literature.

The United States will continue to have a large domestic market, English will continue to be the language of international business, and technological excellence will continue to typify many American industries. Nonetheless, the domain of business has rapidly moved beyond national boundaries; the limitations of monolingualism have become more apparent; and sustained technological superiority in many industries has become a cherished memory. The intense global competition in the 1990s renders parochialism self-defeating. No nation can afford to act as if it is alone in the world (parochialism) or as if it is superior to other nations (ethnocentrism). The United States's economy, like that of all other nations, is inextricably linked to the health of other economies. Like businesspeople the world over, Americans must now compete and contribute based on world-class standards and on a global scale.

Global versus Domestic Organizations

Two fundamental differences between global and domestic organizations are geographic dispersion and multiculturalism. The term *geographic dispersion* refers to the spread of global organizations' operations over vast distances worldwide. Whether organizations produce in multiple countries or only export to them, whether employees work as expatriates or only travel abroad, whether legal ownership involves joint ventures, wholly owned subsidiaries, or strategic alliances, global firms must manage despite the added complexity of working in many countries simultaneously. Geographic dispersion confronts organizations with fluctuations in exchange rates, substantial transportation and communication costs, varying customs regulations, and many other complexities determined by greater distances and national borders.

Multiculturalism, the second fundamental dimension of a global firm, means that people from many cultures (and frequently many countries) interact regularly. Domestic firms can be multicultural if their employees or clients include more than one culture. For example, many organizations in Quebec, Canada, employ Anglophones (English speakers) and Francophones (French speakers) to work within the same organization, as do many companies in California that hire Hispanic and Asian as well as Anglo-Saxon employees."[6] Multiculturalism adds to the complexity of global firms by increasing the number of perspectives, approaches, and business methods represented within the organization. Whereas most international business books have focused on understanding and managing geographical dispersion, this book focuses primarily on managing multiculturalism and raises such questions as: How do people vary across cultures? How do cultural differences affect organizations? When do global managers recognize cultural differences? What are the best strategies for managing corporate multiculturalism?

WHAT IS CULTURE?

To understand the differences between domestic and global management, it is necessary to understand the primary ways in which cultures around the world vary. Anthropology has produced a literature rich in descriptions of alternative cultural systems, containing profound implications for managers working outside of their native country.

Anthropologists define culture in many ways. *Culture* is "that complex whole which includes knowledge, belief, art, law, morals, customs and any capabilities and habits acquired by a . . . [person] as a member of society" (62:1). It is "a way of life of a group of people, the configuration of all the more or less stereotyped patterns of learned behavior, which are handed down from one generation to the next through the means of language and imitation" (6:4). After cataloging more than one hundred different definitions of culture, anthropologists Kroeber and Kluckhohn (38:181) offered one of the most comprehensive and generally accepted definitions:

> Culture consists of patterns, explicit and implicit, of and for behavior acquired and transmitted by symbols, constituting the distinctive achievement of human groups, including their embodiment in artifacts; the essential core of culture consists of traditional (i.e., historically derived and selected)

ideas and especially their attached values; culture systems may, on the one hand, be considered as products of action, on the other, as conditioning elements of future action.

Culture is therefore (12:19)

a.   Something that is shared by all or almost all members of some social group,

b.   Something that the older members of the group try to pass on to the younger members, and

c.   Something (as in the case of morals, laws and customs) that shapes behavior, or . . . structures one's perception of the world.

Managers frequently see culture as "the collective programming of the mind which distinguishes the members of one human group from another . . . the interactive aggregate of common characteristics that influence a human group's response to its environment" (31:25). In general, we see people as being from different cultures if their ways of life as a group differ significantly, one from the other.

Cultural Orientations

The cultural orientation of a society reflects the complex interaction of values, attitudes, and behaviors displayed by its members. As shown in Figure 1-1, individuals express culture and its normative qualities through the values that they hold about life and the world around them. These values in turn affect their attitudes about the form of behavior considered more appropriate and effective in any given situation. The continually changing patterns of individual and group behavior eventually influence the society's culture, and the cycle begins again. What are the differences among values, attitudes, and behavior?

Values

A value is that which is explicitly or implicitly desirable to an individual or a group and which influences the selection from available modes, means, and ends of action. Values can be both consciously and unconsciously held (36). Values therefore reflect relatively general beliefs that either define what is right and wrong or specify general preferences (10:23). Research has shown that personal values affect corporate strategy (22;26;28;30;53;54;57;66) and that managerial values affect all forms

Figure 1-1   *Influence of Culture on Behavior*

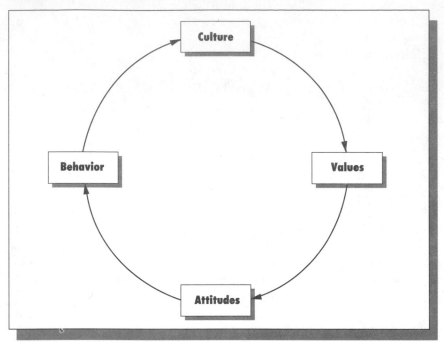

of organizational behavior (7;21;50;51), including selection and reward systems (10); superior/subordinate relationships (44); and group behavior, communication, leadership, and conflict management styles (40). For example, Latin American managers consider loyalty to the family to be very important—a value that leads them to hire members of their own family whenever possible. American managers strongly believe in individual achievement—a value that leads them to emphasize a candidate's track record and performance on qualifying exams rather than family membership. In both cases a strongly held value influences managerial behavior.

Attitudes

An attitude expresses values and disposes a person to act or to react in a certain way toward something. Attitudes are present in the relationship between a person and some kind of object. For example, market research has shown that French Canadians have a positive attitude toward pleasant or sweet smells, whereas English Canadians prefer smells with efficient or clean connotations.   Advertisements for Irish Spring soap directed at French Canadians therefore stress the pleasant smell, whereas the ads for English Canadians stress the inclusion of effective deodorants.[7]

Behavior

Behavior is any form of human action. For example, based on their culture, Middle Easterners stand closer together (a behavior) than do North Americans, whereas Japanese stand farther apart than do either North Americans or Middle Easterners. Latin Americans touch each other more frequently during business negotiations than do North Americans, and both touch more frequently than do Japanese. People's behavior is defined by their culture.

Cultural Diversity

Diversity exists both within and among cultures; however, within a single culture certain behaviors are favored and others repressed. The norm for a society is the most common and generally most acceptable pattern of values, attitudes, and behavior. For example, in global business a man wearing a dark gray business suit reflects the norm through a favored behavior, whereas a man wearing a green business suit would violate the norm. A cultural orientation describes the attitudes of most of the people most of the time, not all of the people all of the time. Accurate stereotypes reflect societal or cultural norms.

Societies enforce norms by communicating disapproval toward transgressors—people who engage in prohibited behavior. Some norms, such as laws, may be very important; whereas other norms, such as customs and habits, may be less important. A norm's importance is measured by how severely society condemns those who violate it. In the United States, for example, an important norm proscribes bribery. Companies caught using bribery to increase their business are publicly prosecuted and fined, both of which reflect severe cultural sanctions. A less important norm in the United States is the tradition of people saying "Good morning" when greeting colleagues at the beginning of the day. If I fail to say "Good morning" one day, it is unlikely that society will punish me severely. At worst, my colleagues may assume that I am preoccupied or perhaps tired.

Anthropologists Kluckhohn and Strodbeck (36) discuss a set of assumptions that allows us to understand the cultural orientations of a society without doing an injustice to the diversity within the society.[8] The six assumptions (as adapted by Rhinesmith (53)), are that

1. "There are a limited number of common human problems for which all peoples at all times must find some solutions." For

example, each society must decide how to clothe, feed, and house its people. Each society must decide on systems of communication, education, transportation, health, commerce, and government.

2.   "There are a limited number of alternatives which exist for dealing with these problems." For example, people may house themselves in tents, caves, igloos, single-family dwellings, or apartment buildings, but they cannot survive the winter without some form of housing.

3.   "All alternatives are present in all societies at all times, but some are preferred over others."

4.   "Each society has a dominant profile or values orientation and, in addition, has numerous variations or alternative profiles." For example, people may cure disease with chemotherapy, surgery, acupuncture, acupressure, prayer, or nutrition. The Chinese tend to prefer acupressure and acupuncture; the British prefer chemotherapy and surgery; and the Christian Scientists prefer prayer.

5.   "In both the dominant profile and the variations, there is a rank ordering of preference for alternatives."

6.   "In societies undergoing change, the ordering of preferences will not be clearcut." For example, as the computer revolution changes society, organizations' preferences to communicate using the Internet, fax, telephone, electronic mail, or the postal system become unclear; different organizations make different choices.

These assumptions emphasize that cultural descriptions always refer to the norm or stereotype; they never refer to the behavior of all people in the culture, nor do they predict the behavior of any particular person.

HOW DO CULTURES VARY?

As shown in Table 1-3, six basic dimensions describe the cultural orientations of societies: people's qualities as individuals, their relationship to nature and the world, their relationship to other people, their primary type of activity, and their orientation in space and time (36;40). The six dimensions answer the questions: Who am I? How do I see the world? How do I relate to other people? What do I do? How do I use space and

TABLE 1-3 *Values Orientation Dimensions*

Perception of	Dimensions		
Individual	Good	Good and evil	Evil
World	Dominant	Harmony	Subjugation
Human Relations	Individual	Laterally extended groups	Hierarchical groups
Activity	Doing	Controlling	Being
Time	Future	Present	Past
Space	Private	Mixed	Public

Source: Based on Kluckhohn & Strodbeck (36), as adapted by Lane and diStefano (40).

time? Each orientation reflects a value with behavioral and attitudinal implications. As summarized in Table 1-4, this section presents the six values dimensions with management examples for each. Because many people are familiar with United States's business customs, the examples highlight differences between the United States and a number of other countries.

How People See Themselves

What is the nature of the individual: good or evil? Americans traditionally see people as a mixture of good and evil, capable of choosing one over the other. They believe in the possibility of improvement through change. Some other cultures see people as basically evil—as reflected in the Puritans' orientation—or as basically good—as reflected in utopian societies throughout the ages. Societies that consider people good tend to trust them a great deal, whereas societies that consider people evil tend to suspect and to mistrust them. In high-trust societies, for example, people leave doors unlocked and do not fear being robbed or assaulted. In low-trust societies, people bolt their doors. After making a purchase, people in high-trust societies expect to receive the merchandise and correct change; they do not expect to be cheated. In low-trust societies, *caveat emptor* ("let the buyer beware") rules the marketplace; one can trust only oneself. In many countries people are more trusting in rural communities than in urban centers.

Today many citizens of the United States and Canada lament that their fellow citizens cannot be trusted the way they used to be. For example, a Toronto hotel now posts a sign reminding guests that "Love is leaving the towels." Los Angeles gas stations, to assure that motorists will not drive away without paying, require motorists to pay twenty dollars or sign a credit card slip before filling their gas tanks. A Minneapolis firm, National

TABLE 1-4   *Cultural Orientations and Their
Implications for Management*

Cultural Dimension	*American Cultural Orientation*	*Contrasting Cultural Orientation*
What is the nature of people?	Mixture of good and evil. Change is possible.	Good (Evil) Change is impossible.
Example:	Emphasize training and development; give people the opportunity to learn on the job.	Emphasize selection and fit; select the right person for the job; don't expect employees to change once hired.
What is a person's relationship to the external environment, including nature?	People dominant over nature and other aspects of the external environment.	Harmony (Subjugation)
Example:	Policy decisions made to alter nature to fulfill people's needs— i.e., building dams, roads.	Policy decisions made to protect nature while meeting people needs.
What is a person's relationship to other people?	Individualistic	Group (Hierarchical or Lateral)
Example:	Personnel director reviews academic and employment records of candidates to select the best person for the job.	Personnel director selects the closest relative of the chief executive as the best person for the job.
Example:	Decisions are made by individuals.	Decisions are made by the group
What is the primary mode of activity?	Doing	Being (Controlling)
Example:	Employees work hard to achieve goals; employees maximize their time at work.	Employees work only as much as needed to be able to live; employees minimize the time at work.
How do people see space?	Private	Public
Example:	Executive holds important meetings in a large office behind closed doors and has the secretary screen interruptions.	Executive holds important meetings in a moderate-sized office or in an open area, with open doors and many interruptions from employees and visitors.
What is a person's temporal orientation?	Future/Present	Past (Present)
Example:	Policy statement refers to 5- and 10-year goals while focus is kept on this year's bottom line and quarterly reports; innovation and flexibility to meet a dynamic, changing future are emphasized.	Policy statements this year reflect policy statements 10 years ago; the company strives to use tradition to perform in the future as it has in the past.

Adapted from Kluckhohn and Strodbeck (36), diStefano (18); also see Lane and diStefano (40).

Source: Nancy J. Adler, "Women as Androgynous Managers: A Conceptualization of the Potential for American Women in International Management." Reprinted with permission from *International Journal of Intercultural Relations*, vol. 3, no. 6 (1979) p. 411. Copyright 1979 by Pergamon Press, Ltd. Adapted by Adler, 1996.

Credential Verification Service, makes a profitable business of exploiting the lack of trust among corporate recruiters and job candidates by exposing résumé deception. Out of 233 personnel officers responding to a survey of *Fortune 500* companies, only one said that deception by applicants for executive positions was diminishing (42:85). To add to this mistrust, many people find it more difficult to trust foreigners than citizens of their own country.

Managers in the People's Republic of China describe their approach as combining the extremes of good (Confucian tradition) with evil (the tradition of Lao Tzu)—a marriage of opposites. They also describe their belief that peasants are good and rich people are not so good, as reflected in a story told among people living in Tianjin, the fourth largest city in the People's Republic of China:

> At the Sino-Franco joint venture wine factory in Tianjin between France's Remy Martin and China's Dynasty, a French director left his wallet filled with French francs in a ped-a-cab. The peasant ped-a-cab driver waited all day outside the factory to return the wallet to the Frenchman.

Perhaps because people fear the unknown, they frequently tend to assume that evil intentions motivate foreigners' behavior. For example, Canadian government officials thought the Inuits, a native people, were evil when they burned down the doors in their Canadian-built public housing projects. The officials misinterpreted the Inuits' behavior as vandalism and therefore judged it to be evil, whereas the Inuits had actually altered the houses to fit their normal—doorless—life-style. The Canadian government condemns the destruction of property, whereas the Inuits condemn closed doors that separate people from family members and neighbors.

Apart from their tendencies toward good or evil, can human beings improve themselves? Societies and organizations vary in the extent to which they believe that adults can change or improve. Organizations that believe people can change, for example, emphasize training and development, whereas organizations that believe people are incapable of change emphasize selection systems. With today's computer and information systems revolution, some organizations choose to replace many of their current administrative support personnel and to hire information systems experts in their place. Other companies retrain their current employees to use the new state-of-the-art technology. The first strategy—hiring exclusively new employees—assumes that change is not possible, whereas the second strategy—training present employees—implies that change is possible. North Americans' emphasis on M.B.A. education and executive development seminars strongly reflects their belief that change is possible. The Chinese saying that the "Chinese . . . strive to become better and, when better, to become perfect" also reflects a strong belief in the ability of adults to change. As one Shanghai executive exclaimed, applying the belief to his own career path, "I was trained as an engineer and now I am an export/import manager. I changed!"

Perception of the Individual:
GOOD VERSUS EVIL

Can a Bosnian Trust a Canadian Working in Sweden?

A Young Canadian in Sweden found summer employment working in a restaurant owned by Bosnians. As the Canadian explained, "I arrived at the restaurant and was greeted by an effusive Bosnian man who set me to work at once washing dishes and preparing the restaurant for the June opening.

"At the end of the first day, I was brought to the back room. The owner took an old cash box out of a large desk. The Bosnians owner counted out my wages for the day and was about to return the box to the desk when the phone rang in the front room. The owner hesitated: should he leave me sitting in the room with the money or take it with him? Quite simply, could he trust me?

"After a moment, the man got up to answer the phone, leaving me with the open money box. I sat there in amazement: how could he trust me, someone he had known for less than a day, a person whose last name and address he didn't even know?"

This incident contrasts perceptions of individuals as good or evil. The Bosnian manager saw individuals as good and inherently trustworthy. For this reason, he could leave his new employee alone with the money without worrying that the Canadian would steal it before he returned. The Canadian employee's surprise that this stranger trusted him with the money is a reflection of a North American's values orientation toward individuals. Believing that people are capable of both good and evil, North Americans would proceed more cautiously than did the Bosnian. If the Canadian had been in the owner's shoes, he probably would have taken the cash box with him to the other room to answer the telephone, fearing that the money might be stolen.[9]

People's Relationship to the World

What is a person's relationship to the world? Are people dominant over their environment, in harmony with it, or subjugated by it? North Americans generally see themselves as dominant over nature. Other societies, such as the Chinese and Navaho, attempt to live in harmony with nature. They see no real separation between people and their natural environment, and their beliefs allow them to live at peace with the environment. In contrast to both of these orientations, a few remote tribal societies see people as subjugated by nature. In these cultures people accept, rather than interfere with, the inevitable forces of nature.

How does an organization see its environment? Are the relevant external environments—economic, social, cultural, political, legal, and technological—seen as stable and predictable or as random, turbulent, and unpredictable? Does an organization assume that it can control its environment, that it must harmonize with it, or that it will be dominated by it?

North Americans' approach to agriculture exemplifies the dominance orientation. By assuming, for instance, that people can and ethically should modify nature to enhance their own well-being, dominance-oriented agribusiness executives use fertilizers and insecticides to increase crop yields. By contrast, harmony-oriented farmers attempt only to plant the "right" crops in the "right" places at the "right" time of the year in order to maintain the soil in good condition. Farmers subjugated by nature hope that sufficient rain will fall, but they do not construct irrigation systems to assure sufficient water for their crops. Although they hope or pray that pests will not attack their crops, they refuse to use insecticides.

Other examples of North Americans' dominance orientation include astronauts' conquest (dominance) of space; economists' structuring of markets; sales representatives' attempts to influence buyers' decisions; and, perhaps most controversial today, bioengineering and genetic programming. Perhaps the contrasting relationships become clearer in the sayings of three societies:

Saying	Culture	Meaning
Ayorama: "It can't be helped"	Inuit—Canada	Reflects subjugation
En Shah Allah: "If God is willing"	Moslem—Arab	Reflects harmony with nature and submission to God
Can Do: "I will do it"	American	Reflects dominance

Perception of the World:
DOMINANCE VERSUS HARMONY

Feng Shui

When the Hong Kong branch of a North American bank moved to a new location, the expatriate executive was asked to choose between two offices. He selected the one that was larger, regularly shaped, and adjacent to the vice-president's office. His Chinese clients, however, became uncomfortable visiting him in his new office. One client with whom he was particularly friendly explained why: "The room has bad *feng shui.*" *Feng shui,* or "wind water," are earth forces, which the Chinese believe can cause success or failure. *Feng shui* reflects the belief that people and their activities are affected by the layout and orientation of their workplaces and homes. The goal of *feng shui* is to be in harmony with the environment.

The expatriate executive faced a dilemma. As a reflection of power and status in the North American context, he had chosen his new office because of its size and proximity to the seat of power. In contrast, the Chinese clients believed that it was a poor location because it had bad *feng shui,* and predicted poor success in business unless he changed offices.

Ultimately, on the recommendation of his Chinese clients, the executive moved into a smaller office, where the space was awkwardly cut up by a pillar. On the advice of his Chinese clients, he placed a mirror on the pillar to overcome this drawback. There were no dire consequences or business failures; his clients were comfortable with the new office and chose to continue to do business with him.

North American and Chinese perceptions of the world clearly differ. North Americans want to control nature, whereas the Chinese want to be in harmony with nature. The expatriate executive had originally chosen his office based on reasons that appeared rational from his cultural perspective of dominance—he wanted to maximize his status and influence through office size and proximity. But to the Chinese, his decision was not rational; the room was unlucky because it lacked harmony with nature. The expatriate was sensitive to Chinese cultural values and changed offices.[10]

A society's orientation toward the world is pervasive. For example, in news reporting, when Sir Edmund Hillary reached the top of Mt. Everest, the Western (dominance-oriented) press reported it as "Man conquers mountain"; in contrast, the Chinese (harmony-oriented) press reported it as "Man befriends mountain." Religious writings similarly reflect a people's cultural orientation. For example, the Bible states in Genesis, "Let them have dominion over the earth"; whereas the Tao Te Ching states, "Those who would take over the earth and shape it to their will, I notice, never succeed"—a dominance orientation contrasted with one of harmony.

Personal Relationships: Individualism or Collectivism

Americans are individualists; they use personal characteristics and achievements to define themselves, and they value individual welfare over that of the group. By contrast, in group-oriented societies people define themselves as members of clans or communities and consider common goals and the group's welfare most important. Lateral group membership includes all who are currently members of a particular family, community, or organization; hierarchical group membership includes those members of the particular group from prior generations.

The United States is strongly individualistic and weak on its loyalty to groups, teams, and communities. For example, Americans praise their sports heros by singling out individual excellence: "Mark Smith and the team trounced the opposition." They praise corporate performance by singling out and rewarding the chief executive officer (CEO). General Electric's outstanding financial performance is often attributed to CEO Jack Welch, as in the subtitle of the book *How Jack Welch Is Making General Electric the World's Most Competitive Company* (64). Compared with people in more group-oriented societies, Americans are more geographically mobile and their relationships, especially with co-workers, are less permanent. Due to its individualistic orientation, the United States has been described as a temporary society with temporary systems, uprootedness, disconnectedness, nonpermanent relationships, and mobility (8). More group-oriented societies, such as Japan, China, and the Israeli Kibbutzim, emphasize group harmony, unity, and loyalty. Individuals in these societies frequently fear being personally ostracized or bringing shame to their family or group for behavior that deviates from the norm.

Personnel policies also follow either individual or group orientations. Individual-oriented personnel directors tend to hire those best qualified to do the job based on personal skills and expertise. Individualistic applicants will therefore submit résumés listing personal, educational, and professional achievements. Group-oriented personnel directors also tend to hire those most qualified, but the prime qualifications they seek are trustworthiness, loyalty, and compatibility with co-workers. They hire people who are well known to them, including friends and relatives of people already working for the organization. Therefore, rather than sending well-prepared résumés listing individual achievements, applicants seek introductions to the personnel director through a mutual friend or relative; and initial discussions center on mutual friends, family, or community members. The managing director of one group-oriented company in Ghana expressed his belief that only people who are known by other employees in the company can possibly be trusted to act responsibly.

The personnel managers' actions can appear biased, illogical, and unfair when viewed from the perspective of a contrasting culture. Many individualistic North Americans see group-oriented hiring practices as nepotism because they see these practices only from their own culture's perspective. Many more group-oriented Latin Americans question the ethics of North American managers, who choose not to be loyal to their friends and family (66).

The organization of firms in individualistic and collective societies differs. In individualistic societies, such as those of Canada and the United States, organization charts generally specify individual positions, each with a detailed job description listing formal duties and responsibilities. By contrast, organization charts in more group-oriented societies, such as Hong Kong, Indonesia, and Malaysia, tend only to specify sections, departments, and divisions, except for the top one or two positions (52). Group-oriented societies describe assignments, responsibilities, and reporting relationship in collective terms.

The individual versus group orientation also influences decision making. In North America, individuals make decisions. North Americans, therefore, make decisions relatively quickly, although implementation frequently gets delayed while the decision maker explains the decision and gains concurrence from other members of the organization. By contrast, in Japan, a group-oriented culture, many people make the decision rather than just one. The process of group decision making is less flexible and more time-consuming than the individualistic system because concurrence must be achieved prior to making the decision. However, since all parties already understand and concur, the Japanese can implement a decision almost immediately after it is made.

Personal Relationships:
INDIVIDUALISM VERSUS COLLECTIVISM
The German Won't Hire the Serbian's Daughter

Rade, an engineer who had immigrated to Western Germany from the former Yugoslavia, worked for a highly respected German engineering firm. His daughter Lana had recently graduated from a prestigious German university. Rade considered it his duty to find his daughter a job, and he wanted his German boss to hire Lana. Although the boss felt Lana was extremely well qualified for the open position, he refused to have a father and daughter working in the same office. The very suggestion of hiring family members was repugnant to him. Rade believed that his boss was acting unfairly—he saw no problem in his daughter working with him in the same office.

The unfortunate outcome was that Lana was neither considered nor hired; the boss lost respect for Rade; and Rade became so upset that he requested a transfer to a new department. Neither Rade nor his boss understood that the conflict was caused by the fundamentally different values orientations in the two cultures.[11]

Activity: Doing or Being

Americans' dominant mode of activity is *doing*, or action. They stress achieving outcomes that they can measure by objective standards; that is, standards believed to be external to the particular individual and capable of being consistently applied to other situations and outcomes. Managers in doing-oriented cultures motivate employees with promises of promotions, raises, bonuses, and other forms of public recognition. The contrasting orientations are *being* and *controlling*. In the *being* orientation, people, events, and ideas flow spontaneously; people stress release, indulgence of existing desires, and living and working for the moment. If managers in *being*-oriented cultures do not enjoy their colleagues and current projects, they quit; they will not work strictly for future rewards. People in *control*-oriented societies restrain their personal desires by detaching themselves from the objects they might desire; such control, they believe, allows each individual to develop as a more integrated person. The *do-er* is more active; the *be-er* is more passive. The *do-er* actively tries to achieve the most in life; the *be-er* wants to experience life.

Activity:
DOING VERSUS BEING

Kashmir Versus Sweden

In the 1980s the United Nations appointed a Swedish army officer as an observer in Kashmir. His job was to travel around the turbulent province situated between Pakistan and India looking for troop movements on each side. The officer and his family moved into a houseboat on the river in Sringar, the capital of the province. As has been customary for Europeans working in Kashmir, the family employed a "boy"—a servant—to perform all the family's household services during their stay. The servant was always very polite and pleasant, cooked delicious meals, and kept the houseboat neat and clean.

The family was very pleased with his work, and after a short time decided to give him a raise. Surprisingly, the servant did not turn up for work the next day, and his little brother arrived in his place. On his new higher salary, the servant had employed his younger brother to work for the family. With the raise he could maintain his own desired standard of living and help his younger brother without personally having to work.

Because the Kashmiri servant was a Hindu, he did not believe that he could improve his standard of living in his lifetime. So by being good and not disturbing the harmony of his circumstances (i.e., by simply *being*), he believed he could be reincarnated into a higher position in his next life. This natural tendency to accept life with no expectations for either improvement or material goods contrasts sharply with the Swedish family's notion of working hard to achieve personal goals and improve one's material lot in this life (i.e., their *doing* orientation). The Swede's surprise at seeing the younger Kashmiri brother arrive for work reflects this contrast.[12]

The doing and being orientations affect planning quite differently. *Being-oriented* managers view time as generational, and therefore believe that planning should allow for the extended time needed for true change to occur. Major projects often need a generation, or certainly a decade, to achieve significant results. *Be-ers* allow change to occur at its own, often slow, pace. They do not push or rush things to achieve short-term results. By contrast, *do-ers* believe that planning can speed up the change process if plans are carefully outlined, specific target dates set, and progress frequently reported (55). *Be-ers* believe that this type of planning is possible but unwise, since it rarely works immediately and is fruitless in the long run.

The activity orientation also explains why people work. To achieve goals, *do-ers* maximize work; to live fully, *be-ers* minimize work. Increasing the salaries of *do-ers* and *be-ers* has opposite effects. Salary increases motivate *do-ers* to work more hours because the rewards are greater; they motivate *be-ers* to work fewer hours because they can earn enough money in less time and still enjoy life. American expatriate managers (*do-ers*), using salary as a motivational tool, made a severe mistake when they raised the salaries of a group of Mexican workers (*be-ers*), only to discover that by doing so they had decreased the total hours that these particular Mexicans wanted to work. Similarly, Canadians working in Malaysia found that workers were more interested in spending extra time with their family and friends than in earning overtime pay bonuses.

Time: Past, Present, or Future

What is the temporal focus of human life? How do societies use time? Are they oriented to the *past*, the *present*, or the *future*? Past-oriented

---

Time:
PAST, PRESENT, OR FUTURE
Bus Schedules in the Bahamas

In the Bahamas, bus service is managed similarly to many taxi systems. Each driver owns his own bus and collects passenger fees for his income. There is no set schedule nor a set time when the bus will run or arrive at a particular location. Everything depends on the driver.

Bus drivers in the Bahamas are present-oriented; what they feel like doing on a particular day at a particular hour dictates what they will actually do. For example, if the bus driver feels hungry, he will go home to eat lunch without waiting for a pre-set lunch hour. Drivers see no need to repeat yesterday's actions today nor to set tomorrow's schedule according to the needs and patterns of yesterday.

This present orientation contrasts sharply with the behavior of bus drivers in New York City, Toronto, Paris, London, and most other urban centers of the Western world. Drivers in these cities have planned schedules that they follow to the best of their ability. Present-oriented behavior has the advantage of flexibility, whereas more future- or past-oriented behavior has the advantage of predictability.[13]

Time:
THE LONG-TERM VERSUS THE SHORT-TERM
A Question of Contracts

The directors of a Japanese firm and a Canadian firm met in Vancouver to negotiate the sale of coal shipments from British Columbia to Japan. The companies reached a stalemate over the length of the contract. The Japanese, ostensibly to reduce the uncertainty in their coal supply and to assure continuous, stable production in Japan, wanted the Canadians to sign a ten-year contract. The Canadians, on the other hand, did not wish to commit themselves to such a lengthy agreement in the event that they could find a more lucrative offer in the interim. Whereas the Japanese wanted to reduce the level of risk in their coal supply, the Canadians expressed their willingness to assume the additional risk of losing a steady buyer for the potential benefits of a more profitable future buyer.

The negotiations had hit a snag. Unless the culturally based time frame of the contract could be resolved, no contract would be signed. A deal that would benefit both parties had a distinct possibility of remaining unconsummated.[14]

---

cultures believe that plans should be evaluated in terms of their fit with the customs, traditions, and the wisdom of society and that innovation and change are justified only according to past experience. By contrast, future-oriented cultures believe that they should evaluate plans in terms of the projected future benefits to be gained. Future-oriented people justify innovation and change in terms of future economic payoffs and have less regard for past social or organizational customs and traditions.

In contrast with most North Americans, many Europeans are more past-oriented. Many Europeans believe that preserving history and continuing past traditions remain important, whereas North Americans give tradition less importance. North American businesspeople focus on the present and near future; they may talk about achieving five- or ten-year plans, but they work toward achieving this quarter's results. North American employment practices also reflect a short-term orientation. Employees who do not perform well during their first year with the organization are fired or at best not promoted. U.S. companies do not give them ten years to demonstrate their worth. By contrast, Japan has a very long-term, future-oriented time horizon. When large Japanese firms hire

---

Time:
A PAST ORIENTATION
The People's Republic of China

Whereas odysseys to outer space lure more future-oriented Americans to movie houses, in China historical dramas have traditionally led box-office sales, and the more ancient the story, the better. Chinese children, so far, have no space-age superman to emulate. Even at play, they pretend to be the Monkey King, the supernatural hero of a famous medieval epic (45:12).

Similarly, Chinese scientists look to the past for inspiration. In the national archives, teams of Chinese meteorologists comb voluminous weather records of the last 300 years in an effort to discover patterns that might help them predict the droughts and floods that still plague the country. Seismologists in charge of improving China's earthquake prediction methods use similar long-term, past-oriented approaches (45).

---

employees, both parties make a commitment for life. Major Japanese firms invest in years of training for each employee because they can expect the employee to work with the firm for thirty to forty years. North American firms invest far less in training because a lifetime commitment between the company and the employee is neither given nor expected.

Societies use different standards of temporal precision. What defines when people arrive late and when they are on time for work, for meetings, or for business lunches? How much variation is allowed? How long do managers expect scheduled appointments to last—five minutes or two hours? What is the typical length of a project assignment—one week or three years? An American engineer working in Bahrain expressed surprise at his Arab client's response to his apologetic explanation that, "Unfortunately, due to unforeseen delays, the new plant would not be ready to open until six months after the originally planned date." The Bahrainian responded; "We have lived for thousands of years without this plant; we easily can wait another six months or a year. This is no problem."

Diversity exists within societies as well as between societies. Past-, present-, and future-oriented people exist within every society. Comparing lawyers and economists in the United States highlights this temporal diversity. American lawyers use a past orientation in citing precedent to adjudicate the outcome of cases, whereas economists use a future orientation in conducting cost-benefit analyses to predict the possible future outcomes of alternative corporate and governmental strategies.

Space: Public or Private

How do people use physical space? Is a conference room, an office, or a building seen as public or private space? When can I enter an office directly, and when must I wait outside until granted permission to enter? The public versus private dimension defines the arrangement of organizational space. North Americans give private offices to more important employees, and even open offices have partitions between desks. They hold important meetings behind closed doors, usually in the executive's large, private office, and generally with minimal interruptions.

The Japanese, by contrast, use no partitions to divide desks; bosses often sit together with their employees in the same large room. Middle Easterners often have numerous people present during important meetings. Both Middle Easterners and Japanese have a more public orientation than do North Americans. By contrast, the Germans and British typically exhibit an even more private orientation than do most North Americans. When visitors meet a German manager for the first time, the German's secretary must generally announce them before the German's closed office door will be opened to admit them.

SUMMARY

Cultures vary in distinct and significant ways. Our ways of thinking, feeling, and behaving as human beings are neither random nor haphazard but rather are profoundly influenced by our cultural heritage. Until we leave our community, we often remain oblivious to the dynamics of our shared culture. As we come in contact with people from other cultures, we become aware of our uniqueness and begin to appreciate our differences. In interacting with foreigners, we learn to recognize and value our fundamental humanity—our cultural similarities and dissimilarities. For years people chose to believe that organizations were beyond the influence of culture and that they were only determined by technology and task. Today we know that work is not simply a mechanistic outgrowth of either technology or task. At every level, culture profoundly influences the behavior of organizations as well as the behavior of people within organizations.

QUESTIONS FOR REFLECTION

1. **Individual Cultural Self-Awareness.**   Using the six Kluckhohn and Strodbeck values orientations summarized in Table 1-4, which values do you think best reflect your personal orientation on each dimension?

2. **National Cultural Self-Awareness.** Describe your country's culture on each of the six values orientations. On which part of the dimension is your country's culture? What concrete evidence do you have? If you were a foreigner observing your country for the first time, what could you observe that would convince you 6f your country's position on each of the values orientations?

3. **Cross-Cultural Awareness.** Think about a cross-cultural situation that you have been in or are currently in (a situation in which you are working with or negotiating with people from another culture). Describe their values orientations. Where do your and their values orientations differ? What problems have been caused or might be caused by the differences in your values orientations? What benefits can you potentially gain by using the cultural differences to your advantage?

4. **Cross-Cultural Interaction Skills.** In reading the international press, select a situation involving people from more than one culture (such as Russians negotiating a trade agreement with Italians). Analyze the situation using at least one of the values dimensions. Indicate how the values differences are helping or hindering the probability of a successful outcome of the situation.

5. **Parochialism and Ethnocentrism.** In which ways is your culture parochial? In which ways is it ethnocentric? Give concrete examples from situations that you have actually observed or that you have read about in the press.

NOTES

1. Blaise Pascal *Pensées*, 60 (294), as sited in Geert Hofstede, *Culture's Consequences* (Beverly Hills, Sage Publications, 1980).

2. Unless otherwise stated, all dollar figures are in U.S. dollars.

3. Arguments for both the pessimistic and optimistic appreciations of shifting world business dynamic summarized by Professor Arshad Ahmad, Concordia University, Montreal, Canada, 1996.

4. Adapted from material originally appearing in the Preface by Nancy J. Adler of Henry W. Lane and Joseph J. diStefano's *International Management Behavior* (Toronto: Nelson Canada, 1988, pp. xiii-xvi).

5. Although the term American literally refers to all peoples from North and South America, it is used in this book as a shorthand way to refer to citizens of the United States of America.

6. Domestic multiculturalism refers to multiple cultures within a particular country. Multiculturalism, as it is used in this book, refers to international multiculturalism; that is, many cultures represented from two or more countries.

7. As conducted and cited by Jim Cornell et al., "Cultural Aspects Influencing Advertising Messages Aimed at French Canadians" (Paper, McGill University), interview with Jacques Grenier of Publi Plus, Inc., March 10, 1982.

8. Kluckhohn and Strodbeck reflect a North American perspective in their work. Their framework is therefore most accurate in describing Western cultures.

9. Stig-Eric Gruman, BCom, McGill University.

10. Anne H. Whetham, MBA, McGill University.

11. Ismail Elkhaby, MBA, McGill University.

12. Franc Malts, MBA, McGill University.

13. Yuk Tsui Grace Seto, BCom, McGill University.

14. John Clancy, BCom, McGill University.

FILM NOTE

The British Broadcasting Corporation video program "World Without Borders" documents the evolution of a multinational firm, Cable and Wireless, from its domestic origins through the multidomestic stage, and into its current multinational and planned transnational strategies. European and North American professors comment on Cable and Wireless's strategy and competitive environment, while presenting frameworks for understanding and managing the evolution of global firms. (Director: Steve Wilkinson, The British Broadcasting Corporation, Open University Production Centre, Walton Hall, Milton Keynes, England MK7 68H; Tel 44-1908-655-343; Fax: 44-1908-655-300)

REFERENCES

1. Adler, N. J. "Cross-Cultural Management Research: The Ostrich and the Trend," *Academy of Management Review,* vol. 8, no. 2 (1983), pp. 226–232.

2. Adler, N. J. "Do MBAs Want International Careers?" *International Journal of Intercultural Relations,* vol. 10, no. 3 (1986), pp. 277–300.

3. Adler, N. J., and Bartholomew, S. "Academic and Professional Communities of Discourse: Generating Knowledge on Transnational Human Resource Management,"*Journal of International Business Studies,* vol. 23, no. 3 (1992), pp. 551–569.

4. Adler, N. J., and Ghadar, F. "International Strategy from the Perspective of People and Culture: The North American Context," in A. M. Rugman, ed.,

Research in Global Strategic Management: Intercultural Business Research for the Twenty-First Century: Canada's New Research Agenda, vol.1 (Greenwich, Conn.: JAI Press, 1990), pp. 179–205.

5. Ball, D. A., and McCulloch, W. H. *International Business: Introduction and Essentials* (Plano, Tex.: Business Publications, 1982).

6. Barnouw, V. *Culture and Personality* (Homewood, Ill.: Dorsey Press, 1963).

7. Bartlett, C. A., and Ghoshal, S. *Managing Across Borders: The Transnational Solution* (Boston: Harvard Business School Press, 1989).

8. Bennis, W., and Slater, P. *The Temporary Society* (New York: Harper & Row, 1968), p. 124.

9. Brown, L. K. "For Women in Business, No Room in the Middle," *New York Times* (December 28, 1981), p. B18.

10. Brown, M. A. "Values—Necessary but Neglected Ingredient of Motivation on the Job," *Academy of Management Review*, vol. 1 (1976), pp. 15–23.

11. *Business and International Education* (Washington, D.C.: American Council of Education, 1977), pp. 9–10.

12. Carrol, M. P. "Culture," in J. Freedman, ed., *Introduction to Sociology: A Canadian Focus* (Scarborough, Ont., Canada: Prentice-Hall, 1982), pp. 19–40.

13. Chandler, C. H., as quoted in C. H. Deutsch, "Losing Innocence, Abroad: American Companies Are Trying to Shake Their Provincialism by Shipping Executives Overseas," *New York Times* (July 10, 1988), Business, pp. 1, 2.

14. *Chicago Tribune* (February 4, 1981), as cited in S. H. Kim, *International Business* (Richmond, Va.: Robert F. Dame, Inc. 1983).

15. Corporate Scoreboard. *Business Week* (July 21, 1980), p. 118; and *1980 World Bank Atlas* (Washington, D.C.: The World Bank, 1981).

16. Daniels, J. D.; Ogram, E. W.; and Radebaugh, L. H. *International Business Environments and Operations*, 3rd ed. (Reading, Mass.: Addison-Wesley, 1982).

17. Dhawan, K. C.; Etemad, H.; and Wright, R. W. *International Business: A Canadian Perspective*. (Reading, Mass.: Addison-Wesley, 1981).

18. diStefano, J. "A Conceptual Framework for Understanding Cross-Cultural Management Problems" (London, Ont., Canada: School of Business Administration, University of Western Ontario, 1972). Also see H. W. Lane and J. diStefano, *International Management Behavior*, 2nd edition (Boston: PWS-Kent, 1992).

19. Dun & Bradstreet, Canada, Ltd. *Canadian Book of Corporate Management*, 1980 (Toronto: Dun & Bradstreet, Canada, Ltd., 1980).

20. Eiteman, D. K., and Stonehill, A. I. *Multinational Business Finance*, 2nd ed. (Reading, Mass.: Addison-Wesley, 1979).

21. England, G. W. *The Manager and His Values: An International Perspective* (Cambridge, Mass.: Ballinger, 1975).

22. Erez, M., and Early, P. C. *Culture, Self-Identity, & Work* (New York: Oxford University Press, 1993).

23. "The Global Economy," *The Economist* (October 1, 1994), pp. 3–4, 14.

24. "Global Strategist," *U.S. News and World Report* (March 7, 1988), p. 50.

25. Godkin, L.; Braye, C. E.; and Caunch, C. L. "U.S.-Based Cross-Cultural Management Research in the Eighties," *Journal of Business and Economic Perspectives*, vol. 15, no. 2 (1989), pp. 37–45.

26. Guth, W. D., and Taguiri, R. "Personal Values and Corporate Strategies," *Harvard Business Review*, vol. 43 (1965), pp. 123–132.

27. Hambrick, D. C.; Korn, L. B; Frederickson, J. W.; and Ferry, R. M. *21st Century Report: Reinventing the CEO.* (New York: Korn/Ferry and Columbia University's Graduate School of Business, 1989), pp. 1–94.

28. Hampden-Turner, C., and Trompenaars, F. *The Seven Cultures of Capitalism: Value Systems for Creating Wealth in the United States, Britain, Japan, Germany, France, Sweden, and the Netherlands.* (New York: Doubleday, 1993).

29. Hamrin, R. D. *Managing Growth in the 1980s* (New York: Praeger, 1980).

30. Hofstede, G. *Cultures and Organizations: Software of the Mind* (London: McGraw-Hill, 1991).

31. Hofstede, G. *Culture's Consequences: International Differences in Work-Related Values* (Beverly Hills, Calif.: Sage, 1980), p. 25.

32. International Monetary Fund and ACLI International, Inc. *Wall Street Journal* (May 28, 1981), p. 50.

33. International Monetary Fund, International Financial Statistics, United Nations Monthly Bulletin of Statistics, and national statistics as cited in *International Trade, 1982/83.* Contracting Parties to the General Agreement on Tariffs and Trade, Geneva, 1983, Appendix Table A4.

34. Jelinek, M., and Adler, N. J. "Women: World Class Managers for Global Competition," *Academy of Management Executive*, vol. 2, no. 1 (1988), pp. 11–19.

35. Kim, S. H. *International Business Finance* (Richmond, Va.: Robert F. Dame, 1983).

36. Kluckhohn, F., and Strodbeck, F. L. *Variations in Value Orientations* (Evanston, Ill.: Row, Peterson, 1961).

37. Korn, L. B. "How the Next CEO Will Be Different," *Fortune* (May 22, 1989), pp. 157–158.

38. Kroeber, A. L., and Kluckhohn, F. *Culture: A Critical Review of Concepts and Definitions*, Peabody Museum Papers, vol. 47, no. 1 (Cambridge, Mass.: Harvard University, 1952), p. 181.   Reprinted with permission of the Peabody Museum of Archaeology and Ethnology, Harvard University.

39. Krugman, P., "Does Third World Growth Hurt First World Prosperity?" *Harvard Business Review* (July-August, 1994), pp. 113–121.

40. Lane, H. W., and diStefano, J. J. *International Management Behavior: From Policy to Practice*, 2nd edition (Boston: PWS-Kent, 1992).

41. Lyles, M. "A Research Agenda for Strategic Management in the 1990s," *Journal of Management*, vol. 27, no. 4 (1990), pp. 363–375.

42. McCain, M. "Résumés: Separating Fact from Fiction," *American Way* (December 1983), p. 85.

43. McEvoy, G. M., and Buller, P. F. "International Human Resource Management Publications: Even in the Eighties & Needs for the Nineties," Utah State University (1992), pp. 1–21.

44. Mankoff, A. W. "Values—Not Attitudes—Are the Real Key to Motivation," *Management Review*, vol. 63, no. 12 (December 1979), pp. 23–29.

45. Mathews, J., and Mathews, L. *One Billion: A China Chronicle* (New York: Ballantine Books, 1983).

46. Mitroff, I. I. *Business Not As Usual* (San Francisco, Calif.: Jossey-Bass, 1987).

47. Parry, T. G. "Foreign Direct Investment and the Multinational Corporation," in Ingo Walter, ed., *Handbook of International Business* (New York: Wiley, 1982), Chapter 16, pp. 4–5.

48. Peng, T. K.; Peterson, M. F.; and Shri, Y. P. "Quantitative Methods in Cross-National Management Research: Trends and Equivalence Issues," *Journal of Organization Behavior*, vol. 12, no. 1 (1990), pp. 87–107.

49. Peters, T. "Competition and Compassion," *California Management Review*, vol. 28, no. 4 (1986), pp. 11–26.

50. Porter, Michael E. *The Competitive Advantage of Nations* (New York: The Free Press, 1990).

51. Posner, B. Z., and Munson, J. M. "The Importance of Values in Understanding Organizational Behavior," *Human Resource Management*, vol. 18 (1979), pp. 9–14.

52. Redding, S. G., and Martyn-Johns, T. A. "Paradigm Differences and Their Relation to Management with Reference to South-East Asia," in G. W. England, A. R. Negandhi, and B. Wilpert, eds., *Organizational Functioning in a Cross-Cultural Perspective* (Kent, Oh.: Kent State University Press, 1979).

53. Rhinesmith, S. H. *Cultural Organizational Analysis: The Interrelationship of Value Orientations and Managerial Behavior* (Cambridge, Mass.: McBer Publication Series Number 5, 1970).

54. Rhinesmith, S. H. *A Manager's Guide to Globalization: Six Keys to Success in a Changing World* (Homewood, Ill.: Business One Irwin, 1993).

55. Rhinesmith, S. H., and Renwick, G. W. *Cultural Managerial Analysis Questionnaire* (New York: Moran, Stahl and Boyer, 1982).

56. Rugman, A. M., and Verbeke, A. "Strategic Responses to Free Trade," in M. Farrow and A. M. Rugman, eds., *Business Strategies and Free Trade, Policy Study No. 5* (Toronto: C.D. Howe Institute, 1988), pp. 13–29.

57. Sackman, S. *Cultural Knowledge in Organizations: Exploring the Collective Mind* (Newbury Park, Calif.: Sage, 1991).

58. Scarangello, A., ed. *American Education Through Foreign Eyes* (New York: Hobbs, Dorman, 1967). Examples contributed by Robert Kohls.

59. Schwab, K., and Smadja, C., "The New Rules of the Game in a World of Many Players," *Harvard Business Review* (July-August 1994), pp. 40–44, 46, 50.

60. Shapiro, A. C. *Multicultural Financial Management*, 4th ed., (Needham Heights, Mass.: Allyn & Bacon, 1992), p. 5.

61. Simon, P. *The Tongue-Tied American: Confronting the Foreign Language Crisis* (New York: Continuum Publishing Corp., 1980).

62. Symington, J. W. "Learn Latin America's Culture," *New York Times* (September 23, 1983). Copyright © 1983/94 by The New York Times Company. Reprinted by permission.

63. Taylor, E. B. *Primitive Culture: Researches into the Development of Mythology, Philosophy, Religion, Language, Arts and Customs*, vol. 1 (New York: Henry Holt, 1977), p. 1.

64. Tichy, N., and Sherman, S. *Control Your Destiny or Someone Else Will: How Jack Welch Is Making General Electric the World's Most Competitive Company* (New York: Currency/Doubleday, 1993).

65. Tinsley, R. L., as quoted in V. V. Merchant's book review of *The Tongue-Tied American: Confronting the Foreign Language Crisis,* in *International Psychologist,* vol. 25, no. 1 (February 1983).

66. Trompenaars, F. *Riding the Waves of Culture: Understanding Cultural Diversity in Business* (London: The Economist Books, 1993).

67. U.S. Department of Commerce. *Survey of Business* (February 1977).

68. Vernon, R. "International Investment and International Trade in the Product Cycle," *Quarterly Journal of Economics*, vol. 8, no. 2 (May 1966), pp. 129–144.

CHAPTER 2
How Do Cultural Differences Affect Organizations?

Deep cultural undercurrents structure life in subtle but highly consistent ways that are not consciously formulated. Like the invisible jet streams in the skies that determine the course of a storm, these currents shape our lives; yet their influence is only beginning to be identified.

— Edward T. Hall (5:12)

People dress differently, eat different foods, and celebrate different holidays in countries around the world. But do those differences affect the ways people work together? Do people organize, manage, and work differently from culture to culture?

WORK BEHAVIOR VARIES ACROSS CULTURES

In what ways does the behavior of people in organizations vary across cultures? Management researchers have found culturally based differences in people's values, attitudes, and behaviors. Each of us has a set of attitudes and beliefs—a set of filters through which we see management situations.

Figure 2-1 shows how managers' beliefs, attitudes, and values affect behavior. To a certain extent, beliefs, attitudes, and values cause both

FIGURE 2-1 *Managerial Attitudes and Employee Behavior:*
A Self-Fulfilling Prophecy

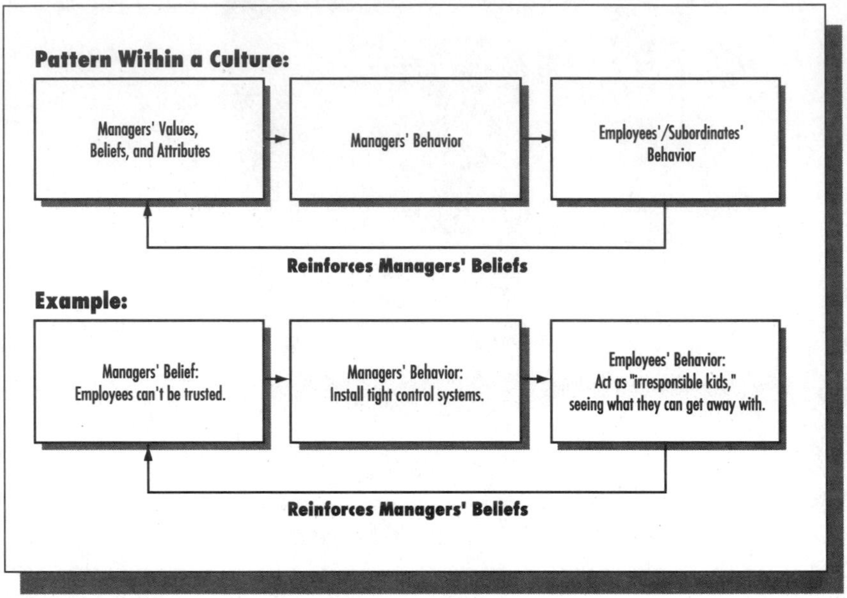

Source: Based on Douglas McGregor, *The Human Side of Enterprise* (New York: McGraw-Hill, 1960).

vicious and benevolent cycles of behavior. Douglas McGregor, an American management theorist, gave us prototypical examples of this pattern in his classical "Theory X" and "Theory Y" managerial styles (13). According to McGregor, Theory X managers do not trust their subordinates and believe that employees will not do a good job unless closely supervised. These managers establish tight control systems—such as time clocks and frequent employee observation—to assure themselves that employees are working. The employees, realizing that management does not trust them, start behaving irresponsibly—they arrive on time only when the time clock is working and only work when the manager is watching. The manager, observing this behavior, becomes more distrustful of the employees and installs even tighter control systems. According to McGregor, the manager's belief that employees cannot be trusted leads to the employees' irresponsible behavior, which in turn reinforces the manager's belief that employees cannot be trusted—a vicious cycle and a counterproductive, yet self-fulfilling, prophecy.

THEORY X OR THEORY Y

Canadian Employees and Filipino Management

A Canadian bank employee gave the following description of his Filipino boss's Theory X approach to management.

"During my employment at the Royal Bank, I had a most unbearable and suspicious supervisor. As an assistant manager, he had authority over all employees on the administrative side, including me. The problem was that he seemed to have a total distrust for his subordinates. He was constantly looking over our shoulders, checking our work, attitudes, and punctuality.

"Although most of his employees resented this treatment, the assistant manager was an extremely conscientious supervisor who honestly believed in what he called 'old-style' management. He believed that employees are lazy by nature. He therefore believed that they must be pressured into working. As the supervisor, he felt justified in treating employees severely.

"I found his attitude condescending and counterproductive. As a group, the employees thought of themselves as basically trustworthy, but we decided that since our boss seemed to have no respect for us we would give him the same treatment in return. The result created a work environment that was filled with mistrust and hostility. The atmosphere affected everyone's work: employees became less and less willing to work, and the assistant manager increasingly believed in the employees' laziness and the need for severity. Luckily, the situation caught the manager's eye and was resolved after lengthy discussions. Only then did it become clear that we were not seeing the situation in the same way at all. From the assistant manager's perspective, he was simply showing his caring and involvement with his subordinates. As he explained, Filipino employees who were not treated like this might have felt neglected and unimportant. Unfortunately, we were not Filipinos and, as Canadians, did not respond as many Filipinos might have responded."[1]

McGregor's Theory Y describes a more benevolent cycle. Managers who trust their employees give them overall goals and tasks without instituting tight control systems or close supervision. The employees, believing that management trusts them, do their best work whether or not their manager is watching them. The manager, seeing that the employees are present and working, becomes even more convinced that they can be trusted. Managers' attitudes influence their own behavior, which in turn influences employees' attitudes and behavior, which then reinforces the managers' original attitudes and behavior.

Managers communicate respect for and trust in their employees in different ways, depending on their cultural background. Managers from more *specific cultures* tend to focus only on behavior that takes place at work, whereas managers from more *diffused cultures* include behavior that takes place in employees' private and professional lives. As a part of a major cross-cultural management study, Fons Trompenaars (16), a world renowned Dutch management researcher, asked managers and employees from around the world if their companies should provide employees with housing. Whereas most managers from such diffused cultures as the former Yugoslavia (89%), Hungary (83%), China (82%), and Russia (78%) believed that the company should provide housing, managers from more specific cultures rejected the idea as interfering with employees' private lives (16:86). Less than 20 percent of managers from such specific cultures as Sweden, the United States, Denmark, Switzerland, the Netherlands, the United Kingdom, Australia, and France believed that providing housing was a good idea (16:86). Managers from diffused cultures communicate their respect by showing concern for an employee's whole life. By contrast managers from specific cultures demonstrate their respect by not intruding in employees' private lives. It is easy to see how misunderstanding and mistrust can grow between managers from one culture and employees from another culture.

Worldwide Differences in Managerial Style

André Laurent (12), a highly acclaimed professor at INSEAD, a leading international management school located in France, studied the philosophies and behaviors of managers in nine Western European countries, the United States, and three Asian countries (Indonesia, Japan, and the People's Republic of China). Laurent asked managers from each country to describe their approach to more than sixty common work situations. He found distinct patterns for managers in each of the countries.

Task and Relationship

In response to the statement, "The main reason for a hierarchical structure is so that everybody knows who has authority over whom," for example, managers from some countries strongly agreed, whereas managers from other countries strongly disagreed. As shown in Table 2-1, most American managers disagree with the statement; they believe that the main reason for a hierarchical structure is to organize tasks and facilitate problem solving around those tasks. Coming from a very task-oriented culture, many Americans believe that an organization with very few hierarchical levels—in which most employees are colleagues rather than bosses and subordinates—can function effectively. They believe that such minimal hierarchy is possible if tasks and roles are very clearly defined and the organization is not too large.

By contrast, many managers from more relationship-oriented cultures, such as most southern Europeans, Asians, Latin Americans, and Middle Easterners, strongly agree with Laurent's statement. Eighty-six percent of the Indonesian managers surveyed believed that the main reason for a hierarchical structure was to have everyone know who has authority over whom. They did not believe that even a small organization could exist, let alone succeed, without a formal hierarchy.

Perhaps these different beliefs explain some potential problems when, for example, Americans work with Indonesians. Americans typically approach a project by outlining the overall goal, designating each of the major steps, and then addressing staffing needs. Their approach goes from task to people. Indonesians, on the other hand, first need to know who will manage the project and who will work on it. Once they know who the leader will be and the hierarchy of people involved, they can assess the project's feasibility. The Indonesians' approach goes from people to task. Both cultures need to understand the project's goals and staffing arrangements, but the importance of each is reversed. An American would rarely discuss who will be the project director before at least

TABLE 2-1   *"The Main Reason for a Hierarchical Structure Is So That Everbody Knows Who Has Authority Over Whom."*

Agreement Rate Across Countries										
United States	Germany	Sweden	Netherlands	Great Britain	Spain	Italy	France	Japan	P.R.C.	Indonesia
17%	26%	30%	31%	34%	34%	42%	43%	50%	70%	83%

Note: P.R.C. refers to the People's Republic of China.

Source: Based on André Laurent, "The Cultural Diversity of Western Conceptions of Management," *International Studies of Management and Organization*, vol. 13 no. 1-2 (Spring-Summer 1983), pp. 75–96. Reprinted by permission of publisher, M. E. Sharpe, Inc., Armonk, N. Y. Updated and expanded, 1993.

broadly defining the project, whereas Indonesians would rarely discuss the feasibility of a project before knowing who will be its leader.

Similarly, in response to the statement, "In order to have efficient work relationships it is often necessary to bypass the hierarchical line," Laurent found large and consistent differences across cultures. As shown in Table 2-2, Swedish managers see the least problem with bypassing. They are task oriented and value getting the job done, which means going to the person most likely to have the needed information and expertise, and not necessarily to their boss. Most Swedish managers believe that a perfect hierarchy—in which their boss knows everything—is impossible; they therefore see bypassing as a natural, logical, and appropriate way for employees to work in complex and changing organizations.

By contrast, most Italians, being more relationship oriented than the Swedes, consider bypassing the boss as an act of insubordination. Most Italian managers believe that frequent bypassing indicates a poorly designed organization. Italians therefore respond to bypassing by reprimanding the employee or redesigning the hierarchical reporting structure. Imagine the potential for frustration and subsequent failure when Swedes and Italians form joint ventures and strategic alliances with each other. When Swedish employees begin working in a typically Italian organization, they will attempt to accomplish their work goals responsibly by continually bypassing hierarchical lines and going directly to the people in the organization who they believe have the information and expertise they need. Because the Swedes do not consult their new Italian boss, the Italian will assume that the Swedes are insubordinate and hence a threat to both the joint venture and the project. In the reverse situation, the Swedish boss, frustrated with the Italian subordinates' constant communication and

TABLE 2-2   *"In Order to Have Efficient Work Relationships, It Is Often Necessary to Bypass the Hierarchical Line."*

Percent Disagreement Across Countries									
Sweden	United States	Great Britain	France	Netherlands	Germany	Indonesia	Italy	P.R.C.	Spain
26%	32%	35%	43%	44%	45%	51%	56%	59%	74%

Note: P.R.C. refers to the People's Republic of China.

Source: Based on André Laurent, "The Cultural Diversity of Western Conceptions of Management," *International Studies of Management and Organization,* vol. 13, no. 1-2 (1983), pp. 75–96. Reprinted by permission of publisher, M. E. Sharpe, Inc., Armonk, N. Y. Updated and expanded, 1993.

requests for permission and information, will assume that the Italian employees lack initiative and are unwilling both to use their personal judgment and to take risks. Why else, asks the Swedish manager, would the Italians always consult me, the boss, before acting on matters for which the boss need not be consulted? Is either side right? No, they are just different.

Managers: Experts or Problem Solvers?

Laurent found little agreement across national borders on the nature of the managerial role. As shown in Figure 2-2, more than four times as many Japanese and Indonesian managers as American managers agreed with the statement, "It is important for managers to have at hand precise answers to most of the questions that their subordinates may raise about their work." Most American managers believe that the role of the manager is to be a problem solver: managers should help subordinates discover ways to solve problems, rather than simply answering their questions directly. Furthermore, American managers believe that merely providing answers

FIGURE 2-2 *The Manager's Role Varies Across Cultures*

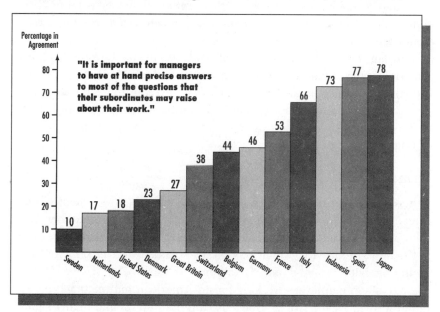

Source: Based on André Laurent, "The Cultural Diversity of Western Conceptions of Management," *International Studies of Management and Organization*, vol. 13, no. 1-2 (Spring-Summer 1983), pp. 75–96. Reprinted by permission of publisher, M. E. Sharpe, Inc., Armonk, N. Y. Updated to add Spain, 1993.

discourages subordinates' initiative and creativity and ultimately diminishes their productivity. By contrast, the French generally see the manager as an expert. Most French managers believe that they should give precise answers to subordinates' questions in order to maintain their credibility as experts and as managers and that their subordinates' sense of security depends on receiving precise answers. The French believe that people should not hold managerial positions unless they can give precise answers to most work-related questions. (See page 81, the Iranian's view, for another example of the expert perspective.)

Is a manager primarily an expert or a problem solver? Again, there is no one right answer because organizations from different cultures maintain different beliefs. Problems, however, arise when managers from one culture interact with managers and employees from other cultures. When an American manager tells French employees, "I don't know the answer, but maybe if you talk to Simon in marketing he will know," the French employees do not assume that they have received appropriate problem-solving help but rather assume that their boss is incompetent. Similarly, when American employees receive specific answers from a French boss, they may consider the boss egotistical rather than competent: "Why didn't the French boss tell them that Simon in marketing has a better answer?"

Laurent concludes that the national origin of European, North American, and Asian managers significantly affects their views on how effective managers should manage (12:77). Overall, the extent to which managers see organizations as political, authoritarian, role-formalizing, or hierarchical-relationship systems varies according to their country of origin (12).

Dimensions of Difference

Differences in work-related attitudes exist across a wide range of cultures. Geert Hofstede, an eminent Dutch management researcher, corroborated and integrated the results of Laurent's and others' research. In a 40-country study (8), which was later expanded to over 60 countries, including both Oriental and Occidental cultures (4;7;9;10), 160,000 managers and employees working for an American multinational corporation were surveyed twice. Hofstede, like Laurent, found highly significant differences in the behavior and attitudes of employees and managers from different countries who worked for this multinational corporation—differences that did not change over time. Hofstede found that national culture explained more of the differences in work-related values and attitudes than did position within the organization, profession, age, or gender. In summarizing the most important differences, Hofstede initially found that managers and employees vary on four primary dimensions: individualism/collectivism, power distance, uncertainty avoidance, and career success/quality of life.[2] Later, Hofstede and his colleagues identified a fifth dimension, Confucian dynamism (4;10).

Individualism and Collectivism

Individualism exists when people define themselves primarily as separate individuals and make their primary commitments to themselves. Individualism implies loosely knit social networks in which people focus primarily on taking care of only themselves and their immediate families. *Collectivism* is characterized by tight social networks in which people strongly distinguish between their own groups (in-groups, such as relatives, clans, and organizations) and other groups. Collectivists hold primarily common goals and objectives, not individual goals focusing exclusively on self-interest. People in collective cultures expect members of their particular in-groups to look after their members, protect them, and give them security in exchange for members' loyalty. For example, as reported in *The Arab Executive*, two-thirds of all surveyed Arab executives thought employee loyalty was more important than efficiency (14). This dimension reflects similar values to those of the individual/group values orientation discussed in Chapter 1.

Determinism characterizes such collectivist cultures as the Japanese, where people believe that the will of the group should determine members' beliefs and behavior. This belief is reflected in the Japanese saying "The nail that sticks out will be pounded down." By contrast, free will and self-determination characterize individualistic cultures such as that of the United States, where individuals believe that each person should determine his or her own beliefs and behavior. In each nation its beliefs become self-fulfilling. People from individualistic cultures also tend to believe that there are universal values that should be shared by all. People from collectivist cultures, on the other hand, accept that different groups have different values. Being individualistic, most North Americans believe that democracy—especially North American–style democracy—ideally should be shared by all. People from collectivist cultures find such a view hard to understand.

Collectivist cultures control their members more through external societal pressure (shame) whereas individualistic cultures control their members more through internal pressure (guilt). Members of collectivist cultures place importance on fitting in harmoniously and saving face. Members of individualistic cultures place more emphasis on individual self-respect. In many ways the two orientations trade off individual freedom against collective protection: Do I do what is best for me or what is best for the group? Do I take care only of myself or does the group take care of me? Do I expect the boss to hire me because I have the right education and work experience (individual) or because I come from the right family or social class (group)? Do I expect to be promoted on the basis of my performance in the company or on the basis of my seniority with the company? In times of economic recession, do I expect the least productive workers to be laid off or every employee to take a pay cut? Figure 2-3 shows the ranking of countries on the individualism/collectivism dimension and Table 2-3 shows the abbreviations used in Figures 2-3, 2-4, and 2-5.

Fons Trompenaars, a Dutch management researcher who worked for years with Royal Dutch Shell, also found that managers worldwide vary markedly in their orientation toward individualism and collectivism (16). Among other questions, Trompenaars asked managers which of the following two options would be most likely to improve the quality of life (16:47):

a. Giving individuals the maximum opportunity to develop themselves
b. Having individuals continuously taking care of their fellow human beings

The vast majority of American and Canadian managers (79% each), as well as, for example, Norwegian managers (76%), selected the individual freedom option, whereas the majority of managers in Nepal (69%), Kuwait (61%), Egypt (59%), and Eastern Germany (55%) selected the collective option (16:48).

Which is better, individualism or collectivism? The answer is neither and both. As Trompenaars and his British colleague Charles Hampden-Turner point out, in complex societies, forming a synthesis of the two has become increasingly necessary (6). Individualism and collectivism are complements of each other, with their relationship being "essentially circular with two starting points" (16:55). Individualistic and collectivistic cultures

> go through . . . cycles, but starting at different points and conceiving of . . . [each other alternatively] as means or ends. The individualistic culture sees the individual as "the end" and improvements to collective arrangements as the means to achieve it. The collectivist culture sees the group as its end and improvements to individual capacities as a means to that end (16:55).

FIGURE 2-3 *Position of Forty Countries on Power Distance and Individualism/Collectivism*

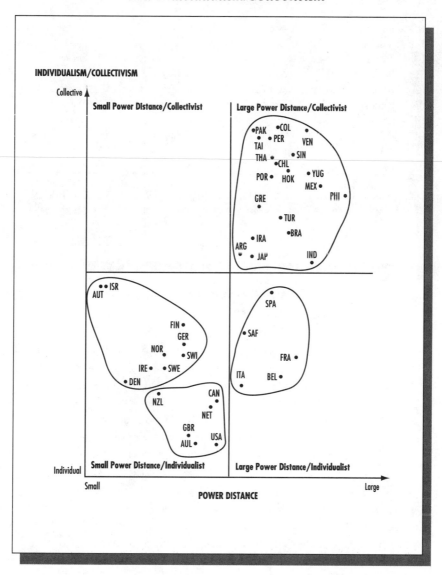

Note: See Table 2-3 for list of abbreviations.

Source: Hofstede, Geert, "Motivation, Leadership, and Organization: Do American Theories Apply Abroad?" Reprinted by permission of the publisher, from *Organizational Dynamics Summer* 1980 © 1980, Dr. Geert Hofstede, et al. American Management Association, New York. All rights reserved.

TABLE 2-3   *Country Abbreviations as Used in Figures 2-3, 2-4, and 2-5*

ARG	Argentina	FRA	France	JAP	Japan	SIN	Singapore
AUL	Australia	GBR	Great Britain	MEX	Mexico	SPA	Spain
AUT	Austria	GER	Germany	NET	Netherlands	SWE	Sweden
BEL	Belgium	GRE	Greece	NOR	Norway	SWI	Switzerland
BRA	Brazil	HOK	Hong Kong	NZL	New Zealand	TAI	Taiwan
CAN	Canada	IND	India	PAK	Pakistan	THA	Thailand
CHL	Chile	IRA	Iran	PER	Peru	TUR	Turkey
COL	Colombia	IRE	Ireland	PHI	Philippines	USA	United States
DEN	Denmark	ISR	Israel	POR	Portugal	VEN	Venezuela
FIN	Finland	ITA	Italy	SAF	South Africa	YUG	Yugoslavia

Source: Hofstede, Geert, "Motivation, Leadership, and Organization: Do American Theories Apply Abroad?" Reprinted by permission of the publisher, from *Organizational Dynamics Summer* 1980 © 1980, Dr. Geert Hofstede, et al. American Management Association, New York. All rights reserved.

INDIVIDUALISM AND COLLECTIVISM

The Pacific Area Travel Association

A global market research firm in Tokyo conducted a survey of travel market potential for the Pacific Area Travel Association (PATA), an organization of national tourist offices from various nations around the Pacific Rim. Although they conducted the survey through a standard questionnaire, each nation was allowed to submit a few of its own open-ended questions.

All countries responded promptly. Of the ten countries surveyed, the U.S. Department of Commerce was the first to send in questions. Individual names were always attached to the letters and faxes from the United States.

Shortly after completing the PATA survey, the company received a contract for a similar study for the Association of Southeast Asian Nations (ASEAN). Due to the similar content, the researchers conducted the ASEAN study in an almost identical fashion to the PATA study. They requested open-ended questions from the national tourism offices of Thailand, the Philippines, Singapore, Malaysia, and Indonesia. Because they had completed the collection of questions in a little over a month for PATA, the company assumed that six weeks would be more than sufficient for the ASEAN nations. They were wrong! The ASEAN nations required a considerably longer time than did the PATA countries. Many letters and faxes had to be exchanged between the Philippines and Tokyo before the market research firm received a final response. Moreover, every communication from the Philippines had a different individual's name on it as its sender.

In thinking over these responses, the survey researchers concluded that the contrast between the Americans' and the Filipinos' responses to the same task stemmed from the relative emphasis on the individual versus the group. Whereas the United States office gave sole responsibility to an individual, the more group-oriented Filipinos delegated the task to a whole department. Since everyone in the office in the Philippines was included, the task naturally took longer.[3]

Power Distance

The second dimension, *power distance*, measures the extent to which less powerful members of organizations accept an unequal distribution of power. To what extent do employees accept that their boss has more power than they have? Is the boss right because he or she is the boss (high power distance) or only when he or she knows the correct answer (low power distance)? Do employees do their work in a particular way because the boss wants it that way (high power distance) or because they personally believe that it is the best way to do it (low power distance)?

In high power distance countries, such as the Philippines, Venezuela, and India, superiors and subordinates consider bypassing to be insubordination; whereas in low power distance countries, such as Israel and Denmark, employees expect to bypass the boss frequently in order to get their work done. When negotiating in high power distance countries, companies find it important to send representatives with titles equivalent to or higher than those of their bargaining partners. Titles, status, and formality command less importance in low power distance countries. As shown in Figures 2-3 and 2-4, the United States ranks relatively low on power distance.

Uncertainty Avoidance

The third dimension, *uncertainty avoidance*, measures the extent to which people in a society feel threatened by ambiguity and therefore try to avoid ambiguous situations by providing greater career stability, establishing more formal rules, rejecting deviant ideas and behavior, and accepting the possibility of absolute truths and the attainment of expertise.

Lifetime employment is more common in high uncertainty avoidance countries such as Japan, Portugal, and Greece; whereas high job mobili-

POWER DISTANCE

An American Executive in London

An American executive went to London to manage the company's British office. Although the initial few weeks were relatively uneventful, it bothered the executive that visitors were never sent directly to his office. A visitor had to first speak with the receptionist, then the secretary, and then the office manager. Finally the office manager escorted the visitor to see the American. The American became annoyed with this practice, which he considered a total waste of time. When he finally spoke with his British employees and urged them to be less formal and to send visitors directly to him, the employees were chagrined.

After a number of delicate conversations, the American executive began to understand the greater stress on formality and hierarchy in England. He slowly learned to ignore his feelings of impatience when the British used their proper channels for greeting guests. As a result, visitors continued to see the receptionist, secretary, and office manager before being sent in to meet the American.[4]

ty occurs more commonly in low uncertainty avoidance countries such as Singapore, Hong Kong, and Denmark. The United States, with its very high job mobility, ranks relatively low on uncertainty avoidance.

As shown in Figure 2-4, common images of organizations vary markedly depending on a country's orientation on power distance and uncertainty avoidance. People in countries such as Denmark that rank low on both dimensions see organizations as resembling *village markets*: the organizations have little hierarchy, everyone talks with everyone else, and risk taking is both expected and encouraged.

Employees in high power distance and low uncertainty avoidance countries such as Singapore and the Philippines tend to view their organizations as *traditional families*. As head of the family, the father protects family members physically and economically. In exchange the family expects loyalty from its members.

Similarly, bosses in Singapore expect to take care of their employees in exchange for employees' loyalty. Employees in countries such as the former Yugoslavia and Mexico, which are high on both dimensions, tend to view their organizations as *pyramids of people* rather than as traditional families. Everyone in the organization knows who reports to whom,

FIGURE 2-4 *Position of Forty Countries on Power Distance and Uncertainty Avoidance*

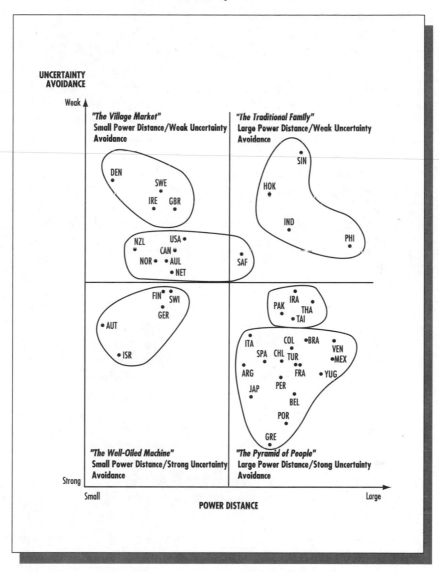

Note: See Table 2-3 for list of abbreviations.

Source: Hofstede, Geert, "Motivation, Leadership, and Organization: Do American Theories Apply Abroad?" Reprinted by permission of the publisher, from *Organizational Dynamics Summer* 1980 © 1980, Dr. Geert Hofstede, et al. American Management Association, New York. All rights reserved.

POWER DISTANCE

The Chinese Dinner Party

One of Canada's leading banks invited a Chinese delegation for dinner. The Canadian host chose to share his hosting responsibilities with a colleague.

The dinner was not a success. Both the Chinese and Canadians remained relatively uneasy throughout the meal. During the dinner, no welcoming speeches or toasts to mutual good health were made. At the end of the meal, the Chinese stood up, thanked the bank officials, declined a ride back to their hotel, and left feeling slighted.

The Canadians also felt upset. They found the departure of the Chinese to be very rude, yet they did not know what they had done wrong to cause the Chinese to leave so abruptly. Despite planning the menu carefully (avoiding such foods as beef and dairy products), providing excellent translation services, and extending normal Canadian courtesies, the Canadians knew something had gone wrong; they were worried and somewhat hurt by the lack of rapport.

When they analyzed the situation, it became clear that the Chinese expectations had not been fulfilled. First, having two people share hosting responsibilities was confusing to the hierarchically minded Chinese. Second, because the Chinese view age as an indication of seniority, they considered the youth of their Canadian hosts as a slight to their own status. Third, in China, the host traditionally offers a welcoming toast at the beginning of the meal, which the guests then reciprocate; by not offering a toast, the Canadians were thought rude.

The specific incident that upset the Canadians—the abrupt departure of the Chinese following the banquet—was, in fact, neither unusual nor a problem: the Chinese retire early and it was getting late.

The Canadians' lack of understanding of the hierarchical nature of Chinese society and the Chinese ways of communicating respect clearly cost them in their business dealings with the visiting delegation.[5]

and formal lines of communication run vertically, never horizontally, across the organization. In the pyramid organization, which operates vertically, management reduces uncertainty by emphasizing who has authority over whom. A pyramid organization resembles a fire department: not only is it clear who is chief, but the fire chief's word becomes law (high power distance). The department clearly defines all procedures and tolerates little or no ambiguity. When the alarm rings, fire fighters do not stop to discuss who will drive the pumper and who will drive the hook and ladder because management has clearly defined their roles and tasks.

In high uncertainty avoidance and low power distance countries such as Israel and Austria, organizations tend to resemble *well-oiled machines*: they are highly predictable without needing a strong hierarchy. Most North American post offices provide excellent examples of this type of organization: they reduce uncertainty by clearly defining roles and procedures.

Career Success and Quality of Life[6]

The fourth dimension contrasts societies focused more narrowly on career success versus those focusing more broadly on the quality of life. The dominant values in *career success* societies emphasize assertiveness and the acquisition of money and things (materialism), while not particularly emphasizing concern for people. The dominant values in *quality-of-life* societies emphasize relationships among people, concern for others, and the overall quality of life.

Societies emphasizing career success tend to define women's and men's roles more rigidly than do quality-of-life societies. For example, women may drive trucks or practice law and men may become ballet dancers or house husbands more easily in societies emphasizing quality of life. As shown in Figure 2-5, the Scandinavian countries strongly emphasize quality of life, the United States emphasizes career success more than quality of life, and Japan and Austria strongly emphasize career success. Japanese and Austrians generally expect women to stay home and to care for children without working outside the home. The United States encourages women to work and gives them a limited amount of support for child care in the form of company-sponsored maternity leave and day-care centers. The Swedes expect women to work; Sweden gives parents the option of paternity or maternity leave to take care of newborn children and the state provides day-mothers to care for older children.

Hofstede's career success/quality-of-life dimension has important implications for motivation in the workplace. Japanese *quality circles*, for example, primarily strive to achieve maximum quality (career success/high uncertainty avoidance); whereas the innovative Swedish work groups—at Volvo, for instance—attempt to enhance job satisfaction and flexibility (quality of life/low uncertainty avoidance). Because societies emphasizing

FIGURE 2-5 *Position of Forty Countries on Uncertainty Avoidance and Career Success/Quality of Life*

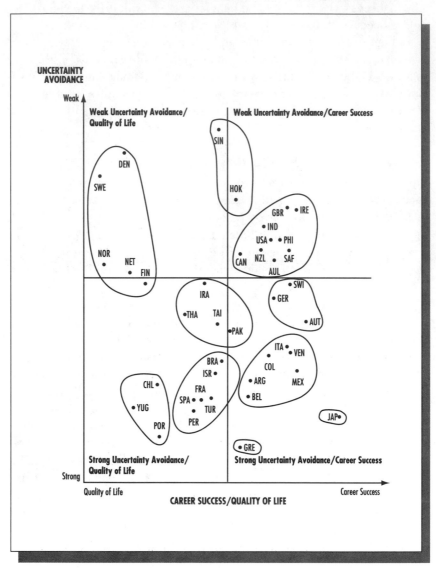

Note: See Table 2-3 for list of abbreviations.

Source: Hofstede, Geert, "Motivation, Leadership, and Organization: Do American Theories Apply Abroad?" Reprinted by permission of the publisher, from *Organizational Dynamics Summer* 1980 © 1980, Dr. Geert Hofstede, et al. American Management Association, New York. All rights reserved.

quality of life also tend to create high-tax environments, extra money often fails to strongly motivate employees (in Sweden, for example). Conversely, societies emphasizing career success tend to develop into lower-tax environments in which extra money or other visible signs of success effectively reward achievement (Mexico and the United States, for example).

Confucian Dynamism

After establishing the first four dimensions, Hofstede and his Hong Kong–based colleague, the eminent cross-cultural psychologist Michael Bond, con-

---

CAREER SUCCESS AND QUALITY OF LIFE

"Inadequate" Business Commitment of Swedish Managers

Swedish policy allows parents to take paternity or maternity leave at their discretion. When the policy was new, the managing director of the Swedish Postal Service created an uproar by announcing his intention to take paternity leave for a number of months to stay home with his new-born child. He explained to the press that executives do not differ from other employees: like other workers, executives also want and need to balance work with family life. In addition, he explained that he believed that an organization that could not function for a period of time without its managing director had no *raison d'être*.

Swedish expatriate managers often do not have the opportunity to explain their desire for balancing their professional and private life to their international colleagues. Swedes frequently surprise their international clients when they expect the work week to end at 5 p.m. on Friday or when they announce their intention to return home at the end of the day on the first plane because they want to spend more time with their families. According to Swedish businesspeople, many foreigners, especially Americans, are willing to work all evening and all weekend to finish an important project; they frequently judge Swedes' behavior as demonstrating an inadequate commitment to work and quickly become annoyed. In actuality, the Swedes are simply demonstrating their strong commitment to quality of life, whereas the Americans and other similar foreigners behave according to their strong commitment to the particular project (*career success* orientation).[7]

ducted the first global management survey ever originally developed with Chinese managers and employees. Based on this survey, they identified a fifth dimension, *Confucian dynamism*, which measures employees' devotion to the work ethic and their respect for tradition (4;10). Many observers attribute the rapid economic growth of Asia's "Four Tigers"—Hong Kong, Singapore, South Korea, and Taiwan—to their extremely strong work ethic and their commitment to traditional Confucian values (10).

Rules and Relationships

Building on the work of Laurent and Hofstede, Trompenaars (16) conducted a major survey of over 15,000 managers in 40 countries. While his results corroborate those of his colleagues, he went beyond their work to document additional dimensions and to highlight some of the ethical issues posed by managers misinterpreting the conflicting cultural signals.

Trompenaars (16:34) asked managers from around the world to consider what they would do in the following situation:

> You are riding in a car driven by a close friend. He hits a pedestrian. You know he was going at least 35 miles per hour in an area of the city where the maximum allowed speed is 20 miles per hour. There are no witnesses. His lawyer says that if you testify under oath that he was only driving 20 miles per hour it may save him from serious consequences. What right has your friend to expect you to protect him?
>
> a. My friend has a definite right as a friend to expect me to testify to the lower figure.
> b. He has some right as a friend to expect me to testify to the lower figure.
> c. He has no right as a friend to expect me to testify to the lower figure.
>
> What do you think you would do in view of the obligations of a sworn witness and the obligation to your friend?
>
> d. Testify that he was going 20 miles an hour.
> e. Not testify that he was going 20 miles an hour.

There was a very wide range of opinions, with more than 90 percent of the managers in Canada (96%), the United States (95%), Switzerland (94%), Australia (93%), Sweden (93%), Norway (93%), and Western Germany (91%) saying that the friend had no right to expect false testimony, that rules were made for everyone, and that therefore they would not testify that their friend was going 20 miles per hour (16:35). By contrast, less than half the managers in South Korea (26%), Venezuela (34%), Russia (42%), Indonesia (47%), and China (48%) would refuse to testify for their friend (16:35).

The underlying difference in response is based on whether the society believes more in universalism or particularism. Universalistic societies, such as Canada and the United States, believe that laws are written for everyone and must be upheld by everyone at all times. The general principle of what is legal, or illegal, takes precedence over the particular details of who is involved in the situation. By contrast, in particularist societies, such as South Korea and Venezuela, the nature of the particular relationship that you have with someone determines how you will act in the situation. To a person from a particularist culture, it makes a difference if someone is or is not a friend or family member. For a person from a universalistic culture, rules are seen as made equally for everyone. Ask yourself what you would do in the situation. Then ask yourself, if it had been your mother or daughter driving the car, would you be more or less likely to testify than you would be for a friend?

Although there is a tendency for firms to become more universalistic as they become more global, the clashes between universalistic and particularistic cultures are legendary. For example, universalistic cultures rely on extensive contracts to document the "rules" of the business relationship, whereas particularistic cultures use much looser written agreements and rely on the strength of their personal relationships to maintain the commitment. Particularists view detailed contracts, and especially penalty clauses, as a sign that they are not trusted and that therefore there is no relationship. They then have little need to adhere to the contract. Interestingly, as many Asian, Middle Eastern, and Latin cultures have shown, personal relationships can, at times, be more durable than contracts, as well as more flexible.

Clearly joint ventures, strategic alliances, and overall business negotiations between universalists and particularists raise ethical questions, from both cultures' perspectives:

> Business people from both societies . . . tend to think [of] each other [as] corrupt. A universalist will say of particularists, "they cannot be trusted because they will always help their friends"; a particularist, conversely, will say of universalists, "you cannot trust them: they would not even help a friend" (16:32).

For example, a team of Brazilian negotiators, coming from a particularistic culture, explained to us that they only tell the truth once they have gotten to know the other party; that is, once they have developed a personal relationship. They described the American and Canadian negotiators, who often accused the Brazilians of lying, as naive for not understanding how negotiations really work. The Americans, for whom truth is an absolute, a "universal" that is unrelated to the particular negotiation or the particular people involved, accused the Brazilians of being deceitful. Americans tell the same "truth" to everyone, without regard for the nature or depth of the relationship. Brazilians tailor their comments, their "truth," to the particular individuals involved.

ARE ORGANIZATIONS BECOMING MORE SIMILAR?

Are organizations becoming more similar worldwide or are they maintaining their cultural dissimilarities? Is the world gradually creating one way of doing business or is the world maintaining a set of distinct markets defined by equally distinct national boundaries, each with its own culturally distinct approach to business?

The question of convergence versus divergence has puzzled global managers for years. If people around the world are becoming more similar, then understanding cross-cultural differences will become less important. If people remain dissimilar, then understanding cross-cultural differences in organizations will become increasingly important.

To clarify this issue, John Child (3), a leading British scholar, compared research on organizations across cultures. Reviewing a myriad of cross-cultural studies, he found one group of highly reputable management scholars repeatedly concluding that the world is becoming more similar and another group of equally reputable scholars concluding that the world's organizations are maintaining their dissimilarity. Looking more closely, Child discovered that most studies concluding convergence focused on macrolevel issues—such as the organization's structure and its technology—whereas most studies concluding divergence focused on microlevel issues—in particular, the behavior of people within organizations. We can therefore conclude that organizations worldwide are growing more similar, while the behavior of people within organizations is maintaining its cultural uniqueness. Organizations in

Canada and Germany may look increasingly similar from the outside, but Canadians and Germans continue to behave differently within their organizations. For example, although both Germans and Canadians install robots in their factories, each culture interacts differently with the robots.

ORGANIZATION CULTURE AND NATIONAL CULTURE

Over the last decade, managers and researchers have increasingly recognized the importance of organization culture as a socializing influence and climate creator (2;11;17). Unfortunately, our understanding of organization culture has tended to limit rather than enhance our understanding of national cultures (1;15). Many managers believe that organization culture moderates or erases the influence of national culture. They assume that employees working for the same organization—even if they are from different countries—are more similar than different. They believe that national differences are only important in working with foreign clients, not in working with international colleagues from the same organization.

Does organization culture erase or at least diminish national culture? Surprisingly, the answer is no. Employees and managers bring their ethnicity to the workplace. As described earlier, Hofstede found striking cultural differences within a single multinational corporation. In his study, national culture explained 50 percent of the differences in employees' attitudes and behaviors. National culture explained more of the differences than did professional role, age, gender, or race (8).

Even more strikingly, Laurent found cultural differences more pronounced among employees from around the world working within the same multinational company than among employees working for organizations in their native lands. After observing managers from nine Western European countries and the United States who were working for companies in their native countries (e.g., Swedish managers working for Swedish companies, Italian managers working for Italian companies, etc.), Laurent replicated his research in one multinational corporation with subsidiaries in each of the ten original countries. He assumed that managers working for the same multinational corporation would be more similar than their domestically employed colleagues, but instead he found the managers maintaining and even strengthening their cultural differences (see Figure 2-6). There were significantly greater differences between managers from the ten countries

FIGURE 2-6 *Organization Culture Magnifies*
Cross-Cultural Differences

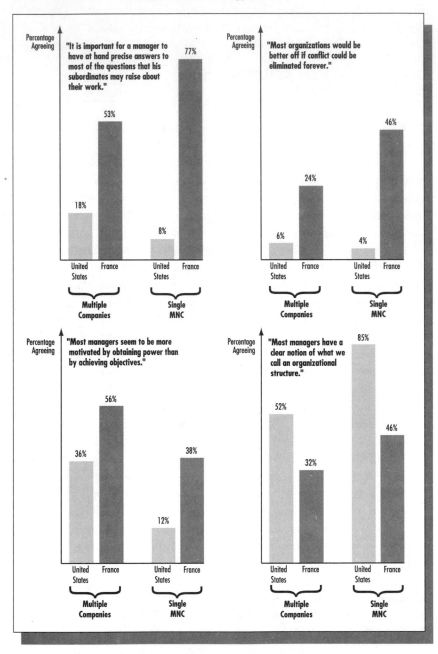

Source: André Laurent, INSEAD. Fontainebleau, France, 1981.

working within the same multinational corporation than there were between managers working for companies in their native countries. When working for a multinational corporation, it appears that Germans become more German, Americans become more American, Swedes become more Swedish, and so on. Surprised by these results, Laurent replicated his research in two additional multinational corporations, each with subsidiaries in the same nine Western European countries and the United States. Similar to the results from the first company, corporate culture did not reduce or eliminate national differences in the second and third corporations. Far from reducing national differences, organizational culture maintains and enhances them.

Why might organizational culture enhance national cultural differences? At this point neither managers nor researchers know the answer. Perhaps pressure to conform to the organization culture of a foreign-owned company brings out employees' resistance, causing them to cling more firmly to their own national identities. Perhaps our ethnic culture is so deeply ingrained in us by the time we reach adulthood that it cannot be erased by any external force. Perhaps other as-yet-unexplained forces are operating. The unambiguous conclusion remains that employees maintain or enhance their culturally specific ways of working when placed within a multinational or global organization.

SUMMARY

Laurent's research documents a wide range of cultural differences in work-related behavior and beliefs. Hofstede's five dimensions—individualism/collectivism, power distance, uncertainty avoidance, career success/quality of life, and Confucian dynamism—along with Trompenaars' additional dimensions, highlight the most important cultural differences for organizations. To manage effectively in a global or a domestic multicultural environment, we need to recognize the differences and learn to use them to our advantage, rather than either attempting to ignore them or simply allowing them to cause problems. Chapter 3 investigates some of the ways in which we perceive, describe, interpret, and evaluate cultural differences. Chapter 4 then explores some of the ways in which organizations can best use those differences to their advantage. The myth that "organizations can be beyond nationality in their design and operations" remains, in reality, a myth.

QUESTIONS FOR REFLECTION

1. **Cultural Self-Awareness.**   Where is your culture on Hofstede's original four dimensions and on universalism/particularism? How is your organizational culture different from your national culture on each of the dimensions?

2. **Cross-Cultural Awareness.**   Select a culture that you have had contact with or are currently working with. How does it differ from your own culture on Hofstede's four dimensions and on universalism/particularism? How might these differences show up in negotiations or ongoing business relationships?

3. **Cultural Self-Identity.**   In what ways are you a product of the culture in which you grew up? How does your personal cultural background affect the ways in which you think and behave? In what ways is your cultural background an advantage to working internationally? In what ways is it a disadvantage?

4. **Cross-Cultural Interpretation.**   In reading the international press, select a situation involving two or more cultures. Analyze the situation using Hofstede's original four dimensions, plus universalism/particularism and task/relationship. How does your cultural analysis help to explain the situation? Given your understanding of the cultural similarities and differences, what would you recommend that each side do (or avoid doing) to resolve the situation?

5. **Cross-Cultural Analysis and Action.**   Interview a colleague about a cross-cultural situation in which he or she is currently involved. Analyze it from a cross-cultural perspective using any of the dimensions discussed in Chapters 1 and 2. What recommendations would you make to your colleague based on your cultural analysis?

NOTES

1. Ken Dang, MBA, McGill University.

2. Hofstede (1980) originally defined this dimension as masculinity/femininity. However, since the dimension does not correspond with contemporary understandings of masculinity and femininity, Adler has changed the title of the dimension to more accurately reflect its underlying meaning. It should be noted that Hofstede never intended to suggest that today's male and female students or managers possess or lack certain attributes that the other gender possesses or lacks.

3. Shigeki Iwashita, MBA, McGill University.

4. Jennifer Oakes, MBA, McGill University.

5. Anne H. Whetham, MBA, McGill University.

6. See note 2 above.

7. Matts Franck, MBA, McGill University.

REFERENCES

1. Adler, N. J. and Jelinek, S. "Is 'Organization Culture' Culture Bound?" *Human Resource Management*, vol. 25, no. 1 (1986), pp. 73–90.

2. Burke, W., ed. "Special Issue on Organizational Culture," *Organizational Dynamics* (Autumn 1983).

3. Child, J. "Culture, Contingency and Capitalism in the Cross-National Study of Organizations," In L. L. Cummings and B. M. Staw, eds., *Research in Organizational Behavior*, vol. 3 (Greenwich, Conn.: JAI Press, 1981), pp. 303–356.

4. Chinese Culture Connection. "Chinese Values and the Search for Culture-Free Dimensions of Culture," *Journal of Cross-Cultural Psychology*, vol. 18, no. 2 (1987), pp. 143–164.

5. Hall, Edward T. *Beyond Culture.* Copyright © 1976, 1981 by Edward T. Hall. Used by permission of Doubleday, a division of Bantam Doubleday Dell Publishing Group, Inc., New York.

6. Hampden-Turner, C. *Charting the Corporate Mind* (Oxford, England: Blackwell, 1991).

7. Hofstede, G. *Cultures and Organizations: Software of the Mind* (London: McGraw-Hill, 1991).

8. Hofstede, G. *Culture's Consequences: International Differences in Work-Related Values* (Beverly Hills: Sage, 1980).

9. Hofstede, G. "Motivation, Leadership, and Organizations: Do American Theories Apply Abroad?" *Organizational Dynamics* (Summer 1980), pp. 42–63.

10. Hofstede, G., and Bond, M. H. "Confucius and Economic Growth: New Trends in Culture's Consequences," *Organizational Dynamics*, vol. 16, no. 4 (1988), pp. 4–21.

11. Jelinek, M.; Smircich, L.; and Hirsch, P., eds. "Organizational Culture" (Special Issue), *Administrative Science Quarterly*, vol. 28 (September 1983), p. 3.

12. Laurent, A. "The Cultural Diversity of Western Conceptions of Management," *International Studies of Management and Organization*, vol. 13, no. 1-2 (1983), pp. 75–96.

13. McGregor, D. M. *The Human Side of Enterprise* (New York: McGraw-Hill, 1960).

14. Muna, F. A. *The Arab Executive* (New York: Macmillan, 1980), Table 6.2.

15. Schneider, S. "National vs. Corporate Culture: Implications for Human Resource Management," *Human Resource Management*, vol. 27, no. 2 (1988), pp. 231–246.

16. Trompenaars, F. *Riding the Waves of Culture: Understanding Cultural Diversity in Business* (London: Economist Books, 1993).

17. Uttal, B. "The Corporate Culture Vultures," *Fortune*, vol. 108, no. 8 (October 17, 1983), pp. 66–72.

C H A P T E R   3

Communicating Across Cultures

If we seek to understand a people, we have to try to put ourselves, as far as we can, in that particular historical and cultural background. . . . It is not easy for a person of one country to enter into the background of another country. So there is great irritation, because one fact that seems obvious to us is not immediately accepted by the other party or does not seem obvious to him at all. . . . But that extreme irritation will go when we think . . . that he is just differently conditioned and simply can't get out of that condition. One has to recognize that whatever the future may hold, countries and people differ . . . in their approach to life and their ways of living and thinking. In order to understand them, we have to understand their way of life and approach. If we wish to convince them, we have to use their language as far as we can, not language in the narrow sense of the word, but the language of the mind. That is one necessity. Something that goes even further than that is not the appeal to logic and reason, but some kind of emotional awareness of other people.

— Jawaharlan Nehru, *Visit to America*

All business activity involves communication. Within the global business environment, activities such as leading, motivating, negotiating, decision making, and exchanging information and ideas are all based on the ability of managers and employees from one culture to communicate successfully with colleagues, clients, and suppliers from other cultures. Communicating effectively challenges managers worldwide even when the work force is culturally homogeneous, but when employees speak a variety of languages and come from an array of cultural backgrounds, effective communication becomes considerably more difficult (10:3–5, 121–128; 16:1).

CROSS-CULTURAL COMMUNICATION

Communication is the exchange of meaning: it is my attempt to let you know what I mean. Communication includes any behavior that another person perceives and interprets: it is your understanding of what I mean. Communication includes sending both verbal messages (words) and nonverbal messages (tone of voice, facial expression, behavior, and physical setting). It includes consciously sent messages as well as messages that the sender is totally unaware of having sent. Whatever I say and do, I cannot *not* communicate. Communication therefore involves a complex multilayered, dynamic process through which we exchange meaning.

Every communication has a message sender and a message receiver. As shown in Figure 3-1, the sent message is never identical to the received message. Why? Communication is not direct, but rather indirect; it is a symbolic behavior. I cannot communicate my ideas, feelings, or information directly; rather, I must externalize or symbolize them before they can be communicated. *Encoding* describes the producing of a symbol message. *Decoding* describes the receiving of a meaning from a symbol message. Message senders must encode their meaning into a form that the receiver will recognize—that is, into words and behavior. Receivers must then decode the words and behavior—the symbols—back into messages that have meaning for them.

For example, because the Cantonese word for *eight* sounds like *faat*, which means prosperity, a Hong Kong textile manufacturer Mr. Lau Ting-Pong paid $5 million in 1988 for car registration number 8. A year later, a European millionaire paid $4.8 million at Hong Kong's Lunar New Year auction for vehicle registration number 7, a decision that mystified the Chinese, since the number 7 has little significance in the Chinese calculation of fortune (20).

Similarly, the members of Hong Kong's prestigious Legislative Council refrained from using numbers ending in 4 to identify their newly installed lockers. Some Chinese consider numbers ending with the digit 4 to be

Figure 3-1 *Cross-Cultural Communication Model*

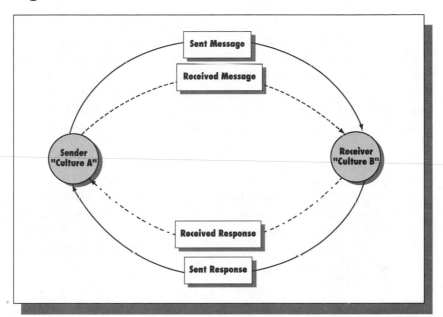

jinxed, because the sound of the Cantonese word *sei* the is same for *four* and *death*. The number 24, for instance, sounds like *yee sei*, or *death-prone* in Cantonese (9).

The process of translating meanings into words and behaviors—that is, into symbols—and back again into meanings is based on a person's cultural background and differs accordingly for each person. The greater the difference in background between senders and receivers, the greater the difference in meanings attached to particular words and behaviors. For example:

A British boss asked a new, young American employee if he would like to have an early lunch at 11 a.m. each day. The employee answered, "Yeah, that would be great!" The boss, hearing the word yeah instead of the word yes, assumed that the employee was rude, ill-mannered, and disrespectful. The boss responded curtly, "With that kind of attitude, you may as well forget about lunch!" The employee was bewildered. What had gone wrong? In the process of encoding agreement (his meaning) into yeah (a word symbol) and decoding the yeah spoken by a new employee to the boss (a word, behavior, and content symbol), the boss received an entirely different message than the employee had meant to send. Unfortunately, as is the case in most miscommunication, neither the sender nor the receiver was fully aware of what had gone wrong and why.

Cross-cultural communication occurs when a person from one culture sends a message to a person from another culture. Cross-cultural miscommunication occurs when the person from the second culture does not receive the sender's intended message. The greater the difference between the sender's and the receiver's cultures, the greater the chance for cross-cultural miscommunication. For example:

A Japanese businessman wants to tell his Norwegian client that he is uninterested in a particular sale. To be polite, the Japanese says, "That will be very difficult." The Norwegian interprets the statement to mean that there are still unresolved problems, not that the deal is off. The Norwegian responds by asking how her company can help solve the problems. The Japanese, believing he has sent the message that there will be no sale, is mystified by the Norwegian's response.

CULTURALLY "BIZARRE" BEHAVIOR

Only in the Eyes of the Beholder

While in Thailand, a Canadian expatriate's car was hit by a Thai motorist who had crossed over the double line while passing another vehicle. After failing to establish that the fault lay with the Thai driver, the Canadian flagged down a policeman. After several minutes of seemingly futile discussion, the Canadian pointed out the double line in the middle of the road and asked the policeman directly, "What do these lines signify?" The policeman replied, "They indicate the center of the road and are there so I can establish just how far the accident is from that point." The startled Canadian became silent. It had never occurred to him that the double line might not mean "no passing allowed."

Unwritten rules reflect a culture's interpretation of its surroundings. A foreign columnist for the English-language *Bangkok Post* once proclaimed that the unwritten traffic rule in Thailand is: "When there are more than three cars in front of you at a stop sign or intersection, start your own line!" This contravenes the Western stay-in-line ethic, of course, but it effectively portrays, albeit in slightly exaggerated fashion, a fairly consistent form of behavior at intersections in Thailand. And it drives non-Thais crazy! (14)

Communication does not necessarily result in understanding. Cross-cultural communication continually involves misunderstanding caused by misperception, misinterpretation, and misevaluation. When the sender of a message comes from one culture and the receiver from another, the chances of accurately transmitting a message are low. People from different countries see, interpret, and evaluate things differently, and consequently act upon them differently. In approaching cross-cultural situations, effective businesspeople therefore *assume difference until similarity is proven*. They recognize that all behavior makes sense through the eyes of the person behaving and that logic and rationale are culturally relative. In cross-cultural business situations, labeling behavior as bizarre usually reflects culturally based misperception, misinterpretation, and misevaluation; rarely does it reflect intentional malice or pathologically motivated behavior.

CROSS-CULTURAL MISPERCEPTION

Do the French and the Chinese see the world in the same way? No. Do Venezuelans and Ghanaians see the world in the same way? Again, no. No two national groups *see* the world in exactly the same way. Perception is the process by which individuals select, organize, and evaluate stimuli from the external environment to provide meaningful experiences for themselves (2;12;16;18). For example, when Mexican children simultaneously view tachistoscopic pictures of a bullfight and a baseball game, they only remember seeing the bullfight. Looking through the same tachistoscope, American children only remembered seeing the baseball game (3). Similarly, adult card players, when shown cards by researchers, fail to see black hearts and diamonds, or red clubs and spades.

Why didn't the children see both pictures? Why did the adults fail to see the unexpected playing card colors? The answer lies in the nature of perception. Perceptual patterns are neither innate nor absolute. They are selective, learned, culturally determined, consistent, and inaccurate.

- Perception is **selective.** At any one time there are too many stimuli in the environment for us to observe. Therefore, we screen out most of what we see, hear, taste, and feel. We screen out the overload and allow only selected information through our perceptual screen to our conscious mind (5).

- Perceptual patterns are **learned.** We are not born seeing the world in one particular way. Our experience teaches us to perceive the world in certain ways.
- Perception is **culturally determined.** We learn to see the world in a certain way based on our cultural background.
- Perception tends to remain **consistent.** Once we see something in a particular way, we continue to see it that way.
- Perception is **inaccurate.** We see things that do not exist and do not see things that do exist. Our background, values, interests, and culture act as filters and lead us to distort, block, and even create what we choose to see and to hear. We perceive what we expect to perceive. We perceive things according to what we have been trained to see, according to our cultural map.

For example read the following sentence:

> FINISHED FILES ARE THE RESULT OF YEARS OF SCIENTIFIC STUDY COMBINED WITH THE EXPERIENCE OF YEARS.

Now, quickly count the number of *F*'s in the sentence. Most nonnative English speakers see all six *F*'s. Many native English speakers only see three *F*'s, they do not see the *F*'s in the word *of* because *of* is not an important word in understanding the sentence's meaning. We selectively see those words that are important according to our cultural conditioning (in this case, our linguistic conditioning). Once we see a phenomenon in a particular way, we usually continue to see it in that way. Once we stop seeing *of*'s, we do not see them again (even when we look for them); we do not see things that do exist. One particularly astute manager at Canadian National Railways makes daily use of perceptual filters to her firm's advantage. She gives reports written in English to bilingual Francophones to proofread and those written in French to bilingual Anglophones. She uses the fact that the English secretaries can "see" more errors—especially small errors—in French and that the French secretaries can "see" more errors in English.

The distorting impact of perceptual filters, which are based on our personal experiences, causes us to see things that do not exist. This phenomenon has been powerfully demonstrated for years in training sessions for executives as well as for other groups.[1] For example, in one session,

Figure 3-2 *Impact of Perceptual Filters*

Source: Rumor Clinic. Anti-Defamation League. Reprinted with permission.

American executives were asked to study the picture shown in Figure 3-2 and then to describe it to a colleague who had not seen the picture. The first colleague then attempted to describe it to a second colleague who had not seen the picture, and so on. Finally, the fifth colleague described his perception of the picture to the group of executives and compared it with the original picture. Among the numerous distortions, the executives, as with other groups, consistently described the black and the white man as fighting; the knife as being in the hand of the black man; and the white man as wearing a business suit and the black man as wearing laborer's overalls. Clearly the inaccurate stereotypes of blacks (as poorer, working class, and more likely to commit crimes) and of whites (as richer, upper class, and less likely to be involved in violent crime) radically altered or shifted the observers' perceptions and totally changed the meaning of the picture (1). The executives' personal experiences, and therefore their perceptual filters, allowed them to see things that did not exist and to miss seeing things that did exist.

CROSS-CULTURAL MISINTERPRETATION

Interpretation occurs when an individual gives meaning to observations and their relationships; it is the process of making sense out of perceptions. Interpretation organizes our experience to guide our behavior. Based on our experience, we make assumptions about our perceptions so we will not have to rediscover meanings each time we encounter similar situations. For example, we make assumptions about how doors work, based on our experience of entering and leaving rooms; thus we do not have to relearn how to open a door each time we encounter a new door. Similarly, when we smell smoke, we generally assume there is a fire. We do not have to stop and wonder if the smoke indicates a fire or a flood. Our consistent patterns of interpretation help us to act appropriately and quickly within our day-to-day world.

Categories

Since we are constantly bombarded with more stimuli than we can absorb and more perceptions than we can keep distinct or interpret, we only perceive those images that may be meaningful to us. We group perceived images into familiar categories that help us to simplify our environment, become the basis for our interpretations, and allow us to function in an otherwise overly complex world. For example, as a driver approaching an intersection, I may or may not notice the number of children in the back seat of the car next to me, but I will notice whether the traffic light is red or green (selective perception). If the light is red, I automatically place it in the category of all red traffic signals (categorization). This time, like prior times, I stop (behavior based on interpretation). Although people are capable of distinguishing thousands of different colors, I do not take the time to notice if the red light in Istanbul is brighter or duller than the one in Singapore or more orange or purple than the one in Nairobi; I just stop. Categorization helps me to distinguish what is most important in my environment and to behave accordingly.

Categories of perceived images become ineffective when we place people and things in the wrong groups. Cross-cultural miscategorization occurs when I use my home country categories to make sense out of situations abroad. For example, a Korean businessman entered a client's office in Stockholm and encountered a woman sitting behind the desk. Assuming that she was a secretary, he announced that he wanted to see Mr. Silferbrand. The woman responded by saying that the secretary would be happy to help him. The Korean became confused. In assuming that most women are secretaries rather than managers, he had misinterpreted the situation and acted inappropriately. His categorization made sense because most women in Korean offices are secretaries, but it proved inaccurate and counterproductive here, since this particular Swedish woman was not a secretary.

Stereotypes

Stereotyping involves a form of categorization that organizes our experience and guides our behavior toward ethnic and national groups. Stereotypes never describe individual behavior; rather, they describe the behavioral norm for members of a particular group. For example, stereotypes of English and French businesspeople, as analyzed by Intercultural Management Associates in Paris, are described as follows:

> We have found that to every set of negative stereotypes distinguishing the British and French there corresponds a particular values divergence that, when recognized, can prove an extraordinary resource. To illustrate: The French, in describing the British as "perfidious," "hypocritical," and "vague," are in fact describing English . . . [managers'] typical lack of a general model or theory and . . . their preference for a more pragmatic, evolutionary approach. This fact is hard for the French . . . to believe, let alone accept as a viable alternative, until, working alongside one another, the French . . . come to see that there is usually no ulterior motive behind . . . English . . . [managers'] vagueness but rather a capacity to think aloud and adapt to circumstances. For [their] part, the English . . . come to see that, far from being "distant," "superior," or "out of touch with reality," the . . . concern [of French managers] for a general model or theory is what lends vision, focus, and cohesion to an enterprise or project, as well as leadership and much needed authority (7).

Stereotypes, like other forms of categories, can be helpful or harmful depending on how we use them. Effective stereotyping allows people to understand and act appropriately in new situations. A stereotype becomes helpful when it is

- *Consciously held.* People should be aware that they are describing a group norm rather than the characteristics of a specific individual.
- *Descriptive* rather than evaluative. The stereotype should describe what people from this group will probably be like and not evaluate those people as good or bad.
- *Accurate.* The stereotype should accurately describe the norm for the group to which the person belongs.

- *The first best guess* about a group prior to having direct information about the specific person or persons involved.
- *Modified*, based on further observation and experience with the actual people and situations.

A subconsciously held stereotype is difficult to modify or discard even after we collect real information about a person, because it is often thought to reflect reality. If a subconscious stereotype also inaccurately evaluates a person or situation, we are likely to maintain an inappropriate, ineffective, and frequently harmful guide to reality. For example, assume that I subconsciously hold the stereotype that Anglophone Québecois[2] refuse to learn French and that therefore they should have no rights within the province (an inaccurate, evaluative stereotype). I then meet a monolingual Anglophone and say, "See, I told you that Anglophones aren't willing to speak French! They don't deserve to have rights here." I next meet a bilingual Anglophone and conclude, "He must be an American because Canadian Anglophones always refuse to learn French." Instead of questioning, modifying, or discarding my stereotype ("Some Anglophone Canadians speak French"), I alter reality to fit the stereotype ("He must be American"). Stereotypes increase effectiveness only when used as a first best guess about a person or situation prior to having direct information. They never help when adhered to rigidly.

Indrei Ratiu (17), in his work with INSEAD, a leading international business school in France, and the London Business School, found that managers identified as "most internationally effective" by their colleagues altered their stereotypes to fit the actual people involved, whereas managers identified as "least internationally effective" continued to maintain their stereotypes even in the face of contradictory information. For example, internationally effective managers, prior to their first visit to Germany, might stereotype Germans as being extremely task oriented. Upon arriving and meeting a very friendly and lazy Herr Schmidt, they would alter their description to say that most Germans appear extremely task oriented, but Herr Schmidt seems friendly and lazy. Months later, the most internationally effective managers would only be able to say that some Germans appear very task oriented, whereas others seem quite relationship oriented (friendly); it all depends on the person and the situation. In this instance, the highly effective managers use the stereotype as a first best guess about the group's behavior prior to meeting any individuals from the group. As time goes on, they modify or discard the stereotype entirely; information about each individual supersedes the group stereotype. By contrast, the least internationally effective managers maintain their stereotypes. They assume that the contradictory evidence in Herr Schmidt's case represents an exception, and they continue to believe that all Germans are highly task oriented. In drawing conclusions too quickly on the basis of insufficient information—premature closure (12)—their stereotypes become self-fulfilling (19).

Canadian psychologist Donald Taylor (4;5;21) found that most people maintain their stereotypes even in the face of contradictory evidence. Taylor asked English and French Canadians to listen to one of three tape recordings of a French Canadian describing himself. In the first version, the French Canadian used the Francophone stereotype and described himself as religious, proud, sensitive, and expressive. In the second version, he used neutral terms to describe himself. In the third version, he used terms to describe himself that contradicted the stereotype, such as not religious, humble, unexpressive, and conservative. After having listened to one of the three versions, each person was asked to describe the Francophone on the tape (not Francophones in general). Surprisingly, people who listened to each of the three versions used the same stereotypic terms—religious, proud, sensitive, and expressive—even when the voice on the tape had conveyed the opposite information. People evidently maintain stereotypes even in the face of contradictory information.

To be effective, global managers therefore become aware of their cultural stereotypes and learn to set them aside when faced with contradictory evidence. They do not *pretend* not to stereotype.

If stereotyping is so useful as an initial guide to reality, why do people malign it? Why do parents and teachers constantly admonish children not to stereotype? Why do sophisticated managers rarely admit to stereotyping, even though each of us stereotypes every day? The answer is that we have failed to accept stereotyping as a natural process and have consequently failed to learn to use it to our advantage. For years we have viewed stereotyping as a form of primitive thinking, as an unnecessary simplification of reality. We have also viewed stereotyping as unethical: stereotypes can be inappropriate judgments of individuals based on inaccurate descriptions of groups. It is true that labeling people from a certain ethnic group as "bad" is not ethical, but grouping individuals into categories is neither good nor bad—it simply reduces a complex reality to manageable dimensions. Negative views of stereotyping simply cloud our ability to understand people's actual behavior and impair our awareness of our own stereotypes. *Everyone* stereotypes.

In conclusion, some people stereotype effectively and others do not. Stereotypes become counterproductive when we place people in the wrong group, when we incorrectly describe group norms, when we inappropriately evaluate the group or category, when we confuse the stereotype with the description of a particular individual, and when we fail to modify the stereotype based on our actual observations and experience.

Sources of Misinterpretation

Misinterpretation can be caused by inaccurate perceptions of a person or situation that arise when what actually exists is not seen. It can be caused by an inaccurate interpretation of what is seen; that is, by using my meanings to make sense out of your reality. An example of this type of misinterpretation (or misattribution) comes from an encounter between an Austrian businessman and a North American.

> I meet my Austrian client for the sixth time in as many months. He greets me as Herr Smith. Categorizing him as a businessman, I interpret his very formal behavior to mean that he does not like me or is uninterested in developing a closer relationship with me. (North American attribution: people who maintain formal behavior after the first few meetings do so because they dislike or distrust the associates so treated.) In fact, I have misinterpreted his behavior. I have used the norms for North American business behavior, which are more informal and demonstrative (I would say "Good morning, Fritz," not "Good morning, Herr Ranschburg"), to interpret the Austrian's more formal behavior ("Good morning, Herr Smith").

Culture strongly influences, and in many situations determines, our interpretations. Both the categories and the meanings we attach to them are based on our cultural background. Sources of cross-cultural misinterpretation include subconscious cultural "blinders," a lack of cultural self-awareness, projected similarity, and parochialism.

Subconscious Cultural Blinders

Because most interpretation goes on at a subconscious level, we lack awareness of the assumptions we make and their cultural basis. Our home culture reality never forces us to examine our assumptions or the extent to which they are culturally based, because we share our cultural assumptions with most other citizens from our country. All we know is that things do not work as smoothly or logically when we work outside our own culture as when we work with people more similar to ourselves. For example:

> Canadians conducting business in Kuwait became surprised when their meeting with a high-ranking official was not held in a closed office and was constantly interrupted. Using the Canadian-based cultural assumptions that important people have large private offices with secretaries to monitor the flow of people into the office, and that important business takes precedence over less important business and is therefore not interrupted, the Canadians interpreted the Kuwaiti's open office and constant interruptions to mean that the official was neither as high ranking nor as interested in conducting the business at hand as they had previously thought. The Canadians' interpretation of the office environment led them to lose interest in working with the Kuwaiti.

The problem is that the Canadians' interpretation derives from their own North American norms, not from Middle Eastern cultural norms. The Kuwaiti may well have been a high-ranking official who was very interested in doing business. The Canadians will never know.

Cases of subconscious cross-cultural misinterpretation occur frequently. For example, in the 1980s a Soviet Russian poet, after lecturing at American universities for two months, said, "Attempts to please an American audience are doomed in advance, because out of twenty listeners five may hold one point of view, seven another, and eight may have none at all" (10). The Soviet poet confused Americans' freedom of thought and speech with his ability to please them. He assumed that one can only please an audience if all members hold the same opinion. Another example of well-meant misinterpretation comes from the United States Office of Education's advice to American teachers working with newly arrived Vietnamese refugee students (22):

> Students' participation was discouraged in Vietnamese schools by liberal doses of corporal punishment, and students were conditioned to sit rigidly and speak out only when spoken to. This background . . . makes speaking freely in class hard for a Vietnamese student. Therefore, don't mistake shyness for apathy.

Perhaps the extent to which this is a culturally based interpretation becomes clearer if we imagine the opposite advice that the Vietnamese Ministry of Education might have given to Vietnamese teachers planning to receive American children for the first time.

Students' proper respect for teachers was discouraged by a loose order and students were conditioned to chat all the time and to behave in other disorderly ways. This background makes proper and respectful behavior in class hard for an American student. Therefore, do not mistake rudeness for lack of reverence.

Lack of Cultural Self-Awareness

Although we may think that a major obstacle in conducting business around the world is in understanding foreigners, the greater difficulty involves becoming aware of our own cultural conditioning. As anthropologist Edward Hall explains, "What is known least well, and is therefore in the poorest position to be studied, is what is closest to oneself" (8:45). We are generally least aware of our own cultural characteristics and are quite surprised when we hear foreigners describe us. For example, many Americans are surprised to discover that foreigners see them as hurried, overly law-abiding, very hard working, extremely explicit, and overly inquisitive (see the box "Cross-Cultural Awareness: Americans as Others See Them"). Many American businesspeople were equally surprised by a *Newsweek* survey reporting the characteristics most and least frequently associated with Americans (see Table 3-1). Asking a foreign national to describe businesspeople from your country is a powerful way to see yourself as others see you.

TABLE 3-1 *How Others See Americans*

Characteristics Most Commonly Associated with Americans*					
France	*Japan*	*Western Germany*	*Great Britain*	*Brazil*	*Mexico*
Industrious	Nationalistic	Energetic	Friendly	Intelligent	Industrious
Energetic	Friendly	Inventive	Self-indulgent	Inventive	Intelligent
Inventive	Decisive	Friendly	Energetic	Energetic	Inventive
Decisive	Rude	Sophisticated	Industrious	Industrious	Decisive
Friendly	Self-indulgent	Intelligent	Nationalistic	Nationalistic	Greedy

Characteristics Least Commonly Associated with Americans*					
Lazy	Industrious	Lazy	Lazy	Lazy	Lazy
Rude	Lazy	Sexy	Sophisticated	Self-indulgent	Honest
Honest	Honest	Greedy	Sexy	Sexy	Rude
Sophisticated	Sexy	Rude	Decisive	Sophisticated	Sexy

*From a list of fourteen characteristics.

Source: Newsweek (July 11,1983), p. 50, Copyright 1981 by Newsweek, Inc. All rights reserved, reprinted by permission.

CROSS-CULTURAL AWARENESS:

Americans As Others See Them

People from other countries often become puzzled and intrigued by the intricacies and enigmas of American culture. Below is a selection of actual observations by people from around the world visiting the United States. As you read them, ask yourself in each case if the observer is accurate and how you would explain the trait in question.

India. "Americans seem to be in a perpetual hurry. Just watch the way they walk down the street. They never allow themselves the leisure to enjoy life; there are too many things to do."

Kenya. "Americans appear to us rather distant. They are not really as close to other people—even fellow Americans—as Americans overseas tend to portray. It's almost as if an American says, 'I won't let you get too close to me.' It's like building a wall."

Turkey. "Once we were out in a rural area in the middle of nowhere and saw an American come to a stop sign. Though he could see in both directions for miles and no traffic was coming, he still stopped!"

Colombia. "The tendency in the United States to think that life is only work hits you in the face. Work seems to be the one type of motivation."

Indonesia. "In the United States, everything has to be talked about and analyzed. Even the littlest thing has to be "Why, Why, Why? I get a headache from such persistent questions."

Ethiopia. "Americans are very explicit; . . . [they] want a 'yes' or 'no.' If someone tries to speak figuratively, the American is confused."

Iran. "The first time . . . my [American] professor told me, 'I don't know the answer, I will have to look it up,' I was shocked. I asked myself, 'Why is he teaching me?' In my country a professor would give the wrong answer rather than admit ignorance."[3]

Another very revealing way to understand the norms and values of a culture is to listen to common sayings and proverbs. What does a society recommend, and what does it prohibit? The box "North American Values: Proverbs" lists some common North American proverbs and the values each teaches.

To the extent that we can begin to see ourselves clearly through the eyes of people from other cultures, we can begin to modify our behavior, emphasizing our most appropriate and effective characteristics and minimizing

NORTH AMERICAN VALUES: PROVERBS

It is evidently much more potent in teaching practicality, for example, to say, "Don't cry over spilt milk" than "You'd better learn to be practical." North Americans have heard this axiom hundreds of times, and it has made its point. Listed below are North American proverbs on the left and the values they seem to be teaching on the right.[4]

Proverb	*Value*
Cleanliness is next to godliness.	Cleanliness
A penny saved is a penny earned.	Thriftiness
Time is money.	Time thriftiness
Don't cry over spilt milk.	Practicality
Waste not; want not.	Frugality
Early to bed, early to rise, makes one healthy, wealthy, and wise.	Diligence; Work ethic
God helps those who help themselves.	Initiative
It's not whether you win or lose, but how you play the game.	Good sportsmanship
A person's home is his castle.	Privacy; Value of personal property
No rest for the wicked.	Guilt; Work ethic
You've made your bed, now sleep in it.	Responsibility
Don't count your chickens before they're hatched.	Practicality
A bird in the hand is worth two in the bush.	Practicality
The squeaky wheel gets the grease.	Aggressiveness
Might makes right.	Superiority of physical power
There's more than one way to skin a cat.	Originality; Determination
A stitch in time saves nine.	Timeliness of action
All that glitters is not gold.	Wariness
Clothes make the man.	Concern for physical appearance
If at first you don't succeed, try, try again.	Persistence; Work ethic
Take care of today, and tomorrow will take care of itself.	Preparation for future
Laugh, and the world laughs with you; weep and you weep alone.	Pleasant outward appearance

those least helpful. To the extent that we are culturally self-aware, we can begin to predict the effect our behavior will have on others.

Projected Similarity

Projected similarity refers to the assumption that people are more similar to you than they actually are or that another person's situation is more similar to your own situation than it in fact is. Projecting similarity reflects both a natural and a common process. American professors asked managers from fourteen countries to describe the work and life goals of a colleague in their work team from another country (6). As shown in Figure 3-3, in every case the managers assumed that their foreign colleagues were more like themselves than they actually were. Projected similarity involves assuming, imagining, and actually perceiving similarity when differences exist. Projected similarity particularly handicaps people in cross-cultural situations. As a South African, I assume that my Greek colleague is more South African than he actually is. As an Egyptian, I assume that my Chilean colleague is more similar to me than she actually is. When I act based on this assumed similarity, I often find that I have acted inappropriately and thus ineffectively.

At the base of projected similarity is a subconscious parochialism. I assume that there is only one way to be: my way. I assume that there is only one way to see the world: my way. I therefore view other people in reference to me and to my way of viewing the world. People may fall into an

Figure 3-3 *Projected Similarity*

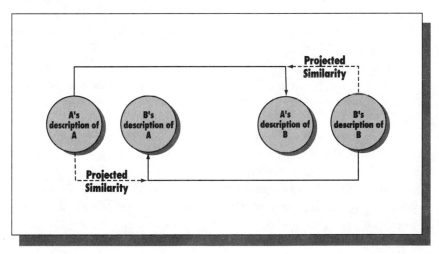

illusion of understanding while being unaware of . . . [their] misunderstand-
ings. "I understand you perfectly but you don't understand me" is an expression typical of such a situation. Or all communicating parties may fall into a
collective illusion of mutual understanding. In such a situation, each party
may wonder later why other parties do not live up to the "agreement" they had
reached (13:3).

Most global managers do not see themselves as parochial. They believe
that as world travelers they are able to see the foreigner's point of view.
This is not always true. The following are examples of projected similarity and consequent cultural misinterpretation:

When Danish managers work with a Saudi and the Saudi states that the plant
will be completed on time, "En shah allah" ("If God is willing"), the Danes
rarely believe that God's will is really going to influence the progress of construction. They continue to see the world from their parochial Danish perspective and assume that "En shah allah" is just an excuse for not getting the
work done, or is meaningless altogether.

Similarly, when Balinese workers' families refuse to use birth control methods,
explaining that it will break the cycle of reincarnation, few Western managers
really consider that there is a possibility that they too will be reborn a number
of times. Instead, they assume that the Balinese either are superstitious, or that
they simply do not understand, or are afraid of, Western medicine.

While it is important to understand and respect the other culture's point of
view, it is not necessary to either accept or adopt it. Understanding and
respect do not imply acceptance. However, a rigid adherence to our own
belief system expresses a form of parochialism, and parochialism underlies projected similarity.

One of the best exercises for developing empathy and reducing both
parochialism and projected similarity is role reversal (see the box "How
Well Do You Know Your International Colleagues?"). Imagine, for example, that you are a businessperson from a culture other than your own.
Imagine the type of family you come from, the number of brothers and sisters you have, the social and economic conditions you grew up with, the
type of education you received, the ways in which you chose your profession and position, the manner in which you were introduced to your spouse,
your goals in working for your organization, and your life goals. Asking
these questions forces you to see the other person as he or she really is, and
not as a mere reflection of yourself. It forces you to see both the similarities

HOW WELL DO YOU KNOW YOUR INTERNATIONAL COLLEAGUES?

Think about a colleague from another culture with whom you are currently working or have worked in the past. See how many of the following questions about him or her you can answer, how many you think you know the answer to but are not certain of (and therefore run a high risk of *projected similarity error*), and how many you do not know at all (and therefore run a high risk of *selective perception error*). If you are still in contact with the colleague, you may want to check the accuracy of your perceptions with him or her after having completed the exercise. Note that the exercise is written as if your international colleague is a woman. If your colleague is a man, just imagine that the questions you ask are about him (instead of *her*).

Family Background

- How large a family does she come from? How many brothers and sisters does she have? Is she the oldest? Youngest?
- From what socioeconomic status is her family? Are they among the richest in the country? The poorest? Did her parents make the family wealth or was it inherited? Is the family highly respected in the community? Why? Why not?
- What religion is she? How important is religion to her? Can you ask her about her religion? Does she want to tell you about her beliefs? How does her religion affect the way she works? How does it affect the way she works with you?
- What type of education did she receive? Did she attend private schools? Public schools? Religious schools? What percent of the people in her country have attained the same level of education? Did she gain entrance into the highest levels of education primarily through performance (tests), money, or personal connections? Did she receive all of her education in her home country? Does she consider her education to be superior or inferior to your own education?
- Is she married? Whom did she marry? Was it an arranged marriage? Does her husband's family influence where she works? Is her closest relationship with her husband? Her mother? Her children?
- Does she have children? How many? What type of relationship does she have with her children? How much time does she spend with her children each day? Would she consider sending her children away to boarding school? What does she see as her responsibility to her children?

- What type of home does she live in? Is it in an elite neighborhood? Is she satisfied with it? Does she live with her extended family (parents, grandparents, aunts, uncles) or her nuclear family?
- As a person, what is most important to her? What are some of her most deeply held values?

Career Background

- Why did she choose the career or profession that she did? Is it what her father did? Is it what her mother did? Is it considered a high status profession?
- Why does she work? For the money? Prestige? Loyalty? Responsibility? Personal satisfaction? Does she have to work to survive economically? Does she come from a culture that "works to live" or "lives to work"?
- What does she need to do to get ahead in her career? How important to her career is the success of her project or alliance with you?
- In her culture, how are people viewed who work with foreigners? Who travel internationally? Who have foreigners as friends?
- Do "fast track" managers in her company (and culture) usually get sent to work abroad or do they usually send just "OK" performers?

Culture

- What does she think about your culture? What does she see as your cultural strengths?   What would she like to learn from your culture? What does she want to learn from you?
- What totally annoys her about your culture? What does she see as your culture's weaknesses? How does she see your culture as getting in the way of working with you?
- In which ways does she see your culture as being ahead of her culture? In which ways does she see her culture as being ahead of your culture? Does she believe in cultural synergy; that is, that you can combine her and your cultures to develop new and innovative approaches to business, including to managerial and organizational challenges?

and the differences, and not simply to imagine similarities when differences actually exist. Moreover, role reversal encourages highly task-oriented businesspeople, such as Americans, to see the person from another culture as a whole person rather than merely as someone with a position and a set of skills needed to accomplish a particular task.

CROSS-CULTURAL MISEVALUATION

Even more than perception and interpretation, cultural conditioning strongly affects evaluation. Evaluation involves judging whether someone or something is good or bad. Cross-culturally, we use our own culture as a standard of measurement, judging that which is like our own culture as normal and good and that which is different as abnormal and bad. Our own culture becomes a self-reference criterion: since no other culture is identical to our own, we tend to judge all other cultures as inferior. Evaluation rarely helps in trying to understand, communicate with, or do business with people from another culture. The following example highlights the consequences of misevaluation:

> A Swiss executive waits more than an hour past the appointed time for his Spanish colleague to arrive and to sign a supply contract. In his impatience he concludes that Spaniards must be lazy and totally unconcerned about business. The Swiss executive has misevaluated his colleague by negatively comparing him to his own cultural standards for business punctuality. Implicitly, he has labeled his own culture's behavior as good ("The Swiss arrive on time and that is good") and the other culture's behavior as bad ("The Spanish do not arrive on time and that is bad").

COMMUNICATION: GETTING THEIR MEANING, NOT JUST THEIR WORDS

Effective cross-cultural communication is possible; however, global managers cannot approach communication in the same way as do domestic managers. First, effective global managers *"know that they don't know."* They assume difference until similarity is proven rather than assuming similarity until difference is proven.

Second, in attempting to understand their colleagues from other cultures, effective global managers emphasize description, by observing what is actually said and done, rather than interpreting or evaluating it. Describing a situation is the most accurate way to gather information about it. Interpretation and evaluation, unlike description, are based more on the observer's own culture and background than on the observed situation. My interpretations and evaluations therefore tell me more about myself than about the actual situation. Although managers, as decision makers, must evaluate people (e.g., performance appraisal) and situations (e.g., project assessment) in terms of organizational standards and objectives, effective global managers delay judgment until they have had sufficient time to observe and interpret the situation from the perspective of all cultures involved.

Third, when attempting to understand or interpret an international situation, effective global managers try to see it through the eyes of their international colleagues. This role reversal limits the myopia of viewing situations strictly from one's own perspective.

Fourth, once effective global managers develop an explanation for a situation, they treat the explanation as a guess (as a hypothesis to be tested) and not as a certainty. They systematically check with colleagues both from home and abroad to make certain that their guesses—their initial interpretations—are plausible. This checking process allows them to converge meanings—to delay accepting their interpretations of the situation until they have confirmed them with others.

Understanding: Converging Meanings

There are many ways to increase the chances for accurately understanding businesspeople from other cultures. The set of recommendations in the box "What Do I Do If They Do Not Speak My Language?" suggests what to do when business colleagues are not native speakers of your language. Each technique is based on presenting the message through multiple channels (for example, stating your position and showing a graph to summarize the same position), paraphrasing to check that colleagues from other cultures have understood your meaning (and not just your words), and converging meanings (always double-checking with the other person to verify that you have communicated what you had intended to communicate).

Standing Back from Yourself

Perhaps the most difficult skill in cross-cultural communication involves standing back from yourself; being aware that you do not know everything, that a situation may not make sense, that your guesses may be wrong, and that the ambiguity in the situation may continue. In this sense the ancient Roman dictum "knowledge is power" becomes true. In knowing yourself, you gain power over your perceptions and reactions; you can control your own behavior and your reactions to others' behavior. Cross-cultural awareness complements in-depth self-awareness. A lack of self-awareness negates the usefulness of cross-cultural awareness.

WHAT DO I DO IF THEY DO NOT SPEAK MY LANGUAGE?

Verbal Behavior

- *Clear, slow speech.* Enunciate each word. Do not use colloquial expressions.
- *Repetition.* Repeat each important idea using different words to explain the same concept.
- *Simple sentence.* Avoid compound, long sentences.
- *Active verbs.* Avoid passive verbs.

Nonverbal Behavior

- *Visual restatements.* Use as many visual restatements as possible, such as pictures, graphs, tables, and slides.
- *Gestures.* Use more facial and appropriate hand gestures to emphasize the meaning of words.
- *Demonstration.* Act out as many themes as possible.
- *Pauses.* Pause more frequently.
- *Summaries.* Hand out written summaries of your verbal presentation.

Accurate Interpretation

- *Silence.* When there is a silence, wait. Do not jump in to fill the silence. The other person is probably just thinking more slowly in the nonnative language or translating.
- *Intelligence.* Do not equate poor grammar and mispronunciation with lack of intelligence; it is usually a sign of nonnative language use.
- *Differences.* If unsure, assume difference, not similarity.

Comprehension

- *Understanding.* Do not just assume that they understand; assume that they do not understand.
- *Checking comprehension.* Have colleagues repeat their understanding of the material back to you. Do not simply ask if they understand or not. Let them explain what they understand to you.

Design

- *Breaks.* Take more frequent breaks. Second language comprehension is exhausting.
- *Small modules.* Divide the material to be presented into smaller modules.
- *Longer time frame.* Allocate more time for each module than you usually need for presenting the same material to native speakers of your language.

Motivation

- *Encouragement.* Verbally and nonverbally encourage and reinforce speaking by nonnative language participants.
- *Drawing out.* Explicitly draw out marginal and passive participants.
- *Reinforcement.* Do not embarrass novice speakers.[5]

One of the most poignant examples of the powerful interplay between description, interpretation, evaluation, and empathy involved a Scottish businessman's relationship with a Japanese colleague. The box "Cross-Cultural Communication: Japanese Pickles and Mattresses, Incorporated" recounts the Scottish businessman's experience.

CROSS-CULTURAL COMMUNICATION

Japanese Pickles and Mattresses, Incorporated

It was my first visit to Japan. As a gastronomic adventurer, and because I believe cuisine is one route that is freely available and highly effective as a first step towards a closer understanding of another country, I was disappointed on my first evening when the Japanese offered me a Western meal.

As tactfully as possible, I suggested that sometime during my stay I would like to try a Japanese menu, if that could be arranged without inconvenience. There was some small reluctance evident on the part of my hosts (due of course to their thought that I was being very polite asking for Japanese food which I didn't really like, so to be good hosts they had to politely find a way of not having me eat it!). But eventually, by an elegantly progressive route starting with Western food with a slightly Japanese bias through to genuine Japanese food, my hosts were convinced that I really wanted to eat Japanese style and was not "posing."

From then on they became progressively more enthusiastic in suggesting the more exotic Japanese dishes, and I guess I graduated when, after an excellent meal one night (apart from the Japanese pickles) on which I had lavished praise, they said, "Do you like Japanese pickles?" To this, without preamble, I said, "No!" To this reply, with great laughter all around, they responded, "Nor do we!"

During this gastronomic getting-together week, I had also been trying to persuade them that I really did wish to stay in traditional Japanese hotels rather than the very Westernized ones my hosts had selected because they thought I would prefer my "normal" lifestyle. (I should add that, at this time, traditional Japanese hotels were still available and often cheaper than, say, the Osaka Hilton.)

Anyway, after the pickles joke, it was suddenly announced that Japanese hotels could be arranged. For the remaining two weeks of my stay, as I toured the major cities, on most occasions a traditional Japanese hotel was substituted for the Western one on my original schedule.

Many of you will know that a traditional Japanese room has no furniture except a low table and a flower arrangement. The "bed" is a mattress produced just before you retire from a concealed cupboard, accompanied by a cereal-packed pillow.

One memorable evening my host and I had finished our meal together in "my" room. I was expecting him to shortly make his "goodnight" and retire, as he had been doing all week, to his own room.

However, he stayed unusually long and was, to me, obviously in some sort of emotional crisis. Finally, he blurted out, with great embarrassment, "Can I sleep with you?!"

As they say in the novels, at this point I went very still! My mind was racing through all the sexual taboos and prejudices my own upbringing had instilled, and I can still very clearly recall how I analyzed: "I'm bigger than he is so I can fight him off, but then he's probably an expert in the martial arts, but on the other hand he has shown no signs of being gay up until now and he is my host and there is a lot of business at risk and there's no such thing as rape, et cetera . . . !"

It seemed a hundred years, though it was only a few seconds, before I said, feeling as if I was pulling the trigger in Russian roulette, "Yes, sure."

Who said that the Orientals are inscrutable? The look of relief that followed my reply was obvious. Then he looked worried and concerned again, and said, "Are you sure?"

I reassured him and he called in the maid, who fetched his mattress from his room and laid it on the floor alongside mine. We both went to bed and slept all night without any physical interaction.

Later I learned that for the traditional Japanese one of the greatest compliments you can be paid is for the host to ask, "Can I sleep with you?" This goes back to the ancient feudal times, when life was cheap, and what the invitation really said was, "I trust you with my life. I do not think that you will kill me while I sleep. You are my true friend."

To have said "No" to the invitation would have been an insult—"I don't trust you not to kill me while I sleep"—or, at the very least, my host would have been acutely embarrassed because he had taken the initiative. If I refused because I had failed to perceive the invitation as a compliment, he would have been out of countenance on two grounds: the insult to him in the traditional context and the embarrassment he would have caused me by "forcing" a negative, uncomprehending response from me.

As it turned out, the outcome was superb. He and I were now "blood brothers," as it were. His assessment of me as being "ready for Japanization" had been correct and his obligations under ancient Japanese custom had been fulfilled. I had totally misinterpreted his intentions through my own cultural conditioning. It was sheer luck, or luck plus a gut feeling that I'd gotten it wrong, that caused me to make the correct response to his extremely complimentary and committed invitation.[6]

SUMMARY

Cross-cultural communication confronts us with limits to our perceptions, our interpretations, and our evaluations. Our cultural perspectives tend to render everything relative and slightly uncertain. Entering a culture that is foreign to us is tantamount to knowing the words without knowing the music, or knowing the music without knowing the beat. Our natural tendencies lead us back to our prior experience: our default option becomes the familiarity of our own culture, thus precluding our accurate understanding of others' cultures.

Strategies to overcome our natural parochial tendencies exist. With care, we can avoid our ethnocentric default options. We can learn to see, understand, and control our own cultural conditioning. When working in other cultures, we can emphasize description rather than interpretation or evaluation, and thus minimize self-fulfilling stereotypes and premature judgments. We can recognize and use our stereotypes as guides rather than rejecting them as unsophisticated simplifications. Effective cross-cultural communication presupposes the interplay of alternative realities. It rejects the actual or potential domination of one reality over another.

QUESTIONS FOR REFLECTION

1. *Stereotyping.*   The most effective global managers use stereotypes. What are some of the ways in which you can use stereotypes to your advantage when working with people from other cultures?

2. *Using Stereotyping.*   What stereotypes do you have concerning lawyers? About South Africans? If you had an appointment with two South African lawyers, what would you expect of them and how would you prepare for the meeting?

3. *Communicating Across Cultures.*   Today many managers work with people from other cultures, both at home and when traveling abroad. What are some of the ways in which your organization could train people to communicate more effectively with people from other cultures?

4. ***Communicating Nonverbally: Cultural Self-Awareness.*** In seeking to understand the importance of nonverbal communication, we must start by examining ourselves. List four examples of nonverbal communication that you commonly use and what each means to you. Then indicate how each might be misinterpreted by someone from another culture.

5. ***Communicating Nonverbally: Cross-Cultural Awareness.*** List four examples of nonverbal communication that managers in other parts of the world use but not managers from your country. Indicate how each might be misinterpreted by colleagues from your country.

NOTES

1. The Anti-Defamation League Rumor Clinic designed the sessions to show how rumors operate and how to distinguish rumors from gossip.

2. Anglophone Québecois are native English speakers living in the predominantly French-speaking province of Quebec, Canada.

3. Individual country quotes taken from John P. Feig and G. Blair, *There Is a Difference*, 2nd ed. (Washington, D.C.: Meridian House International, 1980).

4. List of proverbs and associated values from L. Robert Kohls, *Survival Kit for Overseas Living* (Yarmouth, Me: Intercultural Press, 1979), pp. 30–31.

5. Based on Nancy J. Adler and Moses N. Kiggundu, "Awareness at the Crossroad: Designing Translator-Based Training Programs," in D. Landis and R. Brislin, *Handbook of Intercultural Training: Issues in Training Methodology*, vol. II (New York: Pergamon Press, 1983), pp. 124–150.

6. This is the true experience of a Scottish executive as described to his colleagues after participating in the *Managerial Skills for International Business* executive seminar at INSEAD, in Fontainebleau, France.

REFERENCES

1. Anti-Defamation League Rumor Clinic.

2. Asch, S. "Forming Impressions of Persons," *Journal of Abnormal and Social Psychology*, vol. 40 (1946), pp. 258–290.

3. Bagby, J. W. "Dominance in Binocular Rivalry in Mexico and the United States," in I. Al-Issa and W. Dennis, eds., *Cross-Cultural Studies of Behavior* (New York: Holt, Rinehart and Winston, 1970), pp. 49–56. Originally in *Journal of Abnormal and Social Psychology*, vol. 54 (1957), pp. 331–334.

4. Berry, J.; Kalin, R.; and Taylor, D. "Multiculturalism and Ethnic Attitudes in Canada," in *Multiculturalism as State Policy* (Ottawa: Government of Canada, 1976).

5. Berry, J.; Kalin, R.; and Taylor, D. *Multiculturalism and Ethnic Attitudes in Canada* (Ottawa: Minister of Supply and Services, 1977).

6. Burger, P., and Bass, B. M. *Assessment of Managers: An International Comparison* (New York: Free Press, 1979).

7. Gancel, C., and Ratiu, I. Internal document, Inter Cultural Management Associates, Paris, France, 1984.

8. Hall, E. T. *Beyond Culture* (Garden City, N.Y.: Anchor Press/Doubleday, 1976). Also see E. T. Hall's *The Silent Language* (Doubleday, 1959, and Anchor Books, 1973) and *The Hidden Dimension* (Doubleday, 1966, and Anchor Books, 1969).

9. Ho, A. "Unlucky Numbers Are Locked out of the Chamber," *South China Morning Post* (December 26, 1988), p. 1.

10. Kanungo, R. N. *Biculturalism and Management* (Ontario: Butterworth, 1980).

11. Korotich, V. "Taming of a Desert of the Mind," *Atlas* (June 1977).

12. Lau, J. B., and Jelinek, M. "Perception and Management," in *Behavior in Organizations: An Experiential Approach* (Homewood, Ill.: Irwin, 1984), pp. 213–220.

13. Maruyama, M. "Paradigms and Communication," *Technological Forecasting and Social Change*, vol. 6 (1974), pp. 3–32.

14. Miles, M. *Adaptation to a Foreign Environment* (Hull, Quebec: Canadian International Development Agency, Briefing Centre, (1986).

15. Miller, J. G. "Adjusting to Overloads of Information," in *The Association for Research in Nervous and Mental Disease, Disorders of Communication*, vol. 42 (Research Publications, A.R.N.M.D., 1964).

16. Prekel, T. "Multi-Cultural Communication: A Challenge to Managers," paper delivered at the International Convention of the American Business Communication Association, New York, November 21, 1983.

17. Ratui, I. "Thinking Internationally: A Comparison of How International Executives Learn," *International Studies of Management and Organization*, vol. 13, no. 1-2 (1983), pp. 139–150. Reprinted by permission of publisher, M. E. Sharpe, Inc., Armonk, N.Y.

18. Singer, M. "Culture: A Perceptual Approach," in L. A. Samovar and R. E. Porter, eds., *Intercultural Communication: A Reader* (Belmont, Calif.: Wadsworth, 1976), pp. 110–119.

19. Snyder, M. "Self-Fulfilling Stereotypes," *Psychology Today* (July 1982), pp. 60–68.

20. *South China Morning Post*, "Mystery Man Gives a Fortune for Lucky '7'" (January 22, 1989), p. 3; and "Lucky '7' to Go on Sale" (January 4, 1989), p. 4.

21. Taylor, D. "American Tradition," in R. G. Gardner and R. Kalin, eds., *A Canadian Social Psychology of Ethnic Relations* (Toronto: Methuen Press, 1980).

22. U.S. Office of Education. *On Teaching the Vietnamese* (Washington, D.C.: General Printing Office, 1976).

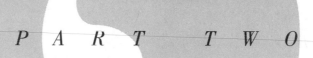

P A R T   T W O

Managing

Cultural

Diversity

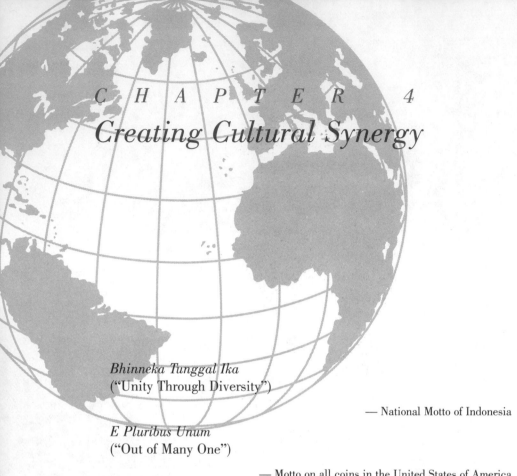

C H A P T E R   4
Creating Cultural Synergy

Bhinneka Tunggal Ika
("Unity Through Diversity")

— National Motto of Indonesia

E Pluribus Unum
("Out of Many One")

— Motto on all coins in the United States of America

Is culture visible? Do managers think that cultural diversity has an impact on organizations? If an impact exists, is it positive or negative, helpful or harmful to organizations? How should businesspeople manage diversity? Should they ignore it, minimize it, or use it? This chapter investigates the invisibility of culture and our own cultural blindness. It describes the potential problems and advantages of working in culturally diverse environments, and presents alternative strategies for managing cultural diversity and its outcomes.

INVISIBLE CULTURE: STRATEGIES FOR RECOGNIZING CULTURE

Culture Is Invisible

Do managers see culture? No. Neither managers nor management scholars generally believe that culture significantly affects the day-to-day operations of organizations. Very often good managers see themselves as beyond passport, and good organizations as beyond nationality.

To better understand the situation, we conducted a study to determine the impact of cultural diversity on organizations (5). We selected Montreal as an ideal location for the study since it has the largest English-speaking population in the predominantly French Canadian province of Quebec. In the study 60 organizational development consultants described the impact, good and bad, of cultural diversity on their organizations and jobs. Two-thirds said they saw no impact whatsoever. Of the remaining one-third, only one consultant saw the impact as positive. Interestingly, although television, radio, and newspaper reports daily attest to Montrealers' recognition of the influence of bilingualism and biculturalism on the social, political, and economic environment of Quebec, the majority of the surveyed consultants saw no influence of culture on the world of work.

Management professors seem to demonstrate an equivalent cultural blindness (2;6;7;9;10). A survey of management research published in 24 academic and professional journals during the 1970s documented that less than 5 percent of the articles refer to either international or domestic multiculturalism in their research designs or results (2). Given the dramatic increase in international business activity over the last decade, one would expect an increase in the proportion of international articles published (6:552). However, trends similar to those in the 1970s continued in the 1980s (13;18;20). Only by 1990 did the proportion of international articles begin to increase, and even then it remained less than 10 percent (6). American researchers have conducted the vast majority of management studies, with the majority focusing on U.S. organizations, and yet they have assumed their findings to be universally true (7;9;10). Management researchers, perhaps to an even greater extent than their corporate colleagues, have ignored the influence of culture on organizations.

Cultural Blindness: Is Seeing Culture Illegitimate?

Cultural diversity, whether international or domestic, does exist and does affect the ways in which we operate within organizations (see Chapters 1 and 2 and references 15, 16, and 24 among others). As one executive recognized, "Local culture affects virtually every aspect of our business." Yet according to two South African managers, "Interest in cultural differences is offensive" (21).

In many instances people associate recognizing cultural differences with simplistic, primitive, immoral thinking. They label managers who recognize the diversity within their organizations as prejudiced, racist, sexist, ethnocentric, and unprofessional. Cultural norms, especially in North America, encourage managers to blind themselves to gender, race, and ethnicity: to see people only as individuals and to attempt to judge them based solely on their professional skills. This approach causes problems because it confuses recognition with judgment. Recognition occurs when a manager realizes that people from different cultural groups behave differently and that that difference affects their relationship to the organization. People from one ethnic group are not inherently any better or worse (judgment) than those from other groups; they are simply different. To ignore cultural differences is unproductive. *Judging* colleagues and clients based on their membership in particular groups fosters prejudice—a prejudgment based on group rather than individual characteristics. Judging cultural differences as good or bad can lead to inappropriate, offensive, racist, sexist, ethnocentric attitudes and behaviors. *Recognizing* differences does not. Choosing not to see cultural diversity limits our ability to manage it—that is, to minimize the problems cultural diversity causes while maximizing the advantages it allows.

When we blind ourselves to cultural diversity, people from other cultures become mere projections of ourselves. As described in Chapter 3, research has demonstrated that we frequently see similarity even when difference exists; we project similarity. As one Canadian manager inaccurately observed, "It is very easy to work with people from other cultures. People are basically the same and have the same needs and aspirations" (8). Although people are not the same, we perceive them to be the same—to have the same needs and aspirations. Cultural blindness is therefore both perceptual and conceptual: we neither see nor want to see differences. All forms of effective cross-cultural management start with a concerted effort to recognize cultural diversity without judging it—to see difference where difference exists.

Diversity Causes Problems

Culture remains generally invisible and, when visible, we usually think it causes problems. People rarely think that cultural diversity benefits organizations. For example, global executives attending management seminars at INSEAD, the leading international management school in France, listed the advantages and disadvantages of cultural diversity to their organizations. Whereas every executive could list disadvantages, less than a third (30%) could list an advantage (8;17). As a typical French executive summarized, "I have been involved in many situations over the years, but I can't think of one made easier because it involved more than one culture." His Danish colleague agreed, "I can think of no situation in my experience where managing ordinary business became easier or more effective because it involved people from more than one culture."

In the Montreal study described earlier (5), only one of the 60 organizational development consultants mentioned an advantage to the organization from cultural diversity. Similarly, the 52 corporate and academic experts from around the world who participated in the McGill International Symposium on Cross-Cultural Management had a considerably harder time identifying the benefits to be gained from diversity than the problems it causes (1). Every manager and academic present could identify a series of diversity-related problems (1).

What types of problems does diversity cause? As shown in Table 4-1, problems most frequently occur in convergent processes, at times when the organization needs employees to think or to act in similar ways. Communication (converging on similar meanings) and integration (converging on similar actions) become more difficult. People from different cultures fail to understand one another; they do not work in the same ways or at the same pace. The potential for increased ambiguity, complexity, and confusion becomes highest when the organization or project requires direction and clarity—convergence.

Diversity also results in problems when managers and employees overgeneralize organizational practices and processes. For example, problems result when managers export marketing campaigns developed in one country without adapting them to another country:

Africa

[One multinational] tried to sell baby food in an African nation by using its regular label showing a baby and stating the type of baby food in the jar. Unfortunately, the local population took one look at the labels and interpreted them to mean the jars contained ground-up babies! Sales, of course, were terrible (22:31).

Cultural diversity causes problems when the organization must reach a single agreement, whether formal or informal:

TABLE 4-1 *Advantages and Disadvantages of Diversity*

Advantages	Disadvantages
Culturally Synergistic Advantages: Organizational Benefits Derived from Multiculturalism	**Disadvantages Due to Cultural Diversity: Organizational Costs Due to Multiculturalism**
Expanding meanings	Diversity increases
Multiple perspectives	Ambiguity
Greater openness to new ideas	Complexity
Multiple interpretations	Confusion
Expanding alternatives	Difficulty converging meanings
Increasing creativity	Miscommunication
Increasing flexibility	Hard to reach agreement
Increasing problem-solving skills	Difficulty converging actions
	Hard to agree on specific actions
Culture-Specific Advantages: Benefits in Working with a Particular Country or Culture	**Culture-Specific Disadvantages: Costs in Working with a Particular Country or Culture**
Better understanding of local employees	Overgeneralizing
Ability to work more effectively with particular local clients	Organizational policies
Ability to market more effectively to specific local customers	Organizational strategies
	Organizational practices
Increased understanding of political, social, legal, economic, and cultural environment of specific countries	Organizational procedures
	Ethnocentrism

Switzerland/Japan

[The settlement of a licensing agreement between a Japanese and a Swiss company] became much more difficult due to big differences in the decision-making and legal systems between the two countries, the inability of the Swiss to understand the Japanese language, the long distances, and the lack of spontaneity. In one's own country, these difficulties would not exist or could easily be overcome (13).

Cultural diversity increases the complexity and difficulty in developing overall procedures:

Personnel Records in Europe

In line with the American parent company's policies, European subsidiaries attempted to design a common system for developing historical medical data on all employees. Human resource managers from the United Kingdom, Germany, Holland, Sweden, Luxembourg, Spain, and Italy convened a meeting to agree on what could be accomplished and how. Despite procedures that worked well in the United States, the American parent company found the variety of national legislation, cultural concerns, and the need for consultation with work councils and trade unions prior to reaching an agreement imposed limitations on the scope of information available. In a domestic setting, the variety of constraints would be reduced and those remaining clearly understood by all persons involved in developing the system. An effective personnel records system would have been much easier to develop if only one country had been involved (8).

Diversity Provides Advantages

Whereas diversity causes the most problems in convergent processes, it leads to the most potential advantages in divergent processes. Diversity becomes most advantageous when the organization wants to expand its perspective, its approach, its range of ideas, its operations, its product lines, or its marketing plans. Diversity can become an advantage in attempting to reposition the organization, launch a new project, create a new idea, develop a new marketing plan, plan a new operation, or assess emerging trends from a new perspective.

As outlined in Table 4-1, some managers describe multicultural organizations as more flexible and open to new ideas. Others stress the ability of multicultural organizations to understand customers' needs better—for example, to tailor their marketing campaigns to the national and cultural preferences of their clients. Still others note the advantages of the multiple perspectives brought to problem solving and the increased ability to avoid *groupthink*.[1] Overall, potential advantages include enhanced creativity, flexibility, and problem-solving skills, especially on complex problems involving many qualitative factors, improved effectiveness in working with culturally distinct client groups, and a heightened awareness of the dynamics and communication patterns within the organization (14;25).

Potential advantages are realized by using cultural diversity as a resource rather than treating it as a liability to the organization. Global managers describe benefits in strategic alliances, joint ventures, global projects, and all types of multinational business. For example, executives described the following benefits from diversity to their companies.

New Product Development

A U.S. pharmaceutical firm developed a new competitive anticancer drug based on an initial discovery made in their Italian subsidiary, research conducted in conjunction with the best-equipped institute for therapeutical research in the world (the U.S.-based National Cancer Institute), new creativity techniques coming out of Sweden, specific new therapy indications from Japan and China, and a major cash flow from Germany and the United States (8).

Accepting New Ideas

New ideas that seemed threatening or absurd when mentioned by someone from one's own country were easier to "hear" when suggested by people from other cultures. For example, during the energy crisis, American and British workers found the low maximum thermostat settings restrictive. When an ex-British-Leyland team then went to Korea to design the Pony car, they found it amazing that the Koreans broke the ice before they could wash their products. Thereafter, the low thermostat settings no longer seemed so restrictive (8).

New Perspectives, Better Communication and Cooperation

A European firm created a Technical and Field Support Center with the involvement of all their European subsidiaries. By involving all countries in defining the "where, how, and why" of operations, the Center avoided one-nation dictatorial decisions, which, in the past, had caused continuous conflicts between countries (8).

New Perspectives—Neutrality

An American/French joint venture required an outside audit of their Algerian subsidiary. The American partner unsuccessfully proposed an American firm. Similarly, the French partner failed in proposing a French firm. The two finally agreed on a French-affiliated office of an American accounting firm that agreed to assign two French-speaking British citizens to do the job. Everybody was happy (8).

Recognizing the Advantages from Diversity

Culture is not one of the ideas readily used by managers or employees to explain the behavior of individuals and teams in organizations. Unless given a model for culture, they often fail to consider it as a possible explanation for variations in organizational functioning. They explain patterns and changes in behavior as caused by influences other than culture. The follow-up to the Montreal organizational development study demonstrated the value of giving managers a cultural diversity model that demonstrates that diversity can lead to both organizational advantages and disadvantages (5). The value of a model for cultural diversity became evident when the follow-up to the organizational development study did not replicate the results of the original interviews. Following the initial 60 interviews, a similar group of 75 Canadian consultants received questionnaires asking them to again describe the impact of culture on their organizations. However, this time the structured questionnaire gave the consultants a model highlighting cultural diversity's possible positive and negative impacts. Unlike the interviewees, the majority of this second group of consultants did see an impact of cultural diversity on their organization and almost half were able to identify potential impacts.

As shown in Figure 4-1, the original interviewees had seen the impact of cultural diversity in one of three ways. Most had seen it as nonexistent, as

FIGURE 4-1   *Alternative Perceptions of the Impact of Cultural Diversity on Organizations*

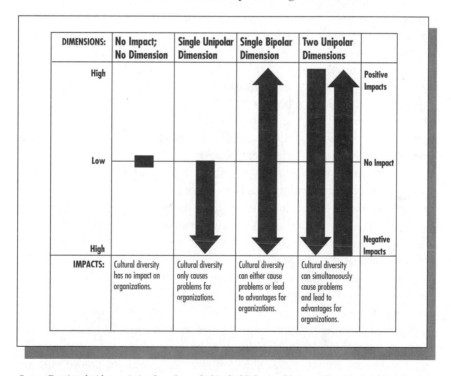

DIMENSIONS:	No Impact; No Dimension	Single Unipolar Dimension	Single Bipolar Dimension	Two Unipolar Dimensions	
High					Positive Impacts
Low					No Impact
High					Negative Impacts
IMPACTS:	Cultural diversity has no impact on organizations.	Cultural diversity only causes problems for organizations.	Cultural diversity can either cause problems or lead to advantages for organizations.	Cultural diversity can simultaneously cause problems and lead to advantages for organizations.	

Source: Reprinted with permission from *Journal of Applied Behavioral Science*, "Organizational Development in a Multicultural Environment," by Nancy J. Adler, vol. 19, no. 3 (Summer 1983), pp. 349–365, copyright 1983 by NTL Institute. Adapted by Adler, 1996.

having no impact whatsoever. Some had seen it as being primarily negative. Only a very few had seen it as being either negative or positive, but not both. In the interviews the consultants had not seen the possibility of cultural diversity simultaneously having both positive and negative impacts. By contrast, the questionnaire respondents saw the possibility of the impact of cultural diversity being simultaneously highly positive and highly negative within the same organization. They did not see positive impacts (advantages) as necessarily related to the lack of negative impacts (problems) (5).

The two parts of the study differed in that the first group, the interviewees, were given neither the concept of culture nor a model of its possible positive and negative impacts, whereas the second group—those who responded to the questionnaire—were explicitly given both. Although it did not occur naturally, it appears that managers can "see" cultural diversity and appreciate its positive and negative impacts if given a model. If culture is not explicitly pointed out, managers remain culture blind.

Strategies for Managing Cultural Diversity

The extent to which managers recognize cultural diversity and its potential advantages and disadvantages defines an organization's approach to managing that diversity (5). As shown in Table 4-2, the most common response of managers to cultural diversity is *parochial*—they do not recognize cultural diversity or its impact on the organization. In parochial organizations, managers believe that "our way is the only way" to organize and manage. The second most common response is *ethnocentric*—members recognize diversity, but only as a source of problems. In ethnocentric organizations, members believe that "our way is the best way" to organize and work; they view all other ways as inferior. Only in those cases in which organization members explicitly recognize the concept of culture can the response to cultural diversity be *synergistic*—seeing cultural diversity as leading to both advantages and disadvantages. Employees and managers using synergistic approaches believe that "our way and their way differ, but neither is inherently superior to the other." They believe that creative combinations of our way and their way produce the best approaches to organizing and working.

Each of the various perceptions and assumptions produces different implications for organizations' approaches to managing diversity. If managers assume the impact of culture to be negligible, as in the case of parochial organizations, their selected strategy will be to ignore cultural diversity. As some parochial managers describe, "Cultural diversity is just not important enough to consider; it is irrelevant." This strategy precludes

TABLE 4-2 *Perceiving and Managing the Impact of Cultural Diversity on Organizations*

Type of Organization	Perception	Strategy	Most Likely Outcomes	Frequency
	What is the perceived impact of cultural diversity on organizations?	How should the impact of cultural diversity on organizations be managed?	What outcomes can managers expect with this perception and strategy?	How common is each of these perceptions and strategies?
Parochial Our way is the only way.	**No impact:** Cultural diversity has no impact on organizations.	**Ignore differences:** Ignore the impact of cultural diversity on organizations.	**Problems:** Problems occur but they are not attributed to cultural diversity.	*Very common*
Ethnocentric Our way is the best way.	**Negative impact:** Cultural diversity causes problems for organizations.	**Minimize differences:** Minimize the source and impact of cultural diversity on organizations. If possible, select a monocultural work force.	**Some problems and few advantages:** Managers reduce problems by reducing diversity; they ignore or eliminate the advantages.	*Common*
Synergistic: Creative combinations of our way and their way may be the best way.	**Potential negative and positive impacts:** Cultural diversity simultaneously leads to problems and advantages for organizations.	**Manage differences:** Train managers and employees to recognize cultural differences and use them to create advantages for the organization.	**Some problems and many advantages:** Managers recognize and realize the advantages to the organizations from cultural diversity. Some problems continue to occur that need to be managed.	*Uncommon*

Source: Adapted in 1996 from Nancy J. Adler, "Organizational Development in a Multicultural Environment," *Journal of Applied Behavioral Science,* vol. 19, no. 3 (Summer 1983), pp. 349–365.

the effective management of diversity. It precludes the possibility of minimizing negative impacts and enhancing positive impacts.

If managers assume that the only impacts of cultural diversity are negative, as in the case of ethnocentric organizations, then their strategy is to minimize the sources and impacts of cultural diversity within the organization. Ethnocentric managers can implement this strategy in a number of ways: for example, by attempting to select a culturally homogeneous work force, or by attempting to socialize all workers into the behavior patterns of the dominant culture. Ethnocentric organizations, by minimizing diversity, preclude the possibility of benefiting from the many cultures present.

If managers see the impacts of cultural diversity as both positive and negative, as in the synergistic approach, then their strategy is to *manage the impacts of cultural diversity rather than managing the diversity itself.* The synergistic approach minimizes potential problems by managing the impacts of cultural diversity, not by attempting to minimize the diversity itself. Similarly, they maximize the potential advantages by managing the impacts of diversity, rather than by ignoring them. Organizations using the synergistic approach train their members to recognize cultural differences and to use those differences to create advantages for the organization.

The first two strategies—ignoring and minimizing cultural difference—occur naturally and are therefore quite common. Only when members of the organization recognize both the cultural diversity and its potential positive impacts does it become probable that they will select to manage the diversity rather than attempting to ignore or minimize it. Cultural diversity potentially has both positive and negative impacts on the organization; the approach to diversity, and not the diversity itself, determines the actual positive and negative outcomes.

CULTURAL SYNERGY

According to Buckminster Fuller, synergy involves "a new way of thinking . . . which helps to free one from outdated patterns and can break the shell of permitted ignorance" (12). Synergy is "the behavior of whole systems that cannot be predicted by the behavior of any parts taken separately. . . . In order to really understand what is going on, we have to abandon starting with parts, and we must work instead from whole to particular" (12). The book *Managing Cultural Synergy* emphasizes that "the very differences in the world's people can lead to mutual growth and accomplishment that is more than the single contribution of each party to the intercultural transaction" (19). It suggests that we can go beyond awareness of our own cultural heritage to produce something greater by cooperation and collaboration. Cultural synergy builds upon similarities and fuses differences resulting in more effective human activities and systems. The very diversity of people can be utilized to enhance problem solving by combined action. Those in international management have unique opportunities to foster synergy on a global basis (19).

Cultural synergy, as an approach to managing the impact of cultural diversity, involves a process in which managers form organizational strategies, policies, structures, and practices based on, but not limited to, the cultural patterns of individual organization members and clients. Culturally synergistic organizations create new forms of management and organization that transcend the distinct cultures of their members (3:172). This approach recognizes both the similarities and the differences among the cultures that compose a global organization and suggests that we neither ignore nor minimize cultural diversity, but rather that we view it as a resource in designing and developing organizational systems (3:172). To a large extent, cultural diversity becomes a key resource in the global learning organization.

A set of assumptions that differs from those most commonly held about cross-cultural interaction within work settings forms the basis of the cultural synergy approach (4). First, as shown in Table 4-3, *homo-geneity*, the belief that all people are basically the same, is the most common assumption—especially in the United States, where it is based on the "melting pot" myth. Cultural synergy, by contrast, assumes *het-erogeneity*. The synergy approach assumes that we are not all the same— that the various groups within society differ and that each maintains its cultural distinctness. Appreciating a pluralistic, rather than a homoge-neous, society underlies the synergy approach. Second, whereas the most commonly held assumption is that the similarities among people are most important, cultural synergy assumes that similarities and dif-ferences share equal importance. Third, whereas the most commonly held assumption posits that "our way is the only way" of living, work-ing, and reaching business goals (parochialism), cultural synergy assumes *equifinality*—that many equivalent ways (*equi*) to live, to work, and to reach a final goal (*finality*) exist, and that no culture's way is inherently superior. Fourth, whereas most people are, to some extent, *ethnocentric* (believing that their way is the best way to live and to work), the synergy approach assumes *cultural contingency*—that the best way depends on the cultures of the people involved.

TABLE 4-3   *Cultural Assumptions and Their Implications for Management*

Common and Misleading Assumptions		Less Common and More Appropriate Assumptions	
Homogeneity	Melting pot myth: We are all the same.	**Heterogeneity**	Image of cultural pluralism: We are not all the same; groups within society differ across cultures.
Similarity	Similarity myth: "They" are all just like me.	**Similarity and Difference**	They are not just like me: Many people differ from me culturally. Most people exhibit both cultural similarities and differences when compared to me.
Parochialism	Only-one-way myth: Our way is the only way. We do not recognize any other way of living or working.	**Equifinality**	Our way is not the only way. There are many culturally distinct ways of reaching the same goal, of working, and of living one's life.
Ethnocentrism	One-best-way myth: Our way is the best way. All other approaches are inferior versions of our way.	**Cultural Contingency**	Our way is one possible way. There are many different and equally good ways to reach the same goal. The best way depends on the culture of the people involved.

Source: Nancy J. Adler, "Domestic Multiculturalism: Cross-Cultural Management in the Public Sector," in William Eddy, ed., *Handbook of Organization Management* (New York: Marcel Dekker, 1983), pp. 481–499. Reprinted from *Handbook of Organization Management*, p. 363, courtesy of Marcel Dekker, Inc. Adapted by Adler, 1996.

In a survey of 145 executives from around the world, 83 percent preferred the synergy approach, yet only a third described their organizations as currently using a synergistic approach for multinational and multicultural problem solving (8). Although global managers clearly recognize the value of approaching problem solving from a synergistic perspective, they also realize that the approach is neither easy nor the traditional approach taken. The following section describes a three-step process for creating synergistic solutions to dilemmas faced by culturally diverse organizations.

Culturally Synergistic Problem Solving

Culturally synergistic organizations reflect the best aspects of all members' cultures in their strategy, structure, and process without violating the norms of any single culture. Managers in synergistic organizations use diversity as a

FIGURE 4-2 *Creating Cultural Synergy*

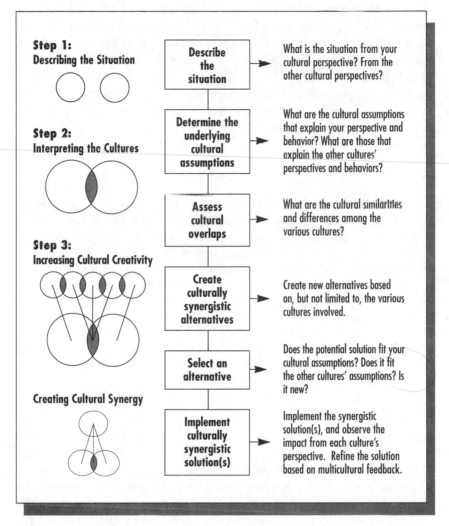

Step 1: Describing the Situation	Describe the situation	What is the situation from your cultural perspective? From the other cultural perspectives?
Step 2: Interpreting the Cultures	Determine the underlying cultural assumptions	What are the cultural assumptions that explain your perspective and behavior? What are those that explain the other cultures' perspectives and behaviors?
	Assess cultural overlaps	What are the cultural similarities and differences among the various cultures?
Step 3: Increasing Cultural Creativity	Create culturally synergistic alternatives	Create new alternatives based on, but not limited to, the various cultures involved.
	Select an alternative	Does the potential solution fit your cultural assumptions? Does it fit the other cultures' assumptions? Is it new?
Creating Cultural Synergy	Implement culturally synergistic solution(s)	Implement the synergistic solution(s), and observe the impact from each culture's perspective. Refine the solution based on multicultural feedback.

Source: Reprinted from W. Warner Burke and Leonard D. Goodstein, eds., *Trends and Issues in OD: Current Theory and Practice.* Copyright © 1980 by Pfeiffer & Company (University Associates, Inc.), San Diego, CA. Used with permission. Adapted by Adler, 1996.

key resource in solving problems. As outlined in Figure 4-2, the process of developing culturally synergistic solutions to organizational problems involves describing the situation from each culture's perspective, culturally interpreting the situation, and developing new culturally creative solutions (3:173).

Step 1: Describing the Situation

What cross-cultural dilemmas does the organization face? What cross-cultural conflicts do managers face? Can the managers describe the conflicts not just from their own perspective, but also from the perspective of each of the various cultures involved? Describing the situation involves one of the most difficult and critical steps in finding solutions to complex multicultural problems. Across cultures, people's divergent values and perceptions magnify the challenges faced in understanding and resolving organizational problems. Some examples involving North American firms include (3:178):

Japan

An American sales manager conveyed the following concern: "I'm an 'open-door manager.' I expect my employees to come to me when they have a problem. But these Japanese never come to you until it's a crisis . . . until it's too late to do anything." To the American manager, the problem had begun weeks earlier. To the Japanese sales representative, the situation only became a "problem" that morning. When questioned later about his behavior, the Japanese salesman explained that "Americans see everything as a problem!" In analyzing the situation, it became clear that people's cultural perspectives determine when they see a situation as a problem. Westerners often see life as a series of problems to be resolved, whereas non-Westerners frequently view life as a series of situations to be accepted (23). Americans therefore define situations as problems much earlier than do the Japanese (3:178).

Egypt

An Egyptian executive, after entertaining his Canadian guest, offered joint partnership in a business venture. The Canadian, delighted with the offer, suggested that they meet again the next morning with their respective lawyers to finalize the details. The Egyptian never arrived. The Canadian wondered what the problem was: Did Egyptians lack punctuality? Was the Egyptian expecting a counteroffer? Or were Egyptian lawyers unavailable in Cairo? None of these explanations proved to be correct, although the Canadian executive considered each of them. The problem was caused by the perceived meaning of inviting lawyers. The Canadian saw the lawyers' presence as facilitating the successful completion of the negotiation; the Egyptian interpreted it as signaling the Canadian's mistrust of his verbal commitment (3:178). Canadians often use the impersonal formality of a lawyer's services to finalize an agreement. Egyptians more frequently depend on a personal relationship developed between bargaining partners for the same purpose.

The first step in the cultural synergy process involves recognizing that a conflict situation exists. Global managers must recognize that a potential problem may exist even when the problem does not make sense from their own cultural perspective (3:178). They must then describe it from each culture's perspective (not just from their own perspective), while refraining from interpreting or evaluating it from any culture's point of view.

Step 2: Culturally Interpreting the Situation

Why do members of different cultures think, feel, and act the way they do? What historical and cultural assumptions must we make to understand the present cross-cultural situation? Once global managers recognize a problem, they can use the synergy approach to analyze it from each culture's perspective. The second step in the cultural synergy process, therefore, involves identifying and interpreting the similarities and differences in thoughts, feelings, and actions among the cultures involved (3:178). All behavior is rational and understandable from the perspective of the person behaving; however, our culturally based perspectives and biases often lead us to misunderstand the logic of other cultures' behavioral patterns (3:179). Whereas a single-culture perspective limits managers' flexibility in global situations, multiple perspectives enhance their understanding and options.

Changing perspectives is achieved through role reversal. During cultural interpretation, managers from each culture attempt to understand the underlying assumptions that lead those in other cultures to behave as they do. During this process, the team identifies similarities and differences between their own culture's assumptions and behaviors and those of other cultures. The following is an example of cross-cultural interpretation:

Iran

An American engineer who was teaching Persians to use a particularly complex technology became disappointed in the progress of his trainees and therefore decided to give them poor performance reviews. One Persian came to the American and queried, "But I thought that you were my friend. Why don't you give me a better review?" The American became furious. Only later, in analyzing and interpreting the underlying cultural assumptions, did the American come to understand the importance Persians place on friendship relative to task accomplishment. Similarly, the Persian came to recognize that Americans base their system of equity solely on competence rather than on competence and relationship (23;24). While both cultures value friendship and achievement, they differ in the relative importance they attach to each (3:179).

Step 3: Increasing Cultural Creativity

Organizations create culturally synergistic alternatives by searching for ways to solve problems—that is, for ways to help people from different cultures enhance their effectiveness and productivity. The question "What can people from one culture contribute to people from another culture?" initiates the search. The answer should be compatible with the cultural assumptions of all represented groups, but it should not imitate any one particular group. Culturally synergistic solutions should be novel and transcend the behavioral patterns of each of the root cultures (3:179). Appropriately selecting the best alternative—evaluation—only becomes possible when preceded by adequately describing and interpretating the situation from a cross-cultural perspective (see Chapter 3). The box "Creating Cultural Synergy: Uruguay and the Philippines" presents an example of the cultural synergy process.

Implementation

Organizations must plan the implementation of culturally synergistic solutions carefully. Before organization members will understand the need for changes based on synergistic problem solving, they must develop cultural self-awareness (an understanding of their own cultural assumptions and patterns of behavior) as well as cross-cultural awareness (an understanding of the other cultures' assumptions and patterns of behavior). Without some understanding of the cultural dynamics involved, proposed changes often appear absurd; with cultural understanding, the organization can solve its problems and implement the changes needed to foster client service, employee effectiveness, and job satisfaction (3:180). The box "Creating Cultural Synergy: Japanese and American Scheduling" highlights a synergistic scheduling plan implemented by an American air freight company for its routes between Japan and the United States.

Strategies That Include Synergy

What strategy do the most effective managers use when working with global strategic alliance and joint venture partners? What approach do managers take in working with global project teams and when negotiating across national borders? Do the most highly effective global managers always use synergy? No.

As shown in Figure 4-3 on page 115, managers have five basic options to choose from in selecting their approach to multicultural situations. In all cross-cultural situations, managers must create a balance between continuing to work in their own way—that is, the way they manage at home—and

CREATING CULTURAL SYNERGY
Uruguay and the Philippines

Situation Description
A Uruguayan doctor at a major California hospital became concerned when he realized that a Filipino nurse was improperly using a particular machine for patient treatment. He instructed the nurse on the proper procedure and asked if she understood. She said she did. Two hours later the patient was doing poorly because the nurse had continued to administer the treatment improperly. The doctor again queried the nurse, and she again affirmed her understanding of the procedure. What went wrong?

Interpretation
In analyzing the situation, the doctor came to understand that many Filipinos will not contradict people in respected positions. To the Filipino nurse, the doctor's status was clearly above hers. He was older; she was younger. He was a doctor; she was a nurse. He was a man; she was a woman. Based on her cultural assumptions, she could not tell the doctor that she did not understand without implying that he had given poor instructions and thus causing him to lose face. The doctor, based on his cultural assumptions, expected "open communication"; he expected the nurse to say whether she understood his instructions and to ask questions if she did not. He considered it a sign of incompetence to assume responsibility for a patient's care without fully understanding the manner of treatment.

Synergistic Solution
After analyzing the situation, the hospital administrator suggested a culturally synergistic solution. Upon giving his initial instructions, the doctor was to ask the nurse to describe the procedure that she would follow. As the doctor listened, he could assess the accuracy of the nurse's understanding and identify areas that needed further explanation. The nurse, never having been asked directly if she understood, would not be forced to say "no" to a superior. The hospital administrator solved the problem without violating either culture's assumptions (3:179–180). The hospital could achieve its goal—the delivery of excellent medical care—without violating the norms of either culture.

adapting to the ways of other cultures. The most highly effective global managers use all five strategic options, selecting a specific option depending on the particular situation and people involved.

CREATING CULTURAL SYNERGY[2]
Japanese and American Scheduling

Situation Description
American sales representatives of a U.S.–based air freight company with extensive Asian operations generally promised customers specific dates and hours for flight arrivals of freight shipments. However, shipments often arrived late. American customers would usually expect, understand, and forgive these delays if given an adequate explanation, whereas Japanese customers expected the company to keep its promises and lost faith in the company when it did not adhere to the promised arrival times. Unlike the Americans, the Japanese sales representatives often refused to promise delivery times until, as the Americans explained, "the plane had arrived on the runway" or, as the Japanese explained, they could be certain that their promises would be kept. However, the Japanese sales representatives' lack of promising did not work with American clients who expected definite timetables; when not given them, they tended to distrust the company's ability to perform its services.

Interpretation
The company needed to design a uniform "promising" system that would be culturally appropriate for both American and Japanese employees and clients. From the American perspective, the system had to be definite enough to develop credibility with American customers. From the Japanese perspective, the promises to customers had to conform to reality sufficiently so that no one would lose face.

Synergistic Solution
After analyzing the underlying cultural dynamics in both systems, the sales representatives agreed that they should begin promising delivery within a range of time, rather than at specific times. For instance, they would promise clients delivery "late morning Thursday," rather than at 11:05 a.m. (scheduled flight arrival time). Thus Americans could continue to promise and the Japanese would rarely promise something that the company could not deliver.

   This solution recognizes the values of both cultures without upsetting either cultures' management practices. As a synergistic solution, it is new and appropriate to both cultures (3:180–181).

FIGURE 4-3 *Global Strategic Options*

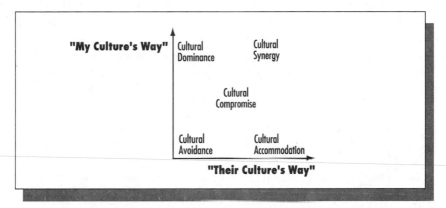

Cultural Dominance

Cultural Synergy

"My Culture's Way"

Cultural Compromise

Cultural Avoidance

Cultural Accommodation

"Their Culture's Way"

Cultural Dominance

The first option is cultural dominance: continuing to do things in the way of your own home culture. Historically, the dominance approach has frequently been used by companies that had considerably more power than their counterparts—for example, because they were larger, more technologically advanced, or more financially successful. On an individual level, managers often choose the cultural dominance approach when they strongly believe their way is the only right way and especially when they perceive the situation to involve a fundamental ethical issue. For example, one Swedish manager refused to lower the safety standards on his company's product, even though the lower standards were legally acceptable in the potential buyer's country. The Swede lost the contract because his bid, which included the higher safety standards, came in too high. Similarly, an American manager refused to accept a small, personal gift from a Korean client because his company, based on American practices, believed that gift giving represented a form of bribery. To the Korean, gift giving represented a form of relationship building. The American's behavior mystified the Korean, "How could a small personal gift be considered a bribe?"

Cultural Accommodation

The second option, cultural accommodation, is the opposite of cultural dominance. Rather than attempting to maintain one's own home country practices when working abroad, managers attempt to imitate the practices of the host culture. When working abroad, they attempt to blend into the local culture. They follow the maxim "When in Rome, do as the Romans do."

Managers who consistently use cultural accommodation are often accused by their home country colleagues of having "gone native," with executives from the home country often fearing that they will no longer fully represent the interests of headquarters.

A German manager used cultural accommodation in Japan when attempting to get a first contract from a particularly important potential Japanese buyer. The German spent the first two weeks in Kobe and Osaka dining and playing golf with the Japanese without scheduling any formal meetings on the product. While the German manager's boss in Munich became annoyed, thinking his colleague had confused a business trip with a vacation, the German manager was accommodating perfectly to the Japanese style of doing business: he was allowing the Japanese to get to know him (relationship building) before focusing on the details of the contract (task focus). The German got the contract.

Managers who learn the local language of countries in which they work are using a cultural accommodation strategy. Similarly, managers who denominate contracts in the local currency are using cultural accommodation. Their accommodation approach allows local managers to continue using their normal, comfortable ways of doing business.

Cultural Compromise

The third approach, cultural compromise, combines the first and second approaches. Using cultural compromise implies that both sides concede something in order to work more successfully with each other. For example, French and Russian potential joint venture partners held initial meetings alternately in Moscow and Paris. Each side had to travel to half the meetings, but neither side experienced the inconvenience of always traveling and working away from their own headquarters.

In compromise solutions the more powerful partner often gives up less than the less powerful partner. However, both sides make concessions for the business relationship to succeed. Home country colleagues often view managers who give up too much as weak and sometimes accuse them of "caving in."

Cultural Avoidance

The fourth approach, cultural avoidance, is the choice to act as if there are no differences—to act as if no conflict exists. This approach, used more frequently by Asian managers than by their Western counterparts, often emphasizes "saving face" over openly and explicitly confronting all the potentially conflictual details inherent in a particular situation. Managers use cultural avoidance most commonly when the unresolved issue is less important than the overall relationship or contract.

For example, in negotiating the final details of a major construction contract in Eastern Malaysia, the Americans thought they had resolved all potential disagreements regarding worker benefits. They were surprised when they saw that the Malaysian version of the benefits agreement included dental care for workers and their families, including the children of the second, third, and fourth wife.[3] Even though the Americans had never considered including dental care, or any other benefits, for the families of workers' second, third, or fourth wife, and they knew that such benefits had never been discussed nor promised, they chose not to confront the Malaysians. Perhaps the Malaysians, based on their cultural tradition, had assumed that "family" meant all wives' families, whereas it had never occurred to the Americans that "family" might mean anything other than one wife's (or husband's) family. Rather than upsetting a project that would be very good for both the Americans and the Malaysians, the Americans chose "not to see" the additional expense in the contract.

Cultural Synergy

As discussed in this chapter, the fifth approach, cultural synergy, develops new solutions to problems that respect each of the underlying cultures but differ from what would be needed in a purely domestic situation. Foreign languages provide an excellent example. When businesspeople meet, they have to use language to communicate. If the two sides speak different native languages, they must choose in which language to communicate. If a British company insists that the working language in its strategic alliance with the Swedes be English, then the British are using a cultural dominance approach. If the Swedes immediately agree, they are choosing to use a cultural accommodation approach. If both sides choose to use interpreters, they are selecting a compromise approach. However, when Norwegians and Austrians choose to speak in English, they are using a synergy approach. In both countries global businesspeople often speak English, the international business language; however, neither the Norwegians nor the Austrians speak English as their native language. English allows the two sides to conduct business without either side capitulating to speak the other's language (and thereby becoming disadvantaged). Similarly, denominating contracts in a basket of currencies becomes a synergistic approach to managing the risk of future exchange rate fluctuations.

SUMMARY

In *Fortune's* cover story on "What the Leaders of Tomorrow See," Corning's CEO asserts, "Future leaders will have to learn how to manage cultural diversity" (11:59). Cultural synergy is a powerful approach to managing the impact of cultural diversity that allows organizations to resolve situations effectively when working across cultures. Synergistic solutions create new forms of managing and organizing by recognizing and transcending the individual ethnic cultures of employees and clients. The synergy approach, far from ignoring the presence of cultural diversity within the organization, recognizes both its potentially positive and negative impacts. Unlike the more common cultural dominance and accomodation approaches, cultural synergy emphasizes managing the impacts of diversity, rather than attempting to eliminate the diversity itself.

The synergy approach to problem solving involves three fundamental steps: cross-cultural situation description, cultural interpretation, and cultural creativity. Global managers first define problems from the perspectives of all cultures involved. Second, they analyze the patterns that make each culture's behavior logical from within its own perspective. Third, they create solutions that foster the organization's effectiveness and productivity without violating the norms of any culture involved.

The synergy approach creates organizational solutions to problems by using cultural diversity as a resource and an advantage to the organization. Synergy is most useful in resolving important issues in which cross-cultural interaction among employees and clients occurs daily. However, organizations should not consider synergy to be the only approach.

In introducing culturally synergistic problem solving to an organization for the first time, managers realize that they are involved in the process of managing change. The most fundamental change is one of perspective: senior executives must guide their organizations toward a more inclusive, global world view. Many organizations have found it helpful to begin the cultural synergy process with cross-cultural management seminars, during which executives, managers, and employees have the opportunity to become more culturally self-aware (recognizing and understanding their own culture's patterns of doing business) and more cross-culturally aware (recognizing and understanding the culturally based work styles of clients and colleagues from other cultures). Following these initial cross-cultural management sessions, organizations begin to more effectively address their culturally based conflict situations. As the organization addresses each new problem from a synergistic perspective, it accumulates the sophistication and experience needed to address future problems. Whereas initial problems often must be addressed explicitly, formally (through workshops, seminars, and structured meetings), and slowly (developing awareness prior to attempting to solve problems), later synergistic problem-solving processes become more implicit, more informal, and considerably less time-consuming. Learning acquired during initial sessions becomes part of the organization's increasingly global perspective and cross-cultural competence.

Cultural synergy is *an* approach, not *the* approach; it is one of five options that highly effective global managers use regularly. The synergistic problem-solving process is not a quick fix. It is a systematic process for increasing the options open to executives, managers, and employees working in increasingly global business environments. Similarly, it is an effective approach for competing successfully in multicultural domestic environments.

QUESTIONS FOR REFLECTION

1. ***Choosing an Approach.*** Select an organizational problem involving more than one culture that you are currently facing or have faced in the past. Describe the process you would recommend for developing a culturally synergistic solution to the problem.

2. ***Cultural Blindness.*** For many organizations, a major problem is cultural blindness. In the organizations that you know, what factors cause managers to remain blind to the impact of cultural diversity? What would you recommend to decrease managers' work-related cultural blindness?

3. ***Creating Cultural Synergy.*** Select a cross-cultural conflict situation that is currently in the news or occurring in an organization. As a consultant, what would you recommend to help the parties involved create a culturally synergistic solution? What might a final culturally synergistic solution look like?

4. ***Developing Skills for Synergy.*** Reflecting on your own personality and work style, what do you see as your greatest skills in being able to create culturally synergistic solutions? In which areas do you need to improve your skills at creating cultural synergy?

5. ***Advantages of Cultural Diversity.*** What are the advantages of using a multicultural senior management team for a company that conducts a substantial portion of its business abroad? What are the advantages of using a team of senior executives selected primarily from the local area? Under what circumstances would you recommend each type of senior executive team?

NOTES

1. The term *groupthink* was first coined by I. L. Janis in his book *Groupthink*, 2nd edition, (Houghton Mifflin Company, 1982). See Chapter 5 for a more in-depth discussion of the topic.

2. Clifford Clarke, President, Clarke Consulting Group, was instrumental in interpreting this cross-cultural air freight situation. His insight and creativity in creating cultural synergy with Japanese organizations continues to advance the insight of the field.

3. According to Islamic tradition, a man may take up to four wives if he can support each of them and their children.

REFERENCES

1. Adler, N. J. "Cross-Cultural Management: Issues to Be Faced," *International Studies of Management and Organization*, vol. 13, no. 1-2 (Spring-Summer 1983), pp. 7–45.

2. Adler, N. J. "Cross-Cultural Management Research: The Ostrich and the Trend," *Academy of Management Review*, vol. 8, no. 2 (April 1983), pp. 226–232.

3. Adler, N. J. "Cultural Synergy: The Management of Cross-Cultural Organizations," in W. W. Burke and L. D. Goodstein, eds., *Trends and Issues in OD: Current Theory and Practice* (San Diego, Calif.: University Associates, 1980), pp. 163–184.

4. Adler, N. J. "Domestic Multiculturalism: Cross-Cultural Management in the Public Sector," in W. Eddy, ed., *Handbook on Public Organization Management* (New York: Marcel Dekker, 1983), pp. 481–499.

5. Adler, N. J. "Organizational Development in a Multicultural Environment," *Journal of Applied Behavioral Science*, vol. 19, no. 3 (Summer 1983), pp. 349–365.

6. Adler, N. J., and Bartholomew, S. "Academic and Professional Communities of Discourse: Generating Knowledge on Transnational Human Resource Management," *Journal of International Business Studies*, vol. 23, no. 3, (1992), pp. 551–569.

7. Adler, N. J., and Boyacigiller, N. "Global Organizational Behavior: Going Beyond Tradition," *Journal of International Management*, vol. 1, no. 1 (1995), pp. 73–86.

8. Adler, N. J., and Laurent, A. Unpublished results from the Cultural Synergy Survey collected at INSEAD in 1980–1983 and in 1982 at major American and Canadian multinationals ($n = 145$).

9. Boyacigiller, N., and Adler, N. J. "The Parochial Dinosaur: The Organizational Sciences in a Global Context," *Academy of Management Review*, vol. 16, no. 2 (1991), pp. 262–290.

10. Boyacigiller, N., and Adler, N. J. "Insiders and Outsiders: Bridging the Worlds of Organizational Behavior and International Management," in Brian Toyne and Doug Nigh, eds., *International Business Inquiry: An Emerging Vision*. (Columbia, S.C.: University of South Carolina Press, 1996), pp. 22–102.

11. Dumaine, B. "What the Leaders of Tomorrow See," *Fortune* (July 3, 1989), pp. 48–62.

12. Fuller, R. B. *Critical Path* (Washington D.C.: St. Martin's Press/World Future Society, 1981).

13 Godkin, L.; Braye, C. E.; Cauch, C. L. "U.S.–Based Cross-Cultural Management Research in the Eighties," *Journal of Business and Economic Perspectives*, vol. 15, no. 2 (1989), pp. 37–45.

14. Hayles, R. "Costs and Benefits of Integrating Persons from Diverse Cultures in Organization," paper presented at the 20th International Congress of Applied Psychology, Edinburgh, Scotland, July 25–31, 1982.

15. Hofstede, G. *Culture's Consequences: International Differences in Work-Related Values* (Beverly Hills, Calif.: Sage, 1980).

16. Laurent, A. "The Cultural Diversity of Western Conceptions of Management," *International Studies of Management and Organization*, vol. 13, no. 1-2 (Spring-Summer 1983), pp. 75–96.

17. Laurent, A., and Adler, N. J. "Managerial Skills for International Business," executive seminars held at INSEAD in Fontainebleau, France, August, 1981–1983.

18. McEvoy, G. M., and Buller, P. F. "International Human Resource Management Publications: Even in the Eighties and Needs for the Nineties," Working Paper. Utah State University, 1992, pp. 1–21.

19. Moran, R. T., and Harris, P. R. *Managing Cultural Synergy* (Houston, Tex.: Gulf Publishing Company, 1981), Chapter 15, p. 3.

20. Peng, T. K.; Peterson, M. F.; and Shyi, Y. P. "Quantitative Methods in Cross-National Management Research: Trend and Equivalence Issues. *Journal of Organizational Behavior*, vol. 12, no. 1 (1990), pp. 87–107.

21. Prekel, T. "Multicultural Communication: A Challenge to Managers," paper delivered at the International Convention of the American Business Communication Association, New York, November 21, 1983, p. 11.

22. Ricks, D. A. *Big Business Blunders: Mistakes in Multinational Marketing* (Homewood, Ill.: Dow Jones–Irwin, 1983).

23. Stewart, E. C. *American Cultural Patterns: A Cross-Cultural Perspective* (Chicago: Ill.: Intercultural Press, 1979).

24. Trompenaars, F., *Riding the Waves of Culture* (London: The Economist, 1993; Burr Ridge, Ill.: Irwin Professional Publishing, 1993, 1994).

25. Ziller, R. C. "Homogeneity and Heterogeneity of Group Membership," in C. G. McClintock, ed., *Experimental Social Psychology* (New York: Holt, Rinehart, and Winston, 1972), pp. 385–411.

CHAPTER 5
Multicultural Teams

It was once said that the sun never set on the British Empire. Today the sun does set on the British Empire, but not on the scores of global corporate empires including those of IBM, Unilever, Volkswagen, and Hitachi.

— Lester Brown, President of Worldwatch Institute (58:320)

International management used to be a minor component of industrial acticity; now it dominates. International management used to involve simply sending one of "our" managers "over there" to sell products to foreign clients; now people from many countries work within our companies, and in many cases, we are the foreigners. International management used to involve sending expatriates to direct operations abroad; now members of corporate boards, executives, managers, and workers represent every nationality. Today more than 10,000 firms headquartered in high-technology, non-Communist countries have operations outside their home nations (see 58:320).

In the 1990s, global business brought cross-cultural contact home to every business. Today, without leaving their own communities, managers may work for a foreign-owned firm, sell to nonnative clients, and negotiate with components suppliers from abroad, while regularly attending meetings with colleagues from around the world. Globally distanced design teams routinely develop revolutionary new products in electronic meetings among experts on five continents, none of whom ever leaves home to participate in the telephone, fax, computer, e-mail and Internet discussions. Cross-cultural dialogue has become the very foundation on which global business is conducted.

MANAGING A MULTICULTURAL WORK FORCE

Both domestically and globally, the multicultural work force has become a reality. However, the impact of multiculturalism varies significantly with the type of environment and the firm's overall strategy. As shown in Figure 5-1, worldwide cultural diversity traditionally has had a minimal impact on domestic firms even when domestic multiculturalism has had a highly significant impact. For example, sophisticated managers in American firms coach their colleagues to appreciate and to effectively manage a work force composed of African-American, Asian-American, Hispanic-American, and Native American women and men. Assuming that the domestic work force is homogeneous or that it is defined by white male norms was never appropriate and is no longer effective.

In multidomestic firms (those which only export or which operate fairly autonomous operations abroad), the impact of culture becomes highly significant. Multidomestic firms must adapt their strategies and their products and services to that of the local culture in each of the countries in which they operate. In multinational firms, because price and cost

Figure 5-1 *Importance of Cultural Diversity*

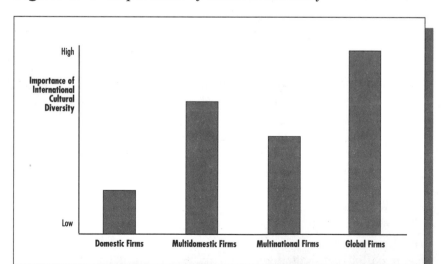

tend to dominate all other considerations, the impact of cultural differences lessens slightly.

By the time firms adopt global strategies, the impact of cultural diversity becomes extremely important. Global firms must understand cultural dynamics to formulate their strategies, to locate production facilities and suppliers worldwide, to design and market culturally appropriate products and services, as well as to manage cross-cultural interaction throughout the organization, from senior executive committees to the shop floor. As more firms move from domestic, multidomestic, and multinational strategies to operating as truly global organizations and alliances, the importance and impact of cultural diversity increase markedly. The impact of cultural diversity, which once was merely "nice to understand," becomes imperative for survival, let alone success (3). (See Chapter 1 for a review of each phase.)

Similar to cultural diversity's increasing importance, the location of its impact varies with changes in the firm's business environment and strategy. As shown in Figure 5-2, worldwide cultural diversity has traditionally affected neither the domestic firm's internal organizational culture nor its external relationship with its clients. Domestic firms work domestically; only domestic multiculturalism has a direct impact on the internal dynamics of the firm as well as on its relationship to its external environment. Today almost no major firms operate in purely domestic environments; few if any have the luxury of operating in a simple, domestic environment free of international influences.

Figure 5-2 *Location of International Cross-Cultural Interaction*

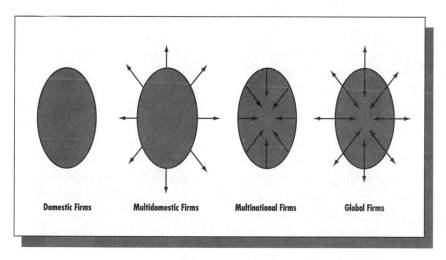

| Domestic Firms | Multidomestic Firms | Multinational Firms | Global Firms |

In multidomestic firms, which focus primarily on exporting and producing abroad, cultural diversity strongly affects relationships external to the firm, especially those with potential buyers and workers in other countries. By contrast, multinational firms place less emphasis on managing cultural differences external to the firm, but increasingly need to manage the growing multinational cultural diversity within the firm. Whereas multidomestic firms primarily use expatriate managers to sell and work abroad, multinational firms hire people from around the world as employees and managers. In multidomestic firms, only expatriates have a high need for developing cultural sensitivity and cross-cultural management skills. By contrast, in multinational firms, because the location of the impact of cultural diversity moves inside the organization and up the levels of hierarchy, many more regular employees and managers need cross-cultural management skills.

Global firms must manage cultural diversity both within the firm and between the firm and its external environment. To work effectively, everyone from the CEO to the lowest level worker needs cross-cultural skills. This progression from culture's relative lack of importance to its critical importance, both with respect to the firm's external environment as well as to its internal organizational culture, underlies today's recognition that executives and managers must know how to work effectively in multinational and multicultural teams if they wish to succeed (3).

How do we manage people who differ from us? Research has shown that the styles of leading, motivating, communicating, decision making, planning, organizing, and staffing vary among countries of the world (see Chapter 6). What happens when people from dissimilar cultures work together on a day-to-day basis within the same organization? How should organizations manage a multinational work force?

This chapter investigates the ways of managing cultural diversity within an organization. It begins with a review of domestic multiculturalism, an important source of multicultural dynamics in teams. It then focuses on cross-cultural interaction within teams: What types of problems can diversity cause within executive and employee teams? What potential benefits emerge from culturally diverse teams? And, most importantly, what does management need to do to maximize the potential benefits and minimize the potential problems caused by diversity?

DOMESTIC MULTICULTURALISM

You do not have to go abroad to meet someone with a cultural background different from your own. With increasing immigration, increasing numbers of people working abroad, and the presence of indigenous ethnic communities, managers who never leave home often face a multicultural work force in local companies and organizations.

Culturally distinct populations live in all countries of the world. Singapore, for example, has four cultural and linguistic groups: Chinese, Malay, Indian, and Eurasian. Belgium has two linguistic groups, French and Flemish. Switzerland has four distinct ethnic communities: French, German, Italian, and Romansh. Canada, a multicultural country by national policy, uses two official languages, English and French. Many countries, including Israel and the United States, have developed historically as havens for immigrants from around the world.

Each population exhibits a culturally unique life-style. Most of us are familiar with the typical foods of the major ethnic groups: no one thinks that spaghetti is Russian, that tortillas are Chinese, or that sushi is Senegalese. But many of us remain unaware of how extensively other cultures' life-styles differ from our own. Even if we consider ourselves internationally sophisticated, many of us fail to recognize the culturally distinct attitudes and behaviors that our fellow citizens bring to the workplace (2).

The city of Los Angeles highlights the pervasiveness of domestic multiculturalism and its impact on the workplace. Since 1970 more than two million foreign immigrants have settled in Los Angeles (8:17). Of Los Angeles' 550,000 school children, 117,000 speak one of 104 languages more fluently than English, including 35 fluent only in Gujarati, a language of western India (8:18). Los Angeles no longer has a majority population but constantly "adjusts to the quirky, polyglot rhythms of 60,000 Samoans and 30,000 Thais, 200,000 Salvadorans and 175,000 Armenians" (8:18). Los Angeles is the second largest Mexican agglomeration after Mexico City (29:52), more Samoans live in Los Angeles than on the island of Samoa four thousand miles away (53:1), and more Israelis live there than in any other city outside of Israel (60). As a former lieutenant governor of California recognized two decades ago, there is one central, inevitable fact: "If the present trends continue, the emerging ethnic groups will constitute more than half the population of California by 1990, and . . . [California] will become the country's first Third World state" (33:35). His prediction has become a reality.

The story reflects the same pattern in other cities and states in the United States. Of the 700,000 largely middle-class Cubans who left Cuba by 1978, more than 60 percent have settled in Dade County, Florida (29:51). More than 1.3 million Puerto Ricans now live in the greater New York City area (29:55). Hawaii has become a domestic microcosm of Eastern and Western cultures. Moreover, there has been a resurgence of ethnic self-identity among both new immigrants and European populations that had seemed all but assimilated (50). Observing these and dozens of other statistics, multiculturalism has become a dominant fact of domestic life in the United States. Americans can no longer forget multiculturalism nor relegate it to the domain of global managers and diplomats.

Perhaps William Somerset Maugham best captured the essence of domestic multiculturalism in 1921 in *The Trembling Leaf* when he described Hawaii, a state whose 900,000 residents represent 29 percent Caucasians, 27.5 percent Japanese, 18 percent Hawaiian and part Hawaiian, 10 percent Filipino, 4.5 percent Chinese, 1 percent each Korean, Samoan, and black, and 8 percent mixed or miscellaneous (25:97).

> It is a meeting place of East and West, the very new rubs shoulders with the immeasurably old . . . you have come upon something singularly intriguing. All these strange people live close to each other, with different languages and different thoughts; they believe in different gods and they have different values; two passions alone they share, love and hunger. And somehow as you watch them, you have an impression of extraordinary vitality.

TASK GROUPS: THE ORGANIZATION IN MICROCOSM

Organizations consist of groups, and groups form the basic structure of organizations. Companies organize their employees into many forms of temporary and permanent work groups, including departments, offices, teams, task forces, subcommittees, committees, commissions, and boards. Such groups vary in quality from poor to excellent, from totally unproductive to highly productive. They can espouse societally desirable values and goals, or society can view their objectives as destructive. They can accomplish much that is good, or they can cause great harm. From the organization's perspective, they can be highly effective or totally ineffective. There is nothing implicitly good or bad, or weak or strong, about a group (38).

The productivity of a work group—or team—depends on its task, its available resources, and its process. The team's goal defines its task, and this task can involve a decision, a recommendation, a project, a report, an action, or a series of actions. The team's resources include the people, information, materials, time, money, and energy available for accomplishing a task. For example, a task force may have three or five people available; it may have one week or four months; it may have a large budget or no budget at all; it may have unlimited computer resources or only very limited access. The team's process "consists of the actual steps taken by an individual or group when confronted by a task. It includes all those intrapersonal and interpersonal actions by which people transform their resources into a product, and all those nonproductive actions that are prompted by frustration, competing motivations, and inadequate understanding" (57:8).

The actual productivity of a team is its potential productivity minus the losses due to faulty process (57:9):

Actual productivity = Potential productivity −
Losses due to faulty process

Actual productivity depends on how well the team works together and uses its resources to accomplish the task.

TYPES OF DIVERSITY IN TEAMS

Team members can have very similar or quite different backgrounds, perspectives, and training (9). Although diversity can refer to many characteristics (gender, race, profession, nationality, age, and experience), this chapter focuses on cultural differences (65). Therefore teams with all members from the same culture are referred to as homogeneous and those with more than one culture as multicultural. Multicultural teams can be divided into three types: those with a single member from another culture (token teams), those with multiple members representing two cultures (bicultural teams), and those with members from three or more cultures (literally, multicultural teams).

Homogeneous Teams

In homogeneous teams, all members share a similar background. Homogeneous team members generally perceive, interpret, and evaluate the world more similarly than do members of heterogeneous teams. For example, a team of male Finnish bankers is homogeneous, based on gender, culture, and profession. A team of Mexican and Panamanian stockbrokers is professionally, but not culturally, homogeneous.

Token Teams

In token teams all but one member comes from the same background. For example, in a team of Australian lawyers and one British attorney, the British attorney would be the token member. In such a token team, the British attorney would probably see and understand situations somewhat differently from the Australians. In the last decade, male management teams began to pay considerable attention to the few token female members. Today many corporations focus significantly more attention on the contributions of their token ethnic members.

Bicultural Teams

In bicultural teams two or more members represent each of two distinct cultures; for example, a fifty-fifty partnership between Peruvians and Bolivians, or a task force composed of Saudi Arabian and Jordanian managers, or a committee with seven Spanish and three Portuguese executives. Bicultural teams must continually recognize and integrate the perspectives of both represented cultures.

Multicultural Teams

In multicultural teams, members represent three or more ethnic backgrounds. United Nations agencies offer good examples of multicultural organizational structures, as do the committees of the European Union (EU) and the Association of Southeast Asian Nations (ASEAN). Today, an increasing number of corporate task forces are globally distanced teams—that is, teams composed of members from around the world who meet electronically. Although often moderated by the economic and political power structure of the represented members, multicultural teams, to work effectively, should recognize and integrate all represented cultures.

Although little research exists describing cross-cultural interaction within work teams, there has been considerable research on the conditions for effective team functioning within the United States (21;23;31;39;42;57;64). A sizable literature also exists describing team behavior in countries around the world (often with American comparisons) (55). Studies include research on such diverse peoples as Hispanics (15), black and white Americans (52), Indians (6;46), Hong Kong and American Chinese (47), Lebanese (17), New Zealanders (7), Arabs (13), Canadians (56), British (41), South Africans, Nigerians, Filipinos (22), and Japanese (14;48). As with other types of organizational behavior, research has demonstrated that the behavior of people in work teams varies across cultures.

CULTURAL DIVERSITY'S IMPACT ON TEAMS

Cultural diversity can have positive and negative impacts on teams (36;43; 44;45;62;63). Diversity augments potential productivity while greatly increasing the complexity of the process that must occur for the team to realize its full potential (57:107). Multicultural teams have more potential for higher productivity than do homogeneous teams, but they also bear the risk of greater losses due to faulty process. As shown in the following model, the actual productivity of multicultural teams can therefore be higher, lower, or the same as that of single-culture teams:

$$(\uparrow \text{ or } \downarrow) \frac{\text{Actual}}{\text{productivity}} = (\uparrow) \frac{\text{Potential}}{\text{productivity}} - (\uparrow) \frac{\text{Losses due to}}{\text{faulty process}}$$

For example, multicultural teams can have many perspectives on a situation (thus increasing potential productivity) (40), but they frequently experience greater difficulty in integrating and evaluating these perspectives (thus causing losses in productivity due to faulty process).

Process Losses in Culturally Diverse Teams

Diversity makes team functioning more difficult because it becomes more difficult to see situations in similar ways, understand them in similar ways, and act on them in similar ways. Diversity makes reaching agreement more difficult. Employees from the same culture are generally easier to manage; they communicate with each other more clearly and trust each other more readily. In culturally diverse teams, misperception, misinterpretation, misevaluation, and miscommunication abound (see Chapter 3). Stress levels increase, with multicultural teams more frequently disagreeing implicitly and explicitly on expectations, the appropriateness of relevant information, and the need for particular decisions. Diversity increases the ambiguity, complexity, and inherent confusion in the team's process (see Chapter 4, Table 4-1). These process losses diminish productivity (34;36).

Cohesiveness involves the ability of individual team members to act as one; the ability of team members, when necessary, to perceive, interpret, and act on the task at hand in similar or mutually agreed upon ways. Because they begin with a less substantial base of similarity, multicultural teams are initially less cohesive than most homogeneous teams.

As shown in Table 5-1, the higher levels of mistrust, miscommunication, and stress present in multicultural teams diminish cohesion. More importantly, these attitudinal and perceptual communication problems also frequently diminish productivity. The main *process problems* experienced by multicultural teams are discussed in the following section.

Attitudinal Problems: Dislike and Mistrust

Culturally diverse teams possess higher levels of mistrust than do their more homogeneous counterparts. Team members often find themselves

Table 5-1   *Advantages and Disadvantages of Diversity in Multicultural Teams*

Advantages	*Disadvantages*

Diversity permits increased creativity
Wider range of perspective
More and better ideas
Less *groupthink*
	Diversity causes a lack of cohesion
	Mistrust
	   Lower interpersonal attractiveness
	   Stereotyping
	   More within-culture conversations

Diversity forces enhanced concentration to understand others'
Ideas
Meanings
Arguments
	Miscommunication
	   Slower speech: Nonnative speakers and translation problems
	   Less accuracy
	Stress
	   More counterproductive behavior
	   Less disagreement on content
	   Tension

Increased creativity can lead to Better problem definition More alternatives Better solutions Better decisions	***Lack of cohesion causes an inability to*** Validate ideas and people Agree when agreement is needed Gain consensus on decisions Take concerted action
Teams can become More effective More productive	***Teams can become*** Less efficient Less effective Less productive

less attracted to people from other cultures than to those from their own culture (59). For example, researchers in Belgium found Walloon and Flemish individuals speaking more frequently to colleagues of their own than of the opposite culture (51). Mistrust, however, results primarily from cross-cultural misinterpretation rather than dislike. For example, many Indian employees look down when acknowledging authority, an attitude that many European and North American managers misinterpret as untrustworthiness. As a result these European and North American managers may fail to develop sufficient trust in their Indian colleagues to delegate or share more than trivial responsibilities.

Perceptual Problems: Stereotyping

Team members often inappropriately stereotype colleagues from other cultures rather than accurately seeing and assessing their skills and potential contributions for accomplishing a particular task (18). For instance, when some members come from higher status cultures and others from lower status cultures, team members tend to talk more to those from the higher status cultures. They assume, usually subconsciously, that national stereotypes apply to each individual in the team. Thus, in initial meetings team members frequently judge those colleagues from the most developed and economically strongest countries more favorably (18). On one particular management team, members assumed that their American colleagues had more technological expertise than did their Moroccan colleagues simply because Morocco is an economically and technologically less developed country. In a parallel situation, an Indian manager described the lack of respect granted him by many of his British colleagues who, he believed, "assume that I am underdeveloped simply because I come from an economically underdeveloped country." Both the initial stereotype and the Indian's resulting frustration diminished the team's productivity.

Communication Problems: Inaccuracy, Misunderstanding, Inefficiency

Diversity causes communication problems (57). It slows down communication when all members do not fluently speak the team's working language (24). In linguistically diverse groups, some members must use a foreign language or employ an interpreter. In both cases communication speed decreases and the chances for errors increase as compared with teams in which all members are native speakers of the same language (24).

Team members from different cultures often disagree over important meanings, such as the causes of events, the determination of admissible evidence, the relevance of specific information, and the possible conclusions that can be drawn (24). In some cases disagreement remains implicit or hidden; members assume they interpret things similarly when in fact the opposite is true. The following incident between an Indian supervisor and his Austrian boss highlights such an implicit misinterpretation:

> When asked if his department could complete a project by a given date, the Indian supervisor said "yes" even though he knew he could not complete the project within the time frame, because he believed that his Austrian manager wanted "yes" for an answer. When the completion date arrived and the Indian had not finished the project, his Austrian manager showed dismay. The Indian's desire to be polite—to say what he thought his manager wanted to hear—seemed more important to him than reporting an accurate assessment of the completion date. Unfortunately, the Austrian manager considered accurate information more important than politeness. Cross-cultural miscommunication interrupted the smooth functioning of work.[1]

Stress

Stress and tension levels in culturally diverse teams often exceed those in single-culture teams (59), due primarily to communication inaccuracies and a lack of trust. For example, the deductive, analytical discussion style of the French often causes stress for the more inductive, pragmatic North Americans: the French continually want to discuss principles and historical precedent whereas the North Americans focus on the details of the immediate situation.[2] Multicultural teams often exhibit symptoms of considerable social stress, including bickering, apathy, single-party (or single-culture) domination of discussions, stubbornness, and reprimanding (24). Multicultural teams can also show "a quiet climate of politeness and gradually increasing friendliness" (51), but according to some researchers, "these [rituals of politeness] have to be seen as the superficial defense of a weak group cohesiveness" (51). This ritual politeness leaves members frustrated and becomes yet another hindrance to team productivity.

Decreased Effectiveness

As has been demonstrated in the previous examples, cultural diversity diminishes effective team functioning in a number of serious ways. Studies show that members of multicultural teams use "more of their time and effort in creating cohesion and solidarity than [do] members of homogeneous groups" (32;51). If unmanaged, cultural differences can paralyze a team's ability to act. For example, as described by one European manager,

In attempting to plan a new project, a three-person team composed of British, French, and Swiss managers failed to reach agreement. To the others, the British manager appeared unable to accept any systematic approach; he wanted to discuss all potential problems before beginning to make a decision. The French and Swiss managers agreed to examine everything before making a decision, but then disagreed on the sequence and scheduling of operations. The Swiss, being more pessimistic in their planning, allocated more time for each suboperation than did the French. As a result, although everybody agreed on its validity, we never started the project. If three Frenchmen, three Swiss, or three British managers had discussed the project, a decision, good or bad, would easily have been made. The project would not have become stalled for lack of agreement.[3]

Potential Productivity: Advantages in Culturally Diverse Teams

Although encountering more process problems, culturally diverse teams also have the potential to achieve higher productivity than do homogeneous teams, primarily because their wider range of human resources allows them to function more creatively. Effective teams need to perceive, interpret, and evaluate situations in numerous ways and then agree on the best decisions and directions. Multicultural teams can more easily consider many alternatives; the team's diversity results in a divergence of ideas. Leaders of all teams constantly balance divergence with convergence; that is, the gathering of new ideas (divergence) with the gaining of agreement on particular decisions and actions (convergence). This balancing of creativity (divergence) and cohesion (convergence) particularly challenges leaders of multicultural teams.

As summarized in Table 5-1, multicultural teams have the potential to invent more options and create more solutions than do single-culture teams. Diversity makes it easier for teams to create more and better ideas. It allows them to avoid the trap of "groupthink" (30). It often forces members to pay closer attention to the contributions of their colleagues. Each of these advantages will be discussed in the following sections (also see Table 4-1).

More and Better Ideas

Due to the varied backgrounds present in multicultural teams, members create more ideas, alternatives, and potential problem solutions than do homogeneous teams (27). Researchers have found that heterogeneous teams also propose more inventive alternatives (26) and higher quality solutions to problems (27). However, heterogeneous teams only realize their potential when they adequately manage the process problems associated with diversity. For example, as described by a manager in a Swedish pharmaceutical firm:

> Product design was traditionally carried out at our Stockholm headquarters. Once, by accident or design, we brought in an international team to discuss the design of a new allergy product. Due to extreme differences in opinion on what constitutes good medical practice, the team designed the new product with maximum flexibility to suit the major demands of each country. Later we discovered that this flexibility was a great advantage in developing and marketing internationally competitive products.[4]

Limited "Groupthink"

Groupthink describes "a mode of thinking that people engage in when they are deeply involved in a cohesive in-group, when the members' striving for unanimity overrides their motivation to realistically appraise alternative courses of action. . . . Groupthink refers to a deterioration of mental efficiency, reality testing, and moral judgment that results from in-group pressures" (30:9). Groupthink constitutes one of the major sources of ineffectiveness in teams.

The three major symptoms of groupthink are (30): overestimates of the team's power and morality, closed-mindedness, and pressures toward uniformity. Compared with their single-culture counterparts, multicultural teams are less likely to prematurely agree on a decision. They are less likely to take part in such counterproductive groupthink behaviors as (30:175):

1. **Self-censorship** of deviations from the apparent team consensus, reflecting every member's inclination to minimize to themselves the importance of their doubts and counterarguments.
2. A **shared illusion of unanimity** concerning judgments conforming to the majority view (partly resulting from self-censorship of deviations, augmented by the false assumption that silence means consent).
3. **Direct pressure** on any member who expresses strong arguments against any of the team's stereotypes, illusions, or commitments, making clear that this type of dissent is contrary to what is expected of all loyal members.
4. The emergence of **self-appointed mindguards**—members who protect the team from adverse information that might shatter their shared complacency about the effectiveness and morality of their decisions.

The consequences of groupthink include incompletely surveying objectives and alternatives, failure to examine risks of preferred choices, failure to reappraise initially rejected alternatives, poor information search, selective bias in processing the information at hand, and failure to work out contingency plans (30:175). Multicultural teams find themselves less susceptible to groupthink because they are less likely to subconsciously limit their perspectives, ideas, conclusions, and decisions to that of the majority or team leadership.

CONDITIONS FOR TEAM EFFECTIVENESS

Multicultural teams have the potential to become the most effective and productive teams in an organization. Unfortunately, they frequently become the least productive. Figure 5-3 shows the relative productivity of a series of four- to six-member problem-solving teams. Culturally diverse teams tend to become either the most or the least effective, whereas single-culture teams tend to be average (35). What differentiates the most from the least effective teams? Why are culturally diverse teams either more or less effective than single-culture teams but rarely equally effective?

Figure 5-3 *Team Effectiveness*

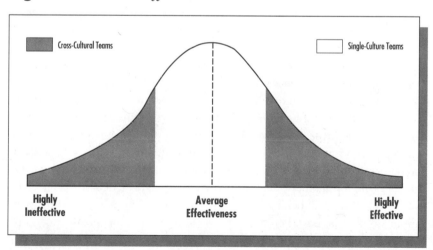

Source: Based on Dr. Carol Kovach's research conducted at the Graduate School of Management, University of California at Los Angeles (UCLA).

Highly productive and less productive teams differ in how they manage their diversity, not, as is commonly believed, in the presence or absence of diversity. When well managed, diversity becomes an asset and productive resource for the team (6;19;27;36;43;44;49;61). When ignored, diversity causes process problems that diminish the team's productivity. Since diversity is more frequently ignored than well managed (see Chapter 4), culturally diverse teams often perform below expectations and below organizational norms.

As shown in Table 5-2, a multicultural team's productivity depends on its task, stage of development, and the ways in which its diversity is managed. Diversity becomes most valuable when the needs for agreement (cohesion) remain low relative to the needs for invention (creativity) and when creativity and agreement can be balanced. The team leader must accurately assess each situation and emphasize those aspects that best fit the team's goals, objectives, and current task.

Task: Innovative or Routine

Whether and how much diversity is desirable depends on the nature of the team's task. When a task requires team members to perform highly specialized roles, it is usually more advantageous to have a diverse team. When everyone must do exactly the same thing, it is generally easier if members think and behave similarly (57:106). For example, corporate consulting teams generally work most effectively when they include many specialities—finance, marketing, production, and strategy experts. Teams assembling radios, on the other hand, generally perform better when all members have the same level of manual dexterity and coordination.

For some tasks the ability of the most or the least competent member determines the team's potential productivity. For other tasks the combination of the abilities of all members determines the team's potential productivity. For example, if a manager decides to give employees a bonus based on the best employee's performance, the team will focus on helping the best employee perform outstandingly. Olympic teams work in this way: a country receives the gold medal for an individual event based on the performance of its top member. Alternatively, if a manager decides to give the entire department a bonus based on the best performance of the worst employee (that is, based on all employees, including the worst, exceeding a certain minimal level), the team will attempt to increase the productivity of the weakest member. This approach reflects the philosophy behind the saying "A chain is only as strong as its weakest link." Alternatively, a manager might choose to give all employees a bonus based on the department's

Table 5-2   *Effectively Managing Diversity*

	Effective	*Ineffective*
Task	Innovative	Routine
Stage	Divergence (earlier)	Convergence (later)
Conditions	Differences recognized	Differences ignored
	Members selected for task-related abilities	Member selected on basis of ethnicity
	Mutual respect	Ethnocentrism
	Equal power	Culturalism dominance
	Superordinate goal	Individual goals
	External feedback	No feedback (complete autonomy)

average productivity. In this case all department members must individually and collectively strive to perform as well as possible. Firms often assess managers using this average scheme: managers' performance appraisals depend on their department's overall (or average) productivity. In some firms managers allow employees to select a reward system. In this case members of each department assess the range of abilities within the department and select a reward scheme accordingly.

Cultural diversity provides the biggest potential benefit to teams with challenging tasks that require innovation. Diversity becomes less helpful when employees are working on simple tasks involving repetitive or routine procedures. With the advent of robots and computer-aided manufacturing, the proportion of challenging, nonroutine tasks increases as does the need for and value of diversity. In general, diversity becomes more valuable during the planning and development phases of projects (the "work" stage referred to in the next section) and less helpful during the implementation phase (the "action" stage). The more senior the team members, the more likely they are to be working on challenging, innovative projects and, therefore, the more likely they are to benefit from diversity. Well-managed diversity has therefore become extremely valuable for senior executive teams both within and across organizations.

Stages: Entry, Work, and Action

Work teams progress through three basic stages: entry, work, and action. Early in its life, a team must develop cohesiveness. Members need to begin to know and to trust each other. After this initial entry stage, creativity becomes central. The team must create ways of defining its objectives, gathering and analyzing information, and developing alternative forms of action. Although tending to hinder the team's initial development, diversity becomes most valuable during this work stage. The team needs creativity (facilitated by divergence) to succeed. During the third and final stage, convergence again becomes important. Teams need to agree, or converge, on which decisions and actions to take. Cohesion, not creativity, fosters agreement. Table 5-3 summarizes some of the advantages and disadvantages caused by diversity at each stage of the team's development.

Entry: Initial Team Formation

In the initial stage, team members need to develop relationships and build trust. Team members from more task-oriented cultures, such as Germany, Switzerland, and the United States, spend relatively little time getting to know each other. Members from more relationship-oriented cultures, such as those in Latin America, the Middle East, and Southern Europe, generally spend more time getting to know their teammates. When people from task- and relationship-oriented cultures join the same team, problems in this initial stage can result. While the task-oriented members become impatient to get down to business, their more relationship-oriented colleagues feel rushed and distrustful of their more hurried team members.

On first meeting, team members generally feel drawn to people who are most similar to themselves. They initially trust those people to whom they feel most attracted. Similarity therefore facilitates initial group formation and visible differences hinder it. For this reason, multicultural teams often find building initial relationships and trust more difficult and time-consuming than do their single-culture counterparts. To counteract this tendency,

Table 5-3 *Managing Diversity Based on the Team's Stage of Development*

Stage	Process	Diversity Makes the Process	Process Bases On
Entry: Initial team formation	Trust building (developing cohesion)	More difficult	Using similarities and understanding differences
Work: Problem description and analysis	Ideation (creating ideas)	Easier	Using differences
Action: Decision making and implementation	Consensus building (agreeing and acting)	More difficult	Recognizing and creating similarities

experienced leaders often focus initially on team members' complementary professional qualifications and equivalent status rather than on the dissimilarities in their cultural backgrounds. Once the members establish professional similarity and respect, they can acknowledge their cultural diversity as a potential team resource rather than an imminent threat.

Work: Problem Description and Analysis

The team next defines its work goals and objectives and assesses its problem-solving potential. During this work stage, the team can use its diversity to generate new perspectives and ideas and thus enhance its ability to create alternative problem definitions and solutions. Although diversity often hinders the team's initial ability to build trust, well-managed diversity can enhance this second work phase. As discussed previously, diverse teams generally are more able to see situations from multiple perspectives, interpret their perceptions in a wide variety of ways, and create more numerous alternatives than can single-culture teams. Multicultural teams rarely succumb to groupthink; that is, to members blindly accepting a single definition of any situation.

Action: Decision Making and Implementation

In this third stage, the team decides what to do and how to do it. Members agree on which alternatives appear best and which action plans appear most effective. Teams reach agreement by building a consensus around a particular perspective. Similar to decision making, implementation also depends on consensus: the team must agree on the best way to proceed. These convergent processes—consensus building, agreement, and concerted action (or implementation)—usually prove easier for single-culture teams than for their multicultural counterparts. The very diversity that makes creating new ideas easier during the second stage renders consensus building and achieving agreement more difficult during this third stage.

MANAGING CULTURALLY DIVERSE TEAMS

Why are only some multicultural teams productive? The most productive multicultural teams learn to use their diversity when it enhances productivity and to minimize the impact of diversity when it diminishes productivity. Team leaders must learn to integrate the team's diversity if the team is to function productively (1;28;43;44;64). "By integrating and building on the diverse perspectives of the various members of a team, solutions and strategies can be developed that produce greater results and are more innovative than the simple addition of each contribution alone" (43:5). Diversity leads to "higher performance only when members . . . [are] able to understand each other, combine, and build on each others' ideas" (44:537); that is, when they communicate effectively with each other. Recent research suggests that all teams need the following communication skills to function effectively: the motivation to communicate, the ability to see situations from another person's perspective, the ability to create a shared social reality, the ability to explain problems appropriately, the ability to establish agreed-upon norms for interacting, and the confidence that other team members are skilled enough to work effectively together (44 based on 10;11). Multicultural teams face substantially greater challenges than do the single-culture teams in developing sufficient communication skills to achieve the prerequisite levels of integration needed for superior performance. Guidelines for increasing integration and minimizing diversity-related productivity losses due to faulty process follow.

Managing Cultural Diversity

Task-Related Selection

Although acknowledging the team's diverse cultural background, leaders should not select members solely for their ethnicity but rather primarily for their task-related abilities. "To maximize team effectiveness, members should be selected to be homogeneous in ability levels (thus facilitating accurate communication) and heterogeneous in attitudes (thus ensuring a wide range of solutions to problems)" (59).

Recognition of Differences

Teams should not ignore or minimize cultural differences: "Many barriers to intercultural communication are due to ignorance of cultural differences rather than a rejection of those differences" (16). Therefore, teams cannot begin to enhance communication without first recognizing and then understanding and respecting cross-cultural differences (12). Research indicates that "culturally trained leader[s], regardless of leadership style . . . achieve . . . high[er] levels of performance and rapport than do non-trained leaders" (20). To enhance the recognition of differences, team members should describe each culture present without initially either interpreting or evaluating it. Before beginning to increase understanding and respect, team members must become aware of their own stereotypes and the ways in which they might inadvertently limit their expectations of fellow team members from other cultures. Once members begin to recognize actual differences—that is, once they can differentiate their stereotypes from the actual personalities and behavior of team members (cultural description)—then they should attempt to understand why members from other cultures think, feel, and act the way they do (cultural interpretation). Subsequently, they should begin to ask what members from each culture can contribute and how their contributions complement those of other members (cultural creativity). In this way, creating effective multicultural teams follows the same process as creating cultural synergy (see Chapter 4).

A Vision or Superordinate Goal

Members of diverse teams generally have more trouble agreeing on their purpose and task than do members of homogeneous teams. In part this is true because teams set their overall purpose during the initial stage of team development—the stage during which individual differences tend to dominate and often interfere with team cohesion. To maximize effectiveness, the leader must help the team agree on a vision or superordinate goal—a goal that transcends their individual differences. Superordinate goals are often defined broadly, thus giving general direction and focus to the team's subsequent activities. Superordinate goals in which success depends on collaboration and cooperation tend to decrease prejudice and increase mutual respect (54). This is particularly true when team members require the continued help of their colleagues to achieve results important to all cultures, as well as to the overall organization.

Equal Power

Teams generally produce more and better ideas if all members participate. Cultural dominance (disproportionate power vested in members of one culture over those from other cultures) is therefore counterproductive because it stifles nondominant team members' contributions. In multinational teams leaders must guard against vesting disproportionate power in host country members, members of the same nationality as the employing organization, members from the most technologically advanced or economically developed countries, or those with ideologies most consonant with their own. Team leaders should distribute power according to each member's ability to contribute to the task, not according to some preconceived gradient of relative cultural superiority.

Mutual Respect

Ethnocentrism reflects a "view of things in which one's own group is the center of everything and all others are scaled and rated with reference to it" (37:8). Prejudice refers to the judging of other groups as inferior to one's own. Equal status, close contact, and cooperative efforts toward a common goal decrease prejudice (4;5). "The greater the opportunity for interethnic contacts, the less prejudiced and more frequent the development of cross-ethnic acceptance and friendship" (59:110). For most teams to work effectively, members must respect each other. Team leaders can enhance mutual respect by selecting members of equal ability, making prior accomplishments and task-related skills known to all team members, and minimizing early judgments based on ethnic stereotypes.

Feedback

Given the different perspectives present, culturally diverse teams have more trouble than do single-culture teams in agreeing collectively on what constitutes a good or bad idea or decision. Whereas single-culture teams rapidly develop judgment criteria based on their similar values, multicultural teams usually experience difficulty and delay before eventually reaching agreement. To encourage effective functioning, managers should give teams positive feedback on their process and output—both as individuals and as a team—early in the team's life together. Positive external feedback (given by a manager who is not on the team) generally aids the team in viewing itself as a team, while additionally serving to teach the team to value its diversity, recognize contributions made by each member, and trust its collective judgment.

SUMMARY

The potential for superior productivity of culturally diverse teams is high—they possess the breadth of resources, insights, perspectives, and experiences that facilitate the creation of new and better ideas. Regrettably, culturally diverse teams rarely achieve their full potential. Process losses due to mistrust, misunderstanding, miscommunication, stress, and a lack of cohesion often negate the potential benefits of diversity to the team. Only if their diversity is well managed can multicultural teams hope to achieve their full potential.

For effective functioning, multicultural teams must therefore: (a) use their diversity to generate multiple perspectives, problem definitions, ideas, action alternatives, and solutions, (b) learn to achieve consensus (agree on specific decisions and directions, despite the diversity), and (c) balance the simultaneous needs for creativity (divergence) with those for cohesion (convergence). If teams fail to generate many ideas, they become no more effective than individuals working alone. If teams fail to achieve consensus, their diversity paralyzes them. If teams fail to balance creativity and cohesion, they become awkwardly inefficient structures adding little value to the organization.

QUESTIONS FOR REFLECTION

1. *Managing Team Diversity.* As a manager, what can you do to help a multinational team work more effectively than a domestic team? What are the major problems that might occur and how best might you handle them?

2. *Multicultural Team Dynamics.* Think of the teams you have worked with or heard about. How have the group dynamics differed in multinational teams, bicultural teams, token teams, and single-culture teams?

3. *Types of Multicultural Teams.* As a senior manager in the automotive industry in charge of two Canadians, a Venezuelan, a German, and three Japanese, would you rather manage them in the research division or on the production line? Why? What differences in management approach would you employ in each situation?

4. *Potential Productivity Losses.* Describe some of the potential productivity losses caused by faulty process. Give examples from the multicultural teams that you have worked with or observed.

5. *Creating Cultural Synergy.* Select a multinational political or economic team that is currently in the news. Using a culturally synergistic approach, how would you manage the team? What outcomes would you strive to achieve?

6. *Increasing Team Effectiveness.* Select a multicultural work team that you are currently involved with or aware of. Analyze the underlying cultural values affecting the team. Suggest ways to manage the team that would increase the probability of achieving synergy.

NOTES

1. The film *Going International*, Part 2, by Copeland Griggs Productions, San Francisco, dramatizes a similar situation between an Indian and an American manager.

2. See the film *The Heart of the Bull*, produced by V. P. Human Resources David Dotlich, which documents the different working styles of French and Americans at the French computer company Groupe Bull.

3. Based on an incident described by a European manager attending the "Managerial Skills for International Business" executive seminar at INSEAD in Fontainebleau, France.

4. See Note 3 above.

FILM NOTE

The two-part British Broadcasting Corporation video program, *It's a Jungle Out There* and *The Survival Guide*, presents the issues faced by multinational teams in learning how to function more effectively. The first part, *It's a Jungle Out There*, presents the experiences of a multinational team from its formation in England through its various experiences on a three-country project in Africa. In the second part, *The Survival Guide*, Professor Nancy J. Adler assesses the areas in which the team functions well and those in which it functions poorly. Professor Adler's commentary is based on *International Dimensions of Organizational Behavior*, including the material presented in Chapter 5. (Director: Steve Wilkinson, The British Broadcasting Corporation, Open University Production Centre, Walton Hall, Milton Keynes, England MK7 68H; Tel: 44-1908-655-343; Fax: 44-1908-655-300) For additional video programs, see Notes 1 and 2 above.

REFERENCES

1. Abramson, F. "Factors Influencing the Entry of Canadian Software Manufacturers into the United States Market." Ph. D. dissertation, The University of Western Ontario, 1992.

2. Adler, N. J. "Domestic Multiculturalism: Cross-Cultural Management in the Public Sector," in W. Eddy, ed., *Handbook of Organization Management* (New York: Marcel Dekker, 1983), pp. 481–499.

3. Adler, N. J., and Ghadar, F. "International Strategy from the Perspective of People and Culture: The North American Context," in A. M. Rugman, ed., *Research in Global Strategic Management: International Business Research for the Twenty-First Century; Canada's New Research Agenda*, vol. 1. (Greenwich, Conn.: JAI Press, 1990), pp. 179–205.

4. Allport, G. W. *The Nature of Prejudice* (Reading, Mass.: Addison-Wesley, 1954), p. 281.

5. Amir, Y. "Contact Hypothesis in Ethnic Relations," *Psychological Bulletin*, vol. 71 (1969), pp. 319–342; and Amir, Y. "The Role of Intergroup Contact in Change of Prejudice and Ethnic Relations," in P. A. Katz, ed., *Toward the Elimination of Racism* (New York: Pergamon, 1976).

6. Anderson, K. "The New Ellis Island," *Time* (June 13, 1983), pp. 16–23.

7. Anderson, L. R. "Leader Behavior, Member Attitudes and Task Performance of Intercultural Discussion Groups," *Journal of Social Psychology*, vol. 69 (1966), pp. 305–319.

8. Anderson, L. R. "Management of the Mixed-Cultural Work Group," *Organizational Behavior and Human Performance*, vol. 31, no. 3 (1983), pp. 303–330.

9. Bass, B. M. "A Plan to Use Programmed Group Exercises to Study Cross-Cultural Differences in Management Behavior," *International Journal of Psychology*, vol. 1, no. 4 (1966), pp. 315–322.

10. Blakar, R. M. *Communication: A Social Perspective on Clinical Issues* (Oslo: Universitetsforlaget, 1984).

11. Blakar, R. M. "Towards a Theory of Communication in Terms of Preconditions: A Conceptual Framework and Some Empirical Explorations," in H. Giles and R. N. St. Clair, eds., *Recent Advances in Language, Communication, and Social Psychology* (London: Lawrence Erlbaum Associates, 1985).

12. Brislin, R. W. *Cross-Cultural Encounters* (New York: Pergamon, 1981).

13. Chemers, M. M.; Fiedler, F. E.; Lekhyananda, D.; and Stolurow, L. M. "Some Effects of Cultural Training on Leadership in Heterocultural Task Groups," *International Journal of Psychology*, vol. 1, no. 4 (1966), pp. 301–314.

14. Davidson, W. H. "Small Group Activity at Musashi Semiconductor Works," *Sloan Management Review*, vol. 23, no. 3 (Spring 1982), pp. 3–14.

15. Delgado, M. "Hispanic Cultural Values: Implications for Groups," *Small Group Behavior*, vol. 12, no. 1 (February 1981), pp. 69–80.

16. Devonshire, C., and Kremer, J. W. *Towards a Person-Centered Resolution of Intercultural Conflicts* (La Jolla, Calif.: Center for the Whole Person).

17. Diab, L. "A Study of Intragroup and Intergroup Competition Among Experimentally Produced Small Groups," *Genetic Psychology Monographs*, vol. 82 (1970), pp. 325–332.

18. Ferrari, S. "Human Behavior in International Groups," *Management International Review*, vol. XII, no. 6 (1972), pp. 31–35.

19. Fiedler, F. E. "The Effect of Leadership and Cultural Heterogeneity on Group Performance: A Test of the Contingency Model," *Journal of Experimental Social Psychology*, vol. 2 (1966), pp. 237–264.

20. Fiedler, F. E.; Meuwese, W. A. T.; and Oonk, S. "Performance on Laboratory Tasks Requiring Group Creativity," *Acta Psychology*, vol. 18 (1961), pp. 110–119.

21. Hackman, J. R. "The Design of Work Teams," in J. W. Lorsch, ed., *Handbook of Organizational Behavior* (New York: Prentice-Hall, 1987), pp. 315–341.

22. Hare, A. P. "Cultural Differences in Performances in Communication Networks in Africa, United States and the Philippines," *Sociology and Social Research*, vol. 54, no. 1 (1969), pp. 25–41.

23. Hare, A. P. *Handbook of Small Group Research* (New York: Free Press, 1976).

24. Hayles, R. "Costs and Benefits of Integrating Persons from Diverse Cultures into Organizations." Paper presented at the 21st International Congress of Applied Psychology, Edinburgh, Scotland, July 1982.

25. Hoefer, H. J. *Hawaii*, 4th ed. (Hong Kong: APA Productions, 1983).

26. Hoffman, L. R. "Homogeneity of Member Personality and Its Effect on Group Problem-Solving," *Journal of Abnormal Psychology*, vol. 58 (1959), pp. 27–32.

27. Hoffman, L. R., and Maier, N. R. F. "Quality and Acceptance of Problem Solutions by Members of Homogeneous and Heterogeneous Groups," *Journal of Abnormal Psychology*, vol. 62, no. 2 (1961), pp. 401–407.

28. Hurst, D. K., Rush, J. C.; and White, R. E. "Top Management Teams and Organizational Renewal," *Strategic Management Journal* (1989), vol. 10 (Special Issue), pp. 87–105.

29. "It's Your Turn in the Sun: Now 19 Million and Growing Fast, Hispanics Are Becoming a Power," *Time*, vol. 112, no. 16 (October 16, 1978), pp. 48–61.

30. Janis, I. L. *Groupthink*, 2nd ed. Copyright © 1982 by Houghton Mifflin Company. Used with permission.

31. Jewell, L. N., and Reitz, H. J. *Group Effectiveness in Organizations* (Glenview, Ill.: Scott, Foresman, 1981).

32. Katz, J.; Goldston, J.; and Benjamin, L. "Behavior and Productivity in Biracial Work Groups," *Human Relations*, vol. 11 (1958), pp. 123–151.

33. Kirsch, J. (citing former Lieutenant Governor of California M. Cymally). "Chicano Power," *New West*, vol. 3, no. 19 (September 11, 1978), pp. 35–46.

34. Kirschmeyer, C., and Cohen, A. "Multicultural Groups: Their Performance and Reactions with Constructive Conflict," *Group and Organization Management*, vol. 17, no. 2 (1992), pp. 153–170.

35. Kovach, C. Based on observations of 800 second-year MBAs in field study teams at UCLA, 1977–1980. Evaluation of teams was conducted by corporate clients and business faculty members in Los Angeles, California, 1980. Originally based on Kovach's paper, "Some Notes for Observing Group Process in Small Task-Oriented Groups," Graduate School of Management, University of California at Los Angeles, 1976.

36. Kumar, K.; Subramanian, R.; and Nonis, S. A. "Cultural Diversity's Impact on Group Process and Performance: Comparing Culturally Homogeneous and Culturally Diverse Work Groups Engaged in Problem-Solving Tasks," *Southern Management Association Proceedings* (1991).

37. Levine, R. A., and Campbell, D. T. *Ethnocentrism* (New York: Wiley, 1972).

38. Likert, R. "The Nature of Highly Effective Groups," in *New Patterns of Management* (New York: McGraw-Hill, 1961).

39. McGrath, J. E. *Groups: Interaction and Performance* (Englewood Cliffs, N.J.: Prentice Hall, 1984).

40. McLeod, P. L. and Lobe, S. A. "The Effects of Ethnic Diversity on Idea Generation in Small Groups," *Academy of Management Best Paper Proceedings* (1992), pp. 227–231.

41. Maier, N. R. F., and Hoffman, L. R. "Group Decision in England and the United States," *Personnel Psychology*, vol. 15, no. 2 (1962), pp. 75–87.

42. Mann, L. "Cross-Cultural Studies of Small Groups," in H. Triandis, ed., *Handbook of Cross-Cultural Psychology*, vol. 5 (Boston: Allyn & Bacon, 1980).

43. Maznevski, M. L. "Process and Performance in Multicultural Teams," working paper. London, Ontario, Canada: The University of Western Ontario, School of Business, 1995, p. 49.

44. Maznevski, M. L. "Understanding Our Differences: Performance in Decision-Making Groups with Diverse Members," *Human Relations*, vol. 47, no. 5 (1994), pp. 531–552.

45. Maznevski, M. L,. and diStefano, J. J. "Synergistic Performance in Multicultural Management Teams: A Communications Perspective," paper presented at the Academy of International Business Annual Meeting, Brussels, 1992.

46. Meade, R. "An Experimental Study of Leadership in India," *Journal of Social Psychology*, vol. 72 (1967), pp. 35–43.

47. Meade, R. "Leadership Studies of Chinese and Chinese-Americans," *Journal of Cross-Cultural Psychology*, vol. 1 (1970), pp. 325–332.

48. Misumi, J. "Experimental Studies on Group Dynamics in Japan," *Psychologia*, vol. 2 (1959), pp. 229–235.

49. Mitchell, R. "Team Building by Disclosure of Internal Frames of Reference," *Journal of Applied Behavioral Science*, vol. 22, no. 1 (1986), pp. 15–28.

50. Novack, M. *The Rise of the Unmeltable Ethnics* (New York: Macmillan, 1972).

51. Rombauts, J. "Gedrag en Groepsbeleving in Etnisch-Homogene en Etnisch-Heterogene Groepen," *Tijdschrift Voor Opvoedkunde*, no. 1 (1962–1963).

52. Ruhe, J., and Eastman, J. "Effects of Racial Composition on Small Work Groups," *Small Group Behavior*, vol. 8, no. 4 (November 1977), pp. 479–486.

53. "The Samoans Among Us," *The Los Angeles Times* (January 2, 1979), p. 1.

54. Sherif, M.; Harvey, O.; White, B.; Hood, W.; and Sherif, C. *Inter-Group Conflict and Cooperation: The Robers Cave Experiment* (Norman, Okla.: Institute of Group Relations, 1961).

55. Shuter, R. "Cross-Cultural Small Group Research: A Review, an Analysis, and a Theory," *International Journal of Intercultural Relations*, vol. 1, no. 1 (Spring 1977), pp. 90–104.

56. Simard, L. M., and Taylor, D. M. "The Potential for Bicultural Communication in a Dyadic Situation," *Canadian Journal of Behavioral Science*, vol. 5 (1973), pp. 211–225.

57. Steiner, I. D. *Group Process and Productivity* (New York: Academic Press, 1972).

58. Toffler, A. *The Third Wave* (New York: William Morrow, 1980).

59. Triandis, H. C.; Hall, E. R.; and Ewen, R. B. "Some Cognitive Factors Affecting Group Creativity," *Human Relations*, vol. 18, no. 1 (February 1965), pp. 33–35.

60. United States Office of Immigration. Personal conversation with immigration official (Los Angeles, Calif., November 1979).

61. Walsh, J. P.; Henderson, C. M.; and Deighton, J. "Negotiated Belief Structures and Decision Performance: An Empirical Investigation," *Organizational Behavior and Human Decision Processes*, vol. 42, no. 2 (1988), pp. 194–216.

62. Watson, W. E., and Kumar, K. "Differences in Decision-Making Regarding Risk-Taking: A Comparison of Culturally Diverse and Culturally Homogeneous Task Groups," *International Journal of Intercultural Relations*, vol. 16, no. 1 (1992), pp. 53–66.

63. Watson, W. E.; Kumar, K.; and Michaelson, L. K. "Cultural Diversity's Impact on Interaction Process and Performance: Comparing Homogeneous and Diverse Task Groups," *Academy of Management Journal*, vol. 36, no. 3 (1993), pp. 590–602.

64. Watson, W. E., and Michaelson, L. K. "Group Interaction Behaviors That Affect Group Performance on an Intellective Task," *Group and Organization Studies*, vol. 13, no. 4 (1988), pp. 495–516.

65. Ziegler, S. "The Effectiveness of Cooperative Learning Teams for Increasing Cross-Ethnic Friendship: Additional Evidence," *Human Organization, The Journal of the Society for Applied Anthropology*, vol. 40, no. 3 (Fall 1981), pp. 264–268.

66. Ziller, R. C. "Homogeneity and Heterogeneity of Group Membership," in C. G. McClintock, ed., *Experimental Social Psychology* (New York: Holt, Rinehart and Winston, 1972), pp. 385–411.

CHAPTER 6
Global Leadership, Motivation, and Decision Making

For all practical purposes, all business today is global. Those individual businesses, firms, industries, and whole societies that clearly understand the new rules of doing business in a world economy will prosper; those that do not will perish.

— Ian Mitroff (78:ix)

Organizations worldwide strive to fulfill their missions. They select leaders who articulate a vision that guides them toward achieving long-term goals and short-term objectives. They expect their leaders to motivate the work force in consistent and effective ways. Corporate leaders continually make decisions that influence the success of entire operations.

This chapter looks at some of the ways corporate vision and leadership vary across cultures, how culture influences motivation, and what the cross-cultural implications are for managerial decision making. Although some principles of leadership, motivation, and decision making apply almost everywhere, the ways in which executives and managers adapt them to local conditions and work situations determine their success or failure (48). Although approaches to leadership, motivation, and decision making are highly interrelated, each will be discussed separately.

Most organization theories (although not influenced by Bruce Springsteen!) were "Made in the U.S.A." and therefore shaped by the political, economic,

151

and cultural context of the United States (18).   Because little research yet exists explaining the specific ways in which either American-based management theories must be altered to become applicable worldwide or, perhaps more importantly, how new management theories indigenous to countries around the world operate, this chapter cannot be as comprehensive as its subject warrants (1;2;3;4;5;17).[1]   Until such knowledge becomes more widely available, it remains best to resist the temptation of assuming universality. As Triandis (108:139) astutely observed, culture's

> influence for organizational behavior is that it operates at such a deep level that people are not aware of its influences. It results in unexamined patterns of thought that seem so natural that most theorists of social behavior fail to take them into account. As a result, many aspects of organizational theories produced in one culture may be inadequate in other cultures.

Prudent managers assume that current American-based theories apply to the United States, not, as is so tempting, to the world at large.

LEADERSHIP

Leaders create vision, the meaning within which others work and live. Managers, by contrast, act competently within a vision. What is our vision of success? What do we want our society to look like? How do we ideally want our organizations to function? Who do we want to lead us? Leadership and vision remain fundamental to the understanding of a people and their institutions. The questions involved are universal, the answers often culturally specific. For example, *The Way of Lao Tzu* captures a traditional Chinese vision of leadership from the sixth century B.C. (111:214).

> I have three treasures. Guard and keep them.
> The first is deep love,
> The second is frugality,
> And the third is not to dare to be ahead of the world.
> Because of deep love, one is courageous.
> Because of frugality, one is generous.
> Because of not daring to be ahead of the world,
>   one becomes the leader of the world.

American Arthur Schlesinger expresses a different leadership vision in *A Thousand Days*—that of former U.S. President John F. Kennedy from the 1960s (91):

> Above all . . . [President Kennedy] gave the world for an imperishable moment a vision of a leader who greatly understood the terror and the hope, the diversity and the possibility, of life on this planet and who made people look beyond nation and race to the future of humanity.

Britain's Anita Roddick, founder and CEO of the highly successful global firm The Body Shop, describes her contemporary vision of "corporate idealism" (89:126):

> Leaders in the business world should aspire to be true planetary citizens. They have global responsibilities since their decisions affect not just the world of business, but world problems of poverty, national security and the environment. Many, sad to say, duck these responsibilities, because their vision is material rather than moral (89:226).

Each vision, although from different cultures and centuries, expresses the tension between one's immediate national concerns and the broader interests of humanity and the future. Research suggests that perceptions of what managers believe they should be doing varies more than their descriptions of what they actually do (112). It is the tension between the reality of our world today and our aspirations for a better world tomorrow that gives rise to the need for societies to select leaders who can articulate a meaningful vision and guide them toward its realization. In *Beyond National Borders*, Kenichi Ohmae (82) captures a vision for Japan as it moves into the twenty-first century:

> Of all the conceivable goals and achievements that Japan might seek to accomplish in the next century, only one, I believe, is worthy of Japan. It is to prove that without wielding military might, by human strength and resourcefulness alone, a major global power can alleviate the earth's disparities and injustices. . . . Now we must begin to think beyond national borders (82:11).

Traditionally, corporate visions have reflected the values and goals of the society in which they were conceived. Today, with the dominant presence of multinational and global firms, corporate visions no longer remain domestic, but are themselves becoming transnational. As witnessed with the economic integration of Europe into the European Union, the founding of the Association of South East Asian Nations (ASEAN) trading block, and the increased trade generated by the North American Free Trade Agreement (NAFTA), national borders are vanishing. Whereas historic feuds remain nationally defined at governmental levels, economic pragmatism vanquishes them at a corporate level. Corporate leaders have chosen to transcend national boundaries in ways that remain outside the realm of government diplomats. As business leaders know, if an idea or action is good for business, it is worth learning and doing no matter where in the world it originated. Corporations, more so than nations, consequently already face the difficult questions involved in integrating visions based on divergent national and cultural values. Their success in defining and implementing transnational visions defines the global corporation's potential for success.

Leadership Theories

Leadership involves the ability to inspire and influence the thinking, attitudes, and behavior of people (11;12;13;14;34;62). The very word *leadership*

> is a relatively new addition to the English language; it appeared approximately 200 years ago in writings about political influence in the British Parliament. However, from Egyptian hieroglyphics, we know that symbols for "leader" existed as early as 5,000 years ago. Simply put, leaders have existed in all cultures throughout history (27:270).

In the past many people assumed that leaders were born, not made, and they attempted to identify the traits of great leaders. Although every society has had its great leaders, researchers have found no consistent set of traits differentiating leaders from other people (105). For example, North Americans value charisma in their leaders and identify such business and political leaders as Lee Iacocca, former CEO of Chrysler Corporation (53), and Ronald Reagan, former president of the United States, as charismatic (23;24). By contrast, Germans do not value charisma in their contemporary leaders, as they associate it with the evil Hitler perpetrated during World War II, in part through his negative charisma. More generally, while the term *leader* evokes a positive image in the United States, people in many parts of the world view it quite negatively (27:271). European Serge Moscovici, for example, writes that for Europeans ". . . everything seems to indicate that leadership is an unintended and undesirable consequence of democracy, or a 'perverse effect' as [is said] . . . in France" (37:241–242).

Researchers have focused on the types of behavior leaders display in various work settings to motivate employees. As described by Levinson in the book *Executive* (66:50), the culture in which leaders grow up strongly influences their attitudes and behaviors.

Consider the implications for leadership of individual attitudes and expectations towards power. As a result of extended experiences with people who have wielded power over them when they were children, adults have expectations about how they should relate to others who have power and how they should behave in return. These attitudes are somewhat modified as a consequence of experiences and teachers, ministers, scout leaders, and other authority figures, but fundamental attitudes toward power are derived from the earliest and most intense experiences with authority figures. . . .

In spite of individual differences, however, these experiences reflect a strong common element in any given culture. As a result, there are generalized expectations about how authority is to be wielded, how the more powerful people should act toward the weaker, and what kinds of behavior the latter might expect from the former. It is expected that one will use social strength according to culturally established norms. Therefore, when acquiring control over others, one also incurs the effects of these expectations about power figures. In short, in a particular culture a person who becomes authoritative in direct relationships to others is expected to act in much the same way as a parent acts in the family. It means that as people develop their expectations of power and attitudes toward it based on their earliest experiences with it, they will tend to work from these attitudes in every encounter. A superior who fails to conform to these expectations will be seen as an inadequate, unfair, or unjust leader.

Douglas McGregor's classic Theory X and Theory Y described two different sets of assumptions about the nature of human beings and what they wanted from their work environment (72) (also see Chapter 2). According to McGregor, Theory X leaders believe they must direct, control, and coerce people in order to motivate them to work. Such leaders assume that the more basic needs for safety and security motivate people. By contrast, Theory Y leaders believe that they must give employees freedom, autonomy, and responsibility in order to motivate them to work. Theory Y leaders assume that higher-order needs for achievement and self-actualization fundamentally motivate people. According to Anita Roddick, CEO of The Body Shop:

[People] . . . are looking for leadership that has vision. If you have a company with itsy-bitsy vision, you have an itsy-bitsy company. . . . If you employ people with small thinking and small ideas, you become a company of dwarves (89:223, 225).

Leaders from different cultures vary in their reasons for making Theory X and Theory Y assumptions. For example, in the United States, many Theory Y managers assume that workers' basic physiological needs for safety and security have been met and that therefore only opportunities to satisfy higher-order needs motivate workers. They believe that denying these opportunities leads to alienation and lower productivity. Theory Y managers in the United States believe that most people can and want to develop interpersonal relationships characterized by trust and open communication. They therefore assume that workers produce more when the workplace is most democratic.

Theory Y managers in the People's Republic of China act similarly, but for very different reasons. According to Oh (81), the pre-1949 Chinese saw satisfaction of lower needs as the main objective of the masses, with higher-order needs going unrecognized for all but upper social class people. After the revolution two types of managers emerged: Reds and Experts. Experts, who possessed extensive technical expertise and were skilled in managing things, tended to use Theory X. Reds, who were more skilled in managing people and possessed political and ideological expertise, tended to use Theory Y. The Reds, believing that Theory Y assumptions were closely tied to the philosophy of Chairman Mao, felt the workplace had to become egalitarian—that all employees had to improve their lot together, both economically and culturally. They believed that management had to give workers' welfare prominence over production, that they had to discourage material incentives that promoted self-interest and competition. Managers had to stress collaboration by replacing individual rewards with collective rewards, encouraging participation in decision making, and emphasizing democracy and decentralization. Both Americans and Chinese agree, for different reasons, that Theory Y organizations can perform efficiently and productively; that is, that industrialization without dehumanization is possible.

The primary assumption behind Theory Y—as well as other classic and contemporary theories, such as employee-empowerment models—is that people are basically good and trustworthy.[2] Managers can therefore delegate tasks, allow employees to structure their own work, and feel no need either to supervise employees closely or to directly control the work flow. Managers combine a strong concern for task with an equally strong concern for the people they supervise. The best managers balance the extent to which they initiate structure and the consideration they show their people based on the nature of the task, the environment, and the skills of the particular people involved. Needless to say, culture is a critical aspect of both the environment and the people.

Cultural Contingency

Some researchers suggest that American approaches to leadership and management apply abroad; for example, in cultures as diverse as the People's Republic of China (81) and the former Yugoslavia (59). Most managers, however, believe that they must adapt their style of leadership to the cultures of employees; that is, they believe that leadership is culturally contingent. In their groundbreaking 1963 research, Haire, Ghiselli, and Porter (39) found that, although the fourteen countries they studied showed more similarities than differences, the countries clustered along ethnic rather than industrial lines. Almost two decades later, Hofstede (57;59) concluded that participative management approaches, including Theory Y, which were strongly encouraged by American theorists and managers, were not suitable for all cultures. Employees in high power distance cultures expect managers to act as strong leaders; they become uncomfortable with leaders delegating discretionary decisions. Some cultures want their managers to act as decisive, directive experts; others want managers to act as participative problem solvers (see Figure 2-4). For example, Laurent (63:75–76) describes his difficulty explaining matrix management to French managers:

> The idea of reporting to two bosses was so alien to these managers that mere consideration of such organizing principles was an impossible, useless exercise. What was needed first was a thorough examination and probing of the holy principle of the single chain of command and the managers' recognition that this was a strong element of their own belief system rather than a constant element in nature.

"Americans' extreme individualism combined with their highly participative managerial climate, may render U.S. management practices unique; that is, differentiated from the approaches in most areas of the world" (27:292;28;46). This conclusion is supported by recent research on leadership that found the United States unique in several respects among all of the Eastern and Western cultures studied (49).

Even among countries culturally well suited to participative management (such as the United States, England, and Sweden), organizations must adapt the form of participation to the local culture (33). Although studies vary in the extent to which they see appropriate leadership styles as similar to those most acceptable in the United States (see, for example, descriptions of managers in Israel (113), Europe (80), India (58), and Germany (110)), today's conclusion is that global managers must be flexible enough to alter their approach when crossing national borders and working with people from other cultures.[3]

MOTIVATION

Beyond culturally appropriate leadership, what causes high employee productivity and job satisfaction? What energizes employees to behave in productive ways? What directs and channels their behavior to accomplish organizational goals? How do organizations maintain desired behavior? What forces in employees and in their environment reinforce or discourage them from following a particular course of action (103)?

One global high-technology firm based in the Silicon Valley in California thought it had the answer. The firm created the "Dragon Slayer Campaign" with posters encouraging employees to "Slay the Dragon." Unfortunately, the American management had not realized that dragons symbolize good luck to the Chinese and that their campaign was not encouraging Chinese employees to cut costs and beat the competition but rather to destroy their good luck. Understandably, Chinese employees forced the firm to take down the posters and to end the campaign.

Numerous motivation theories address these questions and, like the majority of leadership theories, most have been developed and tested in the United States (40). Each attempts to explain why human beings behave in the ways they do and what managers can do to encourage certain types of behavior while discouraging others. Let's look at a few of the historically better recognized motivation theories and determine if they are universal or culture bound.

Maslow's Need Hierarchy

Abraham Maslow (73;74;75), an American psychologist, suggested that human beings' five basic needs form a hierarchy: from physiological, to safety, to social, to esteem, to self-actualization needs. According to Maslow, the higher-order needs (i.e., esteem and self-actualization) only become activated, and thus motivate behavior, after lower-order needs have been satisfied.

Does Maslow's theory, which he based on Americans, hold for employees outside of the United States?[4] Hofstede (48) and Trompenaars (109) suggest that it does not (see Chapter 2). For instance, in countries higher on uncertainty avoidance (such as Greece and Japan) as compared with those lower on uncertainty avoidance (such as the United States),

security motivates most employees more strongly than does self-actualization. Employees in high uncertainty avoidance countries tend to consider job security and lifetime employment more important than holding
a more interesting or challenging job. Social needs tend to dominate the
motivation of workers in countries such as Sweden, Norway, and
Denmark that stress the quality of life (Hofstede's quality-of-life dimension) over productivity (Hofstede's career success dimension).[5] Workers
in more collectivist countries, such as Pakistan, tend to stress social
needs over the more individualistic ego and self-actualization needs
stressed in countries such as the United States. Viewing the conflicting
motivations of individual and group-oriented cultures, managers using
Americans' highly individualist motivation theories must ask

> In what cultural and historical context does the greatest good involve being
> able to break apart from one's collective base to stand alone, self-sufficient
> and self-contained? In the context of an individualistic society in which indi-
> vidualism and self-containment is the ideal, the person who most separates
> self from the group is thereby seen as embodying that ideal most strongly; the
> person who remains wedded to a group is not our [American] esteemed ideal
> (90:776).

Developing countries, in contrast to the United States and many other
developed countries, exhibit relatively high uncertainty avoidance, low individualism, high power distance, and relatively low emphasis on career success (4;46;47;48;55). For example, community dominates individualism in
most East African nations. As explained by Mutiso (79:35), the community

> dominates all aspects of African thought. Dances are communal and worship
> is communal. Property was held communally before the colonial era and there
> are attempts today to reinstate that practice. This inbuilt bias toward the com-
> munity means that individualism is always seen as a deviance.

"The [African] value most clearly approved . . . is traditional communal
responsibility revealed partly in the condemnation of self-seeking individualism" (92:358). Clearly the motivation of employees from more col-
lective-oriented cultures differs from that of their more individualistic,
American counterparts.

Numerous research studies testing Maslow's hierarchy demonstrate
similar but not identical rank ordering of needs across cultures. Studies
include research on such diverse cultures as Peru (104;116), India (56),
the Middle East (4;9;10), Mexico (88), and Anglophone and Francophone

Canada (57).   For example, one study shows that Liberian managers express needs similar to those of managers in South Africa, Argentina, Chile, India, and other developing countries and demonstrate higher security and self-esteem needs than managers in more economically developed countries (50). In another study the need hierarchy of Libyan executives failed to replicate that of executives in the United States; the conclusion is that Maslow's hierarchy varies from culture to culture (20).

Another study found results more consistent with Maslow's findings. In a study involving the United States, Mexico, Puerto Rico, Venezuela, Japan, Thailand, Turkey, and the former Yugoslavia, workers in the twenty-six surveyed industrial plants ranked self-actualization most highly and security as one of the least important needs. In all eight countries, the more highly educated managers ranked self-actualization as more important and security as less important than did their less educated colleagues (87). In a fourteen-country study, Haire et al. (39) found that although managers in each country want similar things from their jobs, they differ in what they think their jobs are currently giving them.

Although the conflicting patterns of research fail to offer definitive conclusions, they strongly indicate that we should not assume that either Maslow's hierarchy or other rankings of motivation hold universally. As aptly summarized by researchers O'Reilly and Roberts (83),

> Studies have found that an individual's frame of reference will determine the order of importance of his needs. It has also been found that his frame of reference is in part determined by his culture. Therefore, it can be said that an individual's needs are partially bound by culture.

Human needs may well include fundamental or universal aspects, but their importance and the ways in which they express themselves differ across cultures.

McClelland's Three Motives

David McClelland, another American theorist, suggested that three important motives drive people: the needs for achievement, power, and affiliation (70). Although McClelland has focused more recently on executives' needs for power (71), he initially emphasized the need for achievement as fundamental in explaining why some societies produce more than others (69). For example, in his famous studies in India, he found that entrepreneurs trained in the need for achievement performed better than did untrained entrepreneurs (also see 51).

Comparative research has shown McClelland's achievement motivation to be relatively robust across cultures. For example, managers in New Zealand appear to follow the same pattern observed in the United States (44). However, similar to his analysis of Maslow's need hierarchy, Hofstede questions the universality of McClelland's three needs (48). Hofstede begins by pointing out that the word *achievement* itself is hardly translatable into any language other than English (48:55). In his research Hofstede found that countries with a high need for achievement also have a high need to produce (Hofstede's career success dimension) and a strong willingness to accept risk (Hofstede's weak uncertainty avoidance). As shown in Figure 2-6, Anglo-American countries such as the United States, Canada, and Great Britain (weak uncertainty avoidance combined with career success) follow the high achievement motivation pattern, and countries such as Chile and Portugal (strong uncertainty avoidance combined with quality of life) follow the low achievement motivation pattern. Although helpful in explaining human behavior, McClelland's three motives have not been shown to be universal (see the box "What Motivates a Person: New Hotel in Tahiti").

Herzberg's Two-Factor Theory

Frederick Herzberg (41;42) suggested that certain extrinsic factors (those associated with the environment surrounding a job) have only the power to demotivate employees, whereas intrinsic factors (those associated with the job itself) have the power to energize, or motivate, people. The extrinsic,

---

WHAT MOTIVATES A PERSON

New Hotel in Tahiti

A major hotel chain chose to develop a new hotel in Tahiti. The developer contracted with a Tahitian skilled in carving large wooden totems. The hotel desired a number of these totems to provide the site with "atmosphere." The Tahitian quoted a price for carving the first totem and then higher and higher prices for each succeeding totem. This, of course, astonished the hotel developer, who asserted that this was "no way to do business. Didn't the Tahitian understand quantity discounts?" The Tahitian artisan, equally mystified, also tried to explain: "No, it is *you* who doesn't understand. Carving the first totem is fun. Carving each additional totem becomes less fun (77:134)."

or potential demotivators, largely correspond to Maslow's lower-order physiological and safety needs. They include factors associated with job dissatisfaction such as working conditions, supervision, relations with coworkers, salary, company policy, and administration. Intrinsic factors, or motivators, largely corresponding to Maslow's higher-order needs, include the work itself, responsibility, recognition for work well done, advancement, and achievement.

More recent research has questioned Hertzberg's two categories. For example, research has shown that people sometimes continue a particular course of action because they have made a prior public commitment to it and not because it continues to be rewarding (102). Similarly, some people, who gain intrinsic satisfaction from a particular activity, switch to explaining their motivation in extrinsic terms after having received an extrinsic reward (retrospective sense-making, see (102), among others). Others indicate that some behavior is random and neither as goal oriented nor as rational as many American models and theories would suggest (85).

Hofstede (48) again points out that culture influences factors that motivate and demotivate behavior. According to his dimensions, it is not surprising that the highly individualistic, productivity-oriented American culture has focused on job enrichment (the restructuring of individual jobs to increase productivity); whereas the more quality-of-life oriented and slightly more collective societies of Sweden and Norway developed sociotechnical systems and new approaches to the quality of working life (such as the restructuring of employees into work groups to achieve the same ends).

Herzberg's two-factor theory has also been tested outside of the United States (45). Results in New Zealand failed to replicate those in the United States. In New Zealand, supervision and interpersonal relationships appear to contribute significantly to satisfaction and not merely to reducing dissatisfaction (44). Similarly, in the Panama Canal Zone, researchers found non–United States citizens (including citizens of the Republic of Panama, the West Indies, Latin America, Europe, Asia, and Canada) cited certain extrinsic factors as satisfiers with greater frequency than did their American counterparts (25).

Similar to other motivation theories, the universality of Herzberg's two-factor theory cannot be assumed. In every culture certain factors act as motivators and others act as demotivators. The specific factors and their relative importance appear particular to each culture and, all too frequently, to each situation. Managers entering a new culture should observe which factors appear important and not assume that their prior experience in other cultures is transferable.

Vroom's Expectancy Theory

Expectancy theories (64;114;115) claim that people are driven by the expectation that their acts will produce results. Workers assess both their ability to perform a task and the probable type of reward for successful performance (for example, continued employment or a paycheck). According to expectancy theories, the likelihood that an action will lead to certain outcomes or goals (E), multiplied by attractiveness of the outcome (V, its valence) equals motivation ($M = E \times V$) (65). Expectancy theories depend on the extent to which employees believe they have control over the outcomes of their efforts as well as on the managers' abilities to identify desired rewards, both of which vary across cultures. Although expectancy theories have clearly advanced our understanding of motivation, they are equally clearly culturally dependent.

A recent review of our understanding of motivation (101:650–651) underscores that "whether the driving force is thought to be prior reinforcement, need fulfillment, or expectancies of future gain, the individual is assumed to be a rational maximizer of personal utility." Unfortunately, this individual, calculative view of motivation has questionable applicability outside of the United States and could indicate "a fundamental omission in our motivation theories" (101:651; also see 18).

For example, in countries where individualism dominates, employees see their relationship with the organization from a calculative perspective; whereas in collectivist societies, the ties between the individual and the organization have a moral component (7;18;80). Clearly people become committed to organizations for very different reasons in individualistic as compared to collectivist societies (102). Employees with collectivist values make organizational commitments because of their ties to managers, owners, and coworkers (collectivism) and much less because of the nature of the job or the particular compensation scheme (individualistic incentives (18)). In Brazil, for example, where people's personal and work lives are highly integrated, it is common for major firms

> . . . to help employees with personal financial problems. For example, because of a lack of public social services, employees may have an illness in the family which puts them in a precarious financial position. The personnel departments of larger Brazilian firms regularly provide assistance to employees in such a situation, thus mitigating the impact of the employees' problems on the functioning of the firm (55:292).

Given its individualistic orientation, it is not surprising that the United States has a very different pattern from Brazil. While Brazilians expect their firms to take care of employees' personal needs, Americans have no such expectations and therefore much less loyalty to their employers. It is not coincidence that the United States (and not Brazil) has the most executive search firms and the highest level of executive and managerial mobility in the world (18).

As discussed in Chapter 1 (see the dominance-harmony dimension, pages 22-25), people in different cultures vary in the amount of control they believe they have over their environment. Most Americans strongly believe that they control the relevant aspects of their environment. American managers believe that they directly influence the world in which they work (that is, they have a high level of internal attribution). For example, most American managers believe that "Where there is a will, there is a way." By contrast, many managers in other parts of the world believe that they only partially control their work environment and the outcomes of their own behavior (that is, they attribute the causes of some events to external circumstances). For example, Moslem managers believe that things will happen only if God wills them to happen (external attribution); Latin American managers believe that it is important to be from the right family and social class (external attribution); Hong Kong Chinese executives believe that there is an element of *joss*, or luck, involved in all transactions (external attribution); whereas most American managers believe that effective problem solving and hard work will get the job done (internal attribution). Expectancy theories work best in explaining cultures that emphasize internal attribution.

The rewards people want from work also vary greatly across cultures. As discussed in reference to Maslow, security is very important to some people, congenial relationships are paramount to others, and individual status and respect (career success) dominate for others. A classic study (95) investigated the work goals of 19,000 employees in a large multinational electrical equipment manufacturer operating in 46 countries and reported the results for the 25 countries with at least 40 employees, including Argentina, Australia, Austria, Belgium, Brazil, Canada, Chile, Colombia, Denmark, Finland, France, Germany, India, Israel, Japan, Mexico, New Zealand, Norway, Peru, South Africa, Sweden, Switzerland, the United Kingdom, the United States, and Venezuela. In these countries the five most important goals concerned achievement, especially individual achievement. Next in importance were the immediate environment, general features of the organization, and employment conditions such as pay and work hours. Some of the major differences among the cultural groups included:

1. English-speaking countries ranked higher on individual achievement and lower on the desire for security.
2. French-speaking countries, although similar to the English-speaking countries, gave greater importance to security and somewhat less to challenging work.
3. Northern European countries expressed less interest in "getting ahead" and work recognition goals and put more emphasis on job accomplishment; in addition, they showed more concern for people and less for the organization as a whole (it was important for them that the job not interfere with their personal lives).
4. Latin American and Southern European countries found individual achievement somewhat less important; Southern Europeans placed the highest emphasis on job security, while both groups of countries emphasized fringe benefits.
5. Germany ranked high on security and fringe benefits and among the highest on "getting ahead."
6. Japan, although low on advancement, also ranked second highest on challenge and lowest on autonomy, with a strong emphasis on good working conditions and a friendly working environment (95).

Expectancy theories are universal to the extent that they do not specify the types of rewards that motivate a given group of workers. Managers themselves must determine the level and type of rewards most sought after by a particular people. Although this study's conclusions support the idea that basic human needs are similar, they highlight that culture and environment determine how these needs can best be met.

Global human resource systems are replete with examples of overgeneralization because of the dominance of American reward structures. For example (as described in Chapter 1), raising the salaries of a particular group of Mexican workers motivated them to work fewer, not more, hours. As the Mexicans explained, "We can now make enough money to live and enjoy life [one of their primary values] in less time than previously. Now we do not have to work so many hours." In another example, an expatriate Canadian manager in Japan decided to promote one of his Japanese sales representatives to manager (a status reward). To the surprise of the Canadian, the promotion diminished the new Japanese manager's performance. Why? Japanese have a high need for harmony—to fit in with their work colleagues. The promotion, an individualistic reward, separated the new manager from his colleagues, embarrassed him, and therefore diminished his motivation to work.

When modified for the extent to which managers believe they control their work environment and for the specific types of rewards desired, expectancy theories appear to hold outside of the United States, even in countries as culturally dissimilar to the United States as Japan (76).

Motivation Is Culture Bound

Most motivation theories in use today were developed in the United States by Americans and about Americans. Of those that were not, many have been strongly influenced by American theories. Americans' strong emphasis on individualism has led to expectancy and equity theories of motivation: theories that emphasize rational, individual thought as the primary basis of human behavior. The emphasis placed on achievement is not surprising given Americans' willingness to accept risk and their high concern for performance. The theories therefore do not offer universal explanations of motivation; rather, they reflect the values system of Americans (48).

Unfortunately, many American as well as non-American managers have treated American theories as the best or only way to understand motivation. They are neither. American motivation theories, although too often assumed to reflect universal values, have failed to provide consistently useful explanations for behavior outside of the United States. Managers must therefore guard against imposing domestic American management theories on their global business practices (54).

DECISION MAKING

"It could be argued that the essence of living is free choice—the process of making decisions. To be deprived of choices is to lose all meaning" (30:59). Decision making plays a central role in managing; for some people decision making *is* managing (94). The higher the level of management, the greater the number and complexity of the decisions made. Leadership involves making decisions that affect whole organizations or units within an organization. Motivation, when viewed from the perspective of decision making, simply becomes the series of choices leaders make in order to influence the behavior of their colleagues and subordinates. Similarly, planning can be viewed as the making of sets of related decisions. Ian Wilson captures the ultimate dilemma faced by all decision makers in observing that "no amount of sophistication is going to allay the fact that all your knowledge is about the past and all your decisions are about the future." Decision makers will always act on the basis of inadequate and incomplete knowledge. Good decision makers in every culture are those who learn to cope with the ambiguity and uncertainty of reality. In the past, managers could successfully base their decisions on their own experience and culture; today that is no longer true.

Organization theorists have argued for years about the theory and reality of how people make decisions. Some believe that managerial decision making reflects a conscious, rational process in which managers select criteria and use them to evaluate alternative solutions to particular problems. For example, in choosing profit maximization as a prime criterion, managers might assess a range of business opportunities relative to their potential to generate profit. Alternatively, an equally rational decision rule might be *satisficing* (i.e., meeting acceptable standards on several criteria rather than maximum standards on a single criterion). When satisficing, managers might assess alternatives until they identify at least one projected to generate a certain acceptable profit level. Without further search they would then select that alternative. Unfortunately, our contact with other cultures has created new problems for us in attempting to use these objective, rational processes. As futurist Robert Theobold (107:42) observed, "We are all having increasing problems as we come to understand that different people have profoundly different visions of reality, and that there is no objective way of sorting out which of these visions is correct."

Other theorists, such as the noted psychoanalyst Sigmund Freud, believe that human decision making is irrational—that forces outside of our conscious control drive decision making. Herbert Simon (93;94), in his administrative theory of individual decision making, describes the process managers use to make decisions as "bounded rationality." According to Simon, managers make choices based on simplified rather than real situations. This "subjective rationality" narrows and alters the objective facts. Since managers from different cultures perceive the world differently, their subjective rationalities differ, as do their ways of simplifying complex realities into perceived environments in which they become capable of making choices.

Along this rational/irrational spectrum, some theorists believe that one best way exists to make decisions; others believe that the best way depends on the particular situation. For example, in certain situations companies should maximize profit, in others they should satisfice, and in still others they should base their decisions on intuition rather than on rational economic analysis. In this section we will look at some of the ways in which decision making is culturally contingent; that is, the ways in which the best way depends on the values, beliefs, attitudes, and behavioral patterns of the people involved. In this sense cultural contingency becomes one more contingency in the fit-models of decision making; the decision-making style must fit the culture.

Decision making involves five basic steps (26, based on 30 & 94):

1. Problem recognition
2. Information search
3. Construction of alternatives
4. Choice
5. Implementation

These steps suggest the following cross-cultural questions: Do managers from different cultures perceive problems in similar ways? Do they gather similar types and amounts of information while investigating a problem? Do they construct similar types of solutions? Do they use similar strategies for choosing between alternatives? Do they implement their decisions in similar ways? The answer to each question is no. As illustrated in Table 6-1, at each step culture influences the ways managers make decisions and solve problems.

Problem Recognition

When is a problem a problem? When do people from different cultures recognize that a problem exists? Based on differences in a society's orientation to activity—to "getting things done" (see Chapter 1)—some cultures emphasize solving problems; others focus on accepting situations as they are. In certain cultures, such as the United States, managers perceive most situations as problems to be solved, as opportunities for improvement through change. Other cultures, such as the Thai, Indonesian, and Malay cultures, tend to see no need to change situations but rather attempt to accept situations as they are.

If a problem-solving manager receives a notice that a prime supplier will be three months late in delivering needed construction materials, she will immediately attempt to speed up delivery or find an alternative supplier. If, by contrast, a situation-accepting manager receives a similar notice of delay, he might simply accept that the project would be delayed. Situation-accepting managers believe that they neither can nor should alter every situation that confronts them. Problem-solving managers believe that they both can and should change situations to their own benefit. Situation-accepting managers generally believe that fate or God's will

TABLE 6-1　*Cultural Contingencies of Decision Making*

Five Steps in Decision Making	Cultural Variations	
1. Problem Recognition	*Problem Solving* We should change situation.	*Situation Acceptance* Some situations should be accepted rather than changed.
2. Information Search	*Gathering "facts"*	*Gathering ideas and possibilities*
3. Construction of Alternatives	*New, future-oriented alternatives* Adults can learn and change.	*Past-, present-, and future-oriented alternatives* Adults cannot change substantially.
4. Choice	*Individual decision making* Decision making responsibility is delegated Decisions are made quickly. Decision rule: Is it true or false?	*Group decision making* Senior managers often make decisions. Decisions are made slowly. Decision rule: Is it good or bad?
5. Implementation	*Slow* Managed from the top Responsibility of one person	*Fast* Involves participation of all levels Responsibility of group

intervene in the production process (external attribution), whereas problem-solving managers are more likely to believe that they are the prime or only influence on the same process (internal attribution). Consequently, while viewing exactly the same situation, American managers might identify a problem long before their Indonesian or Malaysian counterparts would choose to recognize the situation as such. Comparative research has demonstrated that managers' perceptions of situations and their definitions of problems vary across cultures.

Information Search

After recognizing that a problem exists, where does the manager gather information to solve it? The noted psychoanalyst Carl Jung suggested two primary modes of gathering information (i.e., of perceiving): sensing and intuition. Sensors primarily use their five senses to gather information and facts about a situation; intuitive people more frequently use ideas from the past and future as part of their data. Sensors rely on facts and are often more inductive; intuitive people rely more heavily on images and are often more deductive. Cervantes' *Don Quixote*, the prototypical intuitive, captures the thinking pattern of intuitive people:

> When life itself seems lunatic, who knows where madness lies? Perhaps to be too practical is madness. To surrender dreams—this may be madness. To seek treasure where there is only trash. Too much sanity may be madness. And the maddest of all, to see life as it is and not as it should be.[6]

Cultures vary in the extent to which one or the other style of data gathering (of perceiving) dominates. For example, during the 1973 Yom Kippur war in the Middle East, the Americans, as typical sensors, assessed the situation pessimistically for the Israelis because 100 million Arabs were at war with less than 8 million Israelis. The Americans based their perception of the situation on fact-oriented, empirical evidence. The Israelis, who are typically more intuitive, based predictions on their image of the future—the continued existence of a free Jewish state—and therefore remained more optimistic. Moreover, the Israelis felt that the number of Arabs and Israelis was relevant in determining *how* they would fight the war but was irrelevant in influencing their belief about who would win the war. In a similar contrast of perceptual styles, many English Canadians— typically sensors—agonized over Quebec's diminished economic base if the province separated from the rest of Canada. They consequently predicted that people would vote in the 1995 referendum to remain a part of Canada. Many French Canadians, more typically using intuitive perceptions, continued to reiterate their vision of a culturally and linguistically distinct French nation. These French Canadians, while recognizing the economic consequences of separation, considered them less relevant in assessing the validity of their overall goal.

Constructing Alternatives

What types of alternatives do we construct? Are they predominantly new ideas or ideas rooted in the past? Are they ideas that demand large or moderate amounts of change? Based on a culture's underlying values, the types of alternatives vary. For example, more future-oriented cultures, such as California, tend to generate more new alternatives. More conservative, past-oriented cultures, such as England, tend to search for historical patterns on which to base alternatives. Californians, when attempting to minimize urban congestion, would be more likely to consider monorails and "flying cars"; the British are more likely to consider improved traffic control mechanisms. Both societies consider both types of alternatives; but, in each, one type is preferred. Mutiso's observation (79:35) that, for some Africans, "being educated [is] equivalent to rejecting the ways of ancestors" highlights the past orientation and contrasts it with more present and future orientations (see pages 29-32, time dimension).

Similarly, some cultures believe that adults can change, whereas other cultures believe that adults basically remain unchangeable (see pages 20-22, how people see themselves). Cultures that believe in change stress alternatives that include learning and on-the-job training; those believing in permanence stress initial selection. Today a company's orientation toward change is often reflected in its approach to technology: "Can we train our present employees to learn to use robots (change is possible), or must we hire new employees who are already robotics experts (change is impossible)?" Given Americans' strong belief in employees' and managers' ability to change, it is not surprising that the American Society for Training and Development has over 50,000 members.

Choice

Who makes the decisions for a company? Are decisions made quickly or slowly? Are information and alternatives discussed sequentially or holistically? Based on a culture's view of the relationships among people (see pages 25-27 and 47-51), either individuals or groups will hold primary decision-making responsibility. In North American business, individuals usually make decisions. The popular expression "the buck stops here" reflects the belief that ultimately a single person holds responsibility for a particular decision. In Japan groups make decisions; most Japanese would find it inconceivable for an individual to make a decision prior to consulting his or her immediate colleagues and gaining their agreement (31;60;61;84;107).

At what level are decisions made? In more hierarchical cultures (see Hofstede's power distance dimension, page 51), only very senior level managers make decisions. Lower level personnel hold responsibility for implementing decisions. For example, most lower level Indian employees would wonder about the competence of a superior who consulted them on routine decisions. The majority of Indian managers prefer a more directive style, and up to 85 percent of their surveyed subordinates believe they work better under supervision (58). By contrast, most lower level Swedish employees expect to make most of their own decisions about day-to-day operations. Thus, it is not surprising that the Swedes, not the Indians, experimented with some of the first autonomous work groups. At Volvo's Kalmar plant, Swedish management gave groups of employees total responsibility for producing cars (38). The group, not senior management, took responsibility for allocating and scheduling tasks as well as for allocating rewards among workers. Management could only delegate this amount of discretion to the shop floor in a low power distance country.

Are decisions made slowly or quickly? American businesspeople pride themselves in being quick decision makers. In the United States being called "decisive" is a compliment. By contrast, many other cultures downplay time urgency—some cultures even increase a decision's value based on the length of time spent in making it. When managers from quick-paced cultures—such as the United States—attempt to conduct business with people from more slow-paced cultures such as Egypt and Pakistan, the mismatched timing causes problems. Americans, for example, typically become frustrated at Egyptians' slow, deliberate pace and begin to believe that their Middle Eastern counterparts lack interest in doing business. Egyptians, on the other hand, in observing the Americans' "overly hasty race" to make decisions, typically conclude that Americans' unwillingness to take more time reflects the lack of importance they place on the business relationship and the particular agreement being negotiated. Time (as discussed on pages 29-32) is a crucial dimension in understanding business behavior cross-culturally.

How much risk is too much? As described by Hofstede in Chapter 2, cultures vary in their uncertainty avoidance (48). Managers in some cultures take more risks than those from other cultures. The extent to which managers feel willing to experiment, to try previously untried alternatives, depends on their aversion to risk.

In what order do businesspeople discuss alternatives? When do they eliminate alternatives? When do they select one particular alternative? As will be discussed in Chapter 7, some holistic cultures, such as Japan (106) and China, discuss all alternatives before making any decisions; other sequence-oriented cultures, such as the United States, Germany, and Canada, tend to discuss alternatives in a preplanned sequence and to make incremental decisions as each alternative is discussed.

The overall process of decision making can be described in Jungian terms, with some people acting primarily as "thinkers" and others primarily as "feelers." Thinkers generally process data and make decisions by questioning whether an alternative is correct or incorrect, true or false. Feelers, while equally logical, question whether an alternative is good or bad. Thinkers orient themselves around a belief in absolute truth, whereas feelers orient themselves around a model of "fit": Is there a good or bad fit between this alternative and what we are trying to accomplish? In selecting a new manager, the thinker might stress the individual's expertise and track record. The feeler might stress the candidate's ability to fit in with the other members of the organization. Both are equally logical and valid systems for decision making, but each leads to very different choices.

Implementation

If decisions are to have any value, they must be implemented. Again, depending on the culture, implementation can be quick or slow, innovative or disruptive, managed from the top or involving participation from all levels within the organization, and managed by an individual or a group. Some of the most difficult global business decisions involve ethical considerations. In a survey of *Harvard Business Review* readers, almost half agreed that "the American business executive tends not to apply the great ethical laws immediately to work. He is preoccupied chiefly with gain" (19). Only 5 percent listed social responsibility as a factor influencing ethical standards. Half of the respondents attributed unethical practices to superiors who were interested in results no matter how they were attained (19). Global business decisions are often even more difficult to make than domestic decisions because the very basis of what is "right" and "wrong" is culturally determined.

The following excerpt presents four business decisions demanding ethical considerations. As you read each, observe the criteria you would use at each stage of the decision-making process: problem recognition, information search, construction of alternatives, choice, and implementation. To what extent are your criteria culturally determined? Under what conditions would you be willing to modify your perspective and decision?

ETHICAL DECISION MAKING

In each of the following situations, first decide what you would do and why. Note what information you would use to investigate the question, what alternatives you would consider, and what criteria you would use to make the decision. After making your individually arrived-at decision, meet with a group of your colleagues—preferably including people from other cultures—and make a group decision. Again assess the type of information you consider, the range of alternatives you generate, the criteria you use to decide, and your implementation plan. Next, develop a contrasting-culture decision; that is, make the opposite decision based on assumptions of a culture that is very different from your own. Finally, following the suggestions in Chapter 4 for creating synergistic solutions, develop a decision and implementation plan that both you and members of the contrasting culture could accept and support. The situations are not easy. Each is based on a true situation in which at least one manager believed unethical behavior was involved.

Situation 1: Sales Representative in the Middle East

You hold the position of marketing director for a construction company in the Middle East. Your company has bid on a substantial project that it wants very much to get. Yesterday the cousin of the minister who will award the contract suggested that he might be of help. You are reasonably sure that with his help the chances of getting the contract would increase substantially. For his assistance the minister expects $20,000. You would have to pay this in addition to the standard fees to your agent. If you do not make this payment to the minister, you are certain that he will go to your competition (who has won the last three contracts), and they will make the payment (and probably get this contract, too).

Your company has no code of conduct yet, although it formed a committee some time ago to consider one. The government of your country recently passed an Ethical Business Practices Act. The pertinent paragraph is somewhat vague but implies that this kind of payment would probably be a violation of the act. The person to whom you report, and those above him, do not want to become involved. The decision is yours to make.

Situation 2: Hazardous Materials in West Africa

For one year now you have been the international vice president of a global firm that produces and markets chemicals. The minister of agriculture in a small developing country in West Africa has requested a series of large shipments over the next five years of a special insecticide that only your firm prepares. The minister believes that this chemical is the only one that will rid one of his country's crops of a new infestation that threatens to destroy it. You know, however, that one other insecticide would probably be equally effective; it is produced in another country and has never been allowed in your own country.

Your insecticide, MIM, is highly toxic. After years of debate, your government has just passed a law forbidding its use in your country. There is evidence that dangerous amounts are easily ingested by humans through residue on vegetables, through animals that eat the crops, and through the water supply. After careful thought, you tell the minister about this evidence. He still insists on using it, arguing that it is necessary and it will be used "intelligently." You are quite sure that, ten years from now, the insecticide will begin to damage the health of some of his people.

Both the president and executive vice president of your firm feel strongly that the order should be filled. In addition to questioning their own government's position, they are very concerned about the large inventory of MIM on hand and the serious financial setback its prohibition will cause the company. They have made it clear, however, that the decision is up to you.

Although the company has a code of conduct and your government has an Ethical Business Practices Act, neither covers hazardous materials.

Situation 3: The Southeast Asian Advertising Campaign

You are the new marketing manager for a very large, profitable global firm that manufactures automobile tires. Your advertising agency has just presented elaborate plans for introducing a new tire into the Southeast Asian market for your approval. The promotional material clearly implies that your product is better than all local products. In fact, it is better than some, but not as good as others. This material tries to attract potential buyers by explaining that for six months your product will be sold at a "reduced price." Actually, the price is reduced from a hypothetical high price that the firm established only so they could "reduce it." The advertisement further claims that the tire has been tested under the "most adverse" conditions. In reality it has not been tested in the prolonged heat and humidity of the tropics. Finally, your company assures buyers that, riding on your tires, they will be safer in their car than ever before. The truth is, however, that they would be equally safe on a competitor's tire that has been available for two years.

You know your product is good. You also know the proposed advertising is deceptive. Your superior has never been concerned about such practices, believing that advertisements must present your products as distinctive in order to achieve and maintain a competitive edge. Senior management of your company is counting on a very favorable reception for this tire in Southeast Asia. They are counting on you to see that the tire gets this reception.

Whether you go with the proposed advertisement or not is up to you. Your company has a code of conduct and your government has an Ethical Business Practices Act, but neither covers advertising practices.

Situation 4: Cultural Conflict in the Middle East

You became quite upset last week when you read a strong editorial in the *New York Times*, written by a prominent journalist, that strongly criticized your company, especially its major project in a conservative Moslem country.

As the international vice president, you hold responsibility for this project, which is to build and run a large steel plant. Based on the figures, this plant makes a lot of sense, both for your company and for the government of the country that approved the project. But as the journalist pointed out, the company plans to build the steel plant in a rural area, which will have a very disruptive effect upon the values and customs of the people in the whole region. There will be many consequences. The young people from other towns will move to work at the plant, thereby breaking up families and eliminating their primary source of financial and personal security. Working the second or third shift will further interfere with family responsibilities as well as religious observances. Working year round will certainly mean that many people will find themselves unable to return home to help with the harvest. As the company pays the young people more and more, they will gain more influence, thereby overturning century-old patterns of authority.   And, of course, the Westerners who the company brings in will probably not live up to local moral standards nor show due respect for local women.

The journalist ended by charging your company with "cultural imperialism" and claiming that your plant, if actually built and put into operation, would contribute to the disruption of the traditional values and relationships that have provided stability for the country through many generations.

You had known that the new steel plant would cause some social changes, but you had not realized how profound they could be. You have now examined other evidence and discovered that a factory built several years ago by another foreign firm in a similar location is causing exactly these problems—and more. Widespread concern in the country over these problems has become one reason for the increasing influence of traditionalists and nationalists in the country, who argue for getting rid of all foreign firms and their disruptive priorities and practices.

Your company has a code of conduct and your government has an Ethical Business Practices Act, but neither deals with the destruction of traditional values and relationships. You are on your own here. A lot is at stake for the company and for the people of the region into which you had planned to move. The decision is yours.[7]

Britain's Anita Roddick defines corporate leadership as moral leadership:

Authority to lead should be founded on a moral vision rather than a desire to create the biggest or the richest company in the world. I don't understand how anybody can be a leader without a clearly defined moral vision. If your ambitions and interests do not extend beyond the role of making money or expanding your business, as far as I am concerned you are morally bankrupt (89:226).

As global leaders, each of us must define our own moral imperatives. Our moral vision guides our personal and organizational behavior, it frames the goals we set, the trade-offs we are willing to consider, and the decisions we make.

SUMMARY

Effective styles of management vary among cultures. Whereas managers in all countries must lead, motivate, and make decisions, the ways in which they approach these core managerial behaviors remain, in part, determined by their own cultural background and that of their work environment. Far from learning only one way to lead, motivate, and decide, managers working across cultures must become flexible enough to adapt to each particular situation and country. In moving from domestic to global management, leaders must develop a wider range of thinking patterns and behaviors, along with the ability to select the pattern best suited to each particular situation. Effective global managers must become chameleons capable of acting in many ways, not experts rigidly adhering to one approach.

Most management theories have been developed in the United States by Americans. The questions they raise—How can I lead most effectively? How should I motivate the work force? How can I make the best decisions?—are universal, but the solutions remain culturally specific. Rather than being applicable worldwide, many traditional models effectively guide thinking and action only within the American context within which they were developed. Based on the cultural context of their operations, global managers must constantly decide to use more directive or democratic styles of leadership, more individual- or group-oriented motivation schemes, more long-term or short-term criteria for decision making. Their decisions, to be most effective and most appropriate, must depend on the particular culture, industry, organization, and individuals involved. Far from being useless, traditional models guide the questions we ask. Only observation and analysis of each particular culture and situation can guide our answers.

QUESTIONS FOR REFLECTION

1. *World Leaders.* Publicly elected officials often display the leadership values and behaviors of their culture. Select two prominent world leaders and describe their behavior in cultural terms.

2. *Multinational Motivation.* Imagine that you have just been selected to become the new an expatriate managing director in a country in which your company has decided to open a new industrial complex. Neither you nor your company has ever worked in this country before. What would you do to motivate workers from the foreign country to join your company and to work hard. (Note: Select a specific country before describing your motivation plan.)

3. *Global Decision Making.* Your company has just formed a strategic alliance with a company from another part of the world. You have been appointed the

manager of the transition teams which includes executives from Singapore, Switzerland, Mexico, and Canada. Many decisions about the alliance must be made right away. What could you do as team leader to see that the decision-making process in the transition team becomes as effective as possible?

4. ***Cultural Roots of Motivation.*** What are your own assumptions about motivation? Why do you think people work? List your own motivation assumptions and then analyze them from a cross-cultural perspective. In what ways are your assumptions similar to those of most of the people from your country?

CASE FOR REFLECTION

Managing across cultures confronts leaders with profound ethical questions of adhering to the highest standard of integrity while administering culturally appropriate standards of justice. Review the following real situation of "Local Justice and Integrity" (see box), both from the perspective of the North American expatriate managing director who made the decision as well as from the perspective of the local authorities who responded to the information provided to them by the expatriate managing director. Use the Questions for Reflection following the case to guide your analysis. Then imagine that you are on the company's senior management committee, and decide what you would do in the situation.

LOCAL JUSTICE AND INTEGRITY

A major North American company operating in a foreign country discovered one of the local employees stealing company property of minimal value. The managers at the location, all of whom are expatriate Americans, had little doubt as to the employee's guilt.

Following the company's standard worldwide procedure, the American managing director reported the case to the local police. Similar to many other North American companies, this company believed that it was best to let officials from the local culture deal with theft and similar violations in whatever way they found most appropriate, rather than imposing the system of justice from their home culture. The local police arrived at the company, arrested the employee, took him to the station, and interrogated him according to local procedures. The employee confessed. The police then took the employee outside and shot him dead.

The American managing director was devastated. For weeks, he was haunted by the fact that his action, taken because he thought it was culturally appropriate and fair, had led to the murder of an employee.

Questions for Reflection

1. How should employees be treated when they compromise integrity? Does a company's belief in maintaining the highest level of integrity limit its ability to consider possible values differences—and more important- ly, their consequences—between the company's culture and local nation- al cultures?

2. Should companies review their policies on the prevention of theft and the promotion of personal honesty in the light of cultural differences? Can a company use worldwide standards and procedures? Or must companies define integrity issues differently in each country or region of the world?

Senior Management Committee Decision

1. Given the company's belief in maintaining the highest respect for peo- ple and maintaining the highest personal integrity, how should it han- dle future situations such as this?

2. If you were the American managing director, what would you person- ally have done in this situation? Why? Knowing how the situation turned out, what would you recommend that future managing directors do in similar situations?

NOTES

1. University of Pennsylvania Professor Robert House and his worldwide research team are currently conducting a major multidomestic study of leadership to define leadership practices in countries around the world. (See R. J. House; P. Hanges; M. Agar, and A. Ruiz-Quintanilla, *A Multinational Study of Leadership and Organizational Practice.* Study funded by U.S. Department of Education, 1993).

2. Such classic theories as Likert's "System 4" Management (67;68) and Blake and Mouton's "Managerial Grid" (15;16) make assumptions similar to Theory Y; that is, that high concern for people and high productivity go together.

3. For an excellent review of current international cross-cultural leadership research see (27). For other reviews and current research on leadership, see references 6, 8, 21, 22, 29, 32, 35, 36, 52, 81, 96, 97, 98, 99, 100, 117, 118.

4. Although Maslow's hierarchy has been questioned within the United States, it has become one of the accepted bases for explaining and understanding behavior within organizations. Generalizing from this United States–based acceptance to worldwide applicability is questioned in this chapter.

5. Hofstede (47) originally labeled this dimension masculinity/femininity. To better reflect the underlying meaning, it has been relabeled in this book as

career success/quality of life. For a more in-depth discussion of this dimension, see Chapter 2.

6. The quotation is from the play *Man of La Mancha* (as found in Otis L. Guernsey, Jr., New York: Dodd, Mead, 1966, p. 214), which is based on the book *Don Quixote* by Miguel Cervantes.

7. Based on George W. Renwick's and Robert T. Moran's, "Basic Responsibility and International Business Ethics (BRIBE)," American Graduate School of International Management, Glendale, Arizona, January 1982; edited and adapted by Nancy J. Adler, 1996.

REFERENCES

1. Adler, N. J. "Cross-Cultural Management Research: The Ostrich and the Trend," *Academy of Management Review*, vol. 8, no. 2 (1983), pp. 226–232.

2. Adler, N. J., and Bartholomew, S. "Academic and Professional Communities of Discourse: Generating Knowledge on Transnational Human Resource Management," *Journal of International Business Studies*, vol. 23, no. 3 (1992), pp. 551–569.

3. Adler, N. J., and Boyacigiller, N. "Global Management and the 21st Century," in B. J. Punnett and O. Shenkar, eds. *Handbook of International Management Research* (Cambridge, Mass.: Blackwell, 1996), pp. 537–555.

4. Adler, N. J., and Boyacigiller, N. "Global Organizational Behavior: Going Beyond Tradition," *Journal of International Management*, vol. 1, no. 3 (1995a), pp. 73–86.

5. Adler, N. J., and Boyacigiller, N. "Going Beyond Traditional HRM Scholarship," in R. N. Kanungo and D. M. Saunders, eds. *New Approaches to Employee Management*. vol. 3, *Employee Management Issues in Developing Countries* (Greenwich, Conn.: JAI Press, 1995b), pp. 1–13.

6. Al-Gratton, A. A. "Test of the Path–Goal Theory of Leadership in the Multinational Domain," *Group and Organizational Studies*, vol. 10, no. 4 (1985), pp. 429–445.

7. Allen, D. B.; Miller, E. L.; and Nath, R. "North America," in R. Nath, ed., *Comparative Management* (Cambridge, Mass.: Ballinger, 1988), pp. 23–54.

8. Ayman, R. "Leadership Perception: The Role of Gender and Culture," *Leadership Theory and Research* (San Diego: Academic Press, 1993), pp. 137–166.

9. Badawy, M. K. "Managerial Attitudes and Need Orientations of Mideastern Executives: An Empirical Cross-Cultural Analysis," *Academy of Management Proceedings*, vol. 39 (1979), pp. 293–297.

10. Badawy, M. K. "Styles of Mideastern Managers," *California Management Review*, vol. 22, no. 3 (1980), pp. 51–59.

11. Bass, B. M. *Leadership and Performance Beyond Expectations* (New York: Free Press, 1985).

12. Bass, B. M., and Stogdill, R. M. *The Handbook of Leadership*, 3rd ed. (New York: Free Press, 1989).

13. Bennis, W. *Why Leaders Can't Lead: The Unconscious Conspiracy Continues* (San Francisco: Jossey-Bass, 1989).

14. Bennis, W., and Nanus, B. *Leaders* (New York: Harper & Row, 1985).

15. Blake, R. R., and Mouton, J. S. "Motivating Human Productivity in the People's Republic of China," *Group and Organization Studies*, vol. 4, no. 2 (June 1979), pp. 159–169.

16. Blake, R. R., and Mouton, J. S. *The Managerial Grid* (Houston, Tex.: Gulf Publishing,1964).

17. Boyacigiller, N., and Adler, N. J. "Insiders and Outsiders: Bridging the Worlds of Organizational Behavior and International Management," in Brian Toyne and Doug Nigh, eds., *International Business Inquiry: An Emerging Vision* (Columbia, S.C.: University of South Carolina Press, 1996), pp. 22–102.

18. Boyacigiller, N., and Adler, N. J. "The Parochial Dinosaur: The Organizational Sciences in a Global Context," *Academy of Management Review*, vol. 16, no. 2 (April 1991), pp. 262–290.

19. Brenner, S. N., and Molander, E. A. "Is the Ethics of Business Changing?" *Harvard Business Review* (January-February, 1977), pp. 70–71.

20. Buera, A., and Glueck, W. "Need Satisfaction of Libyan Managers," *Management International Review*, vol. 19, no. 1 (1979), pp. 113–123.

21. Chemers, M. M., "A Theoretical Framework for Examining the Effects of Cultural Differences on Leadership." Paper presented at the 23rd International Congress of Applied Psychology, Madrid, Spain, 1994.

22. Chemers, M. M. and Ayman, R. "Directions for Leadership Research," *Leadership Theory and Research* (San Diego: Academic Press, 1993), pp. 321–332.

23. Conger, J. A. *The Charismatic Leader: Behind the Mystique of Exceptional Leadership* (San Francisco: Jossey-Bass, 1989).

24. Conger, J. A., and Kanungo, R. N., eds., *Charismatic Leadership* (San Francisco: Jossey-Bass, 1988).

25. Crabbs, R. A. "Work Motivation in the Culturally Complex Panama Canal Company," *Academy of Management Proceedings* (1973), pp. 119–126.

26. Dewey, J. *How We Think* (Boston: D.C. Heath, 1933).

27. Dorfman, P. W. "International and Cross-Cultural Leadership," in B. J. Punnett and O. Shenkar, eds., *Handbook for International Management Research* (Cambridge, Mass.: Blackwell, 1996), pp. 267–349.

28. Dorfman, P. W., and Howell, J. P. "Dimensions of National Culture and Effective Leadership Patterns: Hofstede Revisited," *Advances in International Comparative Management*, vol. 3 (Greenwich, Conn.: JAI Press, 1988), pp. 127–150.

29. Dorfman, P. W., and Ronen, S. "The Universality of Leadership Theories: Challenges and Paradoxes." Paper presented at the National Academy of Management annual meeting, Miami, Florida, 1991.

30. Driver, M. J. "Individual Decision Making and Creativity," in S. Kerr, ed., *Organizational Behavior* (Columbus, Ohio: Grid Publishing, 1979), pp. 59–91.

31. Drucker, P. F. "What We Can Learn from Japanese Management," *Harvard Business Review* (March–April 1971), pp. 110–122.

32. Erez, M., and Earley, P. C. *Culture, Self-Identity and Work* (New York: Oxford University Press, 1993).

33. Foy, N., and Gadon, H. "Worker Participation Contrasts in Three Countries," *Harvard Business Review* (May–June 1976), pp. 71–84.

34. Gardner, J. W. *John W. Gardner on Leadership* (New York: The Free Press, 1989).

35. Gerstner, C. R., and Day, D. D. "Cross-Cultural Comparison of Leadership Prototypes," *Leadership Quarterly*, vol. 5, no. 1 (1994), pp. 121–134.

36. Graen, G. B. and Wakabayashi, M. "Cross-Cultural Leadership Makings: Bridging American and Japanese Diversity for Team Advantage," *Handbook of Industrial and Organizational Psychology*, vol. 4, 2nd ed. (Palo Alto, Calif.: Consulting Psychologists Press, 1994), pp. 415–446.

37. Grauman, C. F., and Moscovici, S. *Changing Conceptions of Leadership* (New York: Springer-Verlag, 1986).

38. Gyllenhammer, P. G. "How Volvo Adapts Work to People," *Harvard Business Review*, vol. 55, no. 4 (1977), pp. 102–113.

39. Haire, M.; Ghiselli, E. E.; and Porter, L. W. "Cultural Patterns in the Role of the Manager," *Industrial Relations*, vol. 2, no. 2 (February 1963), pp. 95–117.

40. Hammer, W. C. "Motivation Theories and Work Applications," in S. Kerr, ed., *Organizational Behavior* (Columbus, Ohio: Grid Publishing, 1979), pp. 41–58.

41. Herzberg, F. "One More Time: How Do You Motivate Employees?" *Harvard Business Review* (January–February 1968), pp. 54–62.

42. Herzberg, F.; Mausner, B.; and Snyderman, B. *The Motivation to Work*, 2nd ed. (New York: Wiley, 1959).

43. Hessling, P., and Keenen, E. E. "Culture and Subculture in a Decision Making Exercise," *Human Relations*, vol. 22 (1969), pp. 31–51.

44. Hines, G. H. "Achievement, Motivation, Occupations and Labor Turnover in New Zealand," *Journal of Applied Psychology*, vol. 58, no. 3 (1973), pp. 313–317.

45. Hines, G. H. "Cross-Cultural Differences in Two-Factor Theory," *Journal of Applied Psychology*, vol. 58, no. 5 (1973), pp. 375–377.

46. Hofstede, G. *Cultures and Organizations: Software of the Mind* (London: McGraw-Hill, 1991).

47. Hofstede, G. *Culture's Consequences: International Differences in Work-Related Values.* (Beverly Hills: Sage, 1980)

48. Hofstede, G. "Motivation, Leadership and Organization: Do American Theories Apply Abroad?" *Organizational Dynamics*, vol. 9, no. 1 (1980), pp. 42–63.

49. Howell, J. P.; Dorfman, P. W.; Hibino, S.; Lee, J. K; and Tate, U. "Leadership in Western and Asian Countries: Commonalities and Differences in Effective Leadership Processes and Substitutes Across Cultures." Center for Business Research, New Mexico State University, 1994.

50. Howell, P.; Strauss, J.; and Sorensen, P. F. "Research Note: Cultural and Situational Determinants of Job Satisfaction Among Management in Liberia," *Journal of Management Studies* (May 1975), pp. 225–227.

51. Hundal, P. S. "A Study of Entrepreneurial Motivation: Comparison of Fast- and Slow-Progressing Small Scale Industrial Entrepreneurs in Punjab, India," *Journal of Applied Psychology*, vol. 55, no. 4 (1971), pp. 317–323.

52. Hunt, J. W. *Leadership: A New Synthesis* (Newbury Park, Calif.: Sage, 1991).

53. Iacocca, L., and Novak, W. *Iacocca* (New York: Bantam, 1984.)

54. Illman, P. E. "Motivating the Overseas Work Force," in *Developing Overseas Managers and Managers Overseas* (New York: AMACOM, 1980), pp. 83–106.

55. Jaeger, A. M., and Kanungo, R. N., eds., *Management in Developing Countries* (London: Routledge, 1990).

56. Jaggi, B. "Need Importance of Indian Managers," *Management International Review*, vol. 19, no. 1 (1979), pp. 107–113.

57. Jain, C. H., and Kanungo, R. *Behavioral Issues in Management: The Canadian Context* (Toronto: McGraw-Hill Ryerson, 1977), pp. 85–99.

58. Kakar, S. "Authority Patterns and Subordinate Behavior in Indian Organizations," *Administrative Science Quarterly*, vol. 16, no. 3 (September 1971), pp. 298–308.

59. Kaufman, F. "Decision Making—Eastern and Western Style," *Business Horizons*, vol. 13, no. 6 (December 1970), pp. 81–86.

60. Kavcic, B.; Rus, V.; and Tannenbaum, A. S. "Control, Participation, and Effectiveness in Four Yugoslavian Industrial Organizations," *Administrative Science Quarterly*, vol. 16, no. 1 (March 1971), pp. 74–86.

61. Keizan, W. "Decision Making by Socialist Managers in Complex Organizations," *International Studies of Management and Organization*, vol. 9, no. 4 (1979), pp. 63–77.

62. Kotter, J. *The Leadership Factor* (New York: Free Press, 1988).

63. Laurent, A. "The Cultural Diversity of Western Conceptions of Management," *International Studies of Management and Organization*, vol. 13, no. 1-2 (1983), pp. 75–96

64. Lawler, E. E., III. "Job Design and Employee Motivation," *Personnel Psychology*, vol. 22 (1969), pp. 426–435.

65. Lawler, E. E., III. *Pay and Organizational Effectiveness: A Psychological View* (New York: McGraw-Hill, 1971).

66. Reprinted by permission of the publishers from *Executive* by Harry Levinson, Cambridge, Mass.: Harvard University Press, Copyright © 1968, 1981 by the President and Fellows of Harvard College. As cited in R. H. Mason and R. S. Spich, *Management: An International Perspective* (Homewood, Ill.: Irwin, 1987), pp. 190–191.

67. Likert, R. *The Human Organization* (New York: McGraw-Hill, 1967).

68. Likert, R. *New Patterns of Management* (New York: McGraw-Hill, 1961).

69. McClelland, D. C. *The Achieving Society* (Princeton, N.J.: Van Nostrand, 1961).

70. McClelland, D. C.; Atkinson, J. W.; Clark, R. A.; and Lowell, E. L. *The Achievement Motive* (New York: Appleton-Century-Crofts, 1953) .

71. McClelland, D. C., and Burnham, D. H. "Power Is the Great Motivator," *Harvard Business Review*, vol. 54, no. 1 (March–April 1976), pp. 100–110.

72. McGregor, D. *The Human Side of Enterprise* (New York: McGraw-Hill, 1960).

73. Maslow, A. H. *Motivation and Personality* (New York: Harper & Row, 1954).

74. Maslow, A. H. "A Theory of Human Motivation," *Psychology Review* (July 1943), pp. 370–396.

75. Maslow, A. H. *Toward a Psychology of Being* (Princeton, N.J.: Van Nostrand, 1962).

76. Matsui, T., and Terai, I. "A Cross-Cultural Study of the Validity of the Expectancy Theory of Work Motivation," *Journal of Applied Psychology*, vol. 60, no. 2 (1979), pp. 263–265.

77. Miller, J. J., and Kilpatrick, J. A. *Issues for Managers: An International Perspective* (Homewood, Ill.: Irwin, 1987).

78. Mitroff, I. I. *Business Not as Usual* (San Francisco: Jossey-Bass, 1987).

79. Mutiso, G.-C. M. *Socio-Political Thought in African Literature: Weusi* (New York: Barnes and Noble, 1974).

80. Nath, R., and Narayanan, V. K. "A Comparative Study of Managerial Support, Trust, Openness, Decision-Making, and Job Enrichment," *Academy of Management Proceedings*, vol. 40 (1980), pp. 48–52.

81. Oh, T. K. "Theory Y in the People's Republic of China," *California Management Review*, vol. 19, no. 2 (Winter 1976), pp. 77–84.

82. Ohmae, K. *Beyond National Borders* (Homewood, Ill.: Dow Jones-Irwin, 1987).

83. O'Reilly, C. A., and Roberts, K. H. "Job Satisfaction Among Whites and Nonwhites," *Journal of Applied Psychology*, vol. 57, no. 3 (1973), pp. 295–299.

84. Pascale, R. T. "Communication and Decision Making Across Cultures: Japanese and American Comparisons," *Administrative Science Quarterly*, vol. 23 (March 1978), pp. 91–110.

85. Pfeffer, J. *Organizations and Organization Theory* (Boston: Pitman, 1982).

86. Punnett, B. J. "Language, Cultural Values and Preferred Leadership Styles: A Comparison of Anglophones and Francophones in Ottawa," *Canadian Journal of Behavioral Sciences*, vol. 23, no. 2 (1991), pp. 241–244.

87. Reitz, H. J. "The Relative Importance of Five Categories of Needs Among Industrial Workers in Eight Countries," *Academy of Management Proceedings* (1975), pp 270–273.

88. Reitz, J., and Grof, G. *Similarities and Differences Among Mexican Workers, in Attitudes to Worker Motivation* (Bloomington, Ind.: Indiana University, 1973).

89. Roddick, A. *Body and Soul* (New York: Crown, 1991).

90. Sampson, E. D. "Psychology and the American Ideal," *Journal of Personality and Social Psychology*, vol. 35, no. 11 (November 1977), pp. 767–782.

91. Schlesinger, A. M., Jr. *A Thousand Days* (Boston: Houghton Mifflin, 1965).

92. Shelton, A. J. "Behavior and Cultural Value in West African Stories," *Literary Sources for the Study of Culture Contact*, Africa, vol. 34 (1964), pp. 353–359.

93. Simon, H. A. *Administrative Behavior* (New York: The Free Press, 1957).

94. Simon, H. A. *The New Science of Management Decision* (New York: Harper & Row, 1960).

95. Sirota, D., and Greenwood, M. J. "Understanding Your Overseas Workforce," *Harvard Business Review*, vol. 14 (January–February 1971), pp. 53–60.

96. Smith, P. B.; Misumi, S.; Tayeb, M.; Peterson, M.; and Bond, M. "On the Generality of Leadership Style Measures Across Cultures," *Journal of Occupational Psychology*, vol. 62, no. 2 (1989), pp. 97–109.

97. Smith, P. B., and Peterson, M. F. "Leadership as Event-management: A Cross-Cultural Survey Based upon Middle Managers from 25 Nations." Paper presented in the symposium on Cross-Cultural Studies of Event Management at the 23rd International Congress of Applied Psychology, Madrid, Spain, 1994.

98. Smith, P. B., and Peterson, M. F. *Leadership, Organizations and Culture* (London: Sage, 1988).

99. Smith, P. B.; Peterson, M. F.; Misumi, J.; and Bond, M. "A Cross-Cultural Test of Japanese PM Leadership Theory," *Applied Psychology: An International Review*, vol. 41, no. 1 (1992), pp. 5–19.

100. Smith, P. B.; Peterson, M. F.; Misumi, J.; and Tayeb, M. "Testing Leadership Theory Cross-Culturally," *Recent Advances in Social Psychology: An International Perspective* (Amsterdam: North-Holland, 1989), pp. 383–391.

101. Staw, B. M. "Organizational Behavior: A Review and Reformulation of the Field's Outcome Variables," *Annual Review of Psychology*, vol. 35 (1984), pp. 627–666.

102. Staw, B. M. "Rationality and Justification in Organizational Life," in B. M. Staw and L. L. Cummings, eds., *Research in Organizational Behavior*, vol. 2 (Greenwich, Conn.: JAI Press, 1980), pp. 45–80.

103. Steers, R. M., and Porter, L. W., eds., *Motivation and Work Behavior* (New York: McGraw-Hill, 1975).

104. Stephens, D.; Kedia, B.; and Ezell, D. "Managerial Need Structures in U.S. and Peruvian Industries," *Management International Review*, vol. 19 (1979), pp. 27–39.

105. Stogdill, R. M. "Personal Factors Associated with Leadership: A Survey of the Literature," *Journal of Psychology*, vol. 25 (1948), pp. 37–71.

106. Takamiya, S. "Group Decision Making in Japanese Management," *International Studies of Management and Organization*, vol. 2, no. 2 (1972), pp.183–196.

107. Theobald, R. "Management of Complex Systems: A Growing Societal Challenge," in F. Feather, ed., *Through the 80s: Thinking Globally, Acting Locally* (Washington, D.C.: World Future Society, 1980), pp. 42–51.

108. Triandis, H. C. "Dimensions of Cultural Variations as Parameters of Organizational Theories," *International Studies of Management and Organization*, vol. 12, no. 4 (1983), pp. 139-169.

109. Trompenaars, F. *Riding the Waves of Culture* (London: The Economist Books, 1993).

110. Tscheulin, D. "Leader Behavior Measurement in German Industry," *Journal of Applied Psychology*, vol. 57 (1973), pp. 28–31.

111. Tzu, Lao. *The Way of Lao Tzu (tao-te ching): Translated with Introductory Essays, Comments and Notes by Wing-tsit Chan* (Indianapolis, Ind.: Bobbs-Merrill, 1963). As cited in "Lao Leader Behaviors," *Management International Review*, vol. 19 (1979), p. 214. (Lao Tzu wrote in the 6th century B.C.)

112. Van Fleet, D., and Al-Tuhaih, S. "A Cross-Cultural Analysis of Perceived Leader Behaviors," *Management International Review*, vol. 19 (April 1979), pp. 81–88.

113. Vardi, Y.; Shrom, A.; and Jacobson, D. "A Study of Leadership Beliefs of Israeli Managers," *Academy of Management Journal*, vol. 23, no. 2 (1980), pp. 367–374.

114. Vroom, V. H. *Work and Motivation* (New York: Wiley, 1964).

115. Vroom, V. H., and Yetton, P. W. *Leadership and Decision Making* (Pittsburgh, Penn.: University of Pittsburgh Press, 1973).

116. Williams, L. K.; Whyte, W. F.; and Green, C. S. "Do Cultural Differences Affect Workers' Attitudes?" Industrial Relations, vol. 5 (1966), pp. 105–117.

117. Xu, L. C. "A Cross-Cultural Study of the Leadership Behavior of Chinese and Japanese Executives," *Asia Pacific Journal of Management*, vol. 4, no. 3 (1987), pp. 203–209.

118. Yukl, G. A. *Leadership in Organizations*, 3rd ed. (Englewood Cliffs, N.J.: Prentice Hall, 1994).

CHAPTER 7
Negotiating Globally

Let us not be blind to our differences—but let us also direct attention to our common interests and the means by which those differences can be resolved.

— John Fitzgerald Kennedy,
Former President of the United States (32)

Joint ventures, mergers and acquisitions, licensing and distribution agreements, and sales of products and services—a crucial aspect of all such interorganizational relationships involves face-to-face negotiations. As the proportion of international to domestic trade increases, so does the frequency of business negotiations among people from different countries and cultures. To successfully manage such negotiations, businesspeople need to know how to influence and communicate with members of cultures other than their own (2).

A growing literature exists documenting international negotiating styles (37;54). For example, there are descriptions of the negotiating behavior of the French (10;41), Russians (5), Canadians (1), Mexicans (14;56), Brazilians (17;20), Middle Eastern Arabs (39;61); Chinese (3;26;33;34;36;42;46;50) and Japanese (6;19;16;24;48;49;53), among others (4;7;23;25;58). Do Russians bargain with the same expectations and approaches as Arabs? No. Are Arab negotiating styles similar to those of Americans? Again, no. Russians, Arabs, and Americans negotiate in very different ways.

As shown in Table 7-1 (9;15), Russians typically use an axiomatic approach to negotiating—they base their arguments on asserted ideals. Russians generally do not expect to develop a continuing relationship

189

TABLE 7-1   *National Styles of Persuasion*

	North Americans	*Arabs*	*Russians*
Primary Negotiating Style and Process	*Factual:* Appeals made to logic	*Affective:* Appeals made to emotions	*Axiomatic:* Appeals made to ideals
Conflict: Counterparts' Arguments Countered with . . .	Objective facts	Subjective feelings	Asserted ideals
Making Concessions	Small concessions made early to establish a relationship	Concessions made throughout as a part of the bargaining process	Few, if any, concessions made
Response to Counterparts' Concessions	Usually reciprocate counterparts' concessions	Almost always reciprocate counterparts' concessions	Counterparts' concessions viewed as weakness and almost never reciprocated
Relationship	Short term	Long term	No continuing relationship
Authority	Broad	Broad	Limited
Initial Position	Moderate	Extreme	Extreme
Deadline	Very important	Casual	Ignored

Source: Reprinted with permission from *International Journal of Intercultural Relations*, vol. 1, no. 3, Fall 1977. E. S. Glenn; D. Witmeyer; and K. A. Stevenson, "Cultural Styles of Persuasion." Copyright © 1977, Pergamon Press, Ltd.

with their bargaining partners and therefore see little need for relationship building. As a negotiation progresses, Russians make few, if any, concessions and view their counterparts' concessions as signs of weakness. Russians often start with extreme positions, ignore deadlines, and, due to their very limited authority, frequently check back with headquarters.

By contrast, Arabs typically use an affective approach to negotiating (15)—they counter the other side's arguments with emotional appeals based on subjective feelings. Arabs generally want to build long-term relationships with their bargaining partners. Therefore, they are often willing to make concessions throughout the bargaining process and almost always reciprocate their opponents' concessions. Most Arabs do not feel limited by time or authority; they frequently approach deadlines very casually and rarely lack the broad authority necessary to discuss and to agree on all issues pertinent to the negotiation.

Americans differ from both Russians and Arabs. Americans typically use a factual approach to negotiating (15)—they attempt to counter the other side's arguments with logical appeals based on objective facts. Americans make small concessions early in the negotiation in an attempt to establish a relationship, and they generally expect their bargaining partners to do likewise. Americans, far from casual about time and authority, generally take deadlines very seriously and have very broad authority.

What happens when Russians begin negotiating with Arabs or Americans? Who persuades whom when styles of negotiating differ? Who wins when the process of negotiating—the very rules of the game— is defined differently? How can I get what my company and I want from them? To succeed in a global business environment, negotiators must face and solve these questions.

NEGOTIATING GLOBALLY

Negotiation is a process in which at least one individual tries to persuade another individual to change his or her ideas or behavior (8:152); it often involves one person attempting to get another to sign a particular contract or make a particular decision. Negotiation is the process in which at least two partners with different needs and viewpoints try to reach an agreement on matters of mutual interest (8:152). A negotiation becomes cross-cultural when the parties involved belong to different cultures and therefore do not share the same ways of thinking, feeling, and behaving (8:152). All global negotiations are cross-cultural. Some domestic negotiations, in spanning two or more ethnic groups, are also cross-cultural. Therefore, a Singaporian businessperson negotiating a raw materials contract with a Brazilian; a United Nations official negotiating with ambassadors from several countries concerning the agenda for upcoming disarmament talks; Mexican executives involved in joint venture discussions with Swedes; and French- and Flemish-speaking Belgians determining national language legislation are all negotiating cross-culturally.

Negotiation is one of the single most important global business skills (11;12;30;60). Global negotiations contain all of the complexity of domestic negotiations, with the added dimension of cultural diversity. Global managers spend more than 50 percent of their time negotiating (40). As highlighted in Tables 7-1 and 7-2, negotiating styles vary markedly across cultures. Countries vary on such key aspects as the amount and type of preparation for a negotiation, the relative emphasis on task versus interpersonal relationships, the use of general principles versus specific details, and the number of people present and the extent of their influence.

TABLE 7-2 *Negotiation Styles from a Cross-Cultural Perspective*

Japanese	North American	Latin American
Emotional sensitivity highly valued	Emotional sensitivity not highly valued	Emotional sensitivity valued
Hiding emotions	Dealing straightforwardly or impersonally	Emotionally passionate
Subtle power plays; conciliation	Litigation; not as much conciliation	Great power plays; use of weakness
Loyalty to employer; employer takes care of employees	Lack of commitment to employer; breaking ties by either if necessary	Loyalty to employer (who is often family)
Group decision making by consensus	Team provides input to a decision maker	Decisions come down from one individual
Face-saving crucial; decisions often made to save someone from embarrassment	Decisions based on cost-benefit analysis; face-saving not generally important	Face-saving crucial in decision making to preserve honor, dignity
Decision makers openly influenced by special interests	Decision makers influenced by special interests, but often not considered ethical	Inclusion of special interests of decision maker expected and condoned
Not argumentative; quiet when right	Argumentative when right or wrong, but impersonal	Argumentative when right or wrong; passionate
What is down in writing must be accurate, valid	Great importance given to documentation as evidential proof	Impatient with documentation, seen as obstacle to understanding general principles
Step-by-step approach to decision making	Methodically organized decision making	Impulsive, spontaneous decision making
Good of group is the ultimate aim	Profit motive or good of individual ultimate aim	What is good for group is good for the individual
Cultivate a good emotional social setting for decision making; get to know decision makers	Decision making impersonal; avoid involvements, conflict of interest	Personalism necessary for good decision making

Source: Pierre Casse, *Training for the Multicultural Manager: A Practical and Cross-Cultural Approach to the Management of People,* reprinted with permission of Intercultural Press, Inc., Yarmouth, ME. Copyright, 1982. Out of print.

According to global negotiations experts, negotiation is not always the best approach to doing business (43). Sometimes the best strategy is "take it or leave it," other times bargaining, and, on some occasions, negotiations involving problem solving are most appropriate (43:6.24).

Negotiation, compared with bargaining and the take-it-or-leave-it approach, demands more time. Managers should negotiate when the value of the exchange and of the relationship is important; as, for example, within the growing number of global strategic alliances. As summarized in Figure 7-1, negotiating is generally the preferred strategy for creating win-win solutions in the global business environment. Businesspeople should, for example, consider negotiating when any of the following conditions are apparent:

- Their power position is low relative to their counterpart's.
- The trust level is high.
- The available time is sufficient to explore each party's multiple needs, resources, and options.
- Commitment—not mere compliance—is important to ensure that the agreement is carried out.

In discussing negotiation, this chapter uses the terms *negotiator, bargaining partner, counterpart,* and *opponent* interchangeably.

Cultural diversity makes effective communication more difficult (see Chapter 3). Because people from different cultures perceive, interpret,

FIGURE 7-1 *When to Negotiate*

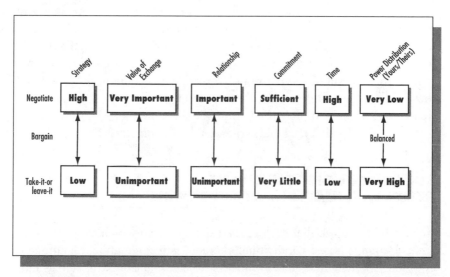

Source: Adapted with permission from Ellen Raider, "Strategy Assessment," in *International Negotiations* (Plymouth, Mass.: Situation Management Systems, 1982), pp. 4–16.

and evaluate the world differently, communicating needs and interests in ways that people from other cultures will understand becomes more difficult, as does fully understanding their words and meanings. Although communicating becomes more difficult, creating mutually beneficial options often becomes easier. When negotiators overcome communication barriers, identifying win-win solutions—mutually beneficial solutions in which both parties gain—becomes easier. For instance, based on their different perspectives, a seller from one culture may no longer want to keep a particular business, whereas a buyer from another culture may find the business an especially attractive prospect.

In negotiations between Americans and Japanese, American owners generally concern themselves more with the viability of an enterprise—with its predicted future cash flow. Japanese buyers, on the other hand, generally show more interest in market share and in the property and physical plant. A Japanese buyer may find an enterprise particularly valuable for one set of reasons, whereas the American owner may place it on the market for an entirely different set of reasons. As another example, Vietnamese, with their high unemployment and low wage rates, may find producing labor-intensive products a more attractive prospect than do Swiss manufacturers who face high wage rates and negligible unemployment. Differences, rather than similarities, form the basis of mutually beneficial solutions. The chances of substantial areas of difference, and therefore substantial areas for mutual gain, generally increase in multicultural situations.

In some cases negotiators go beyond mutually beneficial agreements to create synergistic solutions. Whereas mutually beneficial agreements focus on comparative advantage—the exchange of items more highly valued by one party than the other—synergy uses differences as a resource in creating new solutions that would never have become possible without those differences. Differences, the source of cross-cultural communication complexities and problems, ultimately become the primary resource in creating mutually beneficial, synergistic solutions (see Chapter 4).

SUCCESSFUL NEGOTIATIONS: PEOPLE, SITUATION, AND PROCESS

Research has shown that each of the three areas on which the success of a negotiation is based—individual characteristics, situational contingencies, and strategic and tactical processes—vary considerably across cultures (13;15;16;21). Although all three are important, negotiators have most control over the process—the strategy and tactics. Negotiators can influence the success or failure of a negotiation most directly by managing the negotiating process. This chapter discusses each of the three areas, highlights cultural variations, and recommends the most effective approaches. Effective negotiators base their strategy and tactics on the characteristics of the situation and the people involved. Although global managers would find it easier if there was one best way to negotiate, no such consistency nor any guaranteed formula for success exists.

Qualities of a Good Negotiator

What are the qualities of a good negotiator? According to John Graham's extensive research (16), the answer depends on the culture of the person you ask. As shown in Table 7-3, American managers believe that effective negotiators are highly rational. Brazilian managers, to the surprise of many Americans, hold almost identical perceptions and differ only in replacing integrity with competitiveness as one of the seven most important qualities. By contrast, the Japanese differ quite markedly from both Americans and Brazilians. They stress an interpersonal, rather than a rational, negotiating style. Japanese differ from Americans in stressing both verbal expressiveness and listening ability, whereas Americans only emphasize verbal ability. In contrast to Americans, Brazilians, Japanese, and Chinese managers in Taiwan emphasize negotiators' rational skills and, to a lesser extent, their interpersonal skills. To the Chinese, a negotiator must be an interesting person and should show persistence and determination, the ability to win respect and confidence, preparation and planning skills, demonstrated product knowledge, good judgment, and intelligence.

The role that individual qualities play varies across cultures. According to Graham's research (16), favorable outcomes are most strongly influenced by the negotiator's own characteristics in Brazil, the opponent's characteristics in the United States, the role in Japan (the buyer always does better), and a mixture of the negotiators' and their counterparts' characteristics in Taiwan. Specifically, Brazilian negotiators achieve higher profits when they act more deceptively and in their own self-interest, when they express higher self-esteem, and when their bargaining partners are more honest. American negotiators do better when their counterparts are honest, not self-interested, introverted, not particularly interesting as people, and made to feel uncomfortable by the negotiators' actions. By contrast, Japanese buyers always do better than sellers. Both Japanese buyers and sellers can improve their positions by making their bargaining

TABLE 7-3 *Key Individual Characteristics of Negotiators*

American Negotiators	Japanese Negotiators	Chinese (Taiwan) Negotiators	Brazilian Negotiators
Preparation and planning skill	Dedication to job	Persistence and determination	Preparation and planning skill
Thinking under pressure	Perceive and exploit power	Win respect and confidence	Thinking under pressure
Judgment and intelligence	Win respect and confidence	Preparation and planning skill	Judgment and intelligence
Verbal expressiveness	Integrity	Product knowledge	Verbal expressiveness
Product knowledge	Demonstrate listening skill	Interesting	Product knowledge
Perceive and exploit power	Broad perspective	Judgment and intelligence	Perceive and exploit power
Integrity	Verbal expressiveness		Competitiveness

Source: Professor John Graham, School of Management, University of California at Irvine.

partners feel more comfortable. In Taiwan negotiators do better when they act deceptively and when their counterparts are neither self-interested nor have particularly attractive personalities.

Buyer/Seller Relationship

The hierarchial relationship between buyers and sellers is crucial in understanding how negotiating styles differ across cultures (17). For example, as shown in Figure 7-2, Japanese buyers and sellers have a vertical, hierarchical relationship: buyers generally get most of what they ask for. However, sellers expect buyers to take care of them. When the Japanese explain this system to Americans, the Americans frequently ask, "But won't the seller get taken?" The answer is no, because in Japan management takes care of workers, government takes care of industry, and buyers take care of sellers. *Amae*—indulgent dependence—explains the buyer/seller relationship in Japan.

By contrast, buyers and sellers in the United States have a less hierarchical, more equal, relationship. The American norm is not *amae*, but rather independent competition: "May the best person win." Buyers do not expect to take care of sellers, they expect to take care of themselves by getting the best deal possible for their company.

Predictably, problems arise when Japanese and American buyers and sellers negotiate with each other (24:28–29). From the American perspective, being a buyer in Japan is extremely advantageous. According to some Japanese, "Americans ask for the moon!" Many Japanese, in describing their initial negotiations with Americans, say, "When we first went to the United States, we took a beating. As sellers, we gave the American buyers everything they wanted." But because they were working under a different set of expectations, the Americans did not then "take care of" the Japanese sellers. The Japanese thought the Americans took advantage of them, while the Americans believed they had merely driven a hard bargain.

In the reverse situation, American sellers, not trusting Japanese buyers to take care of them, act as equals. They thus fail to behave with appropriate deference; the Japanese, therefore, perceive them as arrogant. All too frequently, negotiations collapse as a result. Unfortunately, both sides tend to attribute the collapse to unacceptable product or service qualities and price, rather than to the actual cause—cross-cultural differences.

When negotiators bargain with people from many cultures, the most important individual characteristics are good listening skills, an orientation toward people, a willingness to use team assistance, high self-esteem, high aspirations, and an attractive personality, along with credibility and influence within the home organization (22). These individual characteristics, although significant, are not the most important factors determining negotiated outcomes. It is therefore unfortunate that many companies emphasize individual characteristics in selecting members of their negotiating teams rather than training those selected to understand and more skillfully manage the negotiation process.

FIGURE 7-2 *Buyer/Seller Relationship*

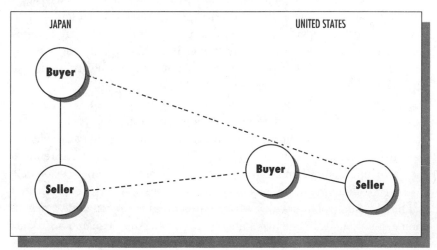

Negotiation Contingencies: Characteristics of the Situation

Situations in which negotiators find themselves vary widely. Effective negotiators recognize and manage the impact of each situational factor on the bargaining process from both their own and their opponents' cultural perspectives. In preparing for global negotiations, they imagine what the situation might look like through the eyes of the other countries' teams: What do they want? What is important to them? Who has power? What is at stake? What is their time frame? Where do they draw their personal and organizational bottom line? Situational contingencies influence success just as individual characteristics do, but they are rarely as critical to success as the strategy and tactics used.

Location

Should you meet at their office, your office, or at a neutral location? Negotiation wisdom generally advises teams to meet at their own or a neutral location. Meeting in another country disadvantages negotiators because it reduces their access to information and increases travel-related stress and cost. Meeting at home allows a team to control the situation more easily. For example, a division of Caterpillar of California increased its control over negotiations by taking international clients out on their yacht. They gained the advantage of removing the client from phones, interruptions, and distractions while severely limiting their access to information.

Many negotiators select neutral locations. Business entertainment has become a common type of neutral location, used primarily to get to know and improve relations with members of the opposing team. Heavy users of business entertainment, the Japanese spend almost two percent of their GNP on entertaining clients—even more than they spend on national defense (1.5%). Americans generally consider this high business entertainment cost absurd, but perhaps Americans' extraordinarily high legal expenses reflect the cost of insufficient relationship building.

In choosing neutral locations, business negotiators often select resorts located geographically somewhere between the bargaining partners. For example, Asian and North American bargainers have traditionally selected Hawaii for business meetings; both sides travel, both sides have reduced access to information, and consequently the incentive increases for both sides to conclude the negotiation as quickly as possible. The cost of travel and hotels usually, but not always, increases pressure to conclude a negotiation expeditiously. In one negotiation between an American and a Russian company, negotiators conducted the sessions at a resort in the south of France. The Russian bargainers made it clear that they did not want to end their "vacation" early by concluding the negotiation prematurely.

Physical Arrangements

In traditional American negotiations, the two teams face each other, often sitting on opposite sides of a boardroom table. Unfortunately, this arrangement maximizes competition. Sitting at right angles, on the other hand, facilitates cooperation. If negotiators view the process as a collaborative search for mutually beneficial outcomes (win-win solutions), the physical arrangements should support cooperation, not competition. As an alternative to the boardroom table, negotiators from both teams may choose to sit on the same side of the table, "facing the problem" (14). In this way they compete with the problem, not with the people. The Japanese, in posting all information related to a negotiation on the walls, structure the environment so that all parties involved "face the problem" holistically.

Participants

Who should attend the formal negotiating sessions? Americans tend to want to "go it alone"—they consider extra team members an unnecessary expense. This strategy is ineffective in global negotiations, where more tends to be better. Why? First, the physical presence of more people communicates greater power and importance—an essential nonverbal message. Second, as discussed earlier, communicating cross-culturally is complex and difficult. Having some team members primarily responsible for listening to conversations and observing nonverbal cues and other members primarily responsible for conducting substantive discussions has proven to be an extremely effective strategy.

The number of teams and audiences present at a negotiation varies. Should the press be present? Will public opinion make it easier or more difficult to develop mutually beneficial solutions? Should the union have direct representation? Should bargainers keep government agencies informed during the negotiation or only present them with the final agreement? The power that government, unions, and public opinion have over business negotiators varies considerably across cultures. For example, negotiating with government officials from such open democracies as Australia, Canada, and New Zealand requires broader public debate than is generally necessary in the more tightly controlled governments of South Korea and Iran, or in communist countries such as North Korea, Cuba, and Albania. Effective global negotiators carefully manage access to the proceedings.

Time Limits

The duration of a negotiation can vary markedly across cultures. Americans, being particularly impatient, often expect negotiations to take a minimum amount of time. During the Paris Peace Talks, designed to negotiate an end to the Vietnam War, the American team arrived in Paris and made hotel reservations for a week. Their Vietnamese counterparts leased a château for a year. As the negotiations proceeded, the frustrated Americans were forced to continually renew their weekly reservations to accommodate the more measured pace of the Vietnamese.

Negotiators generally make more concessions as their deadline approaches. Americans' sense of urgency puts them at a disadvantage with respect to their less hurried bargaining partners. Negotiators from other countries often recognize Americans' time consciousness, achievement orientation, and impatience. They know that Americans will make more concessions close to their deadline (time consciousness) in order to get a signed contract (achievement orientation). For example, one Brazilian company invited a group of Americans to Brazil to negotiate a contract the week before Christmas. The Brazilians, knowing that the Americans would want to return to the United States by Christmas with a signed contract, knew that they could push hard for concessions and an early agreement. The final agreement definitely favored the Brazilians.

Some negotiators attempt to discover their opponents' deadline and refuse to make major concessions until after that deadline has passed. The local team may determine their opponents' deadlines by checking hotel reservations or politely offering to reconfirm return airline tickets. Effective global negotiators determine the best alternative to not meeting their deadline. If they find the best alternative acceptable, they may choose a less hurried pace than they had originally planned or than they typically use at home.

Status Differences

The United States prides itself on its egalitarian, informal approach to life, in which titles do not seem particularly important and ceremonies are often considered a waste of time. American team members often minimize status differences during negotiations: for example, they will use first names to promote equality and informality. Unfortunately this approach, which succeeds at putting Americans at ease, often makes people from other cultures uncomfortable. Most countries are more hierarchical and more formal than the United States, and most negotiators from these countries feel more comfortable in formal situations with explicit status differences. The Japanese, for example, must know the other person's company and position before being able to select the grammatically correct form of address. For this reason, the Japanese always exchange business cards—*meishi*—before a business conversation begins. In Germany negotiators would almost never address colleagues on their own team, let alone those from the other team, by first name. Such informality would severely insult their sense of propriety, hierarchy, and respect.

Age, like title, connotes seniority and demands respect in most countries of the world. Sending a young, albeit brilliant, North American expert to Indonesia to lead a negotiating team is more likely to insult senior Indonesian officials than facilitate a successful exchange of technical information. In almost all cases, North Americans need to increase formality in dress, vocabulary, behavior, and style when working outside of the United States.

NEGOTIATION PROCESS

Process is the single most important factor predicting the success or failure of a negotiation. An effective process includes managing the negotiation's overall strategy or approach, its stages, and the specific tactics used. As with other aspects of negotiating, process varies markedly across cultures (25;31;45;51;60). An effective strategy reflects the situational characteristics and personal backgrounds of the negotiators involved. It balances the position, procedure, timing, and roles of the negotiating partners.

Negotiation Strategy: A Culturally Synergistic Approach

In *Getting to Yes*, based on the work of the Harvard International Negotiation Project, Fisher and Ury (14) propose a principled approach to negotiating. As shown in Table 7-4, this approach involves four steps:

1. Separating the people from the problem
2. Focusing on interests, not on positions
3. Insisting on objective criteria (and never yielding to pressure)
4. Inventing options for mutual gain

Does this principled approach become easier or harder when negotiating globally? Let us analyze the principled approach from a cross-cultural perspective. Cultural differences make communication more difficult. Steps 1, 2, and 3 therefore become more difficult: understanding opponents, their inter-

TABLE 7-4   *Three Approaches to Each Stage of an*
International Negotiation

Traditional Approach (Competitive)	Principled Approach (Collaborative/Individual)	Synergistic Approach (Collaborative/Cultural)
Preparation • Define economic issues	**Preparation** • Define interests	**Preparation** • Cross-Cultural training • Define interests
Relationship Building • Assess counterpart	**Relationship Building** • Separate the people from the problem	**Relationship Building** • Separate the people from the problem • Adjust to their style and pace
Information Exchange • Exchange task-related information • Clarify positions	**Information Exchange** • Exchange task- and participant-related information • Clarify interests	**Information Exchange** • Exchange task- and participant-related information • Clarify interests and customary approaches
Persuasion	**Inventing Options for Mutual Gain**	**Inventing Options for Mutual Gain Appropriate to Both Cultures**
Concessions	**Choice of Best Option** • Insist on using objective criteria • Never yield to pressure	**Choice of Best Option** • Insist on using criteria appropriate to both cultures
Agreement	**Agreement**	**Agreement** • Translate and back-translate agreement • If necessary, renegotiate

Source: The traditional approach is based on John L. Graham and Roy A. Herberger, Jr., "Negotiators Abroad—Don't Shoot from the Hip," *Harvard Business Review*, vol. 61, no. 4 (1983), pp. 160–168. The principled approach is based on Roger Fisher and William Ury, *Getting to Yes* (Boston: Houghton Mifflin Company and Penguin Books, 1981). The synergistic approach is based on Nancy J. Adler (see Chapter 4). The table is adapted from the work of Dr. George Renwick (unpublished).

ests, and their assessment criteria becomes more complex and fraught with cross-cultural communication pitfalls. By contrast, step 4 can become easier. Inventing options for mutual gain requires recognizing and using differences. The fewer the identical items sought by each negotiating team, the greater the chances of simultaneously satisfying all teams' needs. If cross-cultural differences are recognized, clearly communicated, and understood (steps 1, 2, and 3), they can become the very basis for constructing win-win solutions. For example, Western European countries that import Indonesian batiks exchange an economically developed market for a labor-intensive good. The Europeans could not afford to make batiks in Europe, and the Indonesians could not command the price in stable currencies within their own country. This culturally synergistic approach, which uses cultural differences as a resource rather than a hindrance to organizational functioning, allows global negotiators to maximize benefits to all parties. Each step in the principled approach will be discussed as it relates to the four stages of the negotiating process.

Stages of a Negotiation

To prepare for an initial meeting, effective negotiators analyze the situation in terms of their own and their counterparts' needs, goals, and underlying cultural values, determine the limits to their authority, assess power positions and relationships, identify facts to be confirmed, set an agenda, establish overall and alternative concession strategies, and make team assignments. They also determine their *best alternative to a negotiated solution* (14); that is, the most favorable outcome in the event that they fail to reach agreement. This best alternative to a negotiated solution, unlike a conventional *bottom line*, protects negotiators "from accepting terms that are too unfavorable and from rejecting terms it would be in . . . [their] interest to accept (14:104)."

Planning

The Huthwaite Research Group conducted a study in the United Kingdom on the behavior of successful negotiators (43). The researchers interviewed and observed 48 successful negotiators in a total of 102 negotiations. Negotiators were not considered successful unless they were rated as effective by both sides, had a track record of significant success, and had a low incidence of implementation failure. As highlighted in Table 7-5, successful negotiators' planning behavior differed in the following ways from that of their less skilled colleagues (43):

- *Planning time.* Both skilled and average negotiators use about the same amount of time for planning. Evidently "it is not the amount of planning time that makes the difference, but how the time is used" (43).

- *Exploring options.* Skilled negotiators consider twice as wide a range of action options and outcomes as do their less skilled colleagues. The greater the number of options, the greater the chances for success.

- *Establishing common ground.* Although all negotiators focus more on areas of conflict than of agreement, skilled negotiators spend over three times as much attention on common ground.

- *Focusing on long- versus short-term.* All negotiators spend the vast majority of their time on short-term issues. However, skilled negotiators spend more than twice as much time on long-term issues.

- *Setting limits.* Average negotiators set single point objectives, such as requesting $7 per unit. Skilled negotiators set range objectives, such as requesting $5 to $10 per unit. Setting ranges gives skilled negotiators more bargaining flexibility.

TABLE 7-5 *How Successful Negotiators Plan*

Planning Behavior	Skilled Negotiators	Average Negotiators
Planning Time Overall time spent planning	No significant difference	No significant difference
Exploration of Options Number of options and outcomes considered per issue	5.1	2.6
Common Ground Percentage of comments about areas of anticipated common ground	38%	11%
Long Term Percentage of comments about long-term considerations of issues	8.5%	4%
Planned Order: Issues versus Sequences Average use of sequences during planning per session	Issues 2.1	Sequences 4.9
Setting Limits	Range	Fixed-point

Source: Neil Rackham, "The Behavior of Successful Negotiators" (Reston, Va.: Huthwaite Research Group, 1976), as reported in Ellen Raider International, Inc. (Brooklyn, N.Y.), and Situation Management Systems, Inc. (Plymouth, Mass.), *International Negotiations: A Training Program for Corporate Executives and Diplomats* (1982).

- *Using sequence versus issue planning.* Average negotiators use sequence planning. They plan to discuss point A, then point B, then point C, and so on. Skilled negotiators, by contrast, use issue planning—they discuss each issue independently, without any predetermined sequence or order of issues.

Following the preparation, formal negotiations proceed roughly through four stages (18;22):

1. Interpersonal relationship building (learning about the people)
2. Exchanging task-related information (learning about the economic, legal, technical, and logistical issues)
3. Persuading
4. Making concessions and agreements

Countries vary in the emphasis placed on each phase and the style used to approach it. As shown in Table 7-4, effective bargainers can approach each stage of the negotiation through principled strategies: to build interpersonal relationships, principled negotiators separate the people from the problem; to exchange task-related information, principled negotiators focus on interests, not on positions; to effectively persuade the other team, principled negotiators invent options for mutual gain, rather than relying on preconceived positions and high pressure "dirty tricks;" and to make appropriate concessions and reach agreement, principled negotiators insist on using objective decision criteria.

Interpersonal Relationship Building

The first phase of a face-to-face negotiation involves getting to know the other people and helping them to feel comfortable. During relationship building, parties develop respect and trust for members of the other team. In every negotiation, there is the relationship (you and them) and the substance (what you and they want). *Nontask sounding* begins the relationship-building process of discovering general areas of similarity and difference in both the relationship and the substance. Similarities become the basis for personal relationships and trust; differences, the basis for mutual exchange. The strategy of separating the people from the problem implies that negotiators can reject their partners' suggestions without rejecting the people themselves, that they can disagree with their counterparts' analysis without labeling them negatively, and that they can enjoy and trust their counterparts as individuals while rejecting their proposals.

Being particularly task- and efficiency-oriented, Americans usually see little need to "waste time" on getting to know people in nontask-related conversations. Americans want to "get down to business"—to discussing and agreeing on task-related issues—almost immediately, often after only five to ten minutes. The United States' legal system also supports a task-oriented approach. Americans base their transactions on written contracts. Businesspeople in the United States trust the legal system to enforce written agreements (contracts) once all parties involved have signed them. Americans consequently focus on signing contracts rather than developing meaningful relationships with members of the other teams. The American approach and legal system, however, is not replicated in most countries. Many areas of the world have neither strong nor consistently dependable legal systems to enforce contracts. Enforcement mechanisms are personal. People keep commitments to people, not to contracts. People honor contracts if they like and respect the people with whom they are conducting business. They emphasize the relationship, not the written agreement.

Americans need to emphasize building relationships with their global partners. They need to discuss topics other than business, including the arts, history, culture, and current economic conditions of the countries involved. Effective negotiators view luncheon, dinner, reception, ceremony, and tour invitations as times for interpersonal relationship building and therefore as key to the negotiating process. When American negotiators, often frustrated by the seemingly endless formalities, ceremonies, and "small talk," ask how long they must wait before beginning to "do business," the answer is simple: wait until your counterparts bring up business (and they will). Realize that the work of conducting a successful negotiation has already begun, even if business has yet to be mentioned.

Exchanging Task-Related Information

The substance of a negotiation is interests: yours and theirs. Negotiators should therefore focus on presenting their situation and needs, and on understanding their counterparts' situation and needs. Presenting interests—a situation and needs—is not the same as stating a position. A position articulates only one solution for a particular situation from one party's perspective (usually the solution prepared prior to the negotiation). Stating positions limits the ways in which your interests (and by implication, your counterparts' interests) can be met. For example, if, based on an analysis of personal needs (housing, clothing, food, transportation, health care, and entertainment), I tell my employer that I must have a minimum foreign service salary of $100,000 (a position) and she refuses to go above $85,000, we quickly arrive at an impasse. My employer finds my one solution to my needs—$100,000—unacceptable. If, on the other hand, I present my situation and needs, my employer may offer me $85,000 plus company-paid medical insurance, company-owned housing, and use of a company car. Would this offer meet my needs? Perhaps. Would it meet my initial position? No. Focusing on interests rather than positions allows both sides to draw on the widest possible range of mutually agreeable solutions.

In negotiating, cross-cultural miscommunication causes numerous problems. For example, the Iranians' misinterpretation of a bargaining offer presented in English made the Iranian hostage crisis more difficult to resolve:

> In Persian, the word *compromise* apparently lacks the positive meaning it has in English (a "midway solution both sides can live with") and has only a negative meaning ("her virtue was compromised" or "our integrity was compromised"). Similarly, the word *mediator* in Persian suggests "meddler," someone who is barging in uninvited. In early 1980, United Nations Secretary General Waldheim flew to Iran to deal with the hostage question. His efforts were seriously set back when Iranian national radio and television broadcast in Persian a remark he reportedly made on his arrival in Tehran: "I have come as a mediator to work out a compromise." Within an hour of the broadcast, his car was being stoned by angry Iranians (14:34).

A clear understanding of the interests of negotiators from other cultures is difficult. There may be verbal and nonverbal barriers. Misperception, misinterpretation, and misevaluation pervade cross-cultural situations. To begin to understand, effective negotiators try to see the situation from both their own and the other parties' perspectives. Many negotiators use role reversal: they prepare for the negotiation as if they were the other party. This role reversal exercise forces them to appreciate the situation and issues from the other negotiating team's point of view.

Persuading

In principled, synergistic negotiations, bargainers emphasize creating mutually beneficial options, whereas more traditional negotiators often emphasize persuading the other party to accept a particular option. For global negotiators, creating mutually beneficial options is particularly important. (The more common methods of persuasion used both domestically and internationally are reviewed under negotiating tactics.)

In a successful negotiation each party's interests and needs are recognized and satisfied, and therefore all parties win. Effective synergistic negotiators view their counterparts' interests and needs as a part of their own problem. Mutually beneficial options derive from (a) understanding each party's real interests, values, and needs, (b) identifying areas of similarity and difference, and (c) creating new options based primarily on the differences between the parties. Identifying interests more highly valued by one party than the other and using those differences as a resource underlies the creation of mutually beneficial options.

In cross-cultural negotiations, the possibilities for inventing mutually beneficial options exceed those in single-culture situations due to the inherent differences among the parties. For example, if a company tells its employees that they cannot all take their vacations at the same time, management will probably have a problem in selecting who will receive time off during the holiday season. If all employees are Christian, most will want a vacation during Christmas week. If some employees are Christian and others Jewish, some will be happiest with a vacation Christmas week and others with the week of Hanukkah (which rarely coincides with Christmas). Cross-cultural differences, when recognized, facilitate mutually beneficial solutions that are impossible when all employees share similar cultural and religious backgrounds.

Making Concessions and Reaching Agreement

In this fourth stage, principled negotiators insist on using objective criteria in deciding how to make concessions and to reach agreement, rather
than resorting to a series of dirty tricks. Although numerous high-pres-
sure tactics exist, such tactics diminish both the relationships and the
possibility of developing synergistic solutions. (Specific tactics to avoid
will be discussed later.)

Concessions, large or small, can be made at any time during a negotiation. Although the research is not definitive, it appears that negotiators who
make early concessions disadvantage themselves in comparison with those
making fewer concessions primarily at the end of the bargaining sessions
(44). Americans generally negotiate sequentially: they discuss and attempt
to agree on one issue at a time. Throughout the bargaining process,
Americans make many small concessions, which they expect their counterparts to reciprocate; then they finalize the list of concessions into an overall agreement. In some ways, making small concessions reflects
Americans' task-oriented form of relationship building. Negotiators from
many other cultures, unlike most Americans, discuss all issues prior to
making any concessions. These negotiators view concessions as relative
and make them only as they reach a final agreement. This holistic approach
to negotiating is particularly evident in Asia.

Similar to many Asians, most Russian negotiators make very few, if
any, concessions during a negotiation and rarely reciprocate the other
party's concessions. Unlike many of their colleagues, Russian negotiators
generally view concessions as signs of weakness, not as gestures of good-
will, flexibility, or trust. For example, in the seven rounds of postwar
negotiations between the former Soviet and U.S. governments, the United
States made 82 percent of its concessions in the first round, considerably
more than did the Russians (29). Mikhail Gorbachev's and Boris Yeltsin's
styles in implementing political change in the Soviet Union highlight the
Russian approach to negotiation.

No single approach to concessions has proven to succeed more consistently than has any other in global negotiations. Effective global negotiators respect their own and their counterparts' domestic styles, and when
appropriate, adjust accordingly. The following story highlights differences in whom Malaysians and Americans select to negotiate and how
negotiators from these two very different cultures perform.

Contrasting Styles:
MALAYS NEGOTIATING WITH AMERICANS

Americans' patterns of negotiation differ depending on the context. Government officials working out a treaty, for example, negotiate somewhat differently from business executives "hammering out" a contract. The pattern portrayed here is more akin to that of the business executive.

American businesspeople usually begin a series of negotiating sessions in a cordial manner, but they are intent upon "getting things under way." They are very clear as to what they and their company want, when they want it, and how they will go about getting it; they have planned their strategy carefully. And they have done what they could to "psych out" their counterparts with whom they will be negotiating.

From the outset, American negotiators urge everyone to "dispense with the formalities" and get on with the business at hand. As soon as possible they express their determination, saying something like, "O.K., let's get down to brass tacks."

Americans usually state their position (at least their first position) early and definitively. They plan before long to "really get down to the nitty gritty." They want to "zero in" on the knotty problems and get to the point where "the rubber meets the road" (the point, that is, where "the action" begins). Once the negotiations are "really rolling," Americans usually deal directly with obstacles as they come up, trying to clear them away in quick order, and becoming impatient and frustrated if they cannot.

Most of what Americans want to convey, of course, they put into words: spoken words—often many of them.

Their approach, therefore, is highly verbal and quite visible—and thoroughly planned. They have outlined their alternatives ahead of time and prepared their counterproposals, contingencies, back-up positions, bluffs, guarantees, and tests of compliance; all carefully calculated, and including, of course, lots of numbers. Toward the end, they see that some bail-out provisions are included, but they usually don't worry too much about them; making and meeting business commitments "on schedule" is what their lives are all about— they are not too concerned about getting out of the contract. If they have to get out, then they have to, and they will find a way when the time comes.

Americans experience real satisfaction when all the problems have been "worked out," especially if they have been able to get provisions very favorable to their company—and to their own reputation as "tough negotiators." They rest securely when everything is "down in black and white" and the contract is initialed or signed.

Afterwards, Americans enjoy themselves; they relax "over some drinks" and carry on some "small talk" and "joke around" with their team and their counterparts.

Malay patterns of negotiation, as might be expected, differ considerably. When they are buying something, Malays bargain with the merchant; and when they are working, they socialize with their boss and co-workers. Their purpose is to develop some sense of relationship with the other person. The relationship then provides the basis, or context, for the exchange. Malays take the same patterns and preferences into their business-negotiating sessions. When all is said and done, it is not the piece of paper they trust, it is the people—and their relationships with the people.

Malay negotiators begin to develop the context for negotiations through the interaction routines appropriate to this and similar occasions. These routines are as complicated and subtle as customary American routines; they are cordial but quite formal. Like Americans using their own routines, Malays understand the Malay routines but are seldom consciously aware of them. Neither Malays nor Americans understand very clearly the routines of the other.

As the preliminary context is formed, it is important to Malays that the proper forms of address be known beforehand and used, and that a variety of topics be talked about that are unrelated to the business to be transacted. This may continue for quite a while. Malay negotiators want their counterparts to participate comfortably, patiently, and with interest. As in other interaction, it is not the particular words spoken which are of most importance to Malays; rather they listen primarily to the attitudes which the words convey—attitudes toward the Malays themselves and toward the matter being negotiated. Attitudes are important to the relationship. At this point and throughout the negotiations, Malays are concerned as much about the quality of the relationship as the quantity of the work accomplished. Motivation is more important to Malays than momentum.

Malay negotiators, as in other situations, are also aware of feelings—their own and those of their counterparts, and the effects of the exchanges upon both. They are also aware of, and concerned about, how they look in the eyes of their team, how their counterparts look in the eyes of the other team, and how both they and their counterparts will look after the negotiations in the eyes of their respective superiors.

Malays are alert to style, both their own and that of their counterparts. Displaying manners is more important than scoring points. The way one negotiates is as important as what one negotiates. Grace and finesse show respect for the other and for the matter under consideration. Negotiating, like other interaction, is something of an art form. Balance and restraint are therefore essential.

The agenda which Malays work through in the course of the negotiation is usually quite flexible. Their strategy is usually rather simple. Their positions are expressed in more general terms than Americans', but no less strongly held. Their proposals are more offered than argued; they are offered to the other party rather than argued with them.   Malays do not enjoy sparring. They deeply dislike combat.

In response to a strong assertion, Malay negotiators usually express their respect directly by replying indirectly. The stronger the assertion and the more direct the demands, the more indirect the reply—at least the verbal reply.

Malays and their teams usually formulate their positions gradually and carefully. By the time they present their position, they usually have quite a lot of themselves invested in it. Directly rejecting the position, therefore, is sometimes felt to be a rejection of the people. Negotiating for Malays is not quite the game that it is for some Americans.

If Malays and their team have arrived at a position from which they and those whom they represent cannot move, they will not move. If this requires a concession from their counterparts, Malays will not try to force the concession. If the counterparts see that a concession from them is necessary, and make it, Malays, as polite and considerate people, recognize the move and respect the people who made it. A concession, therefore, is not usually considered by the Malay team to be a sign that they can press harder and extract further concessions. Instead, a concession by either side is considered as evidence of strength and a basis for subsequent reconciliation and cooperation.

What about getting out of a contract? Making and meeting business commitments is not what Malays' lives are all about. They have other, often prior, commitments. They therefore enter into contracts cautiously and prefer to have an exit provided.

In addition, Malays are less certain of their control over the future (even their control of their own country) than are Americans. Therefore, promising specific kinds of performance in the future by specific dates in a contract, especially in a long-term contract where the stakes are high, is often difficult for Malays. It is even more difficult, of course, if they are not certain whether they can trust the people to whom they are making the commitment and from whom they are accepting commitments. Malays therefore give a great deal of thought to a contract and to the contracting party before signing it. And they become uneasy if provisions have not been made for a respectable withdrawal should future circumstances make their compliance impossible.[1]

NEGOTIATION TACTICS

Negotiation includes both verbal and nonverbal tactics. Whereas most Americans consider verbal tactics most important, many people from other countries do not agree. According to one study, words communicate only 7 percent of meaning, with tone of voice communicating 38 percent and facial expression 55 percent (38). Both verbal and nonverbal behavior can cause problems cross-culturally. According to global negotiations experts, "It's hard to read the writing on the wall if you don't know the language, much less where to find the wall (43:3.18)." In the following section, we will review some of the most common verbal and nonverbal negotiating tactics. Several "dirty tricks" are outlined, which, although common, do not particularly help in arriving at mutually beneficial agreements.

Verbal Tactics

Negotiators use many verbal tactics. Research (18) has shown that negotiators do better—their profits increase—as: (a) the number of questions asked increases; (b) the number of commitments made prior to the final agreement stage decreases; and (c) the amount of the initial request increases—that is, sellers ask for more and buyers offer less. Consequently, in most cultures, effective negotiators start by having high expectations and making high initial offers (or requests), proceed by asking a lot of questions, and refrain from making very many commitments until the final stage of the negotiation.

Initial Offers

The Chinese (36;42) and Russians (27) habitually use extreme initial offers and requests as their opening bargaining strategy. By contrast, Swedes initially request a price very close to the one they expect to get. Americans, negotiating domestically, consistently reach higher and more satisfactory outcomes using extreme rather than moderate opening offers (44). Other research also suggests that bargainers starting with extreme positions have a higher probability of reaching an agreement (34).

Why do extreme initial positions help? Although not yet thoroughly researched in cross-cultural contexts, some observers believe that an extreme position: (a) demonstrates to counterparts that the negotiator will not be exploited (44), (b) allows the negotiator to gain more than expected, (c) prolongs the negotiating process and thus allows negotiators to gain more information about their counterparts, (d) modifies counterparts' beliefs about the negotiator's preferences, (e) allows more room to make subsequent concessions and thus exhibit cooperation, and (f) communicates the negotiator's willingness to play the game according to "usual" norms (59:727). Exceptions to the advantages of high initial offers also exist. For example, Japanese diplomats who make extreme opening offers in global negotiations often have them treated as phony by the other team (1). More importantly, extreme offers appear to discourage synergistic agreements. The following news report highlights the contrasting expectations of American and Japanese negotiators.

NEGOTIATING FOR OLYMPIC COVERAGE

The Olympic Committee for the Los Angeles Olympics negotiated television broadcasting rights with various countries. From the American Broadcasting Company (ABC), the Olympic Committee received $225 million. From the Japanese, the Committee received $18.5 million. Why did the Japanese pay so much less?

The Japanese originally offered $6 million for the rights and the Olympic Committee countered with $90 million. The Committee's goal was $10 million. The Japanese argued that theirs was a smaller market than that of the United States. Moreover, the Japanese had only one Japanese television station bidding, whereas the Americans had the three major networks bidding up the price (ABC, CBS, and NBC). High expectations (for a low price), convincing arguments (smaller market), and little competition resulted in a final cost to the Japanese network that was twelve times lower than that of their American counterparts.[2]

Range of Tactics

Some of the more common tactics used in negotiating include promises, threats, recommendations, warnings, rewards, punishments, normative appeals, commitments, self-disclosure, questions, and commands. Table 7-6 describes each briefly. The use and meaning of many of these tactics vary across cultures. As shown in Table 7-7, negotiators from Asia (Japanese), North America (Americans), and South America (Brazilians) use different verbal tactics in negotiating (20). For example, Brazilians say no nine times more frequently than do Americans, and almost fifteen times more frequently than do the Japanese. Similarly, Brazilians make more initial concessions than do Americans, who in turn make more than the Japanese (20).

TABLE 7-6 *Verbal Negotiating Tactics*

Tactic	Description	Example
Promise	I will do something you want me to do, if you do something I want you to do. *(conditional, positive)*	I will lower the price by $5 if you increase the order by 100 units.
Threat	I will do something you don't want me to do, if you do something I don't want you to do. *(conditional, negative)*	I'll walk out of the negotiation if you leak this story to the press.
Recommendation	If you do something I want you to do, a third party will do something you want. *(third party positive)*	If you lower your price, all of the teenagers will be able to buy your product.
Warning	If you do something I don't want you to do, a third party will do something you don't want. *(third party negative)*	If you don't settle, the press will spill this whole sordid story on the front page of every newspaper in the country.
Reward	I will give you something positive (something you want) now, on the spot. *(unconditional, positive)*	Let's make it easier on you tomorrow and meet closer to your office. I have really appreciated your willingness to meet at my building.
Punishment	I will give you something negative (something you don't want) now, on the spot. *(unconditional, negative)*	I refuse to listen to your screaming. I am leaving.
Normative Appeal	I appeal to a societal norm.	Everybody else buys our product for $5 per unit.
Commitment	I will do something you want. *(unconditional, positive)*	I will deliver 100 units by June 15.
Self-Disclosure	I will tell you something about myself.	We have had to lay off 100 employees this month. We really need to sign a major contract by the end of the year.
Question	I ask you something about yourself.	Can you tell me more about your Brazilian operation?
Command	I order you to do something.	Lower your price. (or) We are going to talk about delivery now.

The British Huthwaite study, documenting successful negotiators' behavior, analyzed the verbal behavior of skilled and average negotiators (43:6.6–6.13). As shown in Table 7-8, the most skillful British negotiators use fewer irritators, counterproposals, and defend/attack spirals, less argument dilution, and more behavioral labels, active listening, questions, and feeling commentaries. Each of these negotiating tactics is described briefly on pages 216 and 217 (43).

TABLE 7-7 *Cross-Cultural Differences in Verbal Negotiating Behaviors*

Behavior (Tactic)	Average Number of Times Tactic Was Used in Half Hour Negotiating Sessions		
	Japan	United States	Brazil
Promise	7	8	3
Threat	4	4	2
Recommendation	7	4	5
Warning	2	1	1
Reward	1	2	2
Punishment	1	3	3
Normative appeal	4	2	1
Commitment	15	13	8
Self-disclosure	34	36	39
Question	20	20	22
Command	8	6	14
No's (per 30 minutes)	5.7	9.0	83.4
Profit level of first offers (80 max.)	61.5	57.3	75.2
Initial concessions	6.5	7.1	9.4

Source: Based on John Graham, "The Influence of Culture on Business Negotiations," Table 1 and 3, *Journal of International Business Studies*, vol. 16, no. 1 (1985), pp. 81–96.

TABLE 7-8 *How Successful Negotiators Negotiate*

Negotiating Behavior	Skilled Negotiators	Average Negotiators
Use of ***irritators*** per hour of face-to-face negotiating time	2.3	10.8
Frequency of ***counterproposals*** per hour of face-to-face negotiating time	1.7	3.1
Percent of negotiator's time classified as a ***defense/attack spiral***	1.9%	6.3%
Percent of all negotiator's behavior immediately preceded by a ***behavioral label***		
Disagreeing	0.4%	1.5%
All behavior except disagreeing	6.4%	1.2%
Active Listening. Percent of negotiator's time spent		
Testing for understanding	9.7%	4.1%
Summarizing	7.5%	4.2%
Questions, as a percent of all negotiating behavior	21.3%	9.6%
Feelings commentary, giving internal information as a percent of all negotiating behavior	12.1%	7.8%
Argument dilution, average number of reasons given by negotiator to back each argument or case that he or she advances	1.8	3.0

Source: Neil Rackham, "The Behavior of Successful Negotiators" (Reston, Va.: Huthwaite Research Group, 1976) as reported in Ellen Raider International, Inc. (Brooklyn, N.Y.) and Situation Management Systems, Inc. (Plymouth, Mass.), *International Negotiations: A Training Program for Corporate Executives and Diplomats* (1982). Reprinted by permission.

- **Irritators** refer to words that, although having negligible value in persuading counterparts, cause annoyance. Irritators include such phrases as "generous offer," "fair price," and "reasonable arrangement." Average negotiators use over four times as many irritators as do skilled negotiators.

- **Counterproposals** involve negotiators responding to their counterparts' proposals by simply offering their own proposal. Average negotiators use counterproposals twice as frequently as skilled negotiators. Skilled negotiators clarify their understanding of counterparts' suggestions before responding with their own proposals.

- **Defend/attack spiral.** Negotiating, by definition, involves conflict. That conflict often leads to heated, value-laden accusations and defensive statements. Average negotiators frequently respond defensively and often attack the other team, first gently and then harder and harder. Skilled negotiators, by contrast, rarely respond defensively. Although they also rarely attack, when they do so, they hit hard and without warning. Average negotiators attack more than three times as frequently as do skilled negotiators.

- **Behavioral labeling** refers to describing what you plan to say before you say it. For example, "Can I ask a question?" and "Can I make a suggestion?" are behavioral labels for a question and a suggestion. Behavioral labels forewarn counterparts. For all behavior except disagreement, skilled negotiators use labeling over five times as often as their average colleagues. Average negotiators use label disagreement three times as often as do skilled negotiators.

- **Active listening** involves demonstrating to oneself and one's counterpart that the previous statement has been understood. Active listening does not convey agreement or approval—it strictly reflects understanding. Skilled negotiators use two powerful active listening techniques—testing for understanding and summarizing—more than twice as often as their average colleagues.

- **Questions** are a primary source of gathering information. Skilled negotiators use more than twice as many questions as do average negotiators.

- **Feelings commentary** involves describing what a person feels about a situation. A negotiator might say, "I'm uncertain how to react to what you've just said. If the information you've given me is true, then I would like to accept it; yet I feel some doubts inside me about its accuracy. So part of me feels happy and part feels suspicious. Can you help me resolve this?" Skilled negotiators give almost twice as much feelings commentary as do average negotiators.

• *Argument dilution.* Weak arguments generally dilute strong arguments. Skilled negotiators know that the fewer arguments, the better. Average negotiators use almost twice as many reasons to back each of their positions as do skilled negotiators.

In summary, the Huthwaite group found that skilled, British negotiators avoid irritators, counterproposals, defend/attack spirals, and argument dilution. They use behavioral labeling (except for disagreement), active listening, questions, and feelings commentaries. Unfortunately, this important study has not yet been replicated internationally.

Nonverbal Tactics

Nonverbal behavior refers to what negotiators do rather than what they say. It involves how they say their words, rather than the words themselves. Nonverbal behavior includes tone of voice, facial expressions, body distance, dress, gestures, timing, silences, and symbols. Nonverbal behavior is complex and multifaceted—it sends multiple messages, many of which are responded to subconsciously. Negotiators frequently respond more emotionally and powerfully to the nonverbal than the verbal message.

As with verbal behavior (language), nonverbal behavior varies markedly across cultures. As shown in Table 7-9, the extent to which Japanese, Americans, and Brazilians use silence, conversational overlaps, facial gazing, and touching during a negotiation varies considerably (20).

Silence

Japanese use the most silence, Americans a moderate amount, and Brazilians almost none at all. Americans often respond to silence by assuming that the other team disagrees or has not accepted their offer. Moreover, they tend to argue and make concessions in response to silence. This response does not cause problems in negotiating with Brazilians, but it severely disadvantages Americans when they are dealing with Japanese. While the Japanese silently consider the Americans' offer, the Americans interpret the silence as rejection and respond by making concessions (e.g., by lowering the price). Similar dynamics occur when nonnative English speakers negotiate in English. As the nonnative English speakers hesitate, to make certain that they fully understand the meaning of the English words, Americans frequently assume that they are rejecting the Americans' position. Again, they tend to misinterpret the silence as rejection and respond by making unnecessary concessions.

TABLE 7-9 *Cross-Cultural Differences in Nonverbal Negotiating Behaviors*

Behavior (Tactic)	Japanese	Americans	Brazilians
Silent Periods (Number of silent periods greater than 10 seconds, per 30 minutes)	5.5	3.5	0
Conversational Overlaps (Number per 10 minutes)	12.6	10.3	28.6
Facial Gazing (Minutes of gazing per 10 minutes)	1.3	3.3	5.2
Touching (Not including handshaking, per 30 minutes)	0	0	4.7

Source: Based on John Graham, "The Influence of Culture on Business Negotiations," *Journal of International Business Studies,* vol. 16, no. 1 (1985), pp. 81–96.

Conversational Overlaps

Conversational overlaps are the opposite of silent periods—they occur when more than one person speaks at the same time. As shown in Table 7-9 and Figure 7-3, Brazilian negotiators interrupt each other more than twice as often as do either American or Japanese negotiators (20). Moreover, Brazilians frequently talk simultaneously. By contrast, when Japanese or

FIGURE 7-3 *Conversational Overlaps: Who Interrupts Whom*

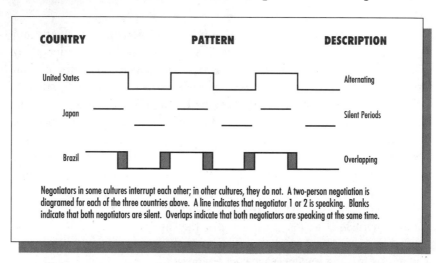

Negotiators in some cultures interrupt each other; in other cultures, they do not. A two-person negotiation is diagramed for each of the three countries above. A line indicates that negotiator 1 or 2 is speaking. Blanks indicate that both negotiators are silent. Overlaps indicate that both negotiators are speaking at the same time.

Source: Based on John Graham, "The Influence of Culture on Business Negotiations," *Journal of International Business Studies,* vol. 16, no. 1 (Spring 1985), pp. 81–96.

American negotiators are interrupted, one or the other speaker generally stops talking—thus minimizing the conversational overlap. Moreover, cultures in which people do not talk while another person is talking generally interpret conversational overlaps as rude and disrespectful behavior.

Facial Gazing

Facial gazing involves looking directly in the face of one's counterpart. Eye contact is one of the most intense forms of facial gazing. The amount of eye contact and facial gazing often communicates the level of intimacy in a relationship—the more eye contact, the more intimacy. Confusion occurs when the appropriate amount of gazing for one culture communicates too much or too little intimacy for people from another culture. In both cases bargaining partners from the other cultures feel uncomfortable. Brazilians use four times as much facial gazing as Japanese, and one and one-half times as much as Americans (20).

Touching

Whether negotiators touch each other during bargaining sessions depends on the cultures involved. Not including handshaking, Brazilian negotiators touch each other almost five times every half hour, whereas there is no physical contact between American or Japanese negotiators (20). Similar to facial gazing, touching communicates intimacy. A hug—a *double embrasso*—in Mexico communicates the development of a trusting relationship, whereas the same gesture offends Germans, for whom it communicates an inappropriately high level of intimacy.

Dirty Tricks

Neither all domestic nor all global negotiators search for mutually beneficial agreements. In attempting to gain the most for themselves, some negotiators resort to "dirty tricks," tactics designed to pressure opponents into undesirable concessions and agreements. Negotiators can reduce the use of dirty tricks by (14) :

1. Not using them themselves;
2. Recognizing them when their counterparts use them, explicitly pointing them out, and negotiating about their use (i.e., establishing the "rules of the game");
3. Knowing what the cost is of walking out if the other party refuses to use principled negotiation (i.e., knowing what the best alternative is to a negotiated solution); and

4.   Realizing that tactics that appear "dirty" to people from another culture may be acceptable to your team.

Avoiding dirty tricks is more complex internationally than domestically. Effective negotiators systematically question their interpretations of counterparts' tactics rather than assuming that their tactics have the same intended meanings as they would at home. Table 7-10 outlines a series of commonly used dirty tricks, including various types of deliberate deception, psychological warfare, and positional pressure tactics (14).

Reviewing the range of dirty tricks from a cross-cultural perspective reveals some of the possible misinterpretations global negotiators face. For example, Brazilians expect more deception among negotiators who do not know each other than do Americans. Brazilians are therefore more likely to use "phony facts" during the initial stages of a global negotiation than are some of their counterparts (20). The recommendation therefore is: "Unless you have good reason to trust someone, don't!" (14).

A negotiating team's discretion (the extent of its authority) varies across cultures. Under communist regimes, Russians and Eastern Europeans traditionally had very limited authority; they had to check with their superiors if they wanted to deviate at all from the planned agenda. Americans, by contrast, have generally had extensive authority; they expect to make the most important decisions at the negotiating table. When the other team has limited authority, experts recommend making all commitments tentative and conditional on the ability of the other party to accept and commit to their side of the deal (15). In cross-cultural business situations, negotiators must remember that the other parties may not be using limited authority as a form of deliberate deception; they may simply come from cultures where the authorities delegate very little discretion to individual team members.

Psychological warfare (tactics designed to make the other person feel uncomfortable) has different meanings in different cultures. For example, a common psychological trick involves too much touching or too little eye contact. As discussed earlier, both extremes make people uncomfortable; both make them want to get out of the situation quickly (and therefore conclude the negotiation as soon as possible). Problems arise in defining appropriate versus extreme amounts of touching and eye contact across cultures. Latins touch much more than Canadians, who in turn touch more than Swedes. Arabs maintain much greater eye contact than do Americans, who in turn use more than the Japanese. What appears to be a dirty trick from a domestic perspective may, in fact, simply express another culture's typical behavior. As with other potentially inappropriate tactics, negotiators must differentiate intended psychological warfare from unintended expressions of a culture's

TABLE 7-10   *What If They Use Dirty Tricks*

Tactic	Example (Ex) and Principled Response (R)
Deliberate Deception	
Phony Facts	R: Unless you have good reason to trust someone, don't.
Ambiguous Authority	R: "Alright. We'll treat it as a joint draft to which neither side is committed," or, "Good, you take it to your boss and I'll sleep on it. Then tomorrow either of us can suggest changes."
Dubious Intentions	R: Call the cards and build in a compliance system. Less than full disclosure is not the same as deception.
Psychological Warfare	Tactics designed to make you feel uncomfortable, so that you will have a subconscious desire to end the negotiation as soon as possible.
Stressful Situation	Ex: Room too hot or too cold, no private place to talk, their turf, too much touching, etc.
	R: Bring it up and change it.
Personal Attacks	Ex: Opponent comments on your clothes, your appearance ("Were you up all night?"), your status (by interrupting with other business, making you wait), your intelligence (making you repeat things, not listening), refusing to make eye contact.
	R: Recognizing it usually nullifies it. Bringing it up usually ends it.
Good Guy/Bad Guy Routine	Ex: "The price is $4,000" (bad guy). "No, $3,800" (good guy).
	R: "Why do you think $4,000 is reasonable; what is your principle?" Followed by a warning: "If $4,000, X will happen."
Positional Pressure Tactics	Bargaining tactics designed to structure a situation so that only one side can effectively make concessions.
Refuse to Negotiate	R: Ask why they refuse to negotiate. Will they be seen as weak? Suggest alternatives: negotiate through third parties, negotiate in private, send letters, etc.
Extreme Demands	Ex: Asking for $100,000 when it is only worth $25,000.
	R: Ask why it is a reasonable demand (price). Bring tactic to their attention.
Escalating Demands	Ex: Making one concession and then adding new demands or reopening old demands.
	R: Call the tactic to their attention and then take a break while you consider which issues you are willing to continue to negotiate on.
Lock-in Tactics	Ex: Committing to a course of action, usually publicly. Paradoxically, you strengthen your bargaining position as you weaken your control over the situation.
	R: Don't take lock-in seriously. Resist lock-in on principle: "I understand you are publicly committed to X, but my practice is never to yield to pressure."
Hard-hearted Partner	Ex: "I would agree, but my partner (i.e., boss) won't."
	R: Get it in writing and/or negotiate directly with hard-hearted partner.
Calculated Delay	Ex: Waiting for the 11th hour. (Danger: If the 11th hour arrives, the other side may continue waiting.)
	R: : Make delaying tactic explicit and negotiate about it. Also create objective deadlines (such as starting to negotiate with another firm).
Take It or Leave It	R: Ignore it. Or, explicitly recognize it, let them know what they have to lose if no agreement is reached, and look for a face-saving way for them to back off.

Source: Based on Roger Fisher and William Ury, *Getting to Yes* (New York: Penguin, 1981).

normal behavior patterns.   Review the two situations "Off the Books Payments" and "Extremely High Freight Forwarding Fees" at the end of the chapter and decide if the parties involved are using dirty tricks or culturally appropriate behavior.

Whose Style to Use?

When should global negotiators continue to use their own cultural style of negotiating and when should they adopt the style of their counterparts? Global negotiations expert Stephen Weiss suggests that negotiators have five options, depending on the nature of the negotiation and the level of cross-cultural knowledge of each of the negotiating teams (52;54;55;57).   As outlined in Figure 7-4, if neither of the teams is familiar with the other's culture, it would be best to consider employing an agent to represent the teams.   If your team has a high knowledge of their culture, but their team has a limited knowledge of your team's culture, you have the option of embracing their cultural approach to negotiating.   If the opposite is true, and they have a high

FIGURE 7-4   *Culturally Responsive Strategies and Their Feasibility*

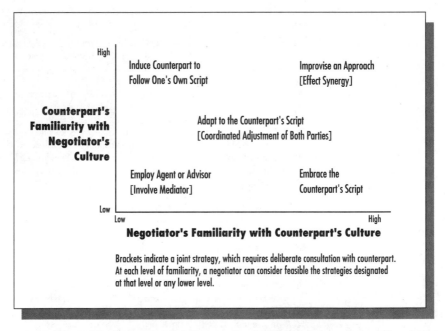

Source: Stephen F. Weiss, "Negotiating with Romans—Part 1," *Sloan Management Review* (Winter 1994), p. 54. Reprinted with permission.

knowledge of your culture while you only have a limited knowledge of their culture, you can attempt to induce your counterparts to follow your culture's approach to negotiating. If both teams have a moderate knowledge of their counterparts' culture, both teams can adapt somewhat to each other's style. In the ideal situation, in which both teams have an in-depth knowledge of the other's culture, the two teams can improvise an approach that works for them both—that is, they can create a culturally synergistic approach to the negotiation (see Chapter 4). Although none of the options guarantees a positive outcome, the higher the cross-cultural knowledge on the part of both of the negotiating teams, the more options remain open to them and the greater their chances of reaching a satisfactory agreement.

SUMMARY

"When in Rome, do as the Romans do"? No, when in Rome, or Beijing, or Prague, act like an effective foreigner. Lucian Pye, in his excellent book, *Chinese Commercial Negotiating Style*, recommends that foreigners conducting business in the People's Republic of China (42:xii)

> (a) practice patience; (b) accept prolonged periods of no movement; (c) control against exaggerated expectations, and discount Chinese rhetoric about future prospects; (d) expect that the Chinese will try to influence by shaming; (e) resist the temptation to believe that difficulties may have been caused by one's own mistakes; and (f) try to understand Chinese cultural traits, but never believe that a foreigner can practice them better than the Chinese.

Pye recommends recognizing and understanding the cultural differences, not trying to become a member of the other culture.

Negotiating styles clearly vary across cultures (2;28;47;48;49;50). Words and behavior that effectively persuade people at home fail to influence bargaining partners from other countries. The cultural context of a negotiation significantly influences who should be a member of the negotiating team, where the negotiation should be conducted, and what approach—including strategy and tactics—negotiators should use. Negotiating globally requires acute observation skills and a more tentative approach to understanding meaning than its domestic counterpart. Not only does negotiating globally imply "not jumping to conclusions," it rarely allows negotiators to conclude the negotiation definitively.

In preparing to negotiate globally, team members should learn as much as possible about the other cultures—their negotiating patterns and especially their style of negotiating with outsiders (2)—and then approach the actual bargaining sessions with as wide a range of options and alternatives—in behavior and substance—as possible. In initial meetings negotiators should emphasize developing a relationship with their bargaining partners (remembering to let them bring up business).   During the discussions negotiators should assume differences exist in negotiating styles until similarity is proven. It is easier to move from an expectation of difference to an acceptance of similarity than to recoup the losses from mistakes incurred in acting as if negotiators from other cultures are just like you when in fact they are not. Effective negotiators have high expectations and make high initial offers (or requests), proceed by asking a lot of questions, and refrain from making many commitments until the final stage of the negotiation. When bargaining, effective negotiators use fewer irritators, counterproposals, and defend/attack spirals, less argument dilution, and more behavioral labels, active listening, and feeling commentaries than do less skilled negotiators.

The most effective negotiators approach bargaining sessions searching for synergistic solutions—solutions in which both sides win. The art of negotiation lies in developing creative options and alternatives, not in using persuasive tactics that more often result in giving offense than in gaining agreement.

QUESTIONS FOR REFLECTION

1. **Stages of a Negotiation.**   Review the four stages of negotiation. Analyze your own negotiating style. Which stages do you emphasize more and which less? In which ways could your natural style of negotiation—the style that you use at home with a domestic counterpart—cause problems when negotiating abroad?

2. **Culturally Synergistic Negotiating.**   Why is a synergistic negotiation style often most effective in negotiations involving representatives from various cultures?

3. **Preparing for a Negotiation.**   How would you prepare for and what would you make certain to do at the first session negotiating with businesspeople from Bombay? From Paris? From Stockholm? From Rio de Janeiro?

4. **Cultural Self-Awareness.**   When negotiators from another culture hear that someone is coming to negotiate with them from your country, what do they expect? What is the stereotype—the most commonly expected behavior—of negotiators from your country? How can you use that stereotype to your advantage? In which ways is the stereotype a disadvantage? In which ways can you overcome the disadvantages associated with the stereotype of negotiators from your culture?

CASES FOR REFLECTION

Global firms are constantly confronted with business situations involving cross-cultural negotiating that challenge their notions of effective and ethical behavior. In the following two situations, "Off the Books Payments" and "Extremely High Freight Forwarding Fees," the senior management team of a major North American-based transnational firm must ethically and effectively manage the immediate situation as well as set a policy that will guide managers' behavior in the future. Analyze each situation from both cultures' perspectives before choosing how to manage the immediate situation or recommending a more general corporate policy governing all such situations.

OFF THE BOOKS PAYMENTS

Prestige, a North American–based global firm, sent American Frank Quick to a certain country to scout out possibilities for increasing the market for a particular Prestige product. Two other global firms compete directly with Prestige for this market, Companies Y and Z.

Frank has spent a year in the country and has made considerable progress. He has made it quite clear to prospective buyers that Prestige offers a much better product than the competition's. Frank has been working especially hard to obtain a large order from the top officials of a large local company, Ajax, Inc., rather than having Ajax place the order with either Company Y or Z.

Ajax presently buys some products from Prestige and some from Companies Y and Z. While admitting that it regards Prestige's products as uniformly superior, Ajax claims it chooses to spread its business among the three suppliers as a hedge against possible failure of supply. Nonetheless, Frank is persisting in his dogged efforts to make Prestige Ajax's sole supplier.

Recently, Ajax's vice president of purchasing invited Frank to his office and informed him that Ajax would be willing to gradually taper off business with Companies Y and Z, primarily because Prestige offers a better product. He adds, however, that under-the-table payments are rather common in his country, and proceeds to hint broadly that he accepts substantial payments from both of the other two companies. Subtly, he indicates that if Prestige pays him an amount equal to the combined payments of Companies Y and Z, Prestige will become his exclusive supplier. However, if Prestige refuses, he will keep Prestige's present contract at its existing level, while expanding Ajax's business with Companies Y and Z, who, he claims, are prepared to make even greater payments than in the past.

Questions for Reflection

1. Under these circumstances, can Prestige continue to conduct any business with Ajax?
2. Does Prestige have an obligation to make public the described under-the-table payments of Companies Y and Z? How much loyalty does Prestige owe to other global firms operating in the host country's business community?
3. Will making this information public force Companies Y and Z to lose their contracts with Ajax? Will such behavior work to Prestige's advantage or disadvantage?

Senior Management Committee Decisions

1. What should Prestige advise Frank to do? What should Prestige's overall policy on such payments be? Should Prestige walk away from companies or individuals who accept under-the-table payments?
2. Should Prestige expose the other companies? Why? Why not? What moral grounds does a company have to try to change the behavior of other companies?
3. What moral grounds does a company have to try to change the country?
4. What would you do if you were in Frank's position?

EXTREMELY HIGH FREIGHT FORWARDING FEES

In a certain Asian host country the only way companies can get raw materials, parts, and finished products through local customs is to use a local freight-forwarding agent at the airport, seaport, or other point of entry. These agents charge forwarding fees that seem extremely high to many outside observers. The explanation, though hard to pin down, appears to be that the freight-forwarding agents use some of the money that companies pay them to make under-the-table payments to local customs officials. When such payments are made, shipments appear to clear customs more quickly, thus helping reduce the companies' cycle time.

Things have long been done this way in this host country, ostensibly because the government underpays local customs officials and offers them annual raises that do not keep pace with inflation. According to common knowledge, the government assumes that the officials will receive part of their income from direct payments from companies and individuals needing customs assistance.

When Prestige, a North American-based global company, originally entered this host country some years ago, it believed that the government did not allow this sort of practice, nor did it take place. However, in the intervening years, the political milieu changed, along with a certain loosening of discipline among civil servants, due in part to surging inflation. Recently, expatriates working in this country for Prestige became increasingly convinced that the situation had become unacceptable, that such payments are not good ethical practice, and that therefore they are not good business practice.

Questions for Reflection

1. Given Prestige's corporate beliefs in the highest level of integrity and the utmost respect for people, what type of respect should Prestige's global managers show to customs and freight-forwarding agents who expect and accept unofficial payments from companies or individuals? How would your behavior change if you knew that typical customs officials in this particular country believe that, far from doing anything unethical, they would be acting unethically, given the inflationary situation, if they failed to accept some additional unofficial payments needed to feed their families and to educate their children? Would knowing the customs agents' appreciation of the situation change your judgment or behavior?
2. Who is to blame? Should Prestige blame the government rather than the individual customs and freight-forwarding agents? Does Prestige have any right to interfere with the procedures of customs and freight-forwarding agents in this, or any other, country?
3. Knowing that such practices exist, what responsibility does Prestige's management have in the host country? Should Prestige make it clear in a quiet but firm way that the company will not participate in such practices? To whom? Are there circumstances under which Prestige should publicly state its position on this issue? What other alternatives does Prestige have?
4. Should an individual Prestige manager who learns about such unofficial payments and reports them to his or her immediate supervisor without apparent effect, report the situation directly to senior management?

Senior Management Committee Decisions

1. What constitutes ethical behavior in this case?
2. What should Prestige's policy be toward such payments in this country? In all countries?
3. How should Prestige implement this policy?
4. As an individual, what would you be willing to do if you were working in this country? What would you be unwilling to do? Why?

NOTES

1. Based on George Renwick, *Malays and Americans: Definite Differences, Unique Opportunities* (Yarmouth, Me.: Intercultural Press, 1985), pp. 51–54; as edited in 1996 by Nancy J. Adler.

2. Example provided by Professor John L. Graham, Graduate School of Management, University of California, Irvine.

REFERENCES

1. Adler, N. J., and Graham, J. L. "Business Negotiations: Canadians Are Not Just Like Americans," *Canadian Journal of Administrative Sciences*, vol. 4, no. 3 (1987), pp. 211–238.

2. Adler, N. J., and Graham, J. L. "Cross-Cultural Interaction: The International Comparison Fallacy," *Journal of International Business Studies*, vol. 20, no. 3 (1989), pp. 515–537.

3. Adler, N. J.; Graham J. L.; and Brahm, R. "Strategy Implementation: A Comparison of Face-to-Face Negotiations in The People's Republic of China," *Strategic Management Journal*, vol. 13, no. 7 (1992), pp. 449–466.

4. Adler, N. J.; Schwartz, T; and Graham, J. L. "Business Negotiations in Canada (French and English Speakers), Mexico and the United States," *Journal of Business Research*, vol. 15, no. 4 (1987), pp. 411–429.

5. Beliaev, E.; Mullen, T.; and Punnett, B. J. "Understanding the Cultural Environment: U.S.A.-U.S.S.R. Trade Negotiation," *California Management Review*, vol. 27, no. 2 (1985), pp. 100–112.

6. Blaker, M. *Japanese International Negotiating Style* (New York: Columbia University Press, 1977).

7. Campbell, N.; Graham, J. L.; Jolibert, A.; and Meissner, H. "Marketing Negotiations in France, Germany, the United Kingdom, and the United States," *Journal of Marketing*, vol. 52, no. 2 (1988), pp. 49–62.

8. Casse, P. *Training for the Cross-Cultural Mind*, 2nd ed. (Washington, D.C.: Society for Intercultural Education, Training, and Research, 1981).

9. Cohen, H. *You Can Negotiate Anything* (Secaucus, N.J.: Lyle Stuart, 1980).

10. Dupont, C. *La Négociation: Conduite, Théorie, Applications* (Paris: Dalloz, 1982).

11. Fayweather, J., and Kapoor, A. "Simulated International Business Negotiations," *Journal of International Business Studies*, vol. 3 (Spring 1972), pp. 19–31.

12. Fayweather, J., and Kapoor, A. *Strategy and Negotiation for the International Corporation* (Cambridge, Mass.: Ballinger, 1976), pp. 29–50.

13. Fisher, G. *International Negotiations: A Cross-Cultural Perspective* (Chicago: Intercultural Press, 1980).

14. Fisher, R., and Ury, W. *Getting to Yes* (Boston: Houghton Mifflin, and New York: Penguin, 1981) .

15. Glenn, E. S.; Witmeyer, D.; and Stevenson, K. A. "Cultural Styles of Persuasion," *International Journal of Intercultural Relations*, vol. 1, no. 3 (1977), pp. 52–66.

16. Graham, J. L. "Brazilian, Japanese, and American Business Negotiations," *Journal of International Business Studies*, vol. 14, no. 1 (1983), pp. 47–61.

17. Graham, J. L. "Deference Given the Buyer: Variations Across Twelve Cultures," in P. Lorange and F. Contractor eds., *Cooperative Strategies in International Business* (Lexington, Mass.: Lexington Books, 1987).

18. Graham, J. L. "An Exploratory Study of the Process of Marketing Negotiations Using a Cross-Cultural Perspective," in R. Scarcella, E. Andersen, and S. Krashen, eds., *Developing Communicative Competence in a Second Language* (Rowley, Mass.: Newbury House Publishers, 1989).

19. Graham, J. L. "A Hidden Cause of America's Trade Deficit with Japan," *Columbia Journal of World Business* (Fall 1981), pp. 5–15.

20. Graham, J. L. "The Influence of Culture on the Process of Business Negotiations," *Journal of International Business Studies*, vol. 16, no. 1 (1985), pp. 81–96.

21. Graham, J. L. "The Problem-Solving Approach to Interorganizational Negotiations: A Laboratory Test," *Journal of Business Research*, vol. 14 (1986), pp. 271–286.

22. Graham, J. L., and Herberger, R. A., Jr. "Negotiators Abroad—Don't Shoot from the Hip," *Harvard Business Review* (July-August 1983), pp. 160–168.

23. Graham, J. L.; Kim, D. K.; Lin, C. Y.; and Robinson, M. "Buyer-Seller Negotiations Around the Pacific Rim: Differences in Fundamental Exchange Process," *Journal of Consumer Research*, vol. 15 (June 1988), pp. 48–54.

24. Graham, J. L., and Sano, Y. *Smart Bargaining: Doing Business with the Japanese* (Cambridge, Mass.: Ballinger, 1984).

25. Harnett, O. L., and Cummings, L. L. *Bargaining Behavior: An International Study* (Houston, Tex.: Dane Publications, 1980).

26. Hofstede, G., and Bond, M. H. "Confucius and Economic Growth: New Trends into Culture's Consequences," *Organizational Dynamics*, vol. 16, no. 4 (1988), pp. 4–21.

27. Ikle, F. C. *How Nations Negotiate* (New York: Harper & Row, 1964), pp. 225–255.

28. Jastram, R. W. "The Nakado Negotiators," *California Management Review*, vol. 17, no. 2 (1974), pp. 88–90.

29. Jensen, L. "Soviet-American Behavior in Disarmament Negotiations," in I. W. Zartman, ed., *The 50 Percent Solution* (New York: Anchor, 1976).

30. Kapoor, A. "MNC Negotiations: Characteristics and Planning Implications," *Columbia Journal of World Business* (Winter 1974), pp. 121–130.

31. Kapoor, A. "Negotiation Strategies in International Business-Government Relations: A Study in India," *Journal of International Business Studies,* vol. 1-2 (Summer 1970), pp. 21–42.

32. Kennedy, J. F. Address given at American University, Washington, D.C., June 10, 1963.

33. Kirkbride, P. S.; Tang, S. F. Y.; and Westwood, R. I. "Chinese Conflict Preferences and Negotiating Behaviour: Cultural and Psychological Influences," *Organizational Studies,* vol. 12, no. 3 (1991), pp. 365–386.

34. Komorita, S. S., and Brenner, A. R. "Bargaining and Concession-Making Under Bilateral Monopoly," *Journal of Personality and Social Psychology,* vol. 9 (1968), pp. 15–20.

35. Krauthammer, C. "Deep Down, We're All Alike, Right? Wrong," *Time* (August 15, 1983), p. 30.

36. Lall, A. *How Communist China Negotiates* (New York: Columbia University Press, 1966).

37. Lewicki, R. J.; Weiss, S. E.; and Lewin, D. "Models of Conflict, Negotiation and Third Party Intervention: A Review and Synthesis," *Journal of Organizational Behavior,* vol. 13 (1992), pp. 209–252.

38. Mehrabian, A., and Ferris, S. R. "Inference of Attitudes from Nonverbal Communication in Two Channels," *Journal of Consulting Psychology,* vol. 31, no. 3 (1967), pp. 248–252. Also see Albert Mehrabian. "Communicating Without Words," *Psychology Today* (September 1968), p. 53.

39. Muna, F. A. *The Arab Mind* (New York: Scribners, 1973).

40. Perlmutter, H. "More than 50 percent of international managers' time is spent in negotiating—in interpersonal transaction time influencing other managers," statement made at Academy of Management Meetings, Dallas, Texas, August 1983, and at The Wharton School, University of Pennsylvania, 1984.

41. Plantey, A. *La Négociation Internationale: Principes et Méthodes* (Paris: Editions du Centre National de la Recherche Scientifique, 1980).

42. Pye, L. *Chinese Commercial Negotiating Style* (Cambridge, Mass.: Oelgeschlager, Gunn and Hain, Publishers, 1982).

43. Raider, E. *International Negotiations: A Training Program for Corporate Executives and Diplomats* (Brooklyn, N.Y.: Ellen Raider International, Inc.; and Plymouth, Mass.: Situation Management Systems, Inc., 1982); and Berlew, D.; Moore, A.; and Harrison, R. *Positive Negotiation Programs* (Plymouth, Mass.: Situation Management Systems, Inc., 1978, 1980, and 1983). Reprinted by permission.

44. Rubin, J. Z., and Brown, B. R. *The Social Psychology of Bargaining and Negotiation* (New York: Academic Press, 1976).

45. Sawyer, J., and Guetzkow, H. "Bargaining and Negotiation in International Relations," in H. C. Kelman, ed., *International Behavior: A Social Psychological Analysis* (New York: Holt, Rinehart and Winston, 1965), pp. 464–520.

46. Tang, S. F. Y., and Kirkbride, P. S. "Developing Conflict Management Skills in Hong Kong: An Analysis of Some Cross-Cultural Implications," *Management Education and Development*, vol. 17, pt. 3 (1986), pp. 287–301.

47. Terasawa, Y. "The Japanese Perspective in International Business Negotiations." Paper presented at the Academy of Management Meetings, Dallas, Texas, August 16, 1983.

48. Tung, R. L. *Business Negotiations with the Japanese* (Lexington, Mass.: Lexington Books, 1984).

49. Tung, R. L. "How to Negotiate with the Japanese," *California Management Review*, vol. 26, no. 4 (1984), pp. 62–77.

50. Tung, R. L. "U.S.-China Trade Negotiations: Practices, Procedures and Outcomes," *Journal of International Business Studies*, vol. 13 (1982), pp. 25–38.

51. Van Zandt, H. F. "How to Negotiate in Japan," *Harvard Business Review* (November-December 1977), pp. 72–80.

52. Weiss, S. E. "Analysis of Complex Negotiations in International Business: The RBC Perspective," *Organization Science*, vol. 4, no. 2 (1993), pp. 269–300.

53. Weiss, S. E. "Creating the GM-Toyota Joint Venture: A Case in Complex Negotiation," *Columbia Journal of World Business*, vol. 22, no. 2 (1987), pp. 23–37.

54. Weiss, S. E. "International Negotiations: Bricks, Mortar, and Prospects," in B. J. Punnett and O. Shenkar, eds., *Handbook for International Management Research* (Cambridge, Mass.: Blackwell, 1996), pp. 209–265.

55. Weiss, S. E. "Negotiating with 'Romans'—Part 1," *Sloan Management Review* (Winter 1994), pp. 51–62.

56. Weiss, S. E. "The Long Path to the IBM-Mexico Agreement: An Analysis of the Microcomputer Investment Negotiations, 1983–1985," *Journal of International Business Studies*, vol. 21, no. 4 (1990), pp. 565–596.

57. Weiss, S. E. "Negotiating with 'Romans'—Part 2," *Sloan Management Review* (Spring 1994), pp. 85–100.

58. Weiss, S. E., and Strip, W. G. "Negotiating with Foreign Business Persons." Working paper # 85–86, New York University, New York, N.Y., 1985.

59. Weiss-Wik, S., "Enhancing Negotiators' Successfulness," *Journal of Conflict Resolution*, vol. 27, no. 4 (1983), pp. 706–739.

60. Wells, L. T. "Negotiating with Third World Governments," *Harvard Business Review* (January-February 1977), pp. 72–80.

61. Wright, P. "Doing Business in Islamic Markets," *Harvard Business Review*, vol. 59, no. 1 (1981), pp. 34*ff*.

PART THREE

Managing

Global

Managers

Cross-Cultural Transitions: Expatriate Employee Entry and Reentry

If a man does not keep pace with his companions, perhaps it is because he hears a different drummer. Let him step to the music which he hears, however measured or far away.

— Henry David Thoreau, *Walden*

Companies send managers to live and work abroad for many reasons, depending primarily on the globalization in their industry and the firm's specific business strategy (2;4;13;20;34;35;41). As shown in Table 8-1, domestic firms, of course, have no business need to send anyone abroad. Multidomestic firms, by contrast, send people abroad to transfer technology, and, more importantly from the perspective of the firm, to maintain control over highly autonomous operations in countries around the world. Multidomestic firms generally select home country nationals—people who are known and trusted at headquarters—and send them abroad as *expatriates* to get a particular job done. Since headquarters often (although generally erroneously) views international operations as simply replicating what has already been achieved at home, multidomestic firms rarely choose high-potential or top performers for expatriate assignments; rather they settle for okay performers. When expatriates from multidomestic firms return home, they often find no job waiting for them, little value given to their expatriate experience, and no benefit from the international experience for their overall career.

TABLE 8-1 *Business Strategy and International Assignments*

Business Strategy	Domestic	Multidomestic	Multinational	Global
Global Assignments	None	Expatriates	Expatriates and Inpatriates	Expatriates, Inpatriates, and Transpatriates
Who Sent	No One	Home country nationals sent abroad	Home country nationals sent abroad and local nationals to headquarters	Any passport; sent from any country to any other country
	—	Okay performers	Good performers	High-potential managers and top executives
Purpose	—	Project (to get job done abroad)	Project and career development	Project, career, and organizational development
Career Impact	—	Negative for domestic career	Good for global career	Essential for executive suite
Professional Reentry	—	Extremely difficult	Somewhat difficult	Easy
Global Organizational Learning	None	None	Limited	Extensive

Luckily for expatriates, their experience improves as firms increase their commitment to global business. In contrast to both domestic and multidomestic firms, multinational firms operate highly integrated global lines of business. Multinational firms also send expatriates abroad; but rather than selecting average performers, they choose their best performers—both senior managers who can take responsibility for worldwide lines of business and more junior high-potential managers who need worldwide experience for their career development. Because multinationals are highly integrated, they stay in close contact with their expatriates while the latter are abroad and carefully fit them back in when they return home. Professional reentry is therefore considerably easier for expatriates returning from international assignments in multinational firms than for those returning to multidomestic firms.

In addition to sending *expatriates*—home country managers—out on assignments abroad, multinationals also bring *inpatriates*—managers from local cultures—in on assignments to the home country to learn about the headquarters' approach to managing. Headquarters then returns the *inpatriates* to their local culture to manage local operations. Unfortunately, corporate learning is generally one-way: while teaching the inpatriates about the headquarters' culture, multinationals rarely spend any time learning from the inpatriates about their countries' cultures and local business environments.

Expatriate assignments in global firms differ markedly from those in domestic, multidomestic, and multinational firms. Because global firms operate in highly competitive, complexly networked global business environments, they need executives who understand the whole world and have had experience working in numerous countries and on several continents. Global firms therefore select the very best people from anywhere in the world to send on assignments to anywhere else in the world. Rather than limiting themselves to transfers into and out of headquarters—that is, either to expatriates (home country nationals sent out to the rest of the world) or inpatriates (people from throughout the world brought into headquarters)— global firms select *transpatriates*. Transpatriates' prime role is organizational development; they act as the "glue" that holds the globally distributed worldwide firm together. For transpatriates to do this effectively, the organization must stay in close contact with its transpatriates and must actively learn as much as possible from them, both while they work abroad and once they have either returned home or moved on to a new global assignment. Unlike their counterparts in domestic, multidomestic, and multinational firms, managers working abroad for global firms find that their experience abroad helps, rather than hinders, their career progress.

Although multidomestic, multinational, and global firms send people abroad for different reasons, in each case the person experiences a predictable series of stages in transferring from a domestic to a global assignment and back home again. As shown in Figure 8-1, organizations recruit potential global managers either from within the company or from other organizations. The company then chooses whether or not to select the candidate, and the recruit chooses whether or not to accept the global assignment. Next, many companies provide orientation sessions describing the international project and local foreign culture as well as the logistical arrangements for moving to a new country (8;9;14). Oriented managers, accompanied by their families, then proceed abroad to accomplish the assignment. Managers come back to their home country and either return to a position within the same organization or leave the organization to find a position elsewhere. Few organizations conduct reentry or debriefing sessions. The complete expatriate global career cycle includes two major international transitions: cross-cultural entry and home country reentry. To succeed, global organizations must understand and manage each phase of the expatriate global career cycle (12;15;18;19;21;22;29;36;38;43;46;47;48;49;50).*

---

*Note that in the following sections, the word *expatriate* is used to refer to *expatriates, inpatriates*, and *transpatriates*.

FIGURE 8-1 *Expatriate Global Career Cycle*

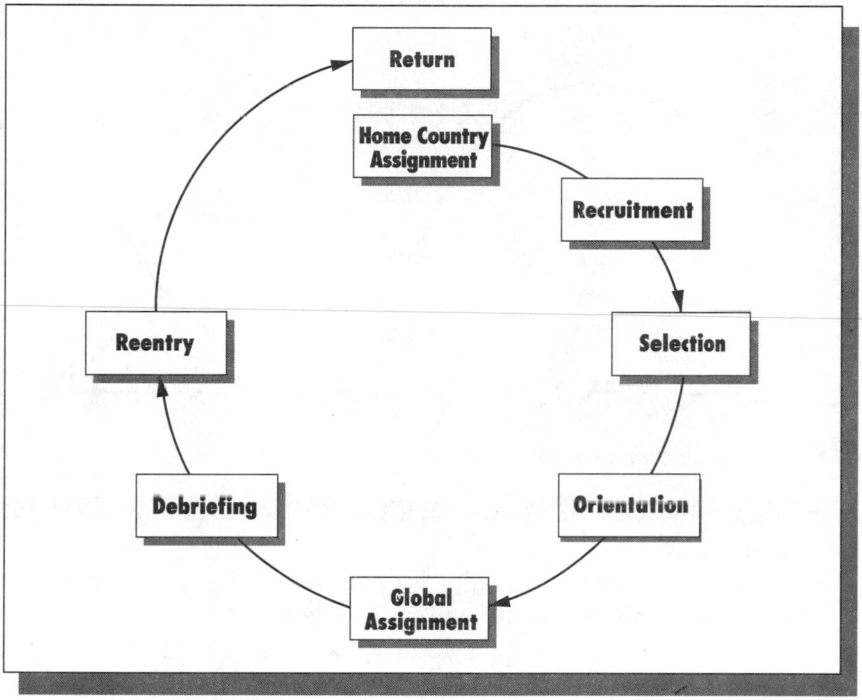

CROSS-CULTURAL ENTRY

Cross-cultural adjustment consists of adjusting to the job, to interacting with host nationals, and to the general nonwork environment (11; also see 10). As shown in Figure 8-2, cross-cultural adjustment to a new country can be described as following a U-shaped curve (27). In the initial phase, at the top of the curve, expatriates enjoy a great deal of excitement as they discover the new culture. Business travelers, as compared with expatriates, often have the luxury of remaining at this stage. This initial phase is often followed by a period of disillusionment, during which time it is no longer romantic to try to take a cab without knowing where to find the taxi stand; nor to wait anxiously on Saturday for the arrival of a letter, only to discover that weekend mail delivery does not exist; nor to try to converse intelligently using a severely limited vocabulary. The bottom of the U-shaped curve is marked by *culture shock*—the frustration and confusion that result from being bombarded by too many new and uninterpretable cues. Following the culture shock phase, expatriates begin adapting to the new culture: they generally begin feeling more positive, working more effectively, and living a

FIGURE 8-2 *Culture Shock Cycle*

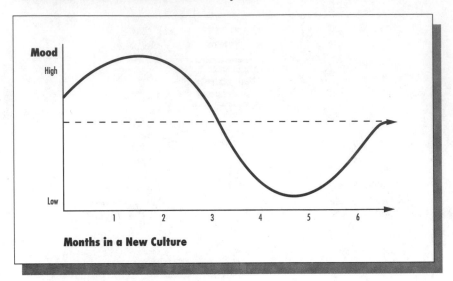

more satisfying life.   Neither the highs of the initial phase nor the lows of the culture shock phase usually mark this subsequent adjustment phase.

Culture Shock

Does everyone suffer from culture shock, or does it only afflict globally inex-
perienced managers and businesspeople moving to very different countries?
Surprisingly, the most effective global managers often suffer the most severe
culture shock (42). By contrast, global managers evaluated as not particularly effective by their colleagues describe themselves as suffering little or
no culture shock. Culture shock is not a disease, but rather the natural
response to the stress of immersing oneself in a new environment.
Economically and linguistically similar countries can cause culture shock as
well as more dissimilar countries. The Quebec-based executive experiences
culture shock arriving in France, as does the Australian transferring to
Canada. Severe culture shock is often a positive sign indicating that the
expatriate is becoming deeply involved in the new culture instead of remaining isolated in an expatriate ghetto. Experienced expatriates therefore
should view culture shock as a sign that they are doing something right, not
wrong. For them, the important question thus becomes how best to manage
the stress caused by culture shock, not how to avoid the culture shock itself.
    What exactly is culture shock? Culture shock is the expatriate's reac-
tion to a new, unpredictable, and therefore uncertain environment (5).   As

discussed in Chapter 3, culture shock results from a breakdown in the global manager's selective perception and effective interpretation systems. Global managers ask the questions "To what should I pay attention?" and "What does it mean?" Millions of sights, sounds, smells, tastes, and feelings bombard global managers, and they find it difficult to know which ones are meaningful and which ones are unimportant and therefore best screened out. Upon entering a new culture, global managers lack an interpretation system based on the local culture and therefore inappropriately and ineffectively use their home culture's interpretive system.

During the initial period in a new culture, global managers often find that other people's behavior does not seem to make sense, and—even more disconcerting—that their own behavior does not produce expected results. They find that the environment makes new demands for which they have neither ready-made answers nor the ability to develop new, culturally appropriate responses. For example, as a North American newly arrived in the Middle East described:

> My third day in Israel, accompanied by a queasy stomach, I ventured forth into the corner market to buy something light and easy to digest. As yet unable to read Hebrew, I decided to pick up what looked like a small yogurt container that was sitting near the cheese. Not being one hundred percent sure it contained yogurt, I peered inside; to my delight, it held a thick, white, yogurt-looking substance. I purchased my "yogurt" and went home to eat—soap, liquid soap! How was I to know that soap came in packages resembling yogurt containers, or that market items in Israel were not neatly divided into edible and inedible sections, as I remembered them in the United States. My now "clean" stomach became a bit more fragile and my confidence waned.

Stress

Change causes stress; expatriates face many changes in leaving their home country and organization and transferring to a new country and a new job. Separation from friends, family, children (perhaps for the first time), and parents (perhaps elderly or ill) increases stress. When expatriates arrive in the new country, different perceptions and conflicting values exacerbate the stress. Global managers see situations that they neither understand nor believe to be ethically correct. For example, some North American expatriates become appalled by the poverty in many developing countries, especially in contrast to their own relatively luxurious international hotels and expatriate homes.

Stress-related culture shock may take many forms: embarrassment, disappointment, frustration, impatience, anxiety, identity confusion, anger, and physiological responses such as sleeplessness, stomachaches, headaches, and trembling hands. As one executive recalled, "There's some kind of traumatic reaction to it. It evidenced itself in my insomnia. There was something there . . . waking up at 4 a.m. every morning." Since culture shock is a sign that the expatriate is beginning to let go of the home culture and engage with the new culture, the appropriate response is not to try to eliminate the culture shock but rather to try to manage the stress it causes.

Successful expatriates use many highly effective and creative stress management mechanisms for coping with culture shock. The best method depends on the particular individual and situation involved. Some people participate in regular physical exercise, some practice meditation and relaxation techniques, and others keep a journal ("Yell at the paper, not at the people!"). Many of the most effective global managers create *stability zones* (42). They spend most of their time totally immersed in the new culture, then briefly retreat into an environment—a stability zone—that closely recreates home. Examples of successful stability zones used by executives include checking into a home country hotel for the weekend, going to an international club and only talking with other compatriots, playing a musical instrument, listening to records, or watching video movies in one's native language.

On the job, managers can reduce the stress caused by culture shock by recognizing it and modifying their expectations and behavior accordingly. They can establish priorities and focus their limited energy on only the most important tasks; they can clearly define their responsibilities and educate the home office concerning the cultural and business difference between the new country, headquarters, and other parts of the world; and they can realize that they will neither work as efficiently nor as effectively, especially initially, in their new position as they did previously. The exact nature of the stability zone and stress management mechanisms is less important than global managers' recognition of the highly stressful nature of moving into a new culture and their development of at least one stress reduction technique that works for them.

Adjustment

After three to six months (depending on the individual and the assignment), most expatriates escape their culture shock "low" and begin living a more normal life abroad. Little by little, they learn what is important and what is meaningful. They learn when "yes" means "yes," when it means "maybe," and when it means "no." They learn what to focus on and what to ignore. They learn to differentiate individual behavior from behavior reflecting a cultural pattern. For example, one expatriate showed his confusion—his inability to differentiate idiosyncratic from culturally patterned behavior—

by asking, "Is it that Budi is lazy while most people from this country work very hard to complete all of their work [idiosyncratic behavior], or is it that most people from this country work slowly and rarely finish their work [behavior reflecting a cultural pattern]?" Moreover, the most successful expatriates begin to learn enough of the local language to make themselves understood in day-to-day conversations.

In addition to time (usually at least three to six months), the key to escaping the culture shock "low" is problem solving. Successful expatriates recognize that the foreign environment makes many demands for which they must find or create solutions. In so doing, they realize that blaming others—host nationals, the company, or one's spouse—for their frustrations, no matter how tempting, is not useful. Ineffective approaches include:

> *Blaming the host nationals.* "These *foreigners* [who, in fact, are the natives] are stupid; anyone who had any intelligence would never have laid out a city this way! Addresses seem to be scattered randomly down the streets."

> *Blaming the company.* "Why didn't the company tell me that the street numbers in Tokyo would not be sequential! How do they expect me to find our clients, let alone make the sales? The least they could have done is give me a map and a guide."

> *Blaming one's spouse.* "Here I've been traveling for the last two weeks, eating strange food, trying to get these foreigners to sign the biggest contract that the firm has ever gotten, and I come home to hear you complaining that the kids can't take a bath because the plumber doesn't speak English. Some help you are!"

Although it is tempting to blame others, it is generally an unproductive stress management technique and never a good problem-solving approach.

The most successful global managers always recognize that they may not fully understand the situation and must find ways to get reliable information and expertise. Their need for immediate decisions versus their lack of sufficient knowledge with which to make those decisions causes both the tension experienced by successful global managers and the large number of inappropriate decisions made by less effective managers. Company-sponsored cross-cultural communication and management programs give expatriates (as well as global business travelers) the skills to manage culture shock and work more effectively worldwide.

Experienced expatriates and host nationals who have previously faced and dealt effectively with the same or similar situations can often best empathize with the newcomer's dilemmas.

> An Italian colleague of mine described the horror of his first day in Philadelphia. He handed his secretary a stack of letters and manuscripts and told her to type them. Each day he expected her to present him with the finished work and each day he received nothing. Only at the end of a disappointing, frustrating, and unproductive week did an Italian friend of his explain that "In the United States, secretaries have more status than in Italy. You must *ask* them *if* they can do your typing, not *tell* them to do your typing. United States organizations are more egalitarian and less hierarchical than Italian firms." Sheepishly, my Italian colleague began to *ask;* slowly, he began to receive typed pages.

Host nationals, although often invaluable as cultural informants, can be somewhat inarticulate in describing their own culture. People do not consciously learn the do's and don'ts of their native culture. Rather, as children, they mimic the behavior of their parents and other adults. Eventually, with maturity, they can perform the behaviors, but they cannot explain them. For example, a Hungarian businessperson meeting with an Arab will not maintain sufficient eye contact. To the Arab, the Hungarian seems shifty-eyed and not to be trusted. If asked, the Arab will not be able to describe how often and how long appropriate eye contact should last. He can do it; he can't explain it. The frustrated Hungarian knows that he is doing something wrong but cannot find out how to behave correctly.

Whatever the source of information, patience and creativity remain essential. Effective global managers "know that they do not know." They recognize that they are in a difficult situation and that they will not act as effectively abroad as they did at home, especially in the initial stages. They recognize the need for good stress management techniques, including stability zones, that will not harm their relationship with colleagues, clients, or family. They also recognize that all members of the family experience culture shock in adjusting to a new country and that the transition often affects the spouse more profoundly than the employee (see Chapter 9). Successful expatriates therefore view cross-cultural adjustment as a systems issue, not as an individual problem (37).

HOME COUNTRY REENTRY[1]

Cross-cultural reentry is the transition from the foreign country back into one's home country (3;16;28;29;33;45;52). Similar to cross-cultural entry, it involves readjusting to the home country work and nonwork environments as well as to interacting again with home country nationals (8). It involves facing previously familiar surroundings after living and working abroad for a significant period of time.   Until the 1980s, companies considered reentry a relatively easy process, but more recently many began to consider it a major problem (39;40).   According to Business International Corporation,

> Repatriating executives from . . . [global] assignments is a top management challenge that goes far beyond the superficial problems and costs of physical relocation. . . . The assumption is that since these individuals are returning home . . . they should have no trouble adapting. . . . However, experience has shown that repatriation is anything but simple (17:65).

Historically, twenty percent of the employees who completed international assignments wanted to leave their firm when they came home. According to a *Wall Street Journal* report surveying thirty-four global companies, "Bosses might quickly become sensitive if they added up the cost to the company of unhappy . . . [returning employees] (51)."

Reentry experiences frequently surprise returnees (16).   When transferring abroad, people generally expect new and unfamiliar situations, whereas they do not expect anything unfamiliar when returning home. Most returnees expect neither reentry shock nor trauma; they expect to slip easily back into their previous organization, job, and lifestyle.

> I don't expect changes. . . . Because it was only a short stay overseas, I expect to just slip right back into my old mold.

> I expect to have the same friends, the same activities, and the same family connections.

> I do not anticipate culture shock at reentry. . . . I don't expect much trauma.

Returnees come back neither to the world they left nor to the world they are expecting. While abroad, the expatriate changes, the organization changes, and the country changes.   Moreover, during the culture shock phase of adjusting to another country, expatriates often idealize their home country, remembering only the good aspects of home—in essence, creating something to hold on to and to dream about.

> As I shivered in Quebec's –35° winter, I remembered Los Angeles' blue sky and sunshine, driving to the beach on a warm January morning. . . . I didn't

remember skies opaque with smog, freeways so clogged with cars that driving anywhere was impossible, nor did I remember my car being broken into while parked at the beach.

When returning home, expatriates face the real changes; the gap between the way it was and the way it is, and the gap between their idealized memories and reality. Most are surprised both at their feelings and at the reality. Returnees often describe reentry as an even more difficult transition than their initial entry into the new country.

> Going home is a harder move. The foreign move has the excitement of being new . . . more confusing, but exciting. Reentry is frightening . . . I'll be happy to be home . . . I really wonder if I can adjust back.

Returnees describe stages similar to those of culture shock—first being in a high mood, quickly plummeting to a very low mood, and then slowly returning to their normal mood. The initial high mood often lasts a very short time, as described by such comments as

> I was pleasantly surprised by neighbors. They really went overboard to welcome us back.

> It's cleaner . . . and just a reasonable number of people . . . fantastic! . . . freedom of mobility . . . quality of life is higher here and I notice it more.

For most returnees the initial high mood lasts less than a month and many report it lasting only a few hours. The low period therefore begins earlier in reentry than in the entry transition. Returnees' lowest times usually occur during the second and third months back. As American managers returning from assignments in South America describe:

> Some of my friends couldn't even imagine the foreign country. . . . They asked me how it was, but they just wanted to hear "fine."

> In Venezuela, getting things done was a hassle . . . and we said, "In the U.S.A. it would be so easy." When we came home, everything was delayed and frustrating. Here in the United States! The U.S.A. was a continual Venezuela story . . . and we had always said, "This will never happen at home . . . HA!"

> Calling friends, my sister, my mom. . . . Everyone was so busy with their lives that they didn't have time to just talk. They cut me off . . . I understand, but . . .

> I came back with so many stories to share, but my friends and family couldn't understand them. It was as if my years overseas were unshareable.

By the sixth month at home, returnees generally accept their situation and report feeling "average"—neither much better nor much worse than usual.

PROFESSIONAL REENTRY

Just as the new environment and lifestyle can cause problems when entering another culture, so too can the professional transition back into the home organization (6;7;8). Professional reentry has often been more difficult than personal reentry, especially for returnees to multidomestic companies in which global experience is not considered critical to overall corporate success (6;7;8;44). Most managers expect a global assignment to help their career; yet historically they have returned to discover that, at best, it had a neutral effect. Multidomestic companies promote fewer than half of their returning expatriate managers (30:1;51). For many, especially in the short run, the career impact is negative. Historically, more than two-thirds of the returnees to multidomestic companies complain of suffering from the out-of-sight, out-of-mind syndrome (30:1;31). As managers returning to various North American companies commented:

> My colleagues react indifferently to my international assignment. . . . They view me as doing a job I did in the past; they don't see me as having gained anything while overseas.

> The organization has changed . . . work habits, norms, and procedures have changed, and I have lost touch with all that. . . . I'm a beginner again!

> I had no specific reentry job to return to. I wanted to leave international and return to domestic. Working abroad magnifies problems while isolating effects. You deal with more problems, but the home office doesn't know the details of the good or bad effects. Managerially, I'm out of touch.

> I lost time. My career stopped when I left and started again when I returned.

Similarly, many managers complain that their reentry jobs bore them (32). Almost half of surveyed repatriated executives found their reentry position less satisfying than their global assignment (4;30). They describe their positions abroad as offering more excitement and challenge. They miss the greater responsibility, authority, status, decision-making autonomy, and variety of their global assignments. Returnees frequently feel disappointed, discouraged, and angry when they realize that their reentry positions do not live up to their expectations:

> I'm bored at work. . . . I run upstairs to see what [another returning colleague] is doing. He says, "Nothing." Me, too.

> In a lot of ways, the red tape and nonsense that we're experiencing now since we reentered are a lot worse. Maybe I didn't recognize these things before [going abroad] or maybe I'd learned to live with them.

> While overseas, I realized that the home office doesn't do anything right . . . bosses call bosses to get anything done. I had to talk to seven people to get one answer. It's a real bureaucracy.

The transition from one organizational culture to another and from one set of organizational assumptions and behaviors to another can be difficult and stressful. Returnees experience organizational culture shock at the same time as they are experiencing societal culture shock. Luckily for returnees, the evolution of corporate strategy and structure from less globally integrated multidomestic structures to today's highly integrated and interdependent multinational and global structures makes professional reentry easier. Due to increased global integration, expatriates are no longer as isolated when abroad nor does the company view their global experience as irrelevant when they return.

Effectiveness

Are returnees effective during their initial period back in the home organization? Yes, and no. As shown in Figures 8-3 and 8-4, returnees and their bosses do not agree: the bosses see returnees as more effective than the returnees see themselves. Historically, returnees described themselves as initially *ineffective* followed by increasing effectiveness. By contrast, home country bosses and colleagues describe the same returnees as initially *effective* followed by increasingly higher effectiveness. Home country bosses, especially in companies with multidomestic strategies, tend to compare expatriates' reentry performance with their prior predeparture performance without realizing that the expatriates have developed professionally while abroad and can therefore handle more responsibility than they could previously. By contrast, returnees generally see themselves as accomplishing relatively little during their first few months back in comparison with the greater breadth and challenge of their work abroad.

Xenophobic Response

In addition to disagreeing about returnees' overall effectiveness, reenterers and their bosses also disagree about which returnees are most effective.

Figure 8-3 *Returnee Assessed Effectiveness Curve*

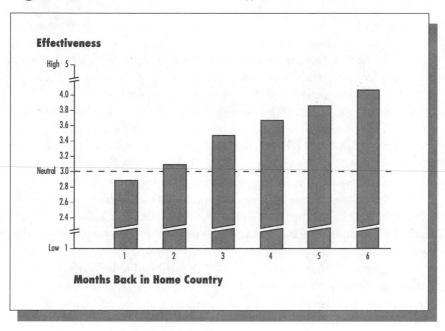

Figure 8-4 *Boss and Colleague Assessed Effectiveness Curve*

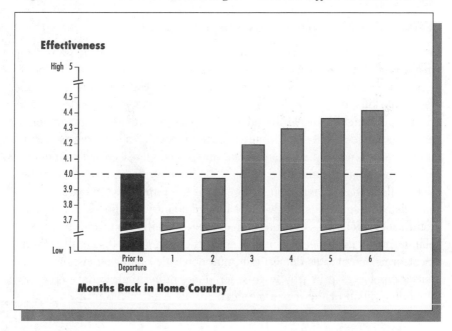

Returnees who see themselves as highly effective are rarely seen as such by their bosses; similarly, returnees who see themselves as ineffective are infrequently rated as such by their bosses. Home country bosses and colleagues generally assess those returnees who appear "least foreign" as most effective—that is, those returnees who do not know or use foreign languages, do not have foreign friends, and were not born in a foreign country. Similarly, they have historically ranked as most effective those returnees who did not explicitly use the skills and learnings gained while abroad on their job back home. This *xenophobic response*—bosses' and colleagues' fear and rejection of things foreign—severely handicaps organizations who want to learn from the experience of their employees around the world. Although multidomestic firms competing primarily in individual domestic markets may have tolerated this response, it is no longer acceptable in today's highly competitive global markets. As experts have said, business today is a learning race and only those companies that learn from their managers and employees worldwide will survive and prosper in the twenty-first century.

In contrast to the assessments of xenophobic home country bosses, returnees themselves rank as most effective those reenterers who recognize and use their global learning and skills to the greatest extent and who are least limited by their home culture. Returnees who speak foreign languages, have foreign friends, and know about foreign cultures rate themselves more highly than do their less globally knowledgeable and involved colleagues.

What Do Managers Learn Abroad?

In reviewing their experiences abroad, returnees report that they improve their managerial skills more than their technical skills. As highlighted in the "Skills Learned Abroad" box, returnees report having enhanced many important professional skills, including those seen as critical for managing in today's rapidly changing, highly competitive, global business environment. In addition to enhanced professional skills, returnees often recognize many personal learnings—most commonly, an improved self-image and increased self-confidence.

When recognized and used, these skills increase the returnee's contribution to the home organization. However, if the returnee's xenophobic boss associates these same skills with the foreign country, the boss's rating of the returnee's effectiveness generally decreases. While both unfortunate and counterproductive, this response is not surprising, given that until recently most firms operated as domestic or multidomestic organizations and transferred employees primarily to get a job done, rather than to develop either the organization or the expatriate's career—as is often the primary goal in today's more globally integrated multinational and transnational organizations. The multidomestic's narrow definition of an expatriate's role, combined with their inherently parochial belief that "our home country's way of working is the best way"—often labeled as the *not-invented-here syndrome*—severely diminishes the value of returnees to the home organization.

SKILLS LEARNED ABROAD[2]

Managerial Skills, Not Technical Skills

Working abroad makes you more knowledgeable about the questions to ask, not the answers.

I learned how to work in two cultures . . . to compromise, not to be a dictator. It's very similar to two domestic cultures . . . like marketing and engineering.

I'm more open-minded . . . more able to deal with a wider range of people . . . because I ran into many other points of view.

Tolerance for Ambiguity

Because I only understood a fraction of what was really going on overseas, maybe 50 percent, I had to make decisions on a fraction of the necessary information. Now I can tolerate nonclosure and ambiguity better.

Things you never thought you'd put up with, you learn to put up with . . . I always thought I was right, until I went overseas.

Multiple Perspective

I learned what it feels like to be a foreigner . . . I could see things from their perspective.

I learned to anticipate . . . it's the role of a diplomat.

Ability to Work with and Manage Others

I increased my tolerance for other people. For the first time, I was the underdog, the minority.

I became a soft-headed screamer. I'm definitely better with others now.

I used to be more ruthless than I am now . . . I was the All-American manager. Now, I stop and realize the human impact more. I use others as resources. I do more communicating with others in the organization.

Transition Strategies

The attitudes (or coping modes) that returnees use to fit back into their formerly familiar home country and home organization vary markedly. As shown in Table 8-2, some returnees become resocialized, some alienated, and others proactive.

Resocialized Returnees

These returnees are the most common among corporate expatriates who work for organizations—such as multidomestic firms—that lack a global orientation. As shown in Table 8-2, resocialized returnees neither recognize nor use their globally acquired skills and learnings. They try to fit back into the domestic corporate structure; that is, to act like managers who have not been away. In treating their experience abroad as nontransferable, they negate the possibility of its enhancing their approach to home country work and life. Historically, because few home organization bosses (especially in multidomestic organizations) appreciated returnees' increased potential contribution, they often felt satisfied with resocialized returnees' fit-back-in strategy (see 24). The resocialized mode precludes both the individual and the organization gaining very much from the expatriate experience. This lack of individual and organizational learning becomes particularly unfortunate today when global firms need continual worldwide learning just to compete, let alone succeed.

Alienated Returnees

These returnees are more common among employees who have had a series of global assignments than those who have had a single such assignment, more common among spouses than employees, and more common among volunteers (e.g., Peace Corps and Canadian University Student Overseas) than among corporate employees. While working abroad, alienated returnees tend to "go native"—they assimilate the values and lifestyle of the foreign culture. When they return, they continue to see the foreign culture as better than their own culture, believing that it offers a richer way of life. They reject their home culture, and in so doing frequently become personally isolated. Alienated returnees, in believing that they cannot fit back in or use their globally acquired skills and learnings in the home environment, often feel professionally unproductive and personally unsatisfied. Similar to resocialized reenterers, alienated reenterers contribute little to the home organization from their international experience. The home organization generally recognizes the alienated returnees' diminished productivity and evaluates them as ineffective.

TABLE 8-2 *Coping Modes: Approaches to the Reentry Transition*

Home Country Orientation		*Foreign Country Orientation*

Resocialized Returnees attempt to fit back in when they return to the home country. They do not recognize learned skills that would be useful at home. In general they are neither aware of changes in themselves nor in their environment. They are rated as highly effective by their bosses and themselves and feel quite satisfied with their reentry positions. Overall, resocialized returnees tend to remove themselves from their international experience. Similarly, while living abroad, most resocialized returnees *reject the foreign country*. Many live in expatriate ghettos separate from the host nationals; many are labeled as "The Ugly Foreigner."

Proactive Returnees attempt to integrate their international and their home country experiences. They are highly aware of changes in themselves and their environment. They recognize and try to use the skills and learning they acquired abroad. Whereas proactive returnees rate themselves as effective and satisfied with their job, their bosses only rate them as moderately so. Proactive expatriates aim to effectively *integrate the home and foreign culture* ways of life; their approach is to attempt to adapt to living abroad.

Alienated Returnees often disassociate themselves from the home culture and home organization. Although they recognize that they have acquired skills and learnings while abroad, they see no way to use them within the home environment. Alienated returnees do not see themselves as particularly effective, nor, in general, do their bosses. They receive the least recognition of the three types of returnees. Similarly, as expatriates, they also *reject the home culture*. Their approach to living abroad is to try *to go* native to attempt to assimilate into the foreign culture.

Proactive Reenterers

These reenterers reject neither their own nor the foreign culture. Rather, they combine aspects of both in creating new approaches to work and to life. Proactive reenterers usually feel optimistic and creative; they recognize and use their globally acquired skills and learnings to contribute within the work environment and to modify their personal lifestyle. Proactive returnees see themselves as more effective and more satisfied with their job than do users of the other coping modes. Proactive reenterers develop a highly sophisticated skill at perceiving their environment—whether abroad or at home—and at describing situations, rather than simply comparing and evaluating them. They are able to identify similarities and differences without needing to classify one as good and the other as bad. Proactive returnees therefore are able to create new, synergistic ways of perceiving and working within the home organization based on both their home country experience and their experience abroad. This synergistic approach—the combining of multiple cultures' ways of working—allows returnees to work more effectively with their colleagues and clients, to make decisions based on a wider range of alternatives, and to act as leaders in the realm of both ideas and action. Proactive returnees' potential for contributing to the organization is great; however, the home organization still must decide to use the returnees' potential contributions and not simply attempt to fit them back in.

Managing Reentry

What makes some returnees more proactive than others? What causes some returnees to fit back in better than others (see 6;7;8;23;25;26)? There are two primary differences between the three coping modes described previously: communication and validation.

Communication

Communication refers to the extent to which expatriates receive information and recognize changes while abroad. Returnees who maintain close contact with the home organization while abroad become more proactive, more effective, and more satisfied in their reentry jobs. Returnees who do best recognize positive and negative changes in themselves, their organization, their industry, and their country. Given the higher levels of integration and interdependence in today's multinational and global organizations—especially in comparison to the multidomestic organizations of the last few decades—today's reenterers are much more likely than their predecessors to receive adequate communication.

Validation

Validation involves the amount of recognition—including promotions—expatriates receive upon returning home. Returnees who receive more recognition from bosses and colleagues for their work abroad as well as for their potential future contributions do better than do less recognized returnees. Returnees whom the company promotes do better than those who are not promoted (25). Organizations that treat expatriates and returnees as if they were "out of sight, out of mind," on vacation, or so far behind that they could not possibly contribute usefully, diminish their proactivity.

Most organizations do not consciously choose to ignore returnees. However, many expatriates return when they complete their global assignment and not necessarily when the company has another appropriate position available. Historically, few companies have used sophisticated global career path systems. One returnee, an engineer, explained that his *Fortune 50* company simply gave him a desk and a phone when he returned and told him to find himself a job within the organization. Another engineer, even though he had no human resource management experience, was put in charge of designing reentry procedures for future expatriates, since "Clearly we don't know what to do with you or with the others who are coming back." External validation—recognizing and valuing global and reentry experiences—is one of the most powerful management techniques for increasing returnees' satisfaction and effectiveness. Equally importantly, it is one of the most effective ways for global companies to gather up-to-date information about the worldwide business environment.

Returnees can facilitate their own reentry by using skills similar to those they used in adjusting abroad. Perhaps most importantly, they must recognize the highly stressful nature of the reentry transition and manage it accordingly. Unfortunately, the very natural assumption of familiarity often blinds returnees to the reality of the reentry transition and strips them of the very skills that they need and so successfully developed while working abroad. Clearly, managers returning to global organizations that operate from an integrated, worldwide perspective find the reentry transition much easier than do those who work either for domestic or multidomestic companies.

UNDERUTILIZED GLOBAL MANAGERS

The global business environment is highly competitive. Success depends on corporate excellence. To compete, today's global companies select the best people and manage them appropriately. Unfortunately, many organizations frequently fail to profit from their employees' global experience. To benefit fully from their investment, the organization and the returnees need to better understand the reentry transition. Both must identify job skills acquired or enhanced abroad and systematically find ways to productively use them. The home organization needs to understand the importance of staying in contact with expatriates, planning for their return, and recognizing the value of their worldwide experience. The attitudes of managers who stay at home must change, as must the evaluation and reward schemes. Increasing effectiveness at each stage in the expatriate global career cycle is neither easy nor superficially accomplished, but rather takes a major commitment on the part of the organization.

Reentry debriefings facilitate the transition back into the home organization as well as significantly increasing home organization learning (36). In a debriefing session, management asks returnees to describe what they learned abroad. Together the returnees and home organization personnel integrate the new appreciations and create synergistic approaches to the ongoing management of worldwide operations. Reentry sessions, rather than focusing on what was learned abroad, emphasize facilitating the transition back into the home organization and home community. As a part of a reentry session, experts describe the reentry transition process on both a personal and a professional level and suggest proactive approaches to managing the transition. By including home country managers in debriefing and reentry sessions, the organization increases the global sophistication of all its managers and significantly decreases organizational parochialism and xenophobia. Both the home-based and expatriate managers learn to transcend their own experience and integrate their perceptions and understandings of the organization on a global basis.

As personnel from the domestic organization become more multicultural and their clientele becomes increasingly global, the need for globally skilled managers also increases. Both companies and expatriates need to cultivate an understanding of the entry and reentry transitions and develop organizational strategies that benefit both parties (41). Companies can no longer afford to send any but their best people abroad. Neither the companies nor the individuals can afford to let the best fail.

SUMMARY

Transitions are a part of the global manager's career path. *Expatriate, inpatriate,* and *transpatriate* managers are selected by the home organization, sent to another country, and returned home again after they have completed global assignments. Transitions, whether entry or reentry, involve managing the stress that accompanies moving into an unfamiliar environment. In moving abroad that stress is caused by culture shock. In moving home it is caused by unmet expectations and a lack of validation. Returning expatriates need to identify what they have learned abroad and how it can benefit the organization. They need to integrate their global perspective with the home country perspective in proactive ways that enhance successful global careers. Organizations need to focus on what they can learn both from expatriates as well as from returnees.

QUESTIONS FOR REFLECTION

1. **Global Skills.** Of the skills learned on a global assignment, which are the most valuable to returning managers? How can the organization best use the returnee's skills?

2. **Managing Reentry.** How might companies best help expatriate managers cope with the reentry transition? What can a home country manager do to make a returnee's transition as easy as possible?

3. **Global Strategy.** Given today's globally competitive business environment, what are the main reasons that companies send managers abroad?

4. **Global Career Planning.** If you were offered an expatriate assignment today to work for three years in an area of the world that is completely new to you, why would you want to go? Why would you reject going?

5. **Managing Culture Shock.** What is culture shock? If you have experienced culture shock, describe what it felt like? What would you recommend to minimize the impact of culture shock on global managers?

CASES FOR REFLECTION

Managing cross-cultural transitions equitably presents challenges for even the most sophisticated global firms. Described in the following boxes are two real situations in which the company must develop an equitable policy both for the immediate situation and for all such future situations in their worldwide operations. For both cases, "Adjusting to America" and "The Morality of Having Fun," analyze the situation from both cultural perspectives before recommending a specific response and a more general corporate policy.

ADJUSTING TO AMERICA

M.B. comes from a country that is culturally quite different from the United States and received his education entirely outside the U.S. He is a devout member of a profoundly different religious tradition that has only recently gained some prominence among Americans.

Prestige, a North American–based global company, regards M.B. as one of its finest young executives. A year ago Prestige offered M.B. a promotion from his current upper middle management position in his native country to a higher position in the United States. M.B. very much looked forward to the new assignment, both for the additional challenge as well as for the opportunity to advance the good of the company. A number of American Prestige managers who had also wanted the position resisted M.B.'s appointment. However, top management's careful assessment convinced them that M.B. was indeed the most qualified person for the job.

M.B.'s wife and two young children felt happy about his success and were eager to be loyal to him. However, they expressed uneasiness about moving to the United States, fearing that it would cause considerable cultural and family adjustment.

As feared, the adjustment to America proved extremely difficult, even though M.B. did everything he could to make his family feel at home. A major problem was the lack of servants. In their home country, M.B. and his wife lived at a high socioeconomic level, with M.B.'s salary allowing them to employ two servants to do the household chores. Indeed, even as children, both M.B. and his wife had grown up in families sufficiently affluent to afford servants to attend to their needs. (In M.B.'s home country, middle-class citizens can easily afford servants who are paid a quite low wage.)

M.B. and his family now feel a deep need for similar services in the United States. Based on his cultural background, M.B., who ordinarily shuns making waves, is now requesting that Prestige provide him with an extra allowance to hire two servants, explaining to the company that this would "only be fair."

Questions for Reflection

1. Prestige regularly gives American expatriates assigned to M.B.'s home country allowances for servants, along with numerous other benefits such as liberal educational allowances for spouses. Does not a policy of the highest respect for people dictate that the company should offer M.B. and his family a lifestyle similar to that which they have grown accustomed since childhood? Is not M.B.'s request reasonable?

2. Should Prestige offer all expatriates transferred to a given country, who hold similar level positions, the same allowances? For example, should Singaporeans transferred by Prestige to a country such as China receive the same allowances as those given to American expatriates of the same grade and position?

Senior Management Committee Decisions

1. Should Prestige pay for two servants for M.B.'s family? Why? Why not?
2. When a company transfers managers and executives across borders, does the highest respect for people mean treating everyone the same? Does it mean treating people as they were treated back home? Does it mean treating people as the host country treats their own citizens? On what principle(s) should Prestige base its corporate expatriate policy?
3. Which parts of the expatriate package should be universal? Which parts should be based on accepted practices in the home country? Which parts should be based on the practices of the host country?

THE MORALITY OF HAVING FUN

I.M. Urgin, a native of a non-Western country, is a devoted family man with three young children. He recently left his senior management position with a local telecommunications company and joined Prestige, a North American-based global company, receiving a raise commensurate with his new, more senior position. I.M. felt thrilled to work for a truly global company.

The new position required I.M. to leave his native country in order to live and work in another country in the region that has a religion, values system, and overall culture quite different from his own. For example, I.M.'s home culture does not consider it bad to frequent prostitutes. Some wives even encourage their husbands to go to prostitutes on occasion, as is the case with I.M.'s wife. By contrast, the new host country holds quite different cultural values concerning prostitution. Prostitution is illegal, although the host country officials often overlook the law.

After arriving in the host country, I.M. continues his previous habits, although on a more limited basis than previously. One of I.M.'s associates at Prestige, a native of the host country, becomes deeply concerned about the legality and morality of I.M.'s actions, and suggests that he stop. I.M. becomes irate. He rigorously defends himself by stating that North American expatriate managers from Prestige living in I.M.'s home country actually form romantic liaisons with local women, including with local Prestige women. I.M. angrily contends that these romantic liaisons create a much more serious problem than going to prostitutes, since the North American men might eventually leave their wives as a result of such relationships. I.M. further argues that in addition to North American culture frowning upon such behavior, it might also upset the local people, with consequent bad effects on the morale of local Prestige workers. I.M. heatedly concludes that "having fun with prostitutes" is much better, and certainly less undesirable, than the North Americans' behavior.

Questions for Reflection

1. Who is to judge the morality here? Must I.M. adhere to the host country's ethics?
2. Does pointing out the new situation by his colleague force I.M. into a new moral context in which formerly innocent acts may now be considered guilty? What if I.M. comes to think of himself as guilty but remains unable to change his behavior?
3. Even if I.M. thinks that he is innocent, does his behavior endanger the integrity of the company? Do the North Americans' "romantic liaisons" in I.M.'s home country endanger the integrity of the company? Does sexual immorality signal a readiness to engage in unethical business practices? How much does an individual's private life impinge on his or her work?
4. Does I.M.'s colleague have any right to report I.M.'s activities to senior management? Does he have a duty to do so?

Senior Management Committee Decision

1. When is the private life behavior of a manager a concern of the company? When it is illegal? When it is immoral? When it reflects badly on the company from any culture's perspective? Never?
2. Should Prestige ask I.M. to stop going to prostitutes? Should the company require that he stop? Similarly, should the company ask the North Americans in I.M.'s home country to stop forming "romanic liaisons" with locals? Should the company require employees to refrain from such behavior?
3. For you personally, what areas of your private life do you believe are of no concern to the company? The way you raise your children? The way you treat your spouse? The way you treat your parents? The way you treat members of the community?

NOTES

1. The research and quotations on reentry, unless otherwise cited, are based on Nancy J. Adler, *Reentry: A Study of the Dynamic Coping Processes Used by Repatriated Employees to Enhance Effectiveness in the Organization and Personal Learning During the Transition Back into the Home Country,* Doctoral disserta-

tion, Graduate School of Management, University of California at Los Angeles (UCLA), 1980. The research is summarized in Nancy J. Adler, "Reentry: Managing Cross-Cultural Transitions," *Group and Organization Studies*, vol. 6, no. 3 (1981), pp. 341–356.

2. Based on Nancy J. Adler, "Reentry: Managing Cross-Cultural Transition," *Group and Organization Studies*, vol. 6, no. 3 (1981), pp. 341–356.

REFERENCES

1. Adler, N. J. "Reentry: Managing Cross-Culture Transitions," *Group and Organization Studies*, vol. 6, no. 3 (1981), pp. 341–356. Copyright 1981. Reprinted by permission of Sage Publications, Inc.

2. Adler, N. J., and Ghadar, F. "Strategic Human Resource Management: A Global Perspective," in Rudiger Pieper, ed., *Human Resource Management in International Comparison* (Berlin: de Gruyter, 1990), pp. 235–260.

3. Austin, C. N. *Cross-Cultural Reentry: An Annotated Bibliography* (Abilene, Tex.: Abilene Christian University Press, 1983).

4. Barham, K., and Antal, A. B. "Competences for the Pan-European Manager," in Paul Kirkbride, ed., *Human Resource Management in Europe* (London: Routledge, 1995), pp. 221–241.

5. Black, J. S. " Locus of Control, Social Support, Stress, and Adjustment in International Assignments," *Asia-Pacific Journal of Management*, vol. 7 (1990), pp. 1–29.

6. Black, J. S., and Gregersen, H. B. "When Yankee Comes Home: Factors Related to Expatriate and Spouse Repatriation Adjustment," *Journal of International Business Studies*, vol. 22, no. 4 (1991), pp. 671–695.

7. Black, J. S.; Gregersen, H. B.; and Mendenhall, M. E. *Global Assignments: Successfully Expatriating and Repatriating International Managers* (San Francisco: Jossey-Bass, 1992).

8. Black, J. S.; Gregersen, H. B.; and Mendenhall, M. E. "Toward a Theoretical Framework of Repatriation Adjustment," *Journal of International Business Studies*, vol. 23, no. 4 (1992), pp. 737–760.

9. Black, J. S., and Mendenhall, M. E. "Cross-Cultural Training Effectiveness: A Review and Theoretical Framework for Future Research," *Academy of Management Review*, vol. 15 (1990), pp. 113–136.

10. Black, J. S.; Mendenhall, M. E.; and Oddou, G. "Toward a Comprehensive Model of International Adjustment: An Integration of Multiple Theoretical Perspectives," *Academy of Management Review*, vol. 16 (1991), pp. 291–317.

11. Black, J. S., and Stephens, G. K. "The Influence of the Spouses on American Expatriate Adjustment in Overseas Assignments," *Journal of Management*, vol. 15 (1989), pp. 529–544.

12. Borg, M. *International Transfers of Managers in Multinational Corporations* (Uppsala, Sweden: Acta Universitatis Upsaliensis, Studia Oeconomiae Negotiorum, no. 27, 1988).

13. Boyacigiller, N. "The Role of Expatriates in the Management of Interdependence, Complexity and Risk in Multinational Corporations," *Journal of International Business Studies*, vol. 21, no. 3 (1990), pp. 357–381.

14. Brewster, C. "Current Issues in Expatriation," *International Studies of Management and Organization* (special issue), vol. 24, no. 3 (1994).

15. Brewster, C. *The Management of Expatriates* (London: Kogan Page, 1991).

16. Brislin, R. W., and Van Buren, H. "Can They Go Home Again?" *International Educational and Cultural Exchange*, vol. 1, no. 4 (1974), pp. 19–24.

17. Business International Corporation. "Successful Repatriation Demands Attention, Care, and a Dash of Ingenuity," *Business International*, vol. 25, no. 9 (1978), pp. 57–65.

18. Copeland, L., and Griggs, L. *Going International* (New York: Random House, 1985).

19. Coyle, W. *On the Move: Minimising the Stress and Maximising the Benefits of Relocation* (Sydney, Australia: Hampden Press, 1988).

20. Derr, C. B., and Oddou, G. "Are U.S. Multinationals Adequately Preparing Future American Leaders for Global Competition?" *International Journal of Human Resource Management*, vol. 2, no. 2 (1991), pp. 227–244.

21. Dowling, P. J. "Human Resource Issues in International Business," *Syracuse Journal of International Law and Commerce*, vol. 13, no. 2 (1986), pp. 255–271.

22. Fayerweather, J. *The Executive Overseas* (Syracuse, N.Y.: Syracuse University Press, 1959).

23. Gregersen, H. B. "Commitment to a Parent Company and a Local Work Unit During Repatriation," *Personnel Psychology*, vol. 45 (1992), pp. 29–54.

24. Gregersen, H. B., and Black, J. S. "Antecedents to Commitment to a Parent Company and a Foreign Operation," *Academy of Management Journal*, vol. 35, no. 1 (1992), pp. 65–90.

25. Gregersen, H. B., and Black, J. S. "Keeping High Performers After International Assignments: A Key to Global Executive Development," *Journal of International Management*, vol. 1, no. 1 (1995), pp. 3–31.

26. Gregersen, H. B., and Black, J. S. "A Multifaceted Approach to Expatriate Retention in International Assignments," *Group and Organization Studies*, vol. 15 (1990), pp. 461–485.

27. Gullahorn, J. T., and Gullahorn, J. E. "An Extension of the U-Curve Hypothesis," *Journal of Social Sciences*, vol. 19, no. 3 (1963), pp. 33–47.

28. Harvey, M. G. "The Other Side of Foreign Assignments: Dealing with the Repatriation Dilemma," *Columbia Journal of World Business*, vol. 17, no. 1, (1982), pp. 53–59.

29. Harvey, M. G. "Repatriation of Corporate Executives: An Empirical Study," *Journal of International Business Studies*, vol. 20 (1989), pp. 131–144.

30. Hazzard, M. S. *Study of the Repatriation of the American International Executive* (New York: Korn/Ferry International, 1981).

31. Howard, C. "The Returning Overseas Executive: Culture Shock in Reverse," *Human Resources Management*, vol. 13, no. 2 (1974), pp. 22–26.

32. "How to Ease Reentry After Overseas Duty," *Business Week* (June 11, 1979), pp. 82–84.

33. Kendall, D. W. "Repatriation: An Ending and a Beginning," *Business Horizons* (November-December 1981), pp. 21–25.

34. Kobrin, S. J. "Expatriate Reduction and Strategic Control in American Multinational Corporations," *Human Resource Management*, vol. 27 (1988), pp. 63 75.

35. Kobrin, S. J. "Is There a Relationship Between a Geocentric Mind-Set and Multinational Strategy?" *Journal of International Business Studies*, vol. 25 (1994), pp. 493–511

36. Mendenhall, M. E., and Oddou, G. R. "Acculturation Profiles of Expatriate Managers: Implications for Cross-Cultural Training Programs," *Columbia Journal of World Business* (Winter 1986), pp. 73–79.

37. Mendenhall, M. E., and Oddou, G. R. "The Dimensions of Expatriate Acculturation: A Review," *Academy of Management Review*, vol. 10, no. 1 (1985), pp. 39–47.

38. Mendenhall, M. E.; Dunbar, E.; and Oddou, G. R. "Expatriate Selection, Training and Career-Pathing: A Review and Critique," *Human Resource Management*, vol. 26, no. 3 (1987), pp. 331–345.

39. Murray, J. A. "International Personnel Repatriation: Cultural Shock in Reverse," *MSU Business Topic*, vol. 21, no. 2 (1973), pp. 59–66.

40. Noer, D. M. "Integrating Foreign Service Employees to Home Organization: The Godfather Approach," *Personnel Journal* (January 1974), pp. 45–51.

41. Osland, J. S. *The Adventure of Working Abroad: Hero Tales from the Global Frontier* (San Francisco: Jossey-Bass, 1995).

42. Ratiu, I. "Thinking Internationally: A Comparison of How International Executives Learn," *International Studies of Management and Organization*, vol. 13, no. 1-2 (1983), pp. 139–150.

43. Selmer, J., ed. *Expatriate Management: New Ideas for International Business* (Westport, Conn.: Quorum Books, 1995).

44. Smith, L. "The Hazards of Coming Home," *Dun's Review* (October 1975), pp. 71–73.

45. Theoret, R.; Adler, N. J.; Kealey, D.; and Hawes, F. *Reentry: A Guide to Returning Home* (Hull, Quebec: Canadian International Development Agency, 1979).

46. Torbiorn, I. *Living Abroad: Personal Adjustment and Personnel Policy in Overseas Setting* (New York: Wiley, 1982).

47. Tung, R. L. "Career Issues in International Assignments," *Academy of Management Executive*, vol. 2, no. 3 (1988), pp. 241–244.

48. Tung, R. L. "Expatriate Assignments: Enhancing Success and Minimizing Failure," *Academy of Management Executive*, vol. 1, no. 2 (1987), pp. 117–126.

49. Tung, R. L. *The New Expatriates: Managing Human Resources Abroad* (Cambridge, Mass.: Ballinger, 1988).

50. Tung, R. L. "Selection and Training Procedures of U.S., European, and Japanese Multinationals," *California Management Review*, vol. 25, no. 1 (1982), pp. 57–71.

51. "Workers Sent Overseas Have Adjustment Problems, a New Study Shows," *Wall Street Journal* (June 19, 1984), p. 1, col. 5.

52. Werkman, S. L. "Coming Home: Adjustment of Americans to the United States After Living Abroad," in G. V. Coelho and P. I. Ahmed, eds., *Uprooting and Development: Dilemmas of Coping with Modernization* (New York: Plenum Press, 1980).

C H A P T E R   9

A Portable Life:
The Expatriate Spouse

We shall not cease from explorations
And the end of all our exploring
Will be to arrive where we started
And know the place for the first time.

— T. S. Eliot (16)

I n an international move, the spouse has the most difficult role of any family member. Whereas employees have the organization and job structure that continue from the home to the new country, and children have the continuity and routine of school, spouses often leave behind many of the most important aspects of their lives, including their friends and activities. More frequently today, spouses must also leave or restructure a job or career in order to follow their partner abroad. Spouses often lose both the structure and the continuity in their lives (11;24;27). The spouse's dissatisfaction, which often leads to early return, is the single most frequently reported reason for failure on a global assignment—nearly half of 300 surveyed companies have brought families home early due to the reported unwillingness or inability of the spouse to adapt. The average cost to the company of repatriating an executive and family exceeds $100,000 (6).

263

The experience of global managers differs markedly from that of their spouses (3;7;8;9;22;26). The spouse generally becomes more immersed in the new culture than does the employee; the challenges to successfully adjusting are therefore both different and greater. This chapter begins by reviewing the historically most common situation faced by spouses in single-career families: that of a wife following her employee husband abroad without having a job of her own. The reason is not that all spouses are wives; they are not. However, to date, companies have sent few married women abroad and even fewer whose husbands accompanied them (2;4;18). The chapter then shifts focus and reviews the situation faced by dual-career couples—a newer and yet increasingly important subset of expatriates. Because the dynamics of single- and dual-career families differ markedly, each is discussed separately.

SINGLE-CAREER COUPLES: THE TRADITIONAL EXPATRIATE'S WIFE

Traditionally, wives have moved from country to country in order to follow their husbands' global careers. What challenges does the wife face in living abroad? How does she adapt to each new culture? How does she create a meaningful, "portable" life for herself—one that proves satisfying in whatever situation she encounters? This section discusses the traditional wife's expatriate cycle: her initial reaction to the international move, her arrival in the foreign country, her approach to creating a new lifestyle, and her return to her home country. Although this cycle takes place concurrently with the employee's global career cycle, its dynamics frequently remain unrecognized by both the couple and the organization.

In a major research study, 197 wives of managers sent abroad by North American corporations and by a government agency (the Canadian International Development Agency) described their experiences of moving and living abroad (5). The women accompanied their expatriate husbands to Asia, Africa, Europe, and Latin America. Some lived abroad in urban centers and others in rural areas; some in economically developed countries and others in extremely poor regions; some in areas linguistically similar to their home country and others in areas in which the language spoken was totally new to them. Their ages and family situations also varied. Although the diversity of their backgrounds and the international environments in which they lived is noteworthy, the challenges they faced in managing the expatriate transitions and creating a meaningful portable life abroad are amazingly similar.

Moving Abroad: Premade Decisions

Companies' involvement in global operations takes many forms, including exporting, subsidiary management, joint ventures, and strategic alliances. Companies therefore transfer employees for a wide variety of reasons (5;12;13;14;15;21;23;29). By contrast, a wife moves abroad because the company has transferred her husband (28). Many couples are unaware of the possibility that they might move abroad. At times wives initially react with surprise or shock.

Argentina

> I just didn't have any idea. I was thoroughly settled in Toronto. We were going to live there the rest of our lives. Our family and friends were all around us and everything was very comfortable . . . I just didn't have any idea of what was ahead of me. I looked it up on the map and I knew it was an awful long way from Toronto. I remembered a little bit from school about Argentina, that Buenos Aires was the capital. But beyond that, it was just like stepping into oblivion. I had no idea what to expect.

Can a wife turn down an expatriate transfer? Although the company and employee usually believe that the wife has a role in deciding whether or not to move abroad, she rarely does. By the time the company identifies an employee that it wants to transfer and announces its decision, it has generally made a large investment in his acceptance. Subtle pressure discourages open discussion of the pros and cons of the international move. The employee often feels he would disappoint the company if he did not accept; his wife feels she would disappoint her husband. The employee often feels he would hinder his career by saying no; his wife feels reluctant to disagree. The couple never mentions concerns that they could have discussed and resolved prior to departure. At a time when communication is critical, open communication is often absent.

Venezuela

> Bill came home in November and asked me what I thought about moving . . . [abroad]. I was silent. Then he told me about what a big promotion it would be and what it would mean for the rest of his career. I told him that I was delighted. The company told us about the things to take and the name of an international school. And we were made busy with the preparations. We left.

"The Carpenter Case" presents the conflicting pressures and dilemmas faced by an American couple when offered the opportunity of a first expatriate assignment.

THE CARPENTER CASE

Tom and Jane Carpenter are a young couple living comfortably in a New England town in the United States. They have three children, Mary 11, Jerry 6, and Ann 3.

Tom works in the headquarters of a manufacturing company as an executive in the engineering department. He has an excellent salary and up until now has been satisfied with his job. A quiet, handsome man about thirty-six years old, he is intelligent, sensitive, ambitious, and known as "a good family man." He has the respect of his colleagues and subordinates. The upper echelons of management regard him as a promising candidate for senior management in this company. Tom is considered a practical man, able to take the changes in life with a basic optimism and adaptability that appear to give him a maturity beyond his years. He likes the material wealth and comfort that his years of conscientious work have produced. He enjoys the status of his company which has an excellent name in its field, being considered one of the most progressive and future-minded of U.S. companies of this type.

If Tom is the practical member of the family, Jane is the "dreamer." She is a pretty, energetic woman of thirty, a good wife and mother and an active member of several committees and voluntary groups. She is strongly attached to both her family and her parents, who are in their early sixties and live in a nearby town. She is sincerely interested in many good causes and always finds the time and energy to devote to them. While she is not a very practical woman by nature, her enthusiasm for her projects is admired by her many friends.

Tom and Jane married early and struggled together for several years until they were able to achieve the comfortable life they now have. Their marital life has been happy and more or less undisturbed, and through the struggle of their earlier years they were able to develop between themselves a rewarding relationship. Although they have traveled to several parts of the U.S. with and without the children, neither Tom nor Jane had traveled abroad until two years ago. At that time Tom, together with three other executives, was sent to Latin America to explore the possibilities of setting up four new plants in different countries in Latin America.

Both Tom and Jane have been feeling more and more relaxed in the past years, since many of their dreams have been realized. They have a good family, financial security, and many friends. They are especially proud of their new home, recently finished. Jane has worked hard to find the furniture and the internal decorations they wanted and now her dream house seems completed. They have both been, so far, generally satisfied with their children, who are well adjusted to their present environment. There have been certain problems with Mary, who is a very sensitive and shy girl, and with Jerry, who has had some difficulties adapting in school. But these were very minor problems and they have not disturbed seriously the otherwise happy family life. Despite this very satisfactory picture of family life, there have recently been more occasions when Tom and Jane have felt (each one without admitting it to the other) that something is "missing."

Tom thinks that his life has become a comfortable routine. The new tasks he is given have less "challenge" and "adventure." For a long while he has been satisfied that his career had a steady development through the years. The time of anxiety and uncertainty has passed, but also with it the time of excitement and the inner feeling of searching and moving. He has begun to feel that he needs a change and it was at that time that he was sent for four months to Latin America. Tom felt that this trip was one of the most interesting and rewarding events of his whole life. Being away for the first time from his family for such a long period, he missed them and he was disappointed because the wives were not allowed to accompany their husbands on that trip. But the prospects of building up their company in Latin America was attractive and he found that he liked to travel, to meet new people, to become acquainted with different ways of living, to be more a part of the "world" and of events outside of their hometown. The three other executives who took the trip with him had about the same feelings as he had. Each seemed to be a little "weary" of being "a little fish" at headquarters. The possibility of being a pioneer in the Latin America division to be created was an exciting prospect. Tom somehow felt reluctant to communicate to Jane all his satisfaction and his thoughts about that trip, as well as the fact that he was hoping to be chosen from among the executives to be responsible for setting up the plants in Latin America.

In a different way, but with the same feeling of restlessness and discontent, there are times now that Jane feels that the pleasant, well-organized life she has is lacking the excitement of unpredictability. She divides her time among many activities, but finds herself at times dreaming about the world outside of her hometown. She wonders at times, like Tom, whether their life has not become too settled, an almost unaltered routine, but unlike Tom, she checks herself by asking the simple question that, after all, isn't this what life really is?

When Tom came home with the news that Mr. Abbott, the president of the company, had offered him the key position in the Latin America operation, she was pleased to hear of the high esteem his superiors had for Tom. Actually, Jane too had been wondering for some time what could be the result of Tom's trip to Latin America.

Although she would have liked to have been able to go with him at that time, the idea that they would have had to leave the children for such a long time forced her to exclude absolutely the possibility of her going, even if the wives of the executives had been allowed to go with them. After that, she used to wonder at times whether the company would choose him, if the decision was made. At that time the idea of having to move to a new environment was not an unpleasant one.

Now that the offer was a firm one, with a high salary, cost of living expenses, opportunity for travel throughout Latin America, she began to have some fears. As Tom talked excitedly about the challenging tasks he would have, her fears seemed to increase. She began to feel more and more that they had little to gain from this experience as regards their family and their life. It was a big step forward in Tom's career, to be sure, but Jane felt that Tom would be successful wherever he was. On the present job, Tom and she shared so much time together, while in the new job, as she understood it, Tom would have to travel a great deal. She was unhappy and ashamed about her fears as opposed to Tom's enthusiasm and obvious willingness to venture ahead.

One evening she tried to sit down by herself and figure out why this new job was not so attractive. There was some urgency for Tom to make up his mind within a week, and she felt the need to understand what this decision to move abroad meant for her and for her family.

She tried to be honest with herself. She naturally had fears about moving to a new environment which was strange and where people spoke another language. She knew that the climate was very different and she believed that the living conditions were likely to offer fewer comforts. She would be far from her friends and her parents. Their furniture would have to be stored, and their new house rented or sold, since it was not clear how many years Tom would need to get the four new plants going.

She felt she would be isolated because she did not think that they could have a close contact with the local people for a long time. Whatever she had heard so far about the personality of the Latin Americans made her fear that close friendships would be difficult to achieve, at least for some time, because she had the impression that they were rather temperamental and unstable. Although she admitted to herself that this impression was based on hearsay and fiction, she somehow could not avoid believing it. She had also heard that there was a great deal of anti-American feeling in the country where they would first live. Furthermore, she wondered whether the sanitary conditions would be dangerous to the health of the children. The company had little experience in Latin America, so it would be likely that they would have to find their own way and learn, probably by hard experience, how to get along in these countries. She realized that what disturbed her more than anything else was probably that Tom was going to travel a lot. Then she would probably have to face a great deal of the problems of their adaptation there alone, while up until this time they had always shared whatever problems they had to face and they supported each other in finding solutions. This also meant that Tom would see more places, meet more people, in general he would enjoy more and probably get more satisfaction out of the whole experience than she and the children would. She was distressed to realize that she was already resentful toward him for that and angry because she could sense that, although he was discussing the problem with her, he had already made up his mind. Jane kept these fears more or less to herself, but she did communicate to Tom her reluctance to go and gave as one of her main reasons her worry about the effect this move was going to have on the education of their children as well as on their health.

Tom sensed most of Jane's fears and he reacted to her expressed doubts by saying that he thought that the children could adapt after a while and that the experience would be a very good one for them. They could learn a new language and they could make new friends after a while. As for themselves, he had the best of memories from his own trip and he believed that they were both going to find this new experience an enriching and rewarding one. He did not underestimate the difficulties involved, but he expressed the belief that they were capable of overcoming them, while enjoying all the advantages that living abroad would offer them. Inwardly Tom was disappointed with Jane's negative reactions and the difficulties she seemed to be having. He had always believed her to be a woman of courage endowed with curiosity and interest for the world outside. In times of crisis previously in their life, she had always proven strong and supportive and she had always shown a spirit of adventure and willingness to go ahead. It was a painful surprise for him to realize that this spirit would operate only in the security of the familiar environment, while a more profound change seemed to appear to Jane as a great threat to herself and her family. He had hoped that she would back him in this decision which was so important to his career. Nevertheless, he maintained his confidence in her and he believed that she would change her mind in time. He called a language school nearby and made plans for both of them to take Spanish lessons.

When Jane's parents came to visit during this period of time, Jane told them of the company's offer to Tom. Her father, who had been ailing for some time, was visibly depressed by the news. Her mother said that this was going to be a great experience for them, "a chance of a lifetime," as she put it. Jane knew that her mother had always regretted not being able to travel abroad. Now she was thrilled that the children were given the opportunity and she promised to come and visit them in Latin America if Tom accepted the job.

Dinner with Mr. Abbott

A few days later, Tom's boss, Mr. Abbott, invited Tom and Jane for dinner, saying that he always talked over a new job abroad with both husband and wife, because he felt that it was very important to take into consideration how the wife felt. Jane had many fears about this dinner. First, she resented being "looked over" by Mr. Abbott who, until now, had not really spent much time with them socially. Second, she did not want to reveal her doubts to Tom's boss, who had a reputation for making quick judgments about people, often not very favorable.

This dinner turned out to be a very pleasant one. Mrs. Abbott helped to put everyone at ease throughout the dinner, talking about her pleasant experience abroad when Mr. Abbott was managing director of a subsidiary branch in Europe. Mrs. Abbott had enjoyed Paris and Rome, but she admitted that she knew little about life in cities like Buenos Aires and Rio.

Mr. Abbott finally turned to Jane and said: "Well, we are very glad you are taking the news of this new assignment for Tom so well. I know you realize what an opportunity this job will be for him. It is a real challenge for him, far greater than what he can get here, you know." Tom hurriedly answered for Jane, who was about to reply to Mr. Abbott: "Jane is really a born traveler. I know that she is looking forward to this. She has already found out how she can take lessons in Spanish." Mr. Abbott seemed pleased. He said: "That is really fine. You know, Tom, that our firm is becoming a global company. There will be few opportunities for executives at headquarters whose international experience is limited. Our policy is to create a management team which could base its decisions on actual experience abroad. Of course, having the kind of wife who is willing to take the risk of going off to the jungle is quite an asset. You are a lucky man, Tom."

While Jane joined in the laughter, she was inwardly very angry. That night, she and Tom had a quarrel which continued for the next few days. Jane resented the fact that the whole discussion was conducted as though Tom had already accepted the job, as well as the fact that she was not given a chance to talk about Tom's work with Mr. Abbott. Tom insisted that Mr. Abbott was not the kind of man to whom one could reveal any doubts about a decision of the company. Discussing the problem the next day with the children confused Tom and Jane more, because the children's reactions were not clear. Mary was unwilling to go, Jerry and Ann seemed excited, but it was more because of the thrill they felt than because they really understood the issue. By now Jane was finding it difficult to sleep, and Tom said that a formal decision was required by next Monday.

They had a long weekend to think over the decision and give a final answer to Mr. Abbott on Monday.[1]

Cross-Cultural Transitions

Expatriates not only experience a grueling physical move abroad, they must also adjust to the new culture and create a meaningful life abroad. Companies generally give considerable attention to the logistics of the transfer itself: what should expatriates pack, which shipper to use, where to stay upon arrival, and so on. They pay much less attention to the skills necessary for adjusting to the new country: good language training; a knowledge of the culture and its people; and an awareness of culturally based differences in values, attitudes, and behaviors. Least attention is paid to assisting the spouse in creating a meaningful portable life abroad. Although rarely recognized as a potent issue by either the employee or the children, the structureless role of the spouse demands explicit attention: if she is to have a fulfilling life abroad, she must create it. The following section reviews the transition itself and the initial adjustment issues confronting the spouse; it then discusses the broader and more fundamental issue of creating a meaningful life abroad.

It's Harder for the Spouse

As mentioned earlier, when a wife moves abroad, she comes into more direct contact with the "foreignness" of the new culture than does her husband. The husband, as a transferred expatriate employee, generally works in the most internationally cosmopolitan strata of society: he meets people who speak English and have met foreigners before. His wife meets much less cosmopolitan people. In caring for her family's daily living needs, she often meets people who do not speak English and have rarely met foreigners. Whereas a global manager often has a secretary and colleagues to translate the language and explain local customs, his wife must depend on her own skills and ingenuity. Whereas a global manager works in an office filled with other expatriates to answer his questions and share his frustrations, his wife often finds herself isolated in her home world. She must confront the differences on her own.

Many wives feel unprepared for their move. They know little about the country, the culture, or the specific location. Their expectations and the foreign reality have little in common. Upon arrival, they often react with surprise and excitement mixed with bewilderment and fear. Below, two expatriate wives describe their arrival in Africa:

Africa

Well, my expectations were very, how would I say, very large. For me, Africa was . . . totally unknown . . . except that I could equate it with wild animals, missionaries, nice black people, and a very different way of life than in Canada. . . . I didn't question anything. I was very young, just married, and very happy to discover a new country. I could imagine that they had modern cities, that Conakry would be a modern city with all the amenities, asked no questions and just left.

Finally I arrived at . . . this hazy airport. . . . I got off the plane, and there were . . . all of these black faces which I wasn't really used to in such mass. So I said, "It's so good to be here and I am so looking forward to getting into the house." . . . . [My husband] didn't know how to say it, but he said, "But we don't have a house." So I burst into tears. I guess it was just the whole stress of thinking that finally I was going to be in a house, and the jet lag, and just being in a completely different culture and a completely different color.

Culture Shock: The Initial Period Abroad

Culture shock, as described in Chapter 8, is the reaction of expatriates to entering a new, unpredictable, and therefore uncertain environment. During the first few months in a new culture, expatriates often find that other people's behavior does not make sense, and even more disconcerting, that their own behavior fails to produce expected results. Wives, being in more direct contact with the foreign culture than employees, describe some of their initial reactions as surprise, bewilderment, and disorientation:

Guinea

Well, then we went into our building, a very modern building. We were on the ninth floor, and the building had no elevators. So we had to walk the nine floors. And then we arrived in this beautiful, huge apartment, with three bathrooms and no water.

Argentina

Everything I was comfortable with in a North American suburban setting, like my shopping, and the schools, and my daily routine, just was drastically different in Argentina. Perhaps the thing that struck me the most was when I set out to do my grocery shopping (which is something that we take for granted with our big supermarkets . . . [in Canada]), I found myself in the biggest supermarket . . . which was just a filthy little dump really, and as I looked around to fill my grocery cart, the only thing I recognized was a box of Quaker Oats. Everything was packaged differently, everything had Spanish names on it, and I couldn't tell salt from icing sugar.

Hong Kong

Before I went to Hong Kong, I'd read a lot of books. I expected the Chinese to be dignified and very courteous. The Cantonese in Hong Kong are the opposite of that. They are very noisy and . . . very pushy. In Argentina, I expected the romantic Latin. Instead, I was annoyed at the "macho-ness" of the men. The reality . . . was disappointing.

Frustration.   The first few months in a foreign culture are rarely easy. The constant frustration of not understanding and not being able to get simple things done follows the initial surprise.

It's the constant minor frustrations . . . the phone never works, the electric power is variable, and, oh yes, filling the water bottles at 4 a.m, just to be sure that we'd have some water.

I had my new Electrolux vacuum cleaner and I tried to show the help how to use it. . . . The next thing I knew they were vacuuming the patio and the grass. They just had no concept of what this [vacuum] was.

We were not aware of the fact that everything seems to be done through a bribe. We were insulted when it was suggested. I think we just didn't understand the culture. So we waited from January until May before our furniture was sprung from customs.

Things can be very difficult . . . [say] you have to put on a dinner party: dinner parties are very important because there is not very much entertainment, so you have to make your own entertainment. You have ten people coming, and there is no electricity, and you have just put the roast in the oven. Right, what do you do? And it's pouring with rain outside so you can't make a barbecue. So you raid the cupboard and find a tin of ham, and you find some tomatoes, and then you find this and that, and you all have a good giggle. You know, really, there is no other way of doing it. You can't get depressed about these things.

I like it . . . but things don't work and it's frustrating. I didn't expect things not to work in Europe. In a developing country, yes, but not in Europe.

While the newness of the environment in large part causes the difficulties, they are exacerbated by insufficient language competence, loneliness, boredom, and a sense of meaninglessness.

Foreign Language Illiteracy.   Whereas most employees have less immediate need for foreign language competence than do their wives, many organizations offer language training only to employees. They expect the wife to enroll on her own in language courses, if she so desires, and often not at the company's expense. Consequently, many wives never become fluent in the local language and therefore have little possibility of becoming fully comfortable living in the new culture.

Italy

I think the most difficult thing when you arrive in a country is not being able to communicate. You feel very isolated because you don't speak the language. So everything becomes very difficult; all small details, everyday life is difficult because you don't know how to communicate.

Mexico

The only foreign language I learned is Spanish . . . and I didn't find it easy. I was embarrassed to speak in case I didn't have it right, and this became a big problem. . . . I would pretend I hadn't been there very long, even when I had been there several months. And I'd have the children speaking for me in the taxi because they could speak far better Spanish than I could.

Argentina

I think the thing that bothered me the most was just my inability to express myself in Spanish. It was a while before I was able to take lessons, and I never did become fluent in the language. I could get by in English in most situations, but it was a little disappointing to see my husband learning Spanish through the office and my children learning it in school and yet I just could never seem to find the time or the concentration to sit down and master this thing.

Loneliness.   The lack of intimate friendships causes a major part of the difficulty during the initial period abroad. Most wives leave their family and friends at home and experience a void upon arrival abroad. The loneliness expresses itself in a number of ways:

> I spent more time alone than anywhere ever. . . . It's hard to spend so much time alone.

> We had a lot of acquaintances, few good friends. . . . You can't make friends until you've learned the language.

> Loneliness is the biggest problem with all the moves. I can remember moving from Mexico to the United States very worried about what we would find there. Looking down at the little family that was in just a shack in Mexico City and envying them because they had the whole family there. And I thought, they are better off than I am.

> . . . In Hong Kong, not long after we arrived, our daughters were going back to school, my husband was going back with them on a business trip, and I felt, well, this is ridiculous. I am the only one here, and the rest of the family is on the other side of the world.

> . . . I think that every country and every move has its low point and then you start going up. . . . I think loneliness is probably the low point.

> When you live abroad and you suffer loneliness, you have to . . . be your own best friend.

> So I was very alone, very lonely, and my husband was not going through the same problems as I. . . . And I felt more lonely because I couldn't share my problems with him. It was very difficult for . . . at least a year or a year and a half.

Boredom and Meaninglessness.   Many wives describe themselves as having hours and hours on their hands with nothing to do. They describe themselves as living in a gilded cage: they have nice homes and servants to do the work but they do not have a meaningful role to fulfill. They no longer feel needed to perform many of the duties that they had previously fulfilled for their families. In addition, many are barred from working or continuing careers outside of the home.

> I was like a prisoner in my own apartment. I had nothing to do. I had no books with me, except for one or two and that's very quickly gone through. . . . I had

absolutely nothing to do. So I started to write letters. That was my only contact with the outside world; and I don't like writing letters!

I felt useless. I was a fifth wheel. There was the maid to do the work and no children that needed my attention.

I was going to be a nurse, but I had to have a work permit . . . so I threw myself into the women's club . . . bridge and golf, empty activities, but they filled my time.

Time . . . trying to find things to do with my time. I spent time sewing and I hate to sew. . . . We got together to crochet and talk. Blah!

After the novelty wears off, you have to find something to do with your time. I worked in a hospital, cooked, gardened. . . . I want to work again.

Separation and a Lack of Support

The expatriate employee's frequent absence compounds the difficulties in adjusting to the new environment. Having just started a new job, a global manager often works long hours. Exacerbating the situation further, many global assignments include regional or worldwide responsibilities and a great amount of travel. Whereas the wife has just given up her friends, activities, and in many cases a job or career to follow her husband and family abroad, her husband continues and increases his major involvement in the job, often to the near exclusion of his wife. Separation and lack of support cause numerous complaints:

My husband wasn't there to help me. He did nothing on the move. He works and travels.

My husband was always away; never available. The men are so busy and the women have nothing to do.

Well, I expected him to travel a little, but I didn't expect it to be so long or so often.

My husband, as well as most of the men in the company, was away probably two weeks out of four. We knew before we left that there was going to be a lot of traveling, but it didn't really make its impact until he was actually doing it.

As shown in Figure 9-1, the husband's work often leaves him least available during the first few months abroad, exactly when his wife needs him the most to help with the logistics of settling in and to provide companionship and support. Unfortunately, the pattern of absent husbands and isolated wives reinforces itself in a vicious cycle. As more problems build up at home, many global managers feel less desire to spend time at home. By their own admission, many spend more time in the office and traveling than the job actually requires. As the wife's situation becomes more difficult, her husband, often feeling guilty at the realization that his career caused the situation in the first place, increasingly avoids home.

Creating a Meaningful Portable Life

Following the initial period of adjustment, the wife faces the hardest task of all: creating a meaningful life abroad. She must identify what she wants to do and find a way to do it in the foreign country. For women who follow their husbands from country to country, it becomes the search for a meaningful portable life.

> Being a transient, I tried to develop those things because . . . it is very difficult for me to have a career. And luckily, I am not a particularly career-minded person. I want to take experiences and opportunities as they come. I want

FIGURE 9-1 *Need Versus Availability Gap*

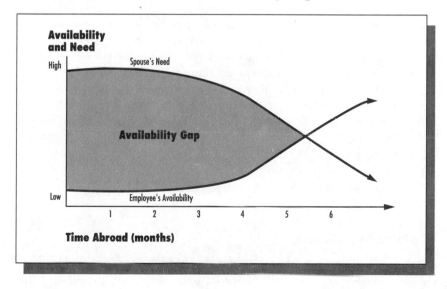

to learn different things, and I want to try different things. I mean, I only have one life. So a career and stepping up the ladder isn't important to me personally, it isn't. But it is important for me to take skills that are portable because, being a transient, you have to have something that you can grasp hold of, that you can take with you, that can be a certain continuity.

Creating a meaningful life abroad remains the most neglected aspect of the spouse's experience abroad. People talk about the initial culture shock, learning a foreign language, and adjusting to the new culture. But adjustment is only half of the challenge; it brings a potentially negative situation to neutral, not to positive. Adjustment only brings the wife to the point where the foreign environment no longer constantly frustrates her; it does not provide motivation, direction, and a meaning to daily life abroad. Introspection and life planning remain necessary for the spouse to answer the questions, "What do I really want to do?" "What would I be happiest having accomplished during my years abroad?" "How can I continue doing the things that I find most important even while I no longer live at home?" The answers to these questions vary. One woman becomes an artist, another a counselor to expatriate families, a third teaches English to immigrant children, a fourth does extensive volunteer work, and a fifth starts her own business. Most simultaneously remain very involved in raising a family. One French Canadian woman, who focused on learning the history, literature, and culture of the country in which she was living, described her growing sense of purpose.

You start to understand the people around you. . . . They are different, but very often the difference is not so evident. But slowly, you go into knowing these differences, and it is a new world that opens up to you . . . . You discover the arts, and the folklore, and how the folklore is lived in the modern world. It is not so evident but there is always something that stays from these roots. You start to see all the small differences that you wouldn't notice if you were just a tourist for a month or so in the country. When you live there, slowly you get to know the people much more, the civilization, how they are and why they are like that, and then I think it is very enjoyable. You are gaining something, it is not just giving.

More frequently today the questions center on identifying ways to continue a career while living abroad.

Returning Home

Expatriates often remember their home country as a more wonderful and perfect place than it actually is. As things get rough abroad and they experience culture shock and difficulties in adjusting to another culture, they dream of how easy and good life will be when they get back home. However, in reality, reentry often presents more challenges than the initial move abroad. Two women, who had lived in a number of countries, capture the difficulty and the disillusionment of returning home.

Quebec

[A French Canadian woman] Coming back was . . . the most difficult move of all. Why was it so difficult? Because . . . you change, the country changes, the people change. You are expecting . . . that you are coming back to your place and that you will feel good right away. . . . It is not true. You come back and you feel like a foreigner in your own country. . . . People deal with you as if . . . you are different. Even your way of speaking the language. So you feel cut off completely and it is your own country. The roots that you were not really consciously, but somehow, dreaming with. You know everybody needs some kind of roots and you come back to these roots and you don't feel well [sic] with them.

England

[A British woman] I was in England recently. I was sitting in the train and I watched two English mums coming from the corner shop, standing and talking. And I said to my husband, "I know exactly what they are going to do, they are going to go home, have a little lunch, have a little sleep, and then they will watch a little bit of tele [television] and maybe do some ironing, then they will get dinner." It is a pity that I am not able to do that anymore. I'm wanting more from life. I am pleased that I have changed, that I have matured, that I have developed, but sometimes it would be easier if I had stayed content with that life. We don't feel we can go back to England. We have been gone too long. . . . They have changed and we have changed.

Recommendations to Single-Career Couples

Expatriate wives offer a range of suggestions for coping with cross-cultural transitions and creating a meaningful portable life abroad, including knowing yourself and what you want out of life and taking responsibility for creating the type of life that you want to live. They recommend treating the move as permanent, no matter how temporary; persevering and being patient. Whereas some recommendations focus on what wives must do for themselves, most recommendations work best if all three—the organization, employee, and spouse—commit themselves to making the transition successful. For example, spouses must ask themselves what they really want out of the time abroad; the company needs to include spouses in a predeparture site visit and, if possible, in selecting a home; and employees, to the extent possible, need to limit their travel during the first three months abroad.

Many companies now interview both the employee and spouse prior to offering an expatriate position (17;19;20). They screen out couples with high probability of failure, including those with excessive alcohol or drug use; indications of rigid and inflexible personalities or lifestyles; communication lacking among the husband, wife, and children; and inappropriate or inadequate coping and stress management mechanisms. Research has shown that the worlds of work and family overlap (10;25). Companies that screen couples recognize that the quality of home life affects the employee's ability to work, and similarly that the very nature of an expatriate assignment strongly influences the family's daily life.

LIVING INTERNATIONALLY: DUAL-CAREER COUPLES

Over the past decade, the number of couples in which both partners have significant careers outside the home has increased dramatically. As discussed in the prior section, historically, most companies selected men for global assignments whose wives either did not work outside of the home or who worked in jobs that they were willing to give up in order to follow their husband abroad. This is no longer true today. Companies today select both women and men for global assignments and, in both cases, their spouses often have careers of their own. Given the recent increase in companies selecting women executives for global assignments who are in dual-career marriages, this section—in a reversal of the prior section—refers to the employee as "she" and to the spouse—her husband—as "he." Needless to say, the labels would be reversed for companies offering a man the global assignment and having his wife follow him abroad as a *trailing spouse*.

When offered a global assignment, dual-career couples must decide for themselves the conditions under which they would accept. The couple, and especially the trailing spouse, often consider a number of options:

- Simply *turning down the global assignment*, although this often results in negative career consequences;
- Finding the trailing spouse a *position in the foreign country*. Ideally, both partners are able to move abroad at the same time, although,

more commonly, they move at different times—with the timing for each move based on the separate needs of her and his career;

- Finding the trailing spouse a *position in the region*, thus becoming a *shorter-distance commuting couple*;
- Having the trailing spouse *remain at home in his current position*, thus becoming a *longer-distance commuting couple*;
- Having the trailing spouse *take a sabbatical*—a career break that allows him to accompany his wife while she works abroad even though he is unable to continue his own career in the particular country;
- *Creating other options* that work for the particular couple and family.

Regional Commuting:
FROM BEIJING TO OSAKA

A major American manufacturing firm transferred a senior engineer to Beijing for a three-year assignment. When her husband discovered that there were no positions available for his specialty in the Chinese capital, he accepted an excellent position in Osaka, Japan. Although the couple could not live together, their commute between Beijing and Osaka was more reasonable than it would have been if he had remained in Chicago.

Leading companies today increase the chances of managers in dual-career marriages finding an acceptable option by offering them services and benefits that traditional single-career couples neither needed nor found valuable. For example, leading companies offer the trailing spouse career counseling and global executive search services. In so doing the company shares responsibility with the couple for finding an appropriate solution. The career counselor initially helps the couple determine if they would find a commuter lifestyle acceptable. Then the counselor helps the trailing spouse decide if he wants to continue his current career or change careers. After lifestyle flexibility and career aspirations are established, the executive search firm conducts a search for professional positions in the same city or region as the employee's global assignment. They then coach the trailing spouse on effective ways to meet and interview with potential employers in the particular country or countries. Simultaneously, most leading companies, rather than explaining why it is impossible to secure a work permit for the trailing spouse in the particular country (as has been so common in the past), take responsibility for securing a work permit (often based on the trailing spouse's own new-found position in the foreign country rather than based on the expatriate employee's position).

A Planned Sabbatical:
A SWEDISH HUSBAND IN HONG KONG

When a New York bank decided to transfer an American woman to a vice president's position in Hong Kong, they told her Swedish economist husband that Hong Kong would not give spouses a work permit. After some reflection, the Swedish economist decided to support his wife's career by taking a sabbatical and following her to Hong Kong without a job. As he thought about his upcoming time in Asia, he looked forward to learning about the Chinese culture and economy and having time to improve his tennis game.

One week after arriving in Hong Kong, the Swedish economist began spending his mornings playing tennis with the other expatriate spouses—the wives of the bank's other executives. Suddenly, to the surprise and amusement of the couple, the bank called and told the Swedish economist that they had found him an ideal position and, based on it, they could obtain a work permit for him.

Whereas the motivation of the bank could certainly be questioned, the outcome benefited all trailing spouses—men and women—who now publicly recognized that the bank could, when motivated, find both appropriate positions and work permits as needed.

Once the couple identifies an acceptable lifestyle and the trailing spouse selects or creates an appropriate position, leading companies support the couple's decisions by offering them a flexible expatriate benefits package tailored to their particular needs. For example, the company might pay for extra plane fares and telephone bills—"staying connected costs"—for commuting couples.

Intercontinental Commuting:
MONTREAL TO LONDON

A major telecommunications company transferred a Montreal woman executive to London for four years. Although her husband, a professor, was able to accompany her to England for the first two years while he wrote his book, he had to return to Montreal to continue teaching at the university for the third and fourth years. To continue spending time with each other during the last two years of the assignment, the couple chose to commute every three weeks between London and Montreal. The telecommunications company supported the decision by allowing the couple to spend less of their expatriate benefits allowance on housing and more on the additional intercontinental airline tickets.

Whereas many companies still falsely believe that transferring dual-career couples poses great obstacles, even more companies erroneously believe that the challenges to sending dual-career couples with children on global assignments remain insurmountable. They are wrong. Many couples report that it is easier, not harder, to maintain the three time-consuming roles of manager, parent, and spouse while abroad on a global assignment than it is at home.

BANGKOK WITH A HUSBAND AND CHILDREN

When a major oil company transferred a geologist to Bangkok, her husband, a diplomat, arranged a transfer to the same city. In describing their global lifestyle, the geologist explained that the availability of household help—including a driver, a nanny for their two small children, and a housekeeper—made it much easier for her to balance her three extremely time-consuming roles—as mother, wife, and geologist—in a way that would be financially impossible for her to achieve in the United States. "Even though everyone thought it would be completely impossible, the expatriate assignment has made my life easier, not more difficult. Time is my scarcest resource, and the household help available in Thailand gives me the time I need to be a good mother, a good wife, and a good manager."

Do all dual-career expatriate couples find good solutions? Unfortunately, no. For example, for husbands who decide to accompany their wives on global assignments without having a position of their own, the cultural dynamics of the local community often make it almost impossible for them to succeed. Few communities in the world offer much social support to a man who chooses to become the primary homemaker in the family or the primary parent. In many communities, such a man is both disparaged and isolated. However, for most couples, acceptable solutions can be found if both the company and the couple actively work to create them, rather than attempting to fit dual-career couples into the lifestyles of their single-career predecessors.

"The O'Connor's Story" presents a dual-career couple faced with making their fourth international move. If you were the couple, what would you do? If you were the company, what would you offer the couple to make certain that the transfer succeeded?

THE O'CONNOR'S STORY

Kelly O'Connor sat in her upstairs study of the Southern California home she shared with her husband Michael and their two children, Kate (6) and James (4). The computer screen in front of her reminded her that she had only four hours to complete a mid-term analysis of downsizing and deliver it to UCLA, an hour away. If the return traffic wasn't bad, she would have 15 minutes to change and straighten the house before Michael arrived for dinner with his law firm's managing partner from New York. She turned away from the computer, reflecting on the decision she and Michael needed to make. Should they move back to Hong Kong?

Early History: The Hong Kong Years 1980-1987

Kelly and Michael had begun their global careers in Hong Kong nearly a decade ago, one year after their marriage in New York. After graduating from Harvard Law School, Michael had gone to work for a New York law firm. A few years later, bored with domestic work, he joined Fishbeck, Rhodes and Goncourt (FR&G) to take a position in Hong Kong.

The early years at FR&G in Hong Kong were thrilling and Michael showed real talent both for handling complex cross-border financing and for working with difficult clients. In addition, he enjoyed the family feeling the firm cultivated by celebrating American and local holidays with the entire staff at a partner's home, sharing practices, and pinch-hitting for each other. The firm recognized Michael's talent by electing him partner two months before Kate was born, and by giving him responsibility for managing the Hong Kong office, the youngest partner ever to be entrusted with line management in the last 50 years of the firm. Under Michael's leadership, the office achieved its best financial year ever.

Kelly's career also progressed in Hong Kong. The major British company she had joined as marketing administrator promoted her to vice-president before she was 30.

The Japan Years: 1987-1989

Recognizing Michael's success at managing the Hong Kong office and concerned about mounting problems in Tokyo, FR&G asked Michael to transfer to Japan. The position they offered him involved responsibility for a start-up operation currently headed by a senior partner whose excesses the firm needed to control. Fortunately, Kelly was able to negotiate a lateral transfer to Tokyo, even though increasing Japanization of her British firm's Tokyo organization had created a difficult working climate for expatriates.

As the family prepared to move to Japan, Kelly discovered that she was pregnant again. At the same time, Michael learned that new Japanese regulations would delay his ability to attain a work permit, thus preventing the rest of the family from accompanying him in dependent status. For the family to continue to live together, Kelly therefore needed to acquire a work permit through her own company and to bring in the children and house-keeper as her dependents. Due to the permit problems, Kelly had to remain in Hong Kong for the first nine months while Michael commuted to Tokyo. Kelly remembers this period as painful and lonely:

> *After seven years in Hong Kong, most of my expatriate friends had come and gone. I became a lame duck in the Hong Kong office, since everyone knew I was expected in Tokyo. And shuttling back and forth between Tokyo and Hong Kong satisfied no one.*
>
> *Fortunately, my second pregnancy was relatively easy, although I almost miscar-ried on a business trip to Perth and, later, the extra weight made me so clumsy that I tripped and broke a toe coming through immigration at Tokyo's Narita Airport, which left me hobbling around for the week of meetings. All the travel and stress finally resulted in the premature birth of my son.*
>
> *As soon as we were able to bring the baby home from the hospital, Michael had to return to Japan. James was so tiny he had to be fed every two hours. I became so exhausted I feared I would sleep through his cries, which were only as loud as a kitten mewing. People from the office sent flowers, but no one visited. My parents flew in from the U.S. to help. Despite my investment in relationships with colleagues, the only people I could count on were family.*

The family finally moved to Tokyo. However, neither Michael's nor Kelly's professional situations were particularly satisfying, and each day brought new annoyances. For example, after having initiated, designed, and analyzed an important market research study, Kelly discovered that a male Japanese colleague planned to present it. When she suggested that this was unfair, her Japanese colleague told her that she could attend the presentation if she took charge of visual aids.

> *At that point, I considered walking out, but I knew I couldn't. Michael still didn't have a residential working permit, so we would have been asked to leave Japan.*

Ultimately the Japanese Ministry informed Michael that his visa applica-tion had been denied, and that he could accept "trainee" status or leave the country within a year. Although Kelly initially felt disappointed, believing that a longer stay in Japan would have offered them useful international experience, she agreed with Michael that "trainee" status was untenable both for practical reasons and for reasons of "face."

When they had agreed to move to Japan, FR&G had promised Michael that he could return to the U.S. office of his choice. As the situation in Japan deteriorated, Kelly and Michael decided to return to Los Angeles and use it as a base for building a new practice. However, several months later, while dodging the half-full packing boxes on the floor of their Japanese home, Michael received a conference call from the Los Angeles managing partner asking him either not to come to Los Angeles or to delay his arrival. Michael explained that it was too late to change the previously agreed-to plans. A month later Michael left Tokyo having turned the operating revenue from a loss to a profit and having brought in the firm's third largest transaction of the year. As they left, Kelly and Michael felt particularly satisfied that they had helped build office morale in Tokyo by introducing family social events similar to those pioneered in Hong Kong.

The Los Angeles Years: 1989 -

Soon after returning to the United States, Michael passed the California State Bar Exam. Kelly settled the children into a rental house, supervised the restoration of their new home, and hunted for a job. The North American headquarters of her British company had originally agreed to transfer her to Los Angeles, but the LA office now nixed the idea. As a consequence, during the following months, Kelly sent out more than 300 résumés, which resulted in about 75 interviews. To her surprise, American firms did not seem to understand or to appreciate her international experience. Few prospective employers had heard of her prior employer—which is one of Britain's largest companies—nor did they seem to understand the British system of titles and responsibility levels used on her résumé. Kelly's salary requirements frequently intimidated potential employers as well. Kelly sought FR&G's help for introductions, but none were forthcoming. In fact, Kelly was rather surprised that after four months in Los Angeles, which included a holiday season, only one couple from the LA office had invited them to their home.

I guess I shouldn't have been so surprised, but I felt like a foreigner in my own country. I didn't know how things worked. With the exception of my family, it was almost as though we had never existed in the U.S. After nine years in Asia, we had no domestic credit record, which even made buying a car difficult. Our Asian credit histories didn't come with us, nor our driving records. We returned to the U.S. with no debt *and tax returns showing more than $400,000 in joint annual income, and yet no one wanted to issue us a credit card. The language, parochialism, and obsessions with cars and breakfast cereals all made me feel like an alien in disguise.*

For years, Kelly had wanted to return to school for an MBA. Given the dismal employment situation in Southern California, she chose to enter UCLA's Executive MBA (EMBA) Program. The two-year program, designed for executives with ten or more years of experience, met on alternate weekends, allowing the participants to continue their careers while getting their MBA.

The Offer to Return to Hong Kong

Shortly after Kelly's initial EMBA orientation, FR&G's Hong Kong office offered Michael the managing partner position for Hong Kong, China and Thailand. Michael's initial instinct was to say no, but he had encountered major political and practice problems in the LA office for which he saw no easy solution. The LA managing partner, who was very senior within the firm, used a laissez-faire management style that created strong competition and practice fiefdoms within the office. There was evidence, for example, that the banking partner with whom Michael thought he shared a practice, was blocking faxes and other business referral communiques intended for him. Oddly enough, a *feng shui* expert* hired by Michael to advise him on the disposition of his new LA office indicated that his good fortune was being blocked in the West. As it happened, the other banking partner held the Western office.

In addition, Michael found the practice in LA less intellectually challenging than his work in Asia. A further consideration was the hint of a recession on the economic horizon. Michael recognized that his two most promising LA clients no longer offered much potential due to internal restructuring and a bankruptcy.

Kelly became concerned that the firm's actions were seriously eroding Michael's self-confidence.

Michael claims that he could have happily stayed in LA in a secondary role in the firm, but I am not so sure. He forgets how depressed he had become. After his success in Hong Kong and Tokyo, Michael expected the firm to reward him. Instead, they held his salary steady the first year he was back, while raising others' salaries. He would come home at night with this hangdog look and absolutely anything to do with the office became a taboo subject. This hurt. By contrast, the people who originally

---

* *Feng shui* (Chinese) translates as "wind water" and is a form of ancient Chinese geomancy for determining the proper positioning of buildings, rooms, and furnishings in relations to the four directions, bodies of water and other topographic criteria with the ultimate aim of ensuring the inhabitants' good fortune.

asked him to go back to Asia were close friends, godparents to our children, and peo-
ple who shared our sense that work could be exciting and rewarding without the back-
biting and private empire building. I encouraged Michael to seriously consider Hong
Kong because I wanted him to enjoy what he was doing again.

While Michael and Kelly considered the Hong Kong offer, the LA managing partner announced his transfer to Sydney. He left a triumvirate in
charge, including the banking partner with the Western office. Prompted
by other partners who lacked confidence in the new management team,
Michael put forward his name, but the New York managing partner rejected it since the firm wanted Michael to go to Hong Kong.

That Spring, Kelly watched several people in her EMBA class lose their
jobs while Michael continued to have limited success developing an independent practice. As the national recession hit Southern California, Michael
and Kelly began to seriously consider moving back to Hong Kong. Kelly,
however, made three stipulations: she wanted an option to return to the U.S.
in three years, to finish her degree within the normal time frame, and to keep
their home. She also encouraged Michael to review the Hong Kong office's
finances before making a final decision and to begin by commuting to ensure
his involvement in any major decisions that might affect them later.

At this point, in order to graduate with her class, Kelly dropped her outside activities and began doubling up on her course load. Michael began
commuting to Hong Kong on a "two-weeks on" and "two-weeks off" basis.
Kate and James went to a local pre-school during the day and stayed with
a baby-sitter in the evenings until Kelly could get home.

Second Thoughts

After four months of commuting, Michael came home one evening and
reported that the firm had told an LA partner, whom the firm had sent to
Tokyo for a two-year assignment and who now wished to return, that he
was unwelcome. Another partner with a young family, who had opened
the Moscow office, was told his compensation would be penalized if he
returned according to the originally agreed-upon timetable. The firm penalized another expatriate partner at the annual compensation meeting for
supposedly treating himself to excessive housing.

The more Michael told me about the schism in the firm between international and
domestic, the more irritated I became. There is something odd about people's inabili-
ty to recognize that when you live abroad you still have a right to a private life. Visitors
from other offices often expect you to personally pick them up at the airport and to pro-
vide personal attention during their entire stay. They seem to expect this as fair rec-

ompense for firm-subsidized housing. Perhaps the partners see expatriates' housing as coming directly out of their pockets. Ultimately, as someone who has now lived and worked both abroad and in the U.S., I can tell you the lifestyle is better in the U.S.

When Michael finally reviewed the Hong Kong office's financial statements, he discovered that it no longer had a banking practice and that the office would probably earn a mere $1.1 million in operating profits in the current fiscal year, before allocating funds to compensate the five partners. This represented $1 million less than in the prior year. Not surprisingly, morale was very low.

In addition, Michael discovered that the firm's new managing partner had reorganized Asia as the first region to operate with a consolidated P & L. The Asia region would be run jointly by the managing partners in Singapore and Japan, with the prospective managing partner of Hong Kong and China (Michael) thus being relegated to a mere consultative role.

At the same time, FR&G's new executive committee formally decided that the firm was compensating expatriates excessively both in housing and in other benefits. As a consequence, the committee lowered both the cost-of-living index and the allowable rent scale for Hong Kong. As part of their cost-cutting, they decided that the Hong Kong office was top-heavy and made contingency plans to lay off two partners.

Kelly became increasingly concerned that not only would the move to Hong Kong entail the usual transition costs in terms of emotions and time, but also that their standard of living would come under heavy pressure from the New York partners who no longer supported FR&G's internationalism:

During our previous time in Hong Kong, FR&G gave partners firm-sponsored club memberships and expense accounts for documentable home business entertaining. These were considered routine costs of doing business, as apartment buildings typically had no recreational facilities and most business entertaining was done at home. When Michael had been managing partner in Hong Kong, we had hosted 6 to 12 people for business-related dinners at least once a week. If anything, FR&G's housing subsidies and expatriate benefits were less generous than those of most other American law firms operating in Hong Kong.

Weighing the Evidence

Kelly couldn't concentrate on her MBA mid-term. Michael had left the final Hong Kong decision up to her, although there was certainly little evidence that he was building a case to stay in Los Angeles.

Both Michael's FR&G experience and her own experience with the British company had convinced Kelly that she had had enough of working for others and of being under their thumbs. She therefore began to think about starting a business, although she wasn't sure what type. She knew she had access to start-up capital and felt confident that over time she could create a business that would serve some of her social goals. The last year had filled her with an almost missionary zeal to make the U.S. more productive; to enjoin business to help in providing better public education for the communities from which they drew their workers; to discover a way to motivate businesses to see the possible synergies in Southern California's increasing cultural diversity rather than just seeing the problems; and to build something her children might inherit, to give them a cultural and family anchor in this rapidly changing world. She audited a class on entrepreneurship, discussed ideas with her business school classmates, and began investigating franchise possibilities.

The years in Hong Kong and Japan had led her to believe in the importance of family taking care of family. Not only did she want to be able to help Kate and James finance college and graduate school, but she also wanted to live near her parents in their senior years. If she said yes to Hong Kong, would the firm really allow them to return in three years?

How much energy would she have at 40? Enough to start again from scratch? Did it make sense to move away from all her UCLA contacts that might help her get a new business off the ground? Did the approach of 1997 and Hong Kong's return to the People's Republic of China pose major political risks for expatriates and foreign businesses in Hong Kong? If she left Los Angeles, what could she build that she could bring back?

Michael was so bright. Couldn't he sidestep the political obstacles at FR&G and build a practice in Los Angeles if he tried? Or find something else? She was tired of the high transition costs of moving: the emotional upheaval, the cultural adjustments, and the long distances from family and friends. She felt weary from trying to build a new life every two or three years, seeing it swept away, and being forced to start over once again.

Kelly worried about moving two small children accustomed to lots of space in their California home back into one of Hong Kong's high rise apartment buildings. Luckily she knew the schools in Hong Kong were good.

Telephone calls poured in nearly every night from friends in Hong Kong and Michael's colleagues trying to convince her to move. Last week, the managing partner in Japan had stopped in LA on just such a mission.

"Analysis Paralysis," Kelly said aloud, turning back to her computer. She glanced at her watch and resolved to put these thoughts to rest: the mid-term deadline was more imminent. Besides, there was an hour commute to UCLA and at least an hour back to decide on the next three years and the rest of her life.[2]

SUMMARY

Today, companies transfer women and men abroad; they transfer both single-career and dual-career couples. In a single-career couple, the spouse's role is the most difficult of all family members'. The spouse—most often the wife—must adjust to the new culture and create a meaningful life for herself abroad. Her adjustment is made more difficult because she interacts with the least internationally sophisticated strata of society. Her ability to lead a meaningful life is challenged by the lack of structure in her life abroad and compounded by all of the activities, friends, and oftentimes a job or career that she has had to leave behind in her home country. Successfully managing the transition and creating a meaningful life abroad demand the involvement of the expatriate employee, the company, and the spouse.

Increasingly today, companies transfer people abroad who are in dual-career marriages. Leading companies assist such couples in identifying options for the trailing spouse, helping him or her find an appropriate position abroad, and supporting the couple's new lifestyle, especially when it involves global commuting. Assuming joint responsibility and using creativity lead to successful dual-career transfers; the inappropriate application of procedures and benefits packages designed primarily for single-career couples does not.

QUESTIONS FOR REFLECTION

1. *Global Human Resource Systems.* What can global firms do to help spouses adapt to a new country and create a meaningful life abroad?

2. *Expatriate Spouses.* If you were asked to move abroad as an expatriate spouse, why would you want to go? Why would you not want to go? What could you do to increase your chances of success? What could your spouse do to increase the chances of your success? What could the company do to increase your chances of success?

3. *Communication: International Decisions.* As a global manager, you have just been offered a very interesting assignment in Poland. As you drive home, you consider how to discuss the topic with your spouse. What are the most important aspects that you would want to discuss? How would you plan to approach to discussion? What are the pros and cons to your approach?

4. *The Trailing Spouse Is the Husband.* Both women and men face very difficult challenges when transferred abroad in the spouse role. Which challenges would be particularly difficult for a male spouse (the husband of a female expatriate manager)? If you were the vice president of human resources for a major

global firm and had chosen to send women abroad as global managers for the first time, what would you do to prepare their husbands for their new role?

NOTES

1. Copyright © by Foulie Psalidas-Perlmutter, Ph.D.

2. Katherine D. D'Arcy. The author drew the material for this case from life experience and framed the issues during an organizational behavior course that focused on the importance of cultural understanding.

FILM NOTE

Material in the section on single-career couples is presented in the video program, *A Portable Life*, which highlights the role of the spouse from the perspectives of four wives of global executives working for Alcan Aluminium Ltd. (see reference 1 in References). *A Portable Life* is available from McGill University, Instructional Communication Centre, 550 Sherbrooke Street West, Suite 400, Montreal, Quebec, Canada H3A 2K6 (telephone: 1-514-398-7200).

REFERENCES

1. Adler, N. J. *Managing International Transitions* (Montreal: Alcan Aluminum Limited, 1980).

2. Adler, N. J. "Pacific Basin Managers; A Gaijin, Not a Woman," *Human Resource Management*, vol. 26, no. 2 (1987), pp. 169–192.

3. Adler, N. J. *Reentry: A Study of the Dynamic Coping Processes Used by Repatriated Employees to Enhance Effectiveness in the Organization and Personal Learning During the Transition Back into the Home Country*. Ph.D. dissertation, University of California, Los Angeles, June 1980.

4. Adler, N. J. "Women in International Management: Where Are They?" *California Management Review*, vol. 26, no. 4 (1984), pp. 122–132.

5. Adler, N. J., and Ghadar, F. "International Strategy from the Perspective of People and Culture: The North American Context," in A. M. Rugman, ed., *Research in Global Strategic Management: International Business Research for the Twenty-First Century: Canada's New Research Agenda*, vol. 1 (Greenwich, Conn.: JAI Press, 1990), pp. 179–205.

6. Baker, J. C. "An Analysis of How the U.S. Multinational Company Considers the Wives of American Expatriate Managers," *Academy of Management Proceedings*, vol. 35 (1975), pp. 258–260.

7. Black, J. S., and Gregersen, H. B. "When Yankee Comes Home: Factors Related to Expatriate and Spouse Repatriation Adjustment," *Journal of International Business Studies*, vol. 22, no. 4 (1991), pp. 671–695.

8. Black, J. S.; Gregersen, H. B.; and Mendenhall, M. E. *Global Assignments: Successfully Expatriating and Repatriating International Managers* (San Francisco: Jossey-Bass, 1992).

9. Black, J. S., and Stephens, G. K. "The Influence of the Spouses on American Expatriate Adjustment in Overseas Assignments," *Journal of Management*, vol. 15 (1989), pp. 529–544.

10. Culbert, S., and Renshaw, J. "Coping with the Stresses of Travels as an Opportunity for Improving the Quality of Work and Family Life," *Family Process*, vol. 11, no. 3 (1972), pp. 321–337.

11. D'Orazio, N. "Foreign Executives' Wives in Tokyo," *Institute of Comparative Culture Business Series*, Bulletin no. 82 (Tokyo: Sophia University, 1981).

12. Edstrom, A., and Galbraith, J. R. "Alternative Policies for International Transfer of Managers," *Management International Review*, vol. 17, no. 2 (1977), pp. 11–22.

13. Edstrom, A., and Galbraith, J. R. "International Transfer of Managers: Some Important Policy Considerations," *Columbia Journal of World Business*, vol. 11 (1976), pp. 100–112.

14. Edstrom, A., and Galbraith, J. "Transfer of Managers as Coordination and Control Strategy in Multinational Organizations," *Administrative Science Quarterly*, vol. 22 (June 1977), pp. 248–263.

15. Edstrom, A., and Lorange, P. "Matching Strategy and Human Resources in Multinational Corporations," *Journal of International Business Studies*, vol. 15 (1984), pp. 125–137.

16. Excerpted from "Little Gidding," from FOUR QUARTETS, copyright 1943 by T. S. Eliot and renewed 1971 by Esme Valerie Eliot, reprinted by permission of Harcourt Brace & Company.

17. "Gauging a Family's Suitability for a Stint Overseas," *Business Week* (April 16, 1979), pp. 127–130.

18. Jelinek, M., and Adler, N. J. "Women: World Class Managers for Global Competition," *Academy of Management Executive*, vol. 2, no. 1 (1988), pp. 11–19.

19. Karras, E. J., and McMillan, R. F. "Interviewing for a Cultural Match," *Personnel Journal* (April 1971), p. 276.

20. Labovitz, G. "Managing the Personal Side of the Personnel Move Aboard," *Advanced Management Journal*, vol. 42, no. 3 (1977), pp. 26–39.

21. Ondrack, D. A. "International Transfers of Managers in North American and European MNEs," *Journal of International Business Studies*, vol. 16 (1985), pp. 1–19.

22. Osland, J. S. *The Adventure of Working Abroad: Hero Tales from the Global Frontier* (San Francisco: Jossey-Bass, 1995).

23. Pazy, A., and Zeira, Y. "Training of Parent-Country Professionals in Host Country Organizations," *Academy of Management Review*, vol. 8, no. 2 (1983), pp. 262–272.

24. Priestoff, N. "The Gaijin Executive's Wife," *The Conference Board Record*, vol. 13, no. 5 (1976), pp. 51–64.

25. Renshaw, J. R. "An Exploration of the Dynamics of the Overlapping Worlds of Work and Family," *Family Process*, vol. 15, no. 1 (1976), pp. 143–165.

26. Selmer, J., ed. *Expatriate Management: New Ideas for International Business* (Westport, Conn.: Quorum Books, 1995).

27. Thompson, A. "Australian Expatriate Wives and Business Success in Southeast Asia," *Euro-Asia Business Review*, vol. 5, no. 2 (1986), pp. 14–18.

28. Wederspahn, G. M. "The Overseas Wife: Excess Baggage," *The Bridge*, vol. 5, no. 4 (1980), p. 16.

29. Zeira, Y., and Harrari, E. "Genuine Multinational Staffing Policy: Expectations and Realities," *Academy of Management Journal*, vol. 20, no. 2 (1979), pp. 327–333.

CHAPTER 10
Global Careers

Ideally, it seems . . . [a global manager] should have the stamina of an Olympic runner, the mental agility of an Einstein, the conversational skill of a professor of languages, the detachment of a judge, the tact of a diplomat, and the perseverance of an Egyptian pyramid builder. [And] that's not all. If they are going to measure up to the demands of living and working in a foreign country, they should also have a feeling for the culture; their moral judgment should not be too rigid; they should be able to merge with the local environment with chameleon-like ease; and they should show no signs of prejudice.[1]

— Thomas Aitken (12)

As globalization evolved from a buzzword to a pervasive reality, demand increased for executives sophisticated in managing the complexities of global business. Corporate and government managers need to be able to think globally. They need to be able to work domestically on international projects as well as abroad on expatriate assignments and business travel. Global business has become so important that organizations can no longer afford to consider candidates for executive positions unless they have had global experience.

According to Colby Chandler (18), the former CEO of Eastman Kodak Company, "These days there is not a discussion or a decision that does not have an international dimension. We would have to be blind not to see how critically important international experience is." The *Wall Street Journal* (15) claims that "intensifying international competition will make the home-grown chief executive obsolete." Duane Kullberg, Arthur Andersen and Company's former chief executive partner, agrees that future American CEOs "will be . . . [people] with experience outside the borders of the U.S. . . . If you go back 20 years, you could be pretty insular and still survive. Today, that's not possible" (15).

WHAT IT TAKES TO REACH THE TOP

North American companies compete with British, French, German, Scandinavian, Chinese, and Korean companies, among others, for global executives to manage their operations around the world (see 30). Yet what it takes to reach the top of a company differs from one country to the next; companies view managerial success through their own cultural blinders (16;17;27). For example, American managers view ambition and drive as the most important characteristic for success; French managers must be labeled as having high potential (27); German managers, more than others, view creativity as essential for career success (27); and their British colleagues see creating the right image and getting noticed for what they do as essential (27).

Similarly, whereas Swiss and German companies respect technical creativity and competence, French and British companies often view managers with such qualities as "mere technicians" (16). Likewise, American companies highly value entrepreneurs, while their British and French counterparts often view entrepreneurial behavior as highly disruptive (16). Similarly, whereas only just over half of Dutch managers see "skills in interpersonal relations and communication" as critical to career success, almost 90 percent of their British colleagues do so (17).

Global management expert André Laurent (27) describes German, British, and French managers' careers as follows (16:10):

German managers, more than others, believe that creativity is essential for career success. In their mind, successful managers must have the right individual characteristics. German managers' outlook is rational: they view the organization as a coordinated network of individuals who make appropriate decisions based on their professional competence and knowledge.

British managers hold a more interpersonal and subjective view of the organizational world. According to them, the ability to create the right image and to get noticed for what they do is essential for career success. British managers view organizations primarily as a network of relationships between individuals who get things done by influencing each other using communication and negotiation.

French managers look at organizations as an authority network where the power to organize and control members stems from their position in the hierarchy. French managers focus on the organization as a pyramid of differentiated levels of power to be acquired or dealt with. They perceive the ability to manage power relationships effectively and to "work the system" as critical to their career success.

As companies integrate their operations globally, these multiple national realities send conflicting messages to success-oriented managers. Affiliates in different countries operate differently and reward different behaviors based on their unique cultural perspectives (17). Regardless of what headquarters desires or designs, no single best way exists to perform or to achieve global career success (17). The challenge for today's global companies is to recognize local differences, while at the same time creating globally integrated career paths for their most senior executives.

Expatriate assignments form a key part of most global managers' careers. Traditionally, North American managers were attracted to working abroad by the financial rewards, increased responsibility, challenge, and independence as well as the unique lifestyle. Yet during the 1970s, a weakened U.S. dollar, inflation, and additional taxes reduced the attractiveness of financial packages. By the 1980s, dual-career marriages complicated transfer decisions as well as exacerbated the financial situation; expatriate salary increases rarely made up for reducing a two-income family to a single salary. Stories of prior expatriates whose careers had been sidetracked while abroad also made many managers hesitant to follow a global career path (5;20;22;24;29;34).

Yet today it is no secret that business faces an environment radically changed from that of even a few years ago, the result of increasingly integrated global competition. The new global environment demands more, not fewer, globally competent managers (8). Rather than sidetracking a manager's career, global experience is rapidly becoming the only route to the top. According to the *New York Times* (18), hands-on global experience has slowly but surely moved out of the "nice but not necessary" category and into the "must have" slot for those on the corporate fast track. Given the increasing demand and potentially diminishing interest in global assignments, what can we predict for the twenty-first century? Will global organizations remain able to attract sufficient numbers of young managers? Are today's young managers interested in global work? What do they see as the advantages and disadvantages of global assignments?

As you read the chapter, ask yourself how prepared you are to work globally. What are your strengths and weaknesses as a global manager?

IS THE TRADITIONAL EXPATRIATE MANAGER EXTINCT?

Traditionally, who was the international executive? According to a study of 1161 expatriates working in forty countries (20), typical American international executives were about 31 years old when they first went abroad, stayed at least three years on each international assignment, and had three such assignments during their career. Expatriate executives were significantly younger than their domestic counterparts; with few exceptions, they were men. Twenty-one percent married foreign women. International executives came from a higher socioeconomic background than their domestic counterparts. Typically, expatriates stayed longer with one company: 41 percent worked for only one firm, 25 percent for only two firms, and 87 percent remained with the same firm after accepting their first international assignment. International executives were better educated than their domestic counterparts: 81 percent graduated from college as compared with less than 70 percent of domestic executives. International executives' education was less specialized than that of domestic executives, with more graduating in liberal arts and fewer in business and engineering.

Today the portrait of the international executive is changing. First, given the increasing importance of global business, more executives manage global projects and work with people from around the world, even if they never leave home. They work for companies from other countries, buy from suppliers in other countries, sell to clients worldwide, and, most significantly, create global strategies with colleagues from many different nations. Second, more fast-track managers are using expatriate assignments to gain the global experience necessary to rise to the top of major, global corporations (9). Third, the number of women seeking global assignments, although still small, is rising (7;10;11;25), with their overwhelming success beginning to break down the gender barrier (4).

To date, the female expatriate managers have been fairly junior within their organizations and careers. Unlike their male counterparts, their average age when they first go abroad is under thirty years old. Also dissimilar to male expatriates, nearly half of the women expatriates are single, with very few having children. Similar to male expatriates, the female expatriates are very well educated and quite internationally experienced. Almost all hold graduate degrees, with an MBA the most common. Over three-quarters have had extensive international interests and experience prior to their companies sending them abroad. For example, more than three-quarters have traveled internationally and almost two-thirds have had an international focus in their studies prior to joining the company. Women expatriate managers generally speak two or three languages, with some speaking as many as six. In addition, most women selected for global assignments demonstrate excellent social skills (4).

TODAY'S GLOBAL CAREERS

Why would today's young managers accept global assignments: for the job challenge, the adventure, the status?   Why would they turn down a global assignment?   We conducted a survey to discover why young managers might accept or reject international assignments and global careers.[2]   Over a thousand graduating MBA students from seven top schools in the United States, Canada, and Europe described their level of interest in global careers, their reasons for accepting or rejecting international assignments, and their assessment of global versus domestic opportunities.

Who Are the Future Global Managers?

The backgrounds of the MBAs from the seven schools showed more similarity than difference.[3]   Although 41 percent had an international focus in their MBA, few had extensive global work experience. Over 80 percent had traveled abroad; few of their friends, however, were from other countries.   As might be expected, European and Canadian MBAs had more international experience than did their American counterparts.

Do Future Managers Want Global Careers?

The future managers showed strong interest in pursuing the global aspects of their careers.[4]   More than four out of five wanted an international assignment at some time during their career. Just under half seriously considered pursuing a global career, including accepting a series of international assignments.   More than a third of the future managers wanted to travel extensively for their job.   Yet, only one-third wanted an international assignment as their first job after graduation. Clearly, most young managers show an interest in global management, but many fewer would like an international assignment "right now."

Do you agree for your career? How would you describe your own interest in international management and a global career? The Careers in Global Management Questionnaire (see box) provides a way to assess your own interest in international assignments and a global career.

CAREERS IN GLOBAL MANAGEMENT QUESTIONNAIRE

Given the substantial increases in global business over the last decade, it has become increasingly important for managers and companies to understand the career aspirations of young managers. This questionnaire allows you to increase your understanding of your own career aspirations.

Background: How Prepared Are You?

1. Including your maternal language, which languages do you speak relatively well?

   _____

2. How many years have you studied outside of your country of citizenship (from age 5 on)?

   _____ total number of years in _____
   country/countries

3. How many months outside your country of citizenship have you traveled, lived, or worked? _____

4. Did either of your parents travel internationally for their work? _____

5. How many of your friends are neither from your country of citizenship nor from the country in which you are currently living?

   _____ none; _____ a few; _____about half; _____ most; _____all

What Are Your Career Plans?

The following section asks you a number of questions about your career plans. In the questions

   Home Country is your country of citizenship.

   An *International Assignment* is one in which the company sends an employee for a single assignment of a year or more to another country.

   A *Global Career* is a series of international assignments in various countries.

   International Travel is a business trip to another country without the employee moving there.

   An *Expatriate* is an employee who is sent by the company to live and work in another country.

How true is each of the following statements for you?

   1. I am seriously considering pursuing a global career. _____

2. I would like my first job after school to be in another country. _____

3. If offered an equivalent position in my home country or in the foreign country of my choice, I would rather work at home. _____

4. While continuing to live in my home country, I would like to travel internationally more than 40 percent (approximately 20 weeks/year) of my time. _____

5. I would like to have an international assignment at some time in my career. _____

6. I would like to follow a global career in which I had a series of international assignments. _____

7. I had never thought about taking an international assignment until I read this questionnaire. _____

There are many reasons why people choose not to pursue a global career. Which of the following would discourage *you* from pursuing a global career or taking an international assignment?

8. I like living in my home country. _____

9. I do not want to learn another language. _____

10. I do not want to adjust to another culture. _____

11. My spouse would not want to move to another country. _____

12. It is not good to move children. _____

13. I want my children to be educated in my home country. _____

14. I do not want to live in:
    a. a country outside my home country _____
    b. North America _____
    c. Europe _____
    d. Latin or South America _____
    e. Asia _____
    f. Africa _____
    g. the Middle East _____
    h. my home country _____
    i. other (specify)

15. International jobs involve too much travel.. _____

16. If I live in a another country, my children will not gain a sense of national identity. _____

17. My spouse would not want to interrupt his or her career. _____

18. I will lose my sense of identity, my roots. _____

19. International assignments put too much strain on a marriage. _____

20. When you are on an international assignment you become "invisible" to the company and tend to be forgotten for promotions. _____

21. It would be difficult to come back home after having lived and worked for a long time in another country. _____

22. I do not want to be exposed to the political instability in some parts of the world. _____

23. I would be more socially isolated and lonely in another country. _____

24. I would be exposed to more personal danger in another country. _____

In comparing potential domestic and global careers, which do you think could give you the greatest professional opportunities?

	Domestic Career	About Same	Global Career
25. I could succeed faster in	_____	_____	_____
26. I could earn a higher salary in	_____	_____	_____
27. I could have greater status in	_____	_____	_____
28. I could be more recognized for my work in	_____	_____	_____
29. I could have a more interesting professional life in	_____	_____	_____
30. I could have a more satisfying personal life in	_____	_____	_____

In comparing women and men, who do you think will have the greater chance of being

	Women	Equal Chances	Men
31. Selected for an international assignment?	_____	_____	_____
32. Effective on an international assignment?	_____	_____	_____
33. Successful in advancing in a global career?	_____	_____	_____
34. Effective on domestic assignments?	_____	_____	_____
35. Successful in advancing in a domestic career?	_____	_____	_____

	Women	Equal Chances	Men
36. Socially isolated and lonely in another country?	———	———	———
37. Exposed to personal danger in another country?	———	———	———

In Your Opinion

1. What are the main reasons that would lead you to accept an international assignment?

   a. _____
   b. _____
   c. _____

2. What are the main reasons why you would turn down an international assignment?

   a. _____
   b. _____
   c. _____

3. What, if any, are the blocks for women successfully pursuing global careers that include international assignments (which do not exist for men)?

   a. _____
   b. _____
   c. _____

Why Future Managers Would Accept an International Assignment

As shown in Table 10-1, the most frequently mentioned reason for accepting an international assignment is the opportunity for cross-cultural and personal growth experiences. Over half the future managers want to see other cultures, travel, learn new languages, and gain a greater understanding of another way of life; that is, they want to expand their horizons. The second reason is the job itself. Forty percent of future managers see global positions—as compared with available domestic positions—as providing more interesting and challenging work, allowing for more autonomy, power, status, and responsibility, and as providing opportunities for more meaningful contributions to the company and society. The third reason is money. More than a quarter of the young managers believe they would earn a higher salary and more benefits in an international than in a domestic position.

TABLE 10-1 *Reasons Young Managers Would Accept International Assignments*

Percent of Future Managers Citing Reason	*Reasons for Accepting an International Assignment*
52	**Cross-Cultural Experience and Personal Growth** See other cultures Learn new languages Gain greater understanding of another way of life Personal growth: expand horizons, broaden background
40	**Job** More interesting and challenging More opportunities, responsibilities, chances for useful work More power, autonomy, status
28	**Money** Higher salary, more fringe benefits, more savings
21	**Career Advancement** Increased exposure Increased opportunities Future domestic promotion
16	**Good Location** Politically stable country Good climate Good social and living conditions Safe English speaking or similar to home country
11	**Satisfying Life** Greater personal freedom More fun, excitement, adventure More variety, less routine, a change Higher quality of life
4	**Spouse and Family** Good situation for the spouse (i.e., job) Good situation for family (education, health facilities) Spouse willing to go
3	**Short Term; Other** No domestic jobs available Women managers respected by local nationals Personal business opportunities available in foreign country Single

Note: 1129 graduating MBAs cited 1867 reasons for accepting international assignments; the most frequently cited reasons are given here. Listed numbers are the percent of MBAs citing the particular reason.

The fourth reason for accepting an international assignment is career advancement. One future manager in five sees expatriate positions as increasing company-wide exposure and thus the potential for promotion. The fifth reason is a good location. Almost 16 percent expressed more willingness to accept an international assignment in a politically stable country with good climate, good social and living conditions, few threats to personal safety, and with an English-speaking population. Young managers are most attracted to countries that are more similar to their own country and more economically developed. The sixth reason is the more satisfying life abroad. Eleven percent look forward to a change—less routine, more fun, more adventure, more excitement, more variety, more personal freedom, and a higher quality of life than they imagine having in their home country.

When the future managers compare the advantages of global versus domestic careers, they see the primary benefits of an international assignment as the greater challenge and responsibility, more interesting work, and better financial rewards. By contrast, they see domestic careers as offering slightly greater status, a more satisfying personal life, more rapid career advancement, and greater recognition for their work than would a global career.

Why Future Managers Would Reject an International Assignment

The future managers identified seven major reasons for turning down an international assignment. As shown in Table 10-2, the most frequently mentioned reason is a bad location. More than half the young managers would reject an assignment if the host country appeared too politically unstable, "uncivilized," dangerous, or hostile towards expatriates, or to have a high potential for war and public violence. The second reason is the job itself and the potentially negative career impact. One-third of the young managers would turn down an international assignment if the job appeared unchallenging or boring. Similarly, a third see international assignments as a bad long-term career strategy. They fear the higher risk of job failure abroad and the possible damage to their career caused by extended isolation from the company's headquarters. They fear being "lost" at reentry and forgotten at times of promotion.

The third reason, also mentioned by one-third of the future managers, describes their concern about spouse and family. Young managers view dual-career marriages as a major problem, especially if the spouse cannot find a suitable position abroad. They also fear the increased marital strain as well as the potentially inadequate educational and medical facilities for children. The fourth reason is money. Nearly one-quarter of the young managers would reject an assignment if the salary and benefits package

TABLE 10-2 *Reasons Young Managers Would Reject*
International Assignments

Percent of Future Managers Citing Reason	Reasons for Rejecting an International Assignment
59	**Location** Politically unstable "Uncivilized" Dangerous Hostility toward expatriates Extreme poverty High potential for war or violence
35	**Job and Career** Boring, unchallenging, professionally uninteresting Not good long-term career strategy Higher risk of job failure Isolation from domestic company Displacement from company's hierarchy: forgotten at promotion time, "lost" at reentry
33	**Spouse and Family** Inadequate medical or educational facilities Children wrong age to move (especially teenagers) Problem of dual-career marriage Spouse unwilling to move Spouse unable to find position to further career
23	**Money** Salary and benefits package inadequate
19	**Unpleasant Life Abroad** Unwillingness to learn new language, adjust to new culture Isolation, loneliness, fear, uncertainty Restrictions on personal life: lack of physical and intellectual freedom, access to people
14	**Disruption to Home Country Life** Disruption to personal and social life Reneging on commitment to family, parents, friends
6	**Contract Too Long; Other** Women not accepted as managers Existing good domestic position Opposition to company's global policies, product, or marketing strategy Too much travel

Note: 1129 graduating MBAs cited 2308 reasons for rejecting international assignments; the most frequently cited reasons are given here. Listed numbers are the percent of MBAs citing the particular reason.

inadequately compensated them for the disruption and additional problems caused by moving and living in another country. Young managers cite potentially unpleasant cross-cultural differences as their fifth reason. Nearly 20 percent reject introducing too much change into their life, learning a new language, adjusting to a new culture, or subjecting themselves to the isolation, loneliness, fear, and uncertainty associated with living abroad. Similarly, one young manager in seven rejects disrupting his or her current, enjoyable home country lifestyle. Other reasons mentioned by some of the young managers include the contract being too long, fear that local nationals would not accept women managers, the assignment requiring too much travel, or unacceptable home company policies toward the host country.

Future managers consistently rate global work as offering greater job satisfaction; domestic work as offering greater organizational recognition and a more satisfying private life. Young managers would accept positions in another country for the cross-cultural experience and opportunity for personal growth, the job itself, and the higher salary and financial benefits. They would reject international assignments due to the negative impact on spouse and family, the personal danger and inconvenience of living in a "bad" location, and the potentially detrimental effect on career advancement both while abroad and when returning home.

Young managers' perceptions of the advantages and disadvantages of living and working abroad reflect those of many managers. Experienced expatriates frequently have described such advantages as increased personal growth opportunities and the inherently more interesting, challenging, and responsible work abroad, as well as traditionally generous salaries and benefit packages. Today's young managers show a greater awareness than their predecessors of the disadvantages of expatriate positions on their private lives and careers. Research has shown that the major cause of failure on international assignments, often leading to early return, is dissatisfaction on the part of the spouse (37; see Chapter 9). Nearly half of 300 surveyed companies have brought families home early due to the spouse's inability to adapt (13). With the increasing prevalence of dual-career couples, the impact of international assignments on the spouse and family will increase, not decrease (see Chapter 9). Young managers appear well aware of these problems.

Potentially negative impacts of international assignments on employees' careers have also become more widely recognized. In the past most expatriates believed that international assignments would help their career; the majority returned to discover the opposite was true (5). Returning employees have all too frequently discovered that home country jobs were at substantially lower levels of responsibility and authority than were their expatriate positions or, more dramatically, that there were no jobs at all to return to (see Chapter 8). Meanwhile, returnees found that domestic colleagues had been promoted while their own career had plateaued.

Today's young managers appear considerably more aware of the hazards of moving abroad and successfully returning home than were the
managers of five, ten, and fifteen years ago.   Future managers consequently are less likely to accept an international assignment that could
jeopardize their career.   Luckily, with increasing globalization and the
parallel rise in importance of global experience and positions, the risks of
derailing one's career by going abroad are diminishing just as young managers' interest is increasing.

WOMEN IN GLOBAL MANAGEMENT

Are women and men equally interested in global careers (10)?   Yes.
Although less than 10 percent of the current North American expatriate
managers are women (1;7), male and female future managers express an
equal interest in accepting international assignments and pursuing global careers (6).

Although equally interested, both young male and female future managers believe that companies offer fewer opportunities for women than for
men in global management.   Similarly, both believe that companies offer
fewer opportunities for women in global management than they offer in
domestic management.   The young managers are right.   In a survey of 60
major North American companies with operations around the world, over
half expressed reluctance to select women managers for international
assignments (1;3;4).   The two primary concerns, expressed by three-quarters of the companies, are their belief that foreigners are so prejudiced
against women managers that they could not succeed, and that the difficulties faced by dual-career couples in moving abroad are insurmountable.   Even with the barriers and hesitance, almost three-quarters of the
companies believe that the number of women working globally will continue to increase (3).

Similar to the companies, over 80 percent of the future managers themselves believe that foreigners' prejudice against women managers poses
the primary barrier to the women's success (2;6).   Over 70 percent label
the home company's reluctance to select women for international assignments and the difficulties faced by global dual-career couples as the second and third most important barriers (6).   Whereas young managers correctly see companies' current selection processes as creating barriers,
neither they nor the companies correctly understand "foreigners' prejudice."   A major study of North American women working in countries

around the world has shown that expatriate women managers are highly successful (4;11;25). As one woman expatriate accurately summarized, "The most difficult job is getting sent, not succeeding once sent" (4).

Why do women succeed as global managers? They succeed because they are seen as *foreigners who happen to be women*, not as women who happen to be foreigners. Although the difference may appear subtle, the effect is huge. Countries such as Japan, Korea, and Saudi Arabia, which promote few of their own women into significant managerial positions, treat foreign women with the respect they accord male expatriate managers. As one woman who works successfully in Hong Kong explained, "It doesn't make any difference if you are blue, green, purple, or a frog, if you have the best product at the best price, the Chinese will buy" (4). In essence, global business pragmatism wins out over prejudice.

Although more barriers may exist for women than for men, today's organizations clearly can select global managers from equally interested groups of young male and female managers. When considering a woman for a global position, companies would be wise (a) not to assume that she does not want to go—she probably does; (b) not to assume that foreigners are so prejudiced that such assignments would be bad for both the company and the woman's career; and (c) not to assume that dual-career issues are insolvable. As discussed in Chapter 9, many North American women expatriates actually find it easier to balance the time-consuming and seemingly conflicting roles of professional, wife, and mother while on a global assignment than at home, because global assignments often provide them with the luxury of a level of household help that they rarely have at home. Luckily, just at the time when the intensity of global competition demands that companies use nothing but their best managers, both the companies and the women are discovering that success is both possible and probable.

WOMEN AND TRANSNATIONAL CORPORATIONS[5]

Given the increasing importance of global and transnational corporations, it is encouraging that their impact on women in management, to date, has been primarily positive. Transnational corporations include women in ways that domestic, multidomestic, and multinational firms did not and do not. First, the extremely competitive business environment forces transnational firms to select the very best people available. The opportunity cost of prejudice—of rejecting women and limiting selection to men—is much higher than in previous economic environments. As *Fortune* succinctly stated, "The best reason for believing that more women will be in charge before long is that in a ferociously competitive global economy, no company can afford to waste valuable brainpower simply because it's wearing a skirt" (19:56).

Second, whereas domestic and multidomestic companies hire primarily local nationals and, therefore, must closely adhere to local norms on hiring—or not hiring—women managers, transnational corporations are not similarly limited. Because the corporate culture of transnational firms is not coincident with the local culture of any particular country, transnationals have greater flexibility in defining selection and promotion criteria that best fit the firm's needs rather than those that most closely mimic the historical patterns of a particular country. Said simply, transnationals can and do hire local women managers even in countries in which the local companies rarely do so.

U.S.–based transnational corporations, for example, have often hired local women managers when local firms would not. This dynamic has been particulary pronounced in Japan, where non-Japanese companies have had difficulty attracting top-ranked male applicants (26;36). American firms have led the way in hiring well-qualified Japanese women, whereas Japanese firms are still extremely reluctant to hire them (35). Interestingly, while still hiring fewer women than most American firms, Japanese transnationals operating in the United States hire more women managers in their American affiliates than they do in their home country operations (33).

By hiring women, transnationals act as role models for firms in many countries that have not seriously considered promoting significant numbers of women into managerial positions. The greater the number of expatriates involved in foreign affiliates, the less likely they are to follow local human resource practices—including being less likely to restrict the number of women mangers (33). The firm's transnational character allows it organizational freedoms and imposes competitive demands not present in domestic or multidomestic environments.

Third, as discussed previously, transnational corporations send women abroad as expatriate managers (7). Because transnationals use expatriate and local managers, they can benefit from the greater flexibility that many cultures afford foreign women. As was described, most countries do not hold foreign women to the same professionally limiting roles that restrict local women (4;25). The outstanding success of the initial group of women expatriate managers in all geographical areas—Africa, the

Americas, Asia, Europe, and the Middle East—is encouraging firms both to continue sending women abroad (4;28) and to begin promoting more local women into management (25).

Fourth, whereas domestic, multidomestic, and multinational firms have been characterized by structural hierarchies, transnationals are increasingly characterized by networks of equals. Recent research suggests that women work particularly well in such networks:

> . . . women . . . are countering the values of the hierarchy with those of the web . . . when describing their roles in their organizations, women usually refer . . . to themselves as being in the middle of things. . . . Inseparable from their sense of themselves as being in the middle . . . [is] women's notion of being connected to those around them (23:45–46,52).

Not surprisingly, transnational firms see women managers as bringing needed collaborative and participative skills to the workplace (31).

Fifth, leading management scholars have identified innovation as a key factor in global competitiveness (14;21;32). An inherent source of innovation is well-managed diversity, including gender diversity (1). Women bring diversity to transnational corporations that have heretofore primarily hired men.

Transnational corporations thus include more women than their predecessors could (or would) and benefit organizationally from their professional contributions in new ways. They benefit both from women's increased representation at all levels of the organization as well as from their unique ways of contributing to the organization that complement those of men.

SUMMARY

Do young managers want global careers? Yes, under certain conditions. Whereas most young male and female managers still see more advantages from domestic than global careers, over 80 percent would like an international assignment at some time during their career. Are women as interested as men in pursuing global careers? Yes, and they are highly successful once sent. Increased competition is forcing global and transnational companies to select the most talented employees for managerial and professional positions, without regard to either nationality or gender. Are young American managers equally as interested in global careers as are their

Canadian and European counterparts? No. From all perspectives, young American managers express less interest in pursuing international assignments and global careers than do their counterparts in other countries.

QUESTIONS FOR REFLECTION

1. *Global Career Planning.*   Why would you personally want to accept an international assignment? Why would you reject an international assignment?

2. *Global Human Resource Systems.*   If you were the vice president of human resources for a major transnational corporation and wanted to attract the very best young managers to accept international assignments, what would you offer them?

3. *Women Expatriate Managers.*   What are some of the best ways to attract women to accept international assignments? What should companies and women do to make certain that their international assignments are successful?

4. *Recruiting a Dual-Career Manager.*   Dual-career marriages have been considered a major problem in global careers. How would you recruit a top manager for an international assignment if the manager's spouse was also a senior manager for another company?

5. *Global Career Planning.*   What kinds of global experiences would you like to have in your career? When? Why?

NOTES

1. The pronoun "he" has been changed in the quote to "they" to include male and female expatriates.

2. This chapter is based, in part, on the study reported in Nancy J. Adler, "Do MBAs Want International Careers?" *International Journal of Intercultural Relations*, vol. 10, no. 3 (1986), pp. 277–300. The research was supported by a grant from the Social Sciences and Humanities Research Council of Canada.   The author thanks Blossem Shaffer for her creative ideas and research assistance in conducting the study.

3. The surveyed MBAs were young (average age 27 years), most were single (68%), approximately a third were women (32%), and most were studying for their MBA in the country in which they were born, held citizenship, and had received their undergraduate education. The most common undergraduate degrees were business and economics (34%) and engineering (11%), while the most common MBA concentrations were finance (44%) and marketing (29%). While 38 percent had no work experience, the majority had worked for a short time (approximately two years) prior to entering the MBA program. Over a third (36%) had never lived abroad. Few of the MBAs' parents had worked internationally. See Table 1 in Adler (1).

4. See Table 2 in Adler (1).

5. This section adapted from Nancy J. Adler's "Competitive Frontiers: Women Managing Across Borders" (1:23–24).

REFERENCES

1. Adler, Nancy J. "Competitive Frontiers: Women Managing Across Borders," in N. J. Adler and D. N. Izraeli, eds., *Competitive Frontiers: Women Managers in a Global Economy* (Cambridge, Mass.: Blackwell, 1994), pp. 22–44.

2. Adler, N. J. "Do MBAs Want International Careers?" *International Journal of Intercultural Relations*, vol. 10, no. 3, (1986), pp. 277–300.

3. Adler, N. J. "Expecting International Success: Female Managers Overseas," *Columbia Journal of World Business*, vol. 19, no. 3 (1984), pp. 79–85.

4. Adler, N. J. "Pacific Basin Managers: A Gaijin, Not a Woman," *Human Resource Management*, vol. 26, no. 2, (1987), pp. 169–191.

5. Adler, N. J. "Re-entry: Managing Cross-Cultural Transitions," *Group and Organization Studies*, vol. 6, no. 3, (1981), pp. 341–356.

6. Adler, N. J. "Women Do Not Want International Careers: And Other Myths About International Management," *Organizational Dynamics*, vol. 13, no. 2 (1984), pp. 66–79.

7. Adler, N. J. "Women in International Management: Where Are They?" *California Management Review*, vol. 26, no. 4 (1984), pp. 78–89.

8. Adler, N. J., and Bartholomew, S. "Managing Globally Competent People," *Academy of Management Executive*, vol. 6, no. 3 (1992), pp. 52–65.

9. Adler, N. J., and Ghadar, F. "Globalization and Human Resource Management," in Alan M. Rugman, ed., *Research in Global Strategic Management: A Canadian Perspective*, vol. 1 (Greenwich, Conn.: JAI Press, 1989), pp. 179–205.

10. Adler, N. J., and Izraeli, D. N. *Competitive Frontiers: Women Managers in a Global Economy* (Cambridge, Mass.: Blackwell, 1994).

11. Adler, N. J., and Izraeli, D. N. *Women in Management Worldwide* (Armonk, N.Y.: M. E. Sharpe, 1988).

12. Aitken, T. "What It Takes to Work Abroad," in T. Aitken, *The Multinational Man: The Role of the Manager Abroad* (New York: Halstead Press, 1973).

13. Baker, J. C. "An Analysis of How the U.S. Multinational Company Considers the Wife of American Expatriate Managers," *Academy of Management Proceedings*, vol. 35 (1975), pp. 258–260.

14. Bartlett, C. A., and Ghoshal, S. *Managing Across Borders: The Transnational Solution* (Boston: Harvard Business School Press 1989).

15. Bennett, A. "Going Global: The Chief Executives in Year 2000 Will Be Experienced Abroad," *Wall Street Journal* (February 27, 1989), pp. A1, A9.

16. Derr, C. B. *Managing the New Careerists* (San Francisco: Jossey-Bass, 1986).

17. Derr, C. B., and Laurent, A. "The Internal and External Careers: A Theoretical and Cross-Cultural Perspective," in M. Arthur, D. T. Hall, and B. S. Lawrence, eds., *The Handbook of Career Theory* (Cambridge, England: Cambridge University Press, 1989).

18. Deutsch, C. H. "Losing Innocence, Abroad," *The New York Times* (July 10, 1988), Business section, pp. 1, 26.

19. Fisher, Anne B. "When Will Women Get to the Top?" *Fortune* (September 21, 1992), pp. 44–56.

20. Gonzales, R. F., and Neghandi, A. R. *The United States Overseas Executive: His Orientations and Career Patterns* (East Lansing, Mich.: Graduate School of Business Administration, Michigan State University, 1967).

21. Hammond, V., and Holton, V. "The Scenario for Women Managers in Britain in the 1990s," in N. J. Adler and D. N. Izraeli, eds. *Competitive Frontiers: Women Managers in a Global Economy* (Cambridge, Mass: Blackwell, 1994) pp. 224–242.

22. Heenan, D. "The Corporate Expatriate: Assignment to Ambiguity," *Columbia Journal of World Business*, vol. 5 (1970), pp. 49–54.

23. Helgesen, S. *The Female Advantage: Women's Ways of Leadership* (New York: Doubleday 1990).

24. Howard, C. "The Returning Overseas Executive: Culture Shock in Reverse," *Human Resources Management*, vol. 13, no. 2 (1974), pp. 22–26.

25. Jelinek, M., and Adler, N. J. "Women: World Class Managers for Global Competition," *Academy of Management Executive*, vol. 2, no. 1 (1988), pp. 11–19.

26. Lansing, P., and Ready, K. "Hiring Women Managers in Japan: An Alternative for Foreign Employers," *California Management Review*, vol. 30, no. 3 (1988), pp. 112–127.

27. Laurent, A. "The Cross-Cultural Puzzle of International Human Resource Management," *Human Resource Management*, vol. 25, no. 1 (1986), pp. 91–102. Copyright 1986 John Wiley & Sons, Inc.

28. Moran, Stahl, and Boyer, Inc. *Status of American Female Expatriate Employees: Survey Results* (Boulder, Colo.: International Division, 1988)

29. Murray, A. "International Personnel Repatriation: Cultural Shock in Reverse," *MSU Business Topics*, vol. 21, no. 2 (1973), pp. 59–66.

30. Perham, J. C. "The Boom in Executive Jobs," *Dun's Review*, vol. 110, no. 5 (1977), pp. 80–81.

31. Perry, N. J. "If You Can't Join 'em, Beat 'em," *Fortune* (September 21, 1992), pp. 58–59.

32. Porter, M. *The Competitive Advantage of Nations* (New York: Free Press, 1990).

33. Rosenzweig, P. M., and Nohria, N. "Influences on Human Resource Management Practices in Multinational Corporations," *Journal of International Business Studies*, 2nd quarter (1994), pp. 229–251.

34. Smith, L. "The Hazards of Coming Home," *Dun's Review* (October 1975), pp. 71–73.

35. Steinhoff, P. G. and Tanaka, K. "Women Managers in Japan," in N. J. Adler and D. N. Izracli, eds., *Competitive Frontiers: Women Managers in a Global Economy* (Cambridge, Mass: Blackwell, 1994), pp. 79–100.

36. Steinhoff, P. G., and Tanaka, K. "Women Managers in Japan," in N. J. Adler and D. N. Izraeli, eds. *Women in Management Worldwide* (Armonk, N.Y.: M.E. Sharpe, 1988), pp. 103–121.

37. Tung, R. L. "U.S. Multinationals: A Study of Their Selection and Training for Overseas Assignments," *Academy of Management Proceedings*, vol. 39 (1979), pp. 298–301.

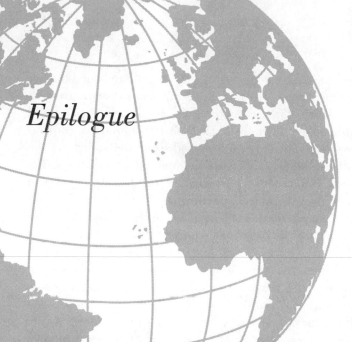

Epilogue

There are good reasons for suggesting that the modern age has ended. Many things indicate that we are going through a transitional period, when it seems that something is on the way out and something else is painfully being born. It is as if something were crumbling, decaying and exhausting itself, while something else, still indistinct, were arising from the rubble. . . .

This state of affairs has its social and political consequences. The planetary civilization to which we all belong confronts us with global challenges. We stand helpless before them because our civilization has essentially globalized only the surface of our lives. . . .

Politicians are rightly worried by the problem of finding the key to insure the survival of a civilization that is global and multicultural. . . . The central political task of the final years of this century, then, is the creation of a new model of co-existence among the various cultures, peoples, races, and religious spheres within a single interconnected civilization. . . . Yes, it is clearly necessary to invent organizational structures appropriate to the multicultural age.

— Vaclav Havel, President of the Czech Republic[1]

Vaclav Havel's appreciation of the transition that the world is now experiencing is certainly important to each of us as human beings. Equally importantly, his appreciation of the world situation challenges us as managers, management scholars, and executives.

The world *has* gotten smaller. Global business has become more important. Managers worldwide are becoming more internationally sophisticated.

It is only as we recognize the extent to which we are culture bound that we can go beyond the limitations of our own necessarily narrow perspectives. It is only as we work globally that we can recognize and benefit from a world economy. We have entered an era in which global organizations, corporations, and alliances determine our economic and social well-being. To the extent that organizations respect individual cultural differences, they allow us to contribute based on our uniqueness. To the extent that they transcend national boundaries, they encourage a world, fraught with wars and animosities, to collaborate and to cooperate. If we fail to recognize cultural differences and choose to maintain staunchly ethnocentric domestic approaches, we condemn the world to divisiveness and its own demise.

In the past, multinational corporations have not been celebrated for their contributions to world peace or understanding. Perhaps it is only today, as we recognize that worldwide understanding and cooperation have become critical for our very survival, that the function of transnational corporations becomes apparent. Governments reflect national boundaries; transnational corporations go beyond national boundaries and national definitions. Corporations can use their transnational status, their creative public-private partnerships, and their ever-expanding networks of alliances in ways that benefit and enrich their worldwide constituencies or in ways that impoverish us all. The challenge is immense. The importance is inestimable.

NOTE

1. Vaclav Havel, President of the Czech Republic, in his speech accepting the Philadelphia Liberty Medal, as published in the *New York Times* as "The New Measure of Man," July 8, 1994, p. A27. Copyright © 1983/94 by The New York Times Company. Reprinted by permission.

Index

319